Science of Memory: Concepts

Science of Memory: Concepts

Edited by

Henry L. Roediger III

James S. McDonnell Distinguished University Professor
at Washington University in St. Louis

Yadin Dudai

Sela Professor of Neurobiology at the Weizmann Institute
of Science, Rehovot, Israel

and

Susan M. Fitzpatrick

Vice President of the James S. McDonnell Foundation

OXFORD
UNIVERSITY PRESS

OXFORD
UNIVERSITY PRESS

Oxford University Press, Inc., publishes works that further
Oxford University's objective of excellence
in research, scholarship, and education.

Oxford New York

Auckland Cape Town Dar es Salaam Hong Kong Karachi
Kuala Lumpur Madrid Melbourne Mexico City Nairobi
New Delhi Shanghai Taipei Toronto

With offices in

Argentina Austria Brazil Chile Czech Republic France Greece
Guatemala Hungary Italy Japan Poland Portugal Singapore
South Korea Switzerland Thailand Turkey Ukraine Vietnam

Published by Oxford University Press, Inc.
198 Madison Avenue, New York, New York 10016
www.oup.com

Oxford is a registered trademark of Oxford University Press

Library of Congress Cataloging-in-Publication Data

Science of memory: concepts / [edited by] Henry L. Roediger III, Yadin Dudai, and Susan M. Fitzpatrick.

p. cm. -- (Science of memory)

Includes bibliographical references and index.

ISBN-13: 978-0-19-531044-3 (pbk.)

1. Memory. I. Roediger, Henry L. II. Dudai, Yadin. III. Fitzpatrick, Susan M., 1956-
BF371.S45 2007
153.1'2--dc22
2006029621

Typeset in Minion by
Cepha Imaging Private Ltd., Bangalore, India

Printed in Great Britain
on acid-free paper by Ashford Colour Press Ltd., Gosport, Hampshire

10 9 8 7 6 5 4 3 2 1

Contents

16. **Phylogeny and evolution**

Epilogue

Preface

Memory is a single term, but with manifold referents. A huge variety of adjectives has been used to modify this noun, so that scholars discuss everything from abstract memory to zebrafish memory. Many different approaches to studying memory have arisen, both humanistic and scientific. Even among scientists who study memory, various methods and lines of attack are used: there are fields devoted to the biochemical, neurobiological, systems neuroscientific, computational and cognitive psychological approaches to studying memory, among others. Each field has its own techniques, methods, experimental preparations and special theories. What, if anything, holds the entire enterprise together? Can we develop a unified science of memory? The *Science of Memory: Concepts* is based on the assumption that the answer to the second question is *yes*. Further, we assume that at least part of the answer to the first question is *concepts*. That is, we believe that cross-disciplinary understanding of key concepts represent a critical element in developing a unified science of memory.

This volume was developed around 16 core concepts of the science of memory, those listed in the Table of Contents on the preceding pages. Each of these concepts was selected for a particular reason and the choices were difficult. Other perfectly plausible candidate concepts exist that we did not include (e.g. reinforcement). The introductory chapter by Dudai, Roediger and Tulving on *Memory concepts* explains and defends our choices. In her concluding chapter, *Remember the future*, Fitzpatrick explains the origin of the enterprise represented in this volume.

Following the introductory chapter on *Memory concepts*, the book is divided into 16 sections, one for each concept. Each section is organized so that a brief defining statement about a concept appears on the first page and then 2–4 short essays about the concept occur next. Authors of each essay were instructed to provide their perspectives on the topic at hand; the essays were their personal testaments, without worrying about satisfying all points of view. The essays are brief, so authors get to the point. We tried to get researchers from different corners of the field to write about the same topic, so even essays on the same subject are heterogeneous. At the end of each section, an integrator was given a bit more space to write an essay assimilating the various viewpoints.

As much as possible, the integrator provided a capstone summary of current understanding of the particular concept for the science of memory.

One primary purpose of this volume is to inform scientists in the various scientific subdisciplines studying memory of the many valid (if multifarious) approaches to their topic. The hope is for all of us to think across our traditional disciplinary boundaries, under the assumption that doing so will enrich the research we conduct within our own traditions.

We hope this book will be read by all researchers interested in scientific approaches to memory. We believe it should be especially useful to graduate students, postdoctoral fellows and young professors getting their start. Many great new discoveries in science have come from a melding of methods or viewpoints, by combining across fields. If this volume leads to some new discoveries of this ilk, the book will be a success.

Henry L. Roediger III
Yadin Dudai
Susan M. Fitzpatrick

Acknowledgments

This volume represents the work of many more people than the three listed on the title page as editors. Endel Tulving was a guiding force throughout, from the initial conception to the final product, and his spirit moved the enterprise along at critical steps over the past several years. The editors thank him for his inspiration, insight and sage advice. The James S. McDonnell Foundation generously provided funding for discussion of the issues covered in this volume at a conference in Palisades, New York. The present book in no way presents a 'conference proceedings' volume, but the conference did enlighten and guide authors of the essays contained in this volume. We would especially like to thank Alene Roth and Brent Dolezalek of the McDonnell Foundation for their enthusiastic and dedicated efforts that kept all the bits and pieces of the project moving forward toward timely completion. Alene took on a lioness's share of the logistical tasks including the all important reminding, prodding and cajoling that authors require to get essays submitted in a timely fashion. Brent, the JSMF web-master, worked quietly behind the scenes so that all web-based electronic transfer of information occurred seamlessly. This volume could not have met its ambitious publication deadlines without his help. Jane McConnell of Washington University provided many services at various points along the way. Catherine Carlin of Oxford University Press first believed in our project and helped us get started. Angela Burke copyedited the entire manuscript and helped to even out style differences among contributors. We also thank Jane Ashley for providing the subject and author indexes, and Helen Hill for shepherding us through the production process. Finally, we thank all the authors whose essays are contained here. Some thought our guidelines and deadlines were impossible to meet, but almost everyone cooperated in a spirit of adventure for this new kind of project. We thank everyone for helping to produce this book.

Henry L. Roediger III
Yadin Dudai
Susan M. Fitzpatrick

Contributors

Michael C. Anderson
Department of Psychology,
University of Oregon, USA

Alan Baddeley
Department of Psychology,
University of York, UK

Robert A. Bjork
Department of Psychology,
University of California,
Los Angeles, USA

Mark E. Bouton
Department of Psychology,
University of Vermont, USA

John T. Bruer
James S. McDonnell Foundation,
USA

Randy L. Buckner
Department of Psychology,
Harvard University, USA

György Buzsáki
Center for Molecular and
Behavioral Neuroscience,
Rutgers University, USA

John H. Byrne
Department of Neurobiology
and Anatomy, The University of
Texas Medical School at Houston,
USA

E.J. Capaldi
Department of Psychological
Sciences, Purdue University, USA

Nicola S. Clayton
Department of Experimental
Psychology, University of
Cambridge, UK

Martin A. Conway
Institute of Psychological Sciences,
University of Leeds, UK

Fergus I.M. Craik
Rotman Research Institute–Baycrest
Centre, University of Toronto, Canada

Lila Davachi
Department of Psychology and
Center for Neural Science, New York
University, USA

Michael Davis
Department of Psychiatry and
Behavioral Sciences, Emory
University, USA

Chris I. De Zeeuw
Department of Neuroscience, Erasmus
Medical Center, The Netherlands

Anthony Dickinson
Department of Experimental
Psychology, University of
Cambridge, UK

Yadin Dudai
Department of Neurobiology,
Weizmann Institute, Israel

Eric Eich
Department of Psychology, University
of British Columbia, Canada

Howard Eichenbaum
Department of Psychology, Boston University, USA

Randall W. Engle
School of Psychology, Georgia Institute of Technology, USA

Michael S. Fanselow
Department of Psychology, University of California, Los Angeles, USA

Susan M. Fitzpatrick
James S. McDonnell Foundation, USA

John M. Gardiner
Department of Psychology, University of Sussex, UK

Susan E. Gathercole
Department of Psychology, University of York, UK

Lynn Hasher
Department of Psychology, University of Toronto, Canada

Michael E. Hasselmo
Department of Psychology, Boston University, USA

Alice F. Healy
Department of Psychology, University of Colorado at Boulder USA

Marcia K. Johnson
Department of Psychology, Yale University, USA

Stanley B. Klein
Department of Psychology, University of California, Santa Barbara, USA

Asher Koriat
Department of Psychology, University of Haifa, Israel

Joseph E. LeDoux
Center for Neural Science, New York University, USA

John E. Lisman
Biology Department & The Benjamin and Mae Volen National Center for Complex Systems, Brandeis University, USA

Elizabeth F. Loftus
Department of Psychology & Social Behavior, University of California, Irvine, USA

Mark A. McDaniel
Department of Psychology, Washington University in St. Louis, USA

Kathleen B. McDermott
Department of Psychology, Washington University in St. Louis, USA

Anthony R. McIntosh
Rotman Research Institute–Baycrest Centre, University of Toronto, Canada

Colin M. MacLeod
Department of Psychology, University of Waterloo, Canada

Randolf Menzel
Institute for Biology–Neurobiology, Free University of Berlin, Germany

Richard G.M. Morris
College of Medicine and Veterinary Medicine, University of Edinburgh, UK

Morris Moscovitch
Department of Psychology,
University of Toronto, Canada

Edvard I. Moser
Center for the Biology of Memory,
Norwegian University of Science and
Technology, Norway

Lynn Nadel
Department of Psychology,
University of Arizona, USA

Steve E. Petersen
Department of Neurology and
Neurological Surgery, Washington
University School of Medicine, USA

Elizabeth A. Phelps
Department of Psychology,
New York University, USA

Suparna Rajaram
Department of Psychology,
Stony Brook University, USA

Robert A. Rescorla
Department of Psychology,
University of Pennsylvania, USA

Henry L. Roediger III
Department of Psychology,
Washington University in St. Louis,
USA

Edmund T. Rolls
Department of Experimental
Psychology, University of Oxford, UK

David C. Rubin
Department of Psychology and
Neuroscience, Duke University, USA

Susan J. Sara
Neuromodulation, Neural Plasticity
and Cognition, Pierre & Marie Curie
University, France

Daniel L. Schacter
Department of Psychology,
Harvard University, USA

Sara J. Shettleworth
Department of Psychology,
University of Toronto, Canada

Alcino J. Silva
Department of Neurobiology,
Psychiatry and Psychology and Brain
Research Institute, University of
California, Los Angeles, USA

Steven M. Smith
Department of Psychology,
Texas A&M University, USA

Norman E. Spear
Department of Psychology,
Binghamton University–SUNY, USA

Larry R. Squire
Veterans Affairs Medical Center
and University of California,
San Diego, USA

Wendy A. Suzuki
Center for Neural Science,
New York University, USA

J. David Sweatt
Department of Neurobiology,
University of Alabama,
Birmingham–Evelyn F. McKnight
Brain Institute, USA

Richard F. Thompson
Neuroscience Program, University
of Southern California, USA

Alessandro Treves
Sector of Cognitive Neuroscience,
International School for Advanced
Studies, Italy

Misha Tsodyks
Department of Neurobiology,
Weizmann Institute, Israel

Endel Tulving
Rotman Research Institute,
University of Toronto, Canada

John T. Wixted
Department of Psychology, University
of California, San Diego, USA

Andrew P. Yonelinas
Department of Psychology,
University of California, Davis, USA

1

Memory concepts

Yadin Dudai, Henry L. Roediger III
and Endel Tulving

A new science of memory is being shaped in front of our very eyes. It rises on the shoulders of giants: psychology, neurobiology and brain research, computational science, philosophy. Each of these parental disciplines contributes a distinctive vocabulary of terms and acronyms, all embedded to some degree or another in zeitgeists and conceptual frameworks. For the practitioners of the science of memory to be able properly to exploit, and benefit from, the rich multidisciplinarity of methods and findings, they must understand the language and *modus operandi* of their colleagues in other subsdisciplines. Such understanding is a *sine qua non* of the success of the venture.

There does exist some commonality in the languages spoken by memory science's parental disciplines already, of course. However, this accord often fails to extend to the level where it would matter most, the level of concepts. The terms may be shared, but the concepts that the terms designate are not. Even some of our most basic terms, such as 'memory' or 'memory systems', stand for rather different entities in different subdisciplines of the science of memory, and sometimes even within a given single subdiscipline.

The project embodied in this volume is an attempt to tackle the problem of the less-than-perfect communication across the discipline boundaries in the new science of memory. We believe that with proper attention, communication and interdisciplinary understanding can be improved. We also believe that a direct confrontation of the issue at what we regard as the most fundamental level of knowledge and analysis—the conceptual level—is the best approach. The discussion of concepts in the contemporary science of memory is underdeveloped. Some exceptions notwithstanding (e.g. Tulving 2000; Dudai 2002a), most practicing students of memory seem to shy away from spelling out and debating the concepts that form, or should form, the foundations of their own science. This project, we hope, will help them overcome their shyness.

What are concepts

The concept of 'concept' is the focus of intense controversies in philosophy and the sciences of the mind (e.g. Laurence and Margolis 1999; Murphy 2002). We are aware of these long-lasting fundamental controversies, as well as of our inability to contribute to their resolution. However, the irony concealed in the attempt to begin a discussion of concepts without even attempting to conceptualize 'concept' did not escape our notice. We could have adopted Bunge's minimalism (1967): concepts are units of thought. Given the scientific context of our discussion, a more formal attempt to delineate the attributes of CONCEPT[1] is desirable and useful, though also potentially controversial and provocative. We think that the most effective way to proceed is to spell out not only what concepts *are*, but also what they *are not*.

Concepts are:

1. Mental representations that encode sets of attributes that describe real or imaginary classes of items, processes or relationships.
2. Always linked to other concepts.
3. Essential elements in mental models and theories.
4. Products of mental models and theories.
5. Ultimately expressed in language.

Concepts are not:

1. Entities with spatial coordinates.
2. The terms in language that are used to express them.
3. Items that can be unveiled in experiments (though data can support or refute their validity).
4. Methods or procedures.

Concepts, conceived in 'mentalese', must be translated into language for the purpose of concretization and communication. This translation is expected to pose an obstacle on the path to shared understanding of nature. Further, scientific disciplines construct languages of some degree of remoteness from natural languages, in which case friction may emerge between the concepts as expressed in the scientific language and the potentially relevant terms in the natural language. The science of the mind is particularly predisposed to such friction, because every human mind harbors an intuitive science of the mind even without being aware of it (e.g. see on the role of metaphor in generating and constraining memory models, Roediger 1980). It is possible that this intuitive

---

[1] Throughout this chapter, we will refer to concepts in small caps.

science of the mind had been shaped by evolution to satisfy autonoetic explanations of certain mental acts, and therefore intuition could make a legitimate guide to some facets of brain output. However, science is not allowed to take this assumption for granted. The intimacy of the mind with itself might actually complicate the proper conceptualization of the science of the mind when the analysis shifts to hidden levels of brain and mind.

Core concepts

The aforementioned treatment of concepts does not differentiate among concepts in a language on the basis of importance, frequency, complexity, ontogeny, kinship, etc. Clearly when one wishes to discuss the conceptual framework of a discipline, not all concepts are to be treated equally. Many concepts are expressed as lexical items in natural languages, e.g. SON, COLOR. Others are common to many scholastic disciplines, e.g. CONCEPT, DIMENSION. Still others are endowed with a specific meaning in a given discipline, e.g. CONSOLIDATION, TRANSFER. Our goal here is to identify, delineate and discuss that set of concepts that define the core of the discipline, in this specific case the science of memory. These are concepts that delineate the domain of knowledge and are necessary for understanding its subject matter, objectives, findings and models. We define these concepts as the core concepts of the discipline. We do not claim that the core concepts that we have selected comprise a unique, let alone definitive set (and see below). Neither do we claim that mastering the core concepts is a sufficient condition for knowledge; many concepts in natural language and in other disciplines, combined with large bodies of data and theory and their interrelations, are required as well. Knowledge of the core concepts, however, is promoted by us as a necessary condition for productive scholarship.

Why concepts

Some scholars believe that bothering with concepts is nonessential and even counterproductive. Their major arguments are briefly cited below. We think that this attitude is a privilege that memory scientists cannot afford. Further, pragmatism, commonly encountered in those who advance the concept that conceptualization is armchair luxury, actually demands proper attention to concepts. The arguments in favor of concepts are listed below as well.

For concepts

The common-ground argument

Neglect of differences in the meaning and usage of concepts could hamper communication, generate confusion, blur research goals and waste mental and physical resources. This is what Socrates' urges Meno to note (Plato, **Meno, 79c,d**):

> Socrates: ... Does anyone know what a part of a virtue is, without knowing the whole?
> Meno: I suppose not.
> Socrates: No, and if you remember, when I replied to you about shape just now,
> I believe we rejected the type of answer that employs terms which are still in question
> and not yet agreed upon.
> Meno: We did, and rightly.
> Socrates: Then please do the same.

The differentiation argument

Concepts are important in the differentiation of a discipline, shaping its identity, delineating its subject matter and guiding its research programs. This is particularly important in young disciplines, and in those that tend to be data driven, like much of contemporary neuroscience. The contribution of concepts, for example NATURAL SELECTION and EVOLUTION, to the evolution of modern biology provides an apt example (Mayr 1982). Another striking example is the role of concepts in defining classical physics, modern physics and the transition between them (Holton 1973). It is noteworthy that although 'interdisciplinarity' has attained the status of a cultural mantra in contemporary culture, the truth is that differentiation into disciplines is critical in ensuring professionalism and in-depth knowledge. It is multidisciplinarity, rather than interdisciplinarity, that is the engine of modern science; therefore, the concepts of each contributing discipline must be mastered before multidisciplinarity consolidates. Last, but not least, as a fringe benefit, conceptualization could assist in tracing and highlighting the historical roots of the evolving discipline, which sometimes may prevent one from reinventing the wheel rather than improving upon it.

The facilitation argument

Conceptualization facilitates the ongoing functionality of the discipline. It does so in multiple ways. It can induce order and coherence, even if only temporary ones, in what otherwise is a rather confusing body of data. It can guide to productive experiments and models. It sometimes provides the opportunity for thought experiments that might filter out superfluous experiments and faulty theories.

The interlevel argument

The science of memory engages extensive interlevel analysis (Dudai 1992). In this type of analysis, a major goal is to produce correspondence rules ('translation rules', 'bridge laws'), which enable shifts from the terminology of one level of analysis to another, and permit formulation of systematic relationships between findings at one level and those at the other. This becomes difficult if the concepts at each level are not defined and their intercorrespondence clarified. An example from the science of memory illustrates the issue: what is the relevance of MEMORY in cellular neuroscience to MEMORY in cognitive neuroscience? Without addressing this, the relationships of findings at the cellular to the cognitive level, and vice versa, remain fuzzy at best.

The real-thing argument

Methods, techniques, fashions, models, all come and go. Core concepts are with us to stay. Physics will always have ENERGY and the science of memory LEARNING. Familiarization with core concepts hence promotes identification of the invariant, elemental problems in the field.

Against concepts

The mental prison argument

Defining concepts may impose our cognitive limitations on nature. Burke (1757) defined it succinctly: 'For when we define, we seem in danger of circumscribing nature within the bounds of our own notions'.

The ignorance argument

This is related to the mental prison argument above, implying that since we are ignorant about most of nature, we could prematurely adopt misnomers or erroneous concepts, only to propagate further ignorance.

The fuzziness argument

Since in reality very few concepts attain the decisiveness demanded from a unique definition of the entity in question, and since often over time exceptions or contradictions are found to interpretations of 'established' concepts, the entire process of conceptualization might be just a useless intellectual game.

The pragmatics argument

The history of science includes many cases in which signal discoveries were made in the absence of conceptualization, often serendipitously. If this pragmatism works well, why bother?

All in all, our view is that the '*for*' far outweigh the '*against*' arguments, though the latter, especially those referring to cognitive limitations and ignorance, should not be belittled, let alone neglected.

The concepts of the science of memory

The set of concepts covered in this volume is the outcome of an iterative exchange among us. We also sought input along the way from invitees to this project. In brief, the concepts in this set are: (1) first and foremost, concepts as defined above, not methods, experimental paradigms, findings or research objectives; (2) deemed by us to express basic ideas in the science of memory that are obligatory for appreciating the discipline; (3) elementary or first order, as opposed to complex or higher order (e.g. TRANSFER versus POSITIVE TRANSFER, NEGATIVE TRANSFER, ANALOGICAL TRANSFER; note that WORKING MEMORY and MEMORY SYSTEMS are considered here as elementary though they are complex in natural language). In addition: (4) even if used in natural language or in folk psychology, they require precise definition, or acquire specific meaning in the science of memory; (5) even if currently used predominantly only in some subdisciplines of the science of memory, their discussion by other subdisciplines is highly valuable for the development of knowledge in the discipline as a whole. All in all, we therefore propose to consider this set as core concepts.

On selection criteria

A few additional considerations will further explain why the 16 key words in the current project were selected to designate the core concepts. Why MEMORY, LEARNING, CODING and REPRESENTATION, PLASTICITY, CONTEXT, ENCODING, WORK-ING MEMORY, CONSOLIDATION, PERSISTENCE, RETRIEVAL, REMEMBERING, TRANSFER, INHIBITION, FORGETTING, MEMORY SYSTEMS, PHYLOGENESIS and EVOLUTION—but not any of the many other terms that dot the pages of learned journals and books, and make their multicolored appearances on countless power-point presentations at meetings and conferences? Where are *amnesia, amygdala, artificial neural networks, compensation, classical and instrumental conditioning, CREB, emotional memory, experimental extinction, false memory, functional neuroimaging, gene expression, habit, habituation, hippocampus, imprinting, learning set, levels of processing, limbic system, long-term potentiation, medial temporal lobe, metamemory, priming, prospective memory, punishment, reward, sensitization, sensory memory, skill* and *state-dependent learning,* to name just a few?

Many popular memory terms received short-shrift because, although at first sight they may appear to refer to concepts, they mostly represent categories that correspond to what 'concepts are not' (see above). These sorts of terms were classified as 'nonconcepts' for the present purposes. Some of them are labels of methods or procedures, some refer to tasks, some to physical objects and still others designate empirical findings, models and other sorts of things that one can intuit as not quite right. For example, *conditioning,* with its many subcategories, did not make the grade because it is easy to think of it primarily as a method, or procedure or a task. The same is true of *functional neuroimaging* and *priming. Amygdala* and *hippocampus,* and all other anatomical terms, were set aside, because they refer to physical objects, entities with spatiotemporal coordinates. Finally, terms such as *false memory*, *imprinting* and *state-dependent learning* failed the grade, because they connote particular kinds of experimental findings more than they point to concept.

Now, we fully realize that the distinction we are making here between concepts and 'nonconcepts' is rather easy to criticize. After all, many concepts are closely tied to things such as methods and findings. ENCODING, CONSOLIDATION and TRANSFER, which appear in our final list of 16, are concepts by definition, but all of them also point to particular methods, and tasks and findings. Yet, *conditioning* and *priming*, which are not on the list, also imply particular methods and tasks, and particular kinds of empirical findings. Therefore, it is easy to ask why they should be classified differently. While admitting to the inevitability of a certain degree of peremptoriness in drawing up the rules of this new game—conceptual analysis of the science of memory—we hope that additional considerations will help.

One such consideration consisted of the idea that the referent of a term should explain something, rather than only describe it. We know that this putative distinction will open another hornet's nest, because countless learned sages of the past have not been able to agree on the reality or usefulness of the distinction. Nevertheless, it did turn out to help us in our deliberations. When we could not see much explanatory surplus meaning in the definition of a term, and decided that it 'just described' something, we skipped it. This is why terms such as *amnesia, habituation, reward* and *skill* did not make it to the final team.

A third difference between our concepts and 'nonconcepts', or perhaps just a corollary of the second, had to do with the requirement that a concept should do a reasonably good job of answering certain kinds of questions that crop up in our science all the time, even if implicitly. These are questions such as 'What (exactly) do you mean when you use the term X?' 'What is X?' and 'What does X do?' Because we are discussing concepts, we note that the 'do' in the last question refers to the (explanatory) role that a given concept is meant to play in a larger scheme of things, such as a model or 'theory'. We could imagine plausible answers to these questions asked about the 16 core concepts, whereas such images might be more difficult to come up with in situations where X refers to venerable expressions such as *association* or *skill*.

The aforementioned considerations did eliminate a number of potential candidates for core concepts, but certainly not all. There are lots of viable candidates left. *Attention, binding, motivation, reinforcement* and many others quickly come to mind as examples. These will have to wait their turn. Some of these, we trust, will be covered in the course of the discussion of the core concepts as defined here; others may get their due when the science of memory project moves on to methods, facts and theories; and still others may triumph in the end as dark horses of the present set. Lastly, we are well aware of the fact that idiosyncrasies are not eliminated by group effort. Paradoxically, they sometimes become reinforced via unwarranted consensual self-contentment. It is quite possible that other teams will come up with somewhat different lists, even if they use similar selection rules. The modest claim we wish to make about the present set is that each term captures an important idea about learning and memory, and that these 16 core terms represent a good starting place.

On the exposition of concepts in this volume

The order in which the set of core concepts appears in this volume is not a given. This order may be construed as reflecting a bias toward an ontogenetic agenda, where 'ontogeny' implies the unfolding of the life history of a platonic memory item. Actually, this coupling of order-of-presentation to order-of-development is mostly a marriage of convenience. After introducing the two meta-concepts of MEMORY and LEARNING, the list proceeds to concepts referring to memory formation (CODING and REPRESENTATION, PLASTICITY, CONTEXT, ENCODING, WORKING MEMORY), maturation and use (CONSOLIDATION, PERSISTENCE, RETRIEVAL, REMEMBERING, TRANSFER) and lack of availability or loss (INHIBITION, FORGETTING). The list concludes with evolutionary issues (MEMORY SYSTEMS, PHYLOGENY and EVOLUTION). We do expect debates about this order even if the biography of a memory item is accepted as a convenient guiding principle. For example, psychologists and neuroscientists may differ on the preferred position of WORKING MEMORY in the list, depending on whether they consider it to be primarily related to the formation or to the use, respectively, of a memory item.

On concepts in an emerging discipline

Pluralism is the ambrosia of science. This appreciation is already connoted by our remark above that other teams might come up with somewhat different lists of core concepts. Even in a mature, paradigmatic science, pluralism impels revaluation of paradigms and ultimately paradigm shifts. Intellectual polyphony is particularly essential in younger disciplines, while bodies of core concepts, research programs, working models and heuristic theories are still being shaped on the basis of the contribution of the source disciplines. A tension is therefore generated between the wish to define and cultivate the identity of the new discipline and the need to remain tuned to what other disciplines have to offer. We are aware of this tension. It is definitely not the intention of this volume artificially to impose a unified view of what each of the core concepts of the science of memory means. Rather, the idea is to present clearly what the different concepts mean to experts from different backgrounds, hoping that this will result in better communication and mutual understanding, less fuzziness and possibly improved research programs, models and theories. This intention is reflected in the structure of the enterprise: for each concept, at least two position papers are presented, followed by an integrative essay. The latter is hence not a jury verdict; it is only an interim report on an intellectual dialogue. The position papers and the integrative attempt should be considered as a trigger for further contemplation of what the science of memory is, and a modest contribution to the maturation of our science.

On concepts as concepts

Finally, glancing at the selection, we cannot refrain from noting that the list reflects some basic controversies in the sciences of concepts and mind, which in turn reflect on the science of memory. Without exceeding too much the scope of this discussion, or promising answers that we cannot deliver, two selected notions are noteworthy. Do the concepts represent natural or artificial types? By natural type we mean a class honored by nature in the absence of obligatory intervention of the human mind. This issue is manifestation of the good old debate on the role of *a priori* and *a posteriori* (valuable concepts *per se*) in the interaction of our mind with the world. We leave it for the reader to take this complex issue from here, only adding that the terms selected for discussion in this book possibly represent a spectrum of more natural to more artificial types of entities. A second, related issue is whether the concepts represent distinctly segregated types of entities in the world, or only prototypes formed in our mind by statistical analysis of properties. The first view is deterministic, the latter statistical. If statistical, we should not aspire to uncover sharp boundaries in taxonomies, e.g. taxonomy of MEMORY SYSTEMS. However, the science of memory—not unlike most other scientific disciplines—is still far away from the point where such fundamental problems of classification impose practical limitations on knowledge.

1

Memory

The most critical concept in the science devoted to its analysis, memory, never had the privilege of sailing the tranquil waters of consensus. Behavioral and brain scientists, their sects notwithstanding, can spend memorable evenings in arguing what is it exactly that 'memory' means. They all seem, however, to base their arguments on the intuitive notion that memory is an imprinting of past experience, be it physical, mental or both. Students of behavior focus on the need to infer the existence of memory from behavior, while, aptly so, students of the brain focus on the need to contemplate memory in terms of neuronal stuff. The focus in multiple branches of the science of memory has shifted over the years toward considering memory as changes in knowledge, or in internal models of the world. According to this view, memory is the retention over time of experience-dependent internal representations or of the capacity to reactivate or reconstruct such representations. This view also epitomizes the notion, spelled out in the Introductory chapter, that concepts make sense only in the context of other concepts; in the present context, the reader is encouraged particularly to consult the concept of coding and representation.

Y.D.

2

Memory: It's all about representations

Yadin Dudai

The concept of memory is deep rooted since pre-scientific times in the behavioral level of description and analysis. This poses two major types of problems. One, how should one distinguish memory from other faculties of the human mind that subserve cognition and behavior. Secondly, given the complex mechanistic and computational vocabulary of contemporary brain research, how should a scientist of memory translate the concept of memory into terms that keep its intuitive and philosophical meanings on the one hand, yet permit analysis of its neuronal substrates and engineering principles on the other. Both types of problems are solvable, though not without the solutions exposing certain inherent weaknesses in the way science attempts to classify the world.

Variations on themes

Classic views of memory, dating back to early philosophy but reformulated over a century ago in the terminology of experimental psychology, share the view that memory refers to changes in the individual's behavior as a result of that individual's experience. A selection of such 'behavioral' definitions is given in Dudai (1992); a terse typical example is 'Lasting change in behavior resulting from previous experience'.

Variations on this classic theme differ in three main aspects. First, an attempt has been made by some authors to incorporate *a priori* into the concept of memory the boundary condition that memory is by definition adaptive, hence is an 'experience-dependent adaptive change in behavior'. This constraint has been ultimately abandoned, and rightly so, because it follows the faulty so-called Panglossian paradigm, which posits that whatever occurs in nature (in this case in the brain) is always guided by beneficial adaptivity (Gould and Lewontin 1979). Secondly, some lasting experience-dependent changes in the individual's behavior have nothing to do with memory as our intuition perceives it, but rather are the outcome of fatigue, intoxication, injury or disease. Therefore, the exclusion clause has been introduced, which defines memory as alteration in behavior provided it is not the consequence of the aforementioned causes. Thirdly, and most importantly, despite the protest of ardent orthodox behaviorists, it has been realized long ago that memory is often manifested as latent changes in behavior rather than overt ones; in other words, proper performance at the time of a particular test should not serve as a defining attribute for the formation of a relevant memory. This led to definitions that refer to memory as the outcome of experience-dependent changes in 'the potential to behave', not solely in actualized behavior. This latter variation on the theme of the behavioral concepts of memory is important indeed, because it introduced 'knowledge', not 'performance', as a critical attribute of memory.

This emphasis on knowledge is, of course, not strikingly original. Plato put it nicely: 'The soul acquires knowledge and is kept going and improved by learning and practice' (*Theaetetus 153b*). An updated modern formulation of the same idea is that memory is 'organized knowledge, which grows and becomes better organized' (Charniak and McDermott 1985). It is noteworthy that this type of thinking implies that memory needs knowledge to start with; to gain knowledge, you must already have to know something that will make this knowledge meaningful and useful. However, the main point, in the context of the present discussion, is that the concept of memory is transformed into the terminology of 'knowledge'. This means that students of the science of memory find themselves facing the problem of how to unveil and measure knowledge, including latent knowledge. Particularly daunting is the task of neuroscientists who seek to identify, let alone quantify, knowledge in the brain.

What knowledge means

I maintain that despite our current inability to identify and quantify knowledge in the brain, or, in other words, decode the language of brain circuits and decipher the precise meaning of their activity, we can, and we should, think about memory in terms of knowledge encoded in brains. Furthermore, we should already now generate the conceptual framework that will fit those future days in which experts will be able to observe a brain circuit in action and tell from its spatiotemporal activity signature what item that circuit encodes at that specific point in time. Moreover, my claim is that by proper conceptual treatment of memories as use-dependent bodies of knowledge, we can unify multi-level approaches to brain research, and relieve reductionistic-oriented experts from the chagrin of trying to figure out the relevance of findings in synapses and individual cells to the actual output of the behaving organism. Proper conceptualization could hence guide practitioners of the science of memory to focus on the proper, restrained level of reduction needed to understand the defining biological phenomena, processes and mechanisms of our memory.

To achieve the aforementioned goal, and in the context of the 'science of memory', I think that the concept of 'knowledge' should be replaced with a related term, better fitted for analysis in the neuroscience. This is 'internal representation'. An internal representation is *a map of event space in the system's coding space* (Cooper 1973; Dudai 1989). In the case of the nervous system, it is, specifically, a *neuronally encoded structured version of the world that could potentially guide behavior* (Dudai 1989, 2002a). It is critical to note that 'internal representation' is here considered in its most reductive sense. The underlying tenet is that nervous systems, be they even the most primitive ones, had evolved to encode representations of facets of the world, and make computations over these representations while keeping the distinctiveness of things represented (parsing) and the relationship among things represented (structure). Internal representations encoded in nervous systems are therefore constructs that vary tremendously in their complexity, from the most elementary ones (e.g. of simple reflexes, encoding the stimulus and its proper response) to the most complex ones in human cognition.

The function of memory is to retain over time experience-created or modified internal representations[2]. Memory is hence the retention over time of experience-dependent internal representations, or of the capacity to reactivate or reconstruct such representations.

Conceptual and practical advantages

Why should we bother to consider memory as lasting experience-dependent internal representations? I think that by doing so we gain the following conceptual and practical advantages.

1. We come to view memory as a cross-level phenomenon or function, which in real life it is. Referring to 'internal representation' implies dealing with the type of information that is encoded in the neuronal substrate but ultimately expressed at the behavioral level. This should appeal to brain scientists, computational neuroscientists and behavioral scientists alike. This should also appeal to neuroscientists working on species ranging from slugs from mathematicians.

---

[2] To escape the Panglossian paradigm noted above, I should stress that this functionalist conceptual framework does not entail assumptions about the origin of the aforesaid function, i.e. whether specifically selected for this function in the course of evolution, or only gained the function as a by-product of other natural selections or of the system's structural constraints. The only relevant point in the context of the present discussion is that that system which we deem a memory system is so deemed by us because it has the capacity to encode models of the world.

2. We focus on what I consider to be the critical obstacle in brain and memory research, namely the identification of the *specific* information that is encoded in neural circuits and of the changes that occur in this information with learning. This as opposed to: (a) types of neural mechanisms, including plasticity mechanisms, which serve as biological vehicles ('tools of neural syntax') to embody representations ('tokens of neural semantics'); (b) changes that are a manifestation of biological house-keeping and homeostasis. Identification of the relevant codes and representations (but see below) could permit at the end of the day molecular, cellular and circuit data to be related to behaviorally relevant memory mechanisms, and distinguish memory-related changes from nonmemory-related changes. In other words, by considering memory as use-dependent, altered or reconstructed representations, we proceed toward construction of translation functions ('bridge rules') among multiple levels of analysis of brain function, from the synaptic via the cellular circuit to the behavior. This is particularly important in the multidisciplinary 'science of memory', in which different experts contribute knowledge from different levels of analysis, some remote from the behavioral output of the intact organism.

3. Alas, at the time of writing, we know only little about how identified brain circuits encode specific pieces of information, even in rather simple systems. However, this is likely to change soon, given the pace of advance of methods and theory. By focusing attention on memory as alteration in internal representations, we hence merge memory research with the most enigmatic and critical cutting edge of neuroscience at large, namely the search for the syntax and semantics of neuronal codes, representations and computations performed over these representations.

Memory, as discussed above, illustrates how a concept, itself a mental construct, can guide research. In this case, by pointing toward the importance of understanding how information is represented in the nervous system, as a prerequisite for understanding how this information changes as a consequence of experience and how the change persists over time. Further, the concept of memory illustrates that despite the great variety of types and manifestations of memory (e.g. see Sections 15 and 16 of this volume), a functional common denominator exists, i.e. memory as alterations in internal representations, which binds the science of memory together. As noted in the introductory chapter to this volume, concepts do not exist in isolation. Among the concepts most intimately related to MEMORY and discussed in companion chapters in this volume, are CODING AND REPRESENTATION, LEARNING, ENCODING, PERSISTENCE, RETRIEVAL and REMEMBERING.

3

Memory: Why the engram is elusive

Morris Moscovitch

Memory is a lasting, internal representation of a past event or experience (or some aspect of it) *that is reflected in thought or behavior*. It follows, therefore, that *memory does not exist until it is recovered*.

Many probably agree with the first part of the definition (especially if we include neural and neurochemical events as underlying representations, see Section 3 of this volume), but at least as many may disagree with the second. Evidence from subjective experience, and from the human and animal laboratory, has shown that memories may momentarily be inaccessible, or difficult to reveal, but that given enough time and the proper cues and testing conditions, those memories can be recovered and demonstrated in thought or behavior. Because memories were only temporarily absent, it is concluded that they had always existed. At a conceptual level, this kind of evidence has supported a concept of memory as a free-standing entity (R.L. Lockhart, personal communication 2005) which exists independently of the operations needed to recover it, and possibly to encode and retain it (see Sections 6, 9 and 10 of this volume).

The concept of memory as a free-standing entity fits the lay person's view nicely, though some dictionary definitions of memory take into account the operations needed to recover the past event or experience (e.g. *Webster's New World Dictionary* 1959; *The American Heritage Dictionary* 1979). It also fits well with most psychologists' and neuroscientists' conception of memory. Although almost everyone concedes that in order to study memory there has to be ultimately some demonstration of a change in behavior (or thought in the case of humans) from which we infer that memory exists, this condition is considered to be only a procedural necessity that may even be eliminated once we can find neural or molecular markers of memory. Indeed, we may already have reached that point. Quite a number of neuroscientists consider themselves as studying memory simply by examining lasting changes in neural activity [e.g. long-term potentiation (LTP)] in the synapse, or in intracellular molecular mechanisms and processes which are induced by a particular event.

The alternative view, that memory does not exist until it is revealed in behavior or thought, conceives of memory not as a free-standing entity, but as linked to a process of recovery and emerging from it. Memory is the product of a process of recovery (an act of memory) rather than an entity which exists independently of that process. This view is at least as old as Semon's (1904) conception of memory, and has a number of more recent incarnations in the work of Tulving (1983), Kolers and Roediger (1984), Whittlesea (2002) and Craik (2002*b*; Chapter 23, this volume), among others. This quote from Craik (2002*b*) captures this view well:

> Where is the percept when we are not perceiving? The question does not make much sense; clearly percepts are not micro-representations waiting patiently for 'their' specific combination of input patterns to activate them. Rather, perceiving is a dynamic process that occurs online in a given time period, and reflects the interaction of incoming sense data with pre-wired and learned processes; this interaction in turn drives behavior and subjective awareness. It is thus perhaps equally meaningless to ask Where is the memory trace when we are not remembering? Again the various behavioral and experiential aspects of remembering occur only during memorial processing, and the hunt for the engram [the physical manifestation of the memory trace that is independent of the operations needed to recover it] may prove as fruitless as the hunting of the Snark. To alter Lewis Carroll's mournful tale only slightly, those pursuing the memory trace may find 'in the midst of their laughter and glee' that the engram has 'softly and suddenly vanished away—for the Trace was a Boojum, you see'.

I agree with all that Craik says except his conclusion. Like many other psychologists and neuroscientists (see a recent paper by Schafe *et al.* 2005), he posits that the engram or memory trace and memory are conflated, whereas I believe, along with Semon (1904) and Tulving (1983), if I understand them correctly, that the two are separate. The engram or memory trace is the representation of an encoded event or experience. It is not yet a memory, but provides the necessary (physical) condition for memories to emerge, just as an external stimulus provides the occasion for a percept to emerge. Put another way, the engram is permissive or necessary for memory but does not suffice for its materialization. A memory emerges when the engram interacts with retrieval cues or information derived from particular environmental conditions, a process which Semon termed "ecphory". The product of this retrieval–engram interaction is a memory. Without retrieval, there is only the engram, and even its existence is inferred from memory's emergence.

The book in the library analogy

Let me illustrate this distinction, and the general point that a memory does not exist until it is recovered, with a simple analogy of looking for a book in a library. Suppose you think a particular book is in the library. You go to the shelf where you believe it was located and it is not there. Does the book exist in the library or not? One possibility is that you looked in the wrong place. You now look up its call number but you discover that the book is not at the location the call number specified. There are now two possibilities: the book is somewhere in the library but you cannot find it, or the book has disappeared. For all intents and purposes, as long as you do not recover the book, you cannot know whether it exists. Saying it is there because there is a record that it possibly existed once (the call number) does not solve the problem, but begs the question.

There are a number of problems with that analogy, but far from undermining the conclusion that a memory does not exist until it is recovered, they only reinforce it. The first problem is that the engram is not like a book. Once written, a book is immutable. That is not true of an engram. Though the engram is the representation of an encoded event, it, too, is subject to change. Moreover, though the book is a bound entity existing in a single location, the engram may consist of information that is not tightly bound, if it is bound at all, and is distributed over many locations. Recovering a memory, therefore, is not like finding a book at a particular single location, but more like assembling the pages of a book which may be scattered in different locations in the library. Finally, unlike a call number which is distinct from the book itself, retrieval cues and processes interact with the engram and influence the memory which is recovered. Depending on the interaction, some 'pages' of the memory may be missing, others may be placed in the wrong sequence, still others may be imported from other books which are related in some way to the cues and the engrams, and some of the cues themselves may be incorporated into the memory that is recovered and change the engram on which it was based (Schacter 1996, 2002). These ideas, that memory is a product of a recovery process, rather than a free-standing entity awaiting discovery, and that it is distinguishable from an engram which itself may be mutable, have a number of implications for the science of memory.

Relevance to research and theory

There is little in this description of the nature of memory that should be surprising to psychologists who work on memory in humans (for reviews, see Schacter 1996, 2002). Though malleable, and sometimes fragile, human memory is sufficiently resilient to support everyday needs and provide an (imperfect) record of past events and experiences. Memory, though not perfect, is good enough. As Schacter rightly observes, memory's deficiencies or imperfections arise as a natural consequences of the operation of the processes and mechanisms on which it is based. Though Schacter did not go so far as to state explicitly that memory does not exist until it is recovered, I believe it is a conclusion that is consistent with the evidence he reviews.

This conclusion applies not only to complex, clearly reconstructive memories, such as recalling a sequence of events that form part of an autobiographical episode, but also to such seemingly simple types of memory which are evident in tests of perceptual and conceptual priming, and even in Pavlovian or classical conditioning (see Section 2 of this volume). Let me give an example from a study on priming that Vriezen, Bellos and I conducted a few years ago (Vriezen *et al.* 1995). Working on the widely held assumption that viewing a stimulus alters its structural representation so that it can be recognized better the next time it is presented (priming), we asked participants to make an animacy judgment on the first presentation and a size judgment on the second, or an identical judgment on both presentations. We fully expected that performance would be better in the identical than the crossed conditions, but predicted that priming, though diminished, would still be observable in the crossed condition. To our surprise, it was completely abolished. These results have been replicated often, and confirmed that priming is altered because some aspect of the 'context' or response has changed (see Schacter *et al.* 2003). It is as if even the simple memory that supports priming did not exist until the retrieval conditions were appropriate for its recovery. As predicted by Vriezen *et al.* and others, viewing the stimulus does effect a change in the structural representation as is evident by alterations in activation in regions of occipital and inferior temporal cortex associated with object perception; nevertheless, these changes in activation in posterior sites are not correlated with priming in the crossed condition (see also Wig *et al.* 2005). The engram may be there, but the implicit memory is not.

As this example illustrates, the definition can accommodate different types of memory, from implicit to explicit, and has the advantage of calling attention to the process of recovery as crucial to our understanding what memory is and how it functions. It also accommodates easily a number of phenomena that are puzzling if we consider memory to be a free-standing entity awaiting discovery, but not if we consider it as being the product of the interaction between engram and retrieval. Among these phenomena are the misinformation effect (in which the cue alters the memory that is retrieved; Loftus *et al.* 1995), confabulation (in which people with damage to ventromedial prefrontal cortex distort past events almost beyond recognition; Gilboa and Moscovitch 2002), the mutability of memory with time, an aspect of which is captured by multiple trace theory of recent and remote memory (Nadel and Moscovitch 1997; Moscovitch *et al.* 2005; Chapter 31, this volume), and re-consolidation (in which memories which were thought to be fully consolidated are 'lost' if an amnestic agent is applied shortly after they are recovered; Dudai 2004; Frankland and Bontempi 2005). The definition also encourages us to consider memory as a process that emerges from underlying representations, and in doing so can alter the representations themselves.

This definition also applies to studies of simpler organisms, such as *Aplysia*, simple preparations, such as hippocampal slices, or even to simple procedures in complex organisms, such as classical eyelid conditioning in mammals. Here, too, the role of retrieval in recovering a memory should not be overlooked. Great strides have been made in identifying the changes at the synaptic and intracellular level needed for engram formation and retention, but little is known about how those changes interact with conditions at retrieval to elicit a memory. Changes which are relatively permanent take a long time to form, and presumably to re-activate, yet they must lead to other changes which can be instantiated quickly to account for the almost instantaneous recovery of even very old memories (see Dudai 2004; and Section 10 of this volume). Conducting studies on retrieval–engram interactions at the synaptic or cellular level, which are analogous to those at the systems level, would be very illuminating in light of the definition we adopted.

Conclusion

The definition of memory for which I argued placed as much weight on retrieval processes as on storage. It follows from the definition that memory does not exist independently of its being retrieved. Such a definition forces us to think of memory as a representation which is created from the interaction of retrieval cues and processes with stored knowledge rather than as an entity awaiting discovery. The implication which this definition has for research and theory was noted.

4

Memory: Delineating the core

Daniel L. Schacter

In a volume concerned with concepts of memory, attempting to delineate and define the notion of memory itself is both important and daunting. The importance of the task should be self-evident: if researchers mean different things when they use the term 'memory', then the resulting misunderstandings and miscommunications are likely to contribute to conceptual confusion in many sectors of the field. Indeed, if students of memory cannot agree on what constitutes the core concept of their discipline, then it is difficult to imagine that they will be able to agree on much else.

The task is daunting because it appears to conflict with one of the major themes in memory research during the past two decades and more: memory is not a single or unitary entity, but instead consists of a number of dissociable underlying forms or systems (Schacter and Tulving 1994). The nature and number of proposed memory forms or systems differ according to the preferences of different theorists, but some of the main contenders are widely agreed on: episodic, semantic, procedural and working memory, not to mention declarative versus nondeclarative memory, and explicit versus implicit memory (see Section 15 of this volume). If memory is not a unitary entity, and multiple forms or systems of memory exist, what is our task in attempting to define memory? What precisely is it that we want to define?

Characterizing memory: seeking the core

If one accepts the premise that memory is a nonunitary entity, there are at least two ways to approach the challenge of conceptualization and definition. The first is to give up on what might seem to some like a futile enterprise and focus attention instead on the specific forms of memory that have been proposed. The second is to seek what is common to the concept of memory across the various forms, i.e. to try to delineate the core of memory itself. What is it about 'memory' that is shared, for example, among episodic memory, semantic memory and procedural memory? In this chapter, I pursue this latter course and try to delineate aspects of 'memory' that are common to various different uses of the term.

Let us begin, then, by focusing on features of three major memory systems: episodic, semantic and procedural. Episodic memory refers to recollecting previous experiences from one's personal past, semantic memory refers to general knowledge of facts and concepts, and procedural memory refers to the acquisition of skills or procedures. I use these three systems as examples because there is reasonably broad agreement concerning their existence and some of their fundamental features (Schacter *et al.* 2000), and because these three forms allow us to sample a broad spectrum of characteristics of memory. If we can come up with a conceptualization of memory that does not exclude any one of these three, then we may well be on the right track in thinking about core features of memory.

For example, memory is sometimes characterized as the recollection or re-experiencing of some aspect of the past in the present. Such a characterization seems innocent enough, but is problematic because it excludes procedural memory. Procedural memory can be expressed without any conscious recollection of the past, as illustrated by amnesic patients who exhibit intact procedural memory for experiences that they do not remember consciously. From this perspective, any attempt to seek the core of memory cannot appeal to conscious recollection or related concepts that exclude implicit or nonrecollective forms of memory such as the procedural system.

At the opposite extreme, we want to make sure that our conceptualization of memory is not so broad that it fails to exclude phenomena that most of us would consider to fall outside the rubric of memory. For instance, consider another seemingly straightforward characterization of memory: the effects of experience that persist over time. Persistence over time is clearly a defining feature of any kind of memory, and such a definition would most certainly include episodic, semantic and procedural forms. However, it would also include many phenomena that we probably do not want to label as 'memory'. Smashing a glass into a wall will produce an effect of experience that persists over time, but not too many of us would want to say that memory is involved, nor would we want to appeal to memory to explain the persisting effects of breaking an arm or a leg.

This problem is not new. Over a century ago, the biologists Hering (1880/1920) and Semon (1904) proposed that memory is a very general property of organic matter that underlies heredity and development as well as retention of personal experience. They were criticized for applying the concept of memory so broadly that it failed to exclude much of anything (for discussion, see Schacter 2001). A similar issue has reared its head in modern discussions of multiple memory systems, especially in analyses of implicit forms of memory such as priming, where some have contended that lax criteria for postulating memory systems could result in postulating a 'memory system' for just about any after-effect of an experience (cf. Roediger *et al.* 1990; Schacter and Tulving 1994). Clearly, there are many persisting after-effects of experience that we want to exclude from our core notion of memory, while at the same time keeping our conceptualization sufficiently broad that we can accommodate episodic, semantic and procedural forms.

One way to address the foregoing concerns, and to exclude persisting after-effects that nobody would want to call 'memory', is to conceive of memory as a *representation* of past experiences that persists over time (e.g. Chapter 2 and Section 3 of this volume). The emphasis on representation here acknowledges that the persisting change in the nervous system that we call memory involves a code that models or stands for some event or set of events in the external world. It is the absence of such representation in examples such as broken glass or legs that allows us to reject these occurrences as instances of memory. At the same time, an emphasis on representation still allows us comfortably to include episodic, semantic and procedural forms of memory within the spirit of our general conceptualization. However, even this seemingly straightforward characterization is not without problems and complications, which we can best appreciate by considering some of the different senses in which 'memory' is typically used by scientists and laypersons alike.

Multiple senses of memory

One problem in attempting to delineate a core concept of memory is that the term is commonly used to refer to different underlying constructs. Tulving (2000) distinguished among six different uses of 'memory', and no doubt one could come up with many additions to his list. For the purpose of the present discussion, I consider four different senses of memory delineated by Tulving (2000): (1) the neurocognitive capacity to encode, store and retrieve information; (2) a hypothetical store in which information is held; (3) the information in that store; and (4) an individual's phenomenal awareness of remembering something.

Attempting to delineate a core concept of memory means committing, implicitly or explicitly, to one of these (or other) senses of memory. We have already considered and rejected number 4 on this list, because defining memory as 'an individual's phenomenal awareness of remembering something' excludes procedural memory and related implicit/nonconscious forms. We can also easily reject sense number 2, because the notion of a 'memory store', though widely used in everyday parlance about memory, is not a concept to which many contemporary students would subscribe. Cognitive psychologists have long abandoned the idea of a 'memory store' in favor of a more processing-oriented view of memory (e.g. Craik and Lockhart 1972), and most neuroscientists conceive of memory storage as a distributed process, with a variety of brain regions participating in storage (e.g. Squire and Kandel 1999).

Consider next sense number 3 in the list: memory conceived as the information that is stored. When we think of memory in the manner I suggested earlier— as a representation of past experiences that persists over time—we are identifying memory with stored information. The potential problem here is that the term 'memory' is being used too narrowly. Over a century ago, Semon (1904) saw the need to distinguish between 'stored information' specifically and 'memory' more generally; he coined the term 'engram' to refer to the former. However, as Semon understood, and as has been articulated especially forcefully by Tulving (1983) in discussions of episodic memory, it is a mistake to equate the concepts of 'memory' and 'engram'. The engram is an important contributor to memory, but the character of memory is also influenced by the retrieval environment—the cues that guide the retrieval process, the state of the rememberer, and so forth (see, for example, Schacter 1996, p. 70; Chapter 3, this volume).

A conceptualization of memory that recognizes the role of the retrieval environment can build on the aforementioned notion of memory as a representation of past experiences that persists over time by adding the important idea that memory also entails the expression of a representation in cognition or behavior. Such a conceptualization brings us closer to using 'memory' in the first of the four senses delineated by Tulving (2000), i.e. as the neurocognitive capacity to encode, store and retrieve information. It seems clear that our notion of what constitutes memory should not exclude any of the three major components (encoding, storage and retrieval). Equating memory with encoding confuses memory with perceptual and conceptual processing activity, equating memory with storage confuses it with the engram, and equating memory with the products of retrieval confuses it with remembering.

Framing the issue in this manner, we are reminded of the importance of developing research that can allow us to analyze the respective contributions of encoding, storage and retrieval processes to overall memory. Cognitive psychologists have long realized the severe difficulties involved in attempting to separate clearly the contributions of the three components of memory to any particular behavioral effects. For example, many words have been written about such issues as whether the effects of aging or amnesia on memory performance can be attributed to changes in encoding, storage or retrieval, but the issue has generally remained resistant to clear resolution. Functional neuroimaging techniques have helped somewhat, inasmuch as they now allow researchers to seek more clearly for separate encoding and retrieval effects.

They are less easily adapted to isolating storage effects, although some attempts along these lines have been made in studies of short-term or working memory (e.g. Postle *et al.* 2003; Buchsbaum *et al.* 2005). Extending this type of analysis to long-term memory poses a difficult challenge, but future research focused on this issue could help to inform our understanding of the constituents of memory.

In summary, then, we need a concept of memory that is broad enough to include each of the major stages and various forms of memory, while at the same time focused enough to exclude phenomena that lie outside the domain that is ordinarily understood to constitute memory research. Hopefully this chapter and the accompanying chapters in this section take us a small step closer to achieving that goal.

Acknowledgments

Preparation of this chapter was supported by grants from the NIA and NIMH. I thank Donna Addis, Elissa Aminoff, Elizabeth Chua, Rachel Garoff-Eaton, Kelly Giovanello, Angela Gutchess, Elizabeth Kensinger, Dale Stevens and Alana Wong for useful discussion of the issues considered in this chapter.

5

Integrative comments
Memory: Distinctions and dilemmas

Richard G.M. Morris

A volume focusing on the diverse scientific concepts of memory celebrates the sophistication of our contemporary understanding, while also recognizing the outstanding problems to be addressed. The field of research on memory has matured to be one that recognizes the existence of qualitatively different types of memory and is characterized by work at many different levels of disciplinary analysis. It has turned up numerous counterintuitive experimental phenomena in the process of testing specific theories, which vibrantly reflects the extraordinary creativity and energy of researchers all over the world. It is also an endeavor that matters—as parts of this understanding are being put to work effectively in ways ranging from therapeutic applications in the neurological clinic through to the design of digital devices for the knowledge economy. A key issue, drawing upon previous discussion of a definition (Dudai 2002), is to identify the core concept of memory.

The folk psychology of memory

Clearly, memory is part of everyday life. Unlike many other scientific concepts, such as 'gene transcription' or 'coriolis force', the term 'memory' is used colloquially in a variety of different ways that are nonetheless each well understood. People talk about their memory as if it was a 'thing' they had like an organ or limb of their body. They speak of having a good memory or a bad one, implying some sense of how well this thing or device is working. They also speak of memory as information, as in having a memory of something, such as of an event that happened some time ago.

Yet another everyday sense of memory is that it is an action we undertake, as in remembering to do something—be it to buy some milk at the store or knowing how to ride a bicycle. Part of what makes memory an attractive topic for research is that the interested layperson is well aware that memory is integral to their lives, in some sense defining a person's individuality, and that it sometimes fails in either benign or more serious ways (Schacter 2001b).

As such, it is easy to communicate to students and to the interested public at large that a better understanding of the mechanisms of memory would be useful. Clearly, however, one problem is that the concept is actually somewhat ill defined in its lay use. Is it any better as a scientific term?

Scientific concepts of memory

With respect to its scientific analysis, the term 'memory' has its origins in psychology but has since been used in a number of different ways in the different subdisciplines of the neurosciences (Dudai 1989; Tulving 2000). These include the following:

- The capacity to encode, store, consolidate and retrieve information (i.e. *memory processing*)

- A hypothetical store in which information is held (i.e. *a physical device in the brain*)

- The information in such a store (i.e. information content, but not synonymous with physical memory traces or 'engrams')

- The process of retrieving information from a store (*as in the act of remembering*), including an individual's exercise of a previously learned skill (*as in remembering how to ride a bicycle*).

- An individual's phenomenal awareness of remembering something (i.e. not only that one remembers a fact or an event, but the conscious awareness of doing so).

A further key idea in modern research, particularly in neuropsychology, is that it is common to speak of multiple 'types' of memory (Squire 1987; Weiskrantz 1987; Dudai 1989; Baddeley 1990; Schacter and Tulving 1994; Eichenbaum and Cohen 2001). Each qualitatively distinct type of memory is, or at least should be, anchored with respect to such parameters as the type of information represented, the encoding rules, the persistence of the information storage over time, the sensitivity to different kinds of brain damage and the flexibility with which information can be expressed or recalled. However, even this lengthy list of the neuropsychological attributes of different types of memory would not satisfy the molecular neuroscientist who might assert that we will not properly understand memory—any type of memory—until we know the molecules and the cell-biological mechanisms that mediate it (Sweatt 2003). The neurophysiologist, in contrast, may want to focus on the dynamic patterns of neural activity or the alterations in synaptic efficacy that occur when different types of memories get made or retrieved and the mechanisms of synaptic plasticity that mediate the changes in strength of connections between neurons which many suppose to be the physical basis of memory (Bliss and Collingridge 1993; Dudai and Morris 2000; Martin *et al.* 2000). Neuroanatomists may hope they can look at memories down a microscope, and so know where they happen in the brain and whether different types of memory have distinct physical substrates. Each of these sciences has a different vantage point and it may seem foolhardy to claim that any one necessarily offers a better perspective on the topic than any other. There is, however, a measure of conceptual confusion here that it is important to identify.

Engrams versus memories

One important distinction relevant to thinking about these different disciplinary approaches is that between 'engram' and 'memory'. Engrams are putative physical traces in the brain that occur as a result of experience, that last and in some way are important to the later expression of memory. Memory, in contrast, is arguably more of a neurocognitive process by which representations of experience are expressed in language or other aspects of behavior. This distinction is important because it seems clear that when anatomists, physiologists or molecular scientists speak of memory, they may more often be speaking of engrams. This not always the case; a point I shall come back to at the end.

The engram versus memory theme is pursued particularly by Morris Moscovitch (Chapter 3). First, it argues for a fundamental distinction between these two concepts. Secondly, it asserts that memories do not exist separately from the various acts of recall. Memory, for him, is *the product of a process that involves an interaction between engrams and the circumstances and/or cues associated with retrieval.* Drawing upon neuropsychological evidence, and from both explicit and implicit memory tests, he argues that the engram/memory distinction carries with it the logical consequence that memories *never* exist unless expressed—a view that is clearly different from the layman's looser understanding of the concept.

The distinction Moscovitch makes is also analytically helpful as it raises the possibility, indeed the likelihood, that a single engram can contribute to distinct acts of remembering in different retrieval contexts. This should not be taken to imply that engrams are fixed or immutable, like a well-preserved book in a library, because acts of remembering may involve and/or give rise to patterns of neural activity that, in turn, change the very engrams that have themselves participated in that memory's expression. Moscovitch's own 'multiple trace' theory of retrograde amnesia is very much in this spirit (Nadel and Moscovitch 1997). Thus, for him, engrams and memories are distinct, the former being necessary for the latter but not sufficient, and there is a dynamic dialectic between them.

Dan Schacter (Chapter 4, this volume) clearly accepts the engram/memory distinction, but goes on to recognize several different ways in which memory may be conceptualized (as in the bulleted list above). He eventually comes down in favor of the idea that, to have a memory, is to have *the neurocognitive capacity to encode, store and retrieve information*. He explicitly recognizes the existence of multiple types of memory—such as episodic, semantic and procedural—yet shares the hope that we can find some 'core' concept of memory amidst this heterogeneity of types. He rejects any identification of memory as the phenomenological awareness of remembering on the grounds that implicit forms of memory (e.g. sensorimotor skills) lack this attribute.

In keeping with most contemporary cognitive psychologists, Schacter also rejects the idea that the concept of memory should be used to refer to the store in which information is held in the brain. The primary reason for this is that it is now usual to think of memory as a capacity to process information with its expression being, as Moscovitch argued, some interaction between engrams and the retrieval cues present at the time. Schacter also argues against too eclectic a definition of memory that would include any or all effects of experience that persist over time, asserting that a 'representational' component is essential. One ironic illustration of this last point can be made in reference to the graphic artist's pre-digital drawing tool of a 'bendy ruler' that can be molded into a variety of different shapes. Can such a ruler be said to have memory? Once used and the line on paper drawn, the result may well be a representation of something. However, on the less inclusive account of memory that Schacter commends, the ruler itself does not represent the particular shape, it simply holds it over time. Thus, it has certain physical attributes than enable persistence over time, but it does not encode any shape given to it, nor does it store or retrieve it. Its use by the artist enables memory, but it does not itself possess it. A bendy ruler only has memory in a layperson's metaphorical use of the term.

Internal representations over time

In contrast to these two neuropsychological views, Yadin Dudai (Chapter 2, this volume) appears not to accept the engram/memory distinction quite as articulated by Moscovitch and Schacter. His definition is that *memory is internal representations encoded within brains*. However, for him also, the function of memory is to retain representations over time. This definition raises the question of whether Dudai's 'internal representations' are isomorphic with Moscovitch's 'engrams'. I think not. Engrams are putative physical traces in the brain. As such, while memory is representational, engrams are not. In a simple (*sic*) nervous system such as *Aplysia*, an engram may constitute the set of structural and biochemical changes associated with presynaptic facilitation, a physiological process identified as mediating one experience-dependent form of sensitization of a withdrawal reflex. This physical trace is not—on its own—representational in the sense that Dudai's contribution implies. However, in conjunction with specific patterns of sensory activation ('retrieval cues' in Moscovitch's terminology), a memory may be expressed in the form of appropriate behavior. This memory is representational in the sense—albeit a somewhat limited one—that its appropriateness constitutes a primitive representation of a motor response that is fitting to a world that has recently become more dangerous (an augmented tendency to display withdrawal in response to somatosensory stimulation).

Dudai's emphasis on internal representations is intended to capture the notion that memory is about knowledge, that knowledge can be represented in a neural system (even implicit procedural knowledge) and that such representations can truly be said to be in the brain. The motivation for such a definition is to capture the distinction between those experience-dependent changes in nervous systems that have to do with encoded information and those that are merely house-keeping—a task that he (rightly) sees as a fundamental problem for neuroscientists studying the physiological and cell-biological 'correlates' of learning and memory. Numerous such correlates are observed in interventional studies on animals, way beyond the limited picture of brain mechanisms coming from the hemodynamic signals of human functional neuroimaging (fMRI) research, but it is very unclear how to work out which of these correlates really are the substrate of engrams that are necessary for representational knowledge. The boundaries between house-keeping and the mechanisms underlying true information encoding may actually be somewhat indistinct.

The physical basis of memory processing

Essays devoted to trying to pin down the concept of memory cannot resolve this last issue. It will take years of effort and, even then, the boundaries between 'mere' house-keeping and signal transduction involved in information encoding may actually be somewhat indistinct. However, the contrast between the idea that memory is a process that occurs only at the time of retrieval (Moscovitch and Schacter) and memory as internal representations in the brain (Dudai) high-lights a potentially major difference of opinion between neuropsychologically based and neuroscience-oriented concepts of memory. The former most surely accept that searching for the physical basis of memory is a reasonable scientific exercise. If so, then they must accept that retrieval cues also have a physical instantiation, as do the myriad of encoding, consolidation and retrieval processes that enable such cues, engrams and the context of their juxtaposition to result collectively in the expression of memory. Given this, the engram/memory distinction may not be quite as it may have once seemed, as there are many features of memory beyond engrams whose physical basis can be—and are being—investigated. The emergence of such distinctions as retrieval effort versus retrieval success is one notable example of this in neuropsychology, and there are ever more examples of neuroscientists attempting to identify the physical basis of encoding and retrieval processes that are quite distinct from the separate search for the engram. However, then Dudai's dilemma remains. How will we identify which of these correlates are uniquely involved in memory processing and which are involved in house-keeping?

2

Learning

Learning refers to the acquisition of information. Depending on the subdiscipline and the level of analysis, it is meant to denote the formation of item(s) of memory in an individual (psychology and cognition), or of the neuronal changes that are postulated to encode such items of memory in the brain of that individual (neuroscience). Hence, learning may refer to behavioral phenomena and processes, as measured by a change in performance or in the potential to perform, or to the underlying neuronal plasticity phenomena, processes and mechanisms, correlated with, or leading to, the altered behavioral performance. In practice, in cellular and molecular neuroscience, learning may also refer to use-dependent alterations in neuronal or synaptic processes or properties, even if correlation with a change in the behavioral performance is undocumented. Learning can occur intentionally or incidentally, both in real life and in the laboratory setting. Furthermore, even in situations of intentional learning, the participant may acquire information incidentally in addition to the intended study material. This may introduce confounds in the interpretation of the behavioral consequence of a learning situation. The rule of thumb is that learning may occur even when we do not intend it to happen, do not expect it or think that we do not study it. A prominent example is provided by retrieval tests, which are intend to detect and quantify the consequence of past learning, but themselves may induce new learning; the challenge for the investigator is in this case to dissociate the consequence of past experience from the new learning. Finally, when we learn a token of information, we may also learn how to learn more effectively the same or a similar type of information in the future.

Y.D.

6

Learning: A pre-theoretical concept

Robert A. Rescorla

Within the so-called field of 'animal learning' that dominated psychology in the early part of the last century, it was once common for textbooks to begin by giving a definition of 'learning'. This represented a kind of self-confidence, some would say arrogance, that those who studied learning in animals could speak for all scientists interested in learning and memory. A typical example is Kimble's (1961) influential revision of a classic textbook by Hilgard and Marquis: 'Learning is a relatively permanent change in behavior potentiality which occurs as a result of reinforced practice'. Since the 1960s it has become much less common to hazard a definition. In the 1970s, in summarizing the field for neuroscientists, Holland and I deliberately rejected the idea that one should begin with a definition (Rescorla and Holland 1976). Contemporary textbooks in animal learning have by and large adopted the same view, typically simply sidestepping the issue of what learning is and introducing the subject by a kind of historical description.

It is worth keeping in mind why giving definitions of learning fell by the wayside. In my view there are two reasons. First, within the field there seemed to be a broadly shared, if somewhat vague, agreement about what constituted learning and what did not. Obviously there would be fuzzy instances, but the tortured discussions that had attempted to resolve those issues in the past did not seem worth the effort. Rather, workers felt that the time would be better spent getting on with the actual business of investigating learning.

Moreover, such discussions invited a kind of caste system in which some phenomena were admitted into the honorific society called 'learning' whereas others were identified as outcasts. Such distinctions can be useful in providing a partition of what phenomena need attention and in helping scientists limit the range of literature that they need to read. However, they can also lead to hard feelings when pronouncements from the ruling class proclaim some phenomena as less worthy of study than others. Indeed, this is precisely what happened in the early days of study of the neuroscience of learning, in which biologists would bring phenomena to psychologists as an example of the neural basis of learning only to be told by the psychologists that this was not 'real' learning at all. I think that this kind of interaction contributed to the broad use of the term 'plasticity', which avoided the need for certification by the high council of psychologists.

My own view is that the field made the right decision in this regard. Learning seems to me to be a common language term, and the effort to give it a more precise scientific meaning may not be worthwhile. It clearly is applied to a wide range of phenomena that need explanation, but that explanation is likely to be given in terms of more specific scientific concepts at various levels of discourse, including neural and behavioral. Whether or not the various phenomena share anything is a decision to be made at the level of process and theory, not redefinition of a common language term.

Still, there seems at the intuitive level to be something in common with the phenomenon called 'learning'. Certainly laymen and scientists of other fields believe that there is an area here with shared properties and explanations. So let me try my hand at offering some suggestions about how one might go about fleshing out the meaning. Two approaches to doing this seem to me (1) to lay out the shared features of procedures that purport to study learning; in doing so we may make more operational our thinking and (2) to ask what phenomena we are especially eager to contrast with learning phenomena; in doing so we may sharpen what we feel to be the critical features of learning.

Some years ago, Holland and I suggested a framework for the study of learning (Rescorla and Holland 1976). We claimed that all learning paradigms could be characterized in terms of two points in time, what we called 't1', during which the organism has some interaction with the environment, and then 't2', at which the organism is identified as being different as a result. We argued that learning paradigms differed in the particular experiences that they used at t1 and in the different changes in the organism that they measured at t2.

Within the field of animal learning, the primary differential experiences that have been identified as interesting have been given labels, 'habituation', 'Pavlovian conditioning' and 'instrumental learning'. Procedurally these involve experiences at t1 in which the organism receives some stimulus either on its own (habituation), in systematic relation to another stimulus (Pavlovian conditioning) or in systematic relation to its own behavior (instrumental learning). However, other fields addressing learning emphasize instead other experiences.

The question of whether or not learning has occurred is a question of whether or not the t1 experience produced differences that could be measured at t2. Here it is worth noting a technical, but important, detail. In the nature of things, t2 necessarily comes after t1. Consequently, one must be on guard that the differences identified at t2 are really attributable to experiences at t1, not simply autonomous changes with the passage of time. For this reason, I have argued that the study of learning should not properly start with comparisons of the organism at t1 and t2, but rather with comparisons between two different organisms at t2, one of which has had the t1 experience and one of which has been spared that experience. That claim has some far-reaching implications, three of which I cannot resist noting: first, it forces one to confront seriously the question of what is a good comparison treatment at t1 involving not receiving the experience. Secondly, it opens up the class of differences that are taken as evidence at t2 to include behaviors and other features that are not measured at t1. Thirdly, it implies that acquisition curves are useless in the study of learning. Data taken during the t1 acquisition period almost invariably come from animals receiving different treatments dictated by the independent variables of interest. That means that they are not taken under comparable conditions for the different groups. As a result, one cannot be sure any differences reflect differences in learning as distinct from differences in local conditions in which the data are taken. A common t2 test naturally addresses that problem (see Rescorla 1988).

Within behavioral psychology the primary organismic changes that have been emphasized at t2 are behavioral: different abilities of stimuli to produce responses, different abilities to reward, etc. However, presumably these behavioral differences have concomitant neural and molecular changes that could also be used to identify changes. Different subfields have different dependent variables, such as the ability for conscious recall, effects on priming, effects on judgments, etc.

This way of thinking leads to a preliminary specification: 'Learning is the name for a heterogeneous group of processes by which differential environmental experience at one time changes the organism, leading to differential assessment results at a later time'.

Now it is clear that such a t1/t2 framework, although it might be a useful beginning, casts too broad a net, including many phenomena not normally labeled as 'learning'. Indeed, a primary issue in the older attempts to define learning was to exclude from discussion phenomena that looked like learning but were not deemed to be so. Although much effort was wasted here, perhaps there is merit in looking at some instances of t2 change as a result of t1 experiences that seem outside the ballpark. Hearst (1988) provides a typical list: motor fatigue, sensory adaptation, brain damage, disease, motivational factors, aging, poor health, drugs, maturation. The challenge in each of these cases is to devise experimental procedures for the separation. In some instances, this is a matter of picking the proper comparison t1 treatment. In other instances, it may be much more difficult or even impossible.

I believe that one reason the field of animal learning has devoted so much attention to the two learning associative procedures of Pavlovian conditioning and instrumental training is that they seemed to provide a natural and widely accepted way to exclude many of these alternatives. Because both of these are cases involving learning as a result of relationships among elements, a comparison procedure that involves presenting those same events but destroying (or modifying) the relationship provides a powerful way of identifying the critical action of the relationship in producing the t2 behavior change. In contrast, the procedures that produce habituation, repeated presentation of a stimulus, seem more difficult to separate from alternatives such as sensory adaptation and response fatigue.

In any case, one approach to narrowing the field so as to exclude 'nonlearning' is to specify more closely the t1 experiences that count. Another approach is to constrain the nature of the t2 differences that count. I do not myself favor such a constraint, but the field abounds with examples. Perhaps the first was to demand that the change found at t2 be 'relatively permanent', in an attempt to exclude peripheral sensory and motor changes. However, contemporary instances of short-term memory seem to make this less attractive. More specific to animal learning was the demand that new responses to a signal fall in a particular class. In Pavlovian conditioning, it was once common to demand that the conditioned response (CR) look like the unconditioned response (UR); but few would impose such constraints today.

My own view is that it is better to allow the definition to be too broad and to leave it to specific theories and experiments to select among instances. The question of what instances of change are or are not 'learning' will disappear into the question of what underlying mechanisms, specified either at the theoretical or neural level, are responsible for the change. That is a matter for empirical exploration, not pre-experimental rumination. In fact nothing of scientific importance will hang on the decision as to whether to call a particular phenomenon an instance of 'learning'.

So the bottom line is that 'learning' is a pre-theoretical, possibly even a pre-scientific, concept. Although it may serve as an umbrella term (such as 'social psychology' or 'molecular biology') under which to group phenomena or scientific studies, it can be expected to play little role in the development of our understanding of how experience changes behavior. Instead we can expect that more specific concepts, defined with the context of a widely accepted theory, such as 'association', will provide the ideas around which explanations will be organized.

7

Learning: The need for a hybrid theory

Anthony Dickinson

The attempt to define a general, yet inclusive concept of learning has a long and fruitless history in psychology (see Chapter 6, this volume), and therefore a more productive conceptual analysis isolates those basic concepts that have generality across different theories of learning and that bridge the psychological and neurobiological levels of analysis. This approach respects 'memory concepts' as 'products' and 'essential elements' of theories, rather than as ill-defined and fuzzy categories. Students of animal learning are not by nature theoretically profligate, with the result that the last 30 years have seen the development of a variety of learning theories that share common basic concepts. In this chapter, I discuss briefly three concepts that are central to more than one theory: associative strength, associability and prediction error. Each discussion gives a description of the concept, identifies the conceptual issues raised by the various instantiations of each concept, and finally evaluates whether or not the concept bridges between psychology and neurobiology.

Associative strength

This concept refers to the strength of the association between two elements, each of which represent a stimulus or a response. The strength itself is an imperfect representation of the contingency or relationship between the stimuli and responses because it confounds the representation of the contingency with other features of the learning experience, such as the amount and history of training and the magnitude or intensity of the stimulus. The strength is also the vehicle for the processes, excitation and inhibition, by which the associative representation generates retrieval and behavior. The stronger the association, the more activating one element excites or inhibits the other. Finally, the concept delimits the task of a learning theory to that of specifying how a particular learning episode changes associative strength.

There are at least three issues that distinguish the way in which different theories deploy the concept.

1. *Types of associations.* The classic Rescorla–Wagner theory (Rescorla and Wagner 1972) assumes a unitary concept of associative strength, which can take both positive and negative values to represent positive and negative contingencies, respectively. Inherent in this conception, however, is the implication that associative strength can be weakened or, in other words, that unlearning occurs. In the absence of empirical evidence for unlearning, other theorists (Pearce and Hall 1980; Wagner 1981) have assumed that positive and negative contingencies are represented by separate excitatory and inhibitory associations.

2. *Elements of association.* Although most theories assume that the elements of associations represent tonic or phasic stimuli (or responses), some theorists have argued that the target of an association can be another association in order to explain the learning of conditional relationships (Bouton 1994). However, whether the syntax of associationism permits a stimulus to have an associative strength with another association is a matter of dispute.

3. *Directionality of associations.* Most theories assume unidirectional associations to represent predictive/causal relationships. However, others have argued for bidirectional associations (Arcediano *et al.* 2005).

Finally, it should be noted that associative strength is a useful bridging concept in that it can be related to synaptic strength, with changes in associative strength being implemented through the mechanisms of synaptic plasticity, such as long-term potentiation and depression. Alternatively, there is no reason why the concept could not be applied at the systems level of neuro-biological analysis.

Associability

The concept of associability arises from the observation that the rate of learning is determined not only by the contingency between a predictive stimulus and the outcome but also by the properties of these events. The associability of a stimulus or outcome is a determinant of the increment in associative strength that occurs on a learning episode and enters into rules or processes governing changes in associative strength as a learning rate parameter.

The conceptual issues relate to the properties and processes that determine associability.

1. *Salience.* Rescorla and Wagner (1972) assume that associability is fixed parameter of a stimulus that varies with its sensory/perceptual properties.

2. *Learned attention.* To accommodate the fact that the rate of learning to a stimulus can vary with its history, a number of theories assume that associability is determined by the learned attention to the stimulus. For example, Pearce and Hall (1980) argue that a stimulus that has occurred in association with surprising or unexpected outcomes in the recent past have a high associability, whereas, according to Sutherland and Mackintosh (1971), animals attend to stimuli from dimensions that have been good predictors of outcomes.

3. *Predictive relevance.* The rate of learning is determined not only the properties of stimuli and outcomes when considered individually, but also by the conjunction of their properties. For example, flavors are more associable with gastric outcomes than are exteroceptive stimuli, which in turn are more associable with external outcomes. Although such outcome-specific associability appears to have an innate component, Mackintosh (1975) has argued that it can also be learned to the extent that a stimulus has been a relatively good predictor of the outcome in the animal's past history.

The concept of associability has also made a significant contribution to our understanding of the brain processes mediating conditioning, most notably in the hands of Holland, Gallagher and colleagues (see Holland 1997). This research has identified important roles for the amygdala, the septo-hippocampal system and forebrain cholinergic projections in the control of associability. For example, Holland *et al.* (2000) have shown that a common system based on the central nucleus of the amydala mediates visuospatial attention in the rat as well as the modulation of learning by associability processes.

Prediction error

The concept of prediction lies at the heart of most current theories of associative learning because it controls the changes in both associative strength and associability. The prediction error generated by a learning episode is the difference between the associative strength required to predict the outcome and the current associative strength of the predictive stimulus (or stimuli) present on a learning episode. The predictor error provides a measure of the extent to which the occurrence of the outcome is unexpected or surprising and therefore specifies the extent to which more learning is required. When the prediction is zero, the current associative strengths provide an accurate representation of the predictive and causal structure of the environment.

The conceptual issues concern whether or not prediction errors have a direct impact on changes in associative strength or whether their influence is indirect, being mediated by associability.

1. *Direct.* Both Rescorla and Wagner (1972) and Mackintosh (1975) assume that the prediction error has a direct impact on changes in associative strength. Where they differ is in the nature of the prediction error. According to the Rescorla–Wagner rule, a general prediction error encodes how unexpected the outcome is in relation to the associative strength of all the stimuli present on a learning episode, whereas Mackintosh (1975) employs a stimulus-specific prediction error that encodes how surprising is the outcome in relation to the associative strength of the target stimulus alone.

2. *Indirect.* In addition to using a direct stimulus-specific prediction error for the acquisition of associative strength, Mackintosh assumes that changes of associability are governed by prediction errors by allowing a relative assessment of which is the best predictor of the outcome. Pearce and Hall (1980) also assume that the current associability of a stimulus is determined by the general prediction error with which it has been associated in the past.

The last decade has seen an increasing interest in the concept of prediction error in the neuroscience of learning (Schultz and Dickinson 2000). In part, this interest has been stimulated by the finding that dopamine neurons appear to encode a general prediction error by responding to surprising, but not predicted, rewards in standard conditioning procedures, such as blocking (Waelti *et al.* 2001). The concept has also provided the rationale and focus for a number of brain imaging studies of human learning (e.g. Corlett *et al.* 2004).

In summary, associative strength, associability and prediction error are important and valid basic concepts in associative learning. Their importance is reflected by the fact that a variety of theories have incorporated these concepts within their theoretical machinery, whereas their validity is endorsed by their extension from animal to human learning (Dickinson 2001) and by their role as productive concepts in bridging between psychology and neuro-biology. All three concepts are neither too specific nor too general, which allows them to act as both substantive and generative concepts in the analysis of learning. In my view, the current consensus is that one particular instantiation of these concepts cannot do all the theoretical work, and what is required is hybrid theory that integrates these core concepts (Le Pelley 2004).

8

Learning: Challenges in the merging of levels

Elizabeth A. Phelps

As scientists, we use observation to inform our understanding of theoretical concepts that describe patterns existing in the world. Although the principles underlying these concepts should be separable from the types of observations used in the laboratory, in practice this can be difficult to achieve. Learning is a concept especially difficult to define due to the breadth of means that can be used to assess responses one might classify as 'learning'. For example, contemporary psychological and neuroscience research uses verbal reports, motor actions, physiological states, responses of neurons and neurotransmitters, or signals linked to blood flow to indicate learning. This list is not exhaustive. Rather than generating a definition of the concept of learning that captures the similarities among all these measures, this chapter focuses on what I believe is a primary challenge as we move forward in the study of learning. How do we merge the different means of assessment for learning that are observed outside of the nervous system, with the neural mechanisms proposed to underlie learning?

Learning results in a change in the organism with experience. How this change is defined can vary depending on the discipline or approach. However, inherent in the concept of learning is that there is an adaptive change in the response of the organism as a result of a specific experience (see Chapter 64, this volume). Although the term learning has been used to describe changes observed within the nervous system, there is always the strong assumption that these experience-dependent changes underlie behaviors and responses that can be observed outside of the nervous system (Kandel 2004). The observable change in behavior is the primary indication of learning, and changes in the neural substrate are secondary and presumed to underlie these learned behaviors or responses. This chapter focuses on challenges in linking this primary, behavioral indication of learning with cellular and systems neurobiological approaches to learning mechanisms.

Although there has been tremendous progress in understanding the neural substrates of learning, the ability to link these neural mechanisms clearly with observable behaviors has been especially challenging. This is probably most apparent in studies of the cellular mechanisms of learning. It is widely assumed that altering the communication between neurons is the basis for learning (Hebb 1949). Over the last several decades, research on synaptic plasticity has provided elegant models outlining molecular and genetic mechanisms that could underlie learned behaviors. Studies of long-term potentiation (LTP) and long-term depression (LTD) have supported Hebb's original hypothesis by demonstrating that synaptic transmission can be altered with activity (Kandel 2004). Given the experimental constraints of studying activity-dependent synaptic plasticity, most studies (with some exceptions) have not attempted to link these cellular mechanisms directly with learned behaviors, instead focusing on understanding the mechanisms themselves (Kandel 2004). As a result, directly relating these cellular mechanisms to learned behaviors observed in the organism has been difficult, and there has been significant debate as to whether LTP and LTD underlie learning in particular, or are related to other processes effecting the expression of learning (e.g. Shors and Matzel 1997).

However, several studies have shown that manipulating variables, such as genes or N-methyl-D-aspartate (NMDA) receptors, that may be *necessary* for activity-dependent synaptic plasticity, results in impairments in learned behavior (for reviews, see Martin *et al.* 2000; Kandel 2004). In addition, a study examining neurons in a region known to be important for the representation of fear conditioning (i.e. the lateral nucleus of the amygdala) showed changes in cellular responses in this region similar to those observed with mechanistically induced LTP. This change was correlated with the expression of conditioned fear (Rogan *et al.* 1997), consistent with the notion that activity-dependent synaptic plasticity mediates this learning.

What has been more challenging still for researchers is showing that activity-dependent synaptic plasticity is *sufficient* to induce learning (see Martin *et al.* 2000 for a discussion of this topic). Although the complexity of the neural networks that underlie most learned behaviors makes it especially difficult to relate these behaviors to activity-dependent synaptic plasticity, there is correlational evidence for this link. It is less clear if these changes are sufficient for these behaviors (Martin *et al.* 2000), or if these cellular mechanisms also underlie other processes that may be related to the expression of learning (e.g. such as attention, see Shors and Matzel 1997).

Relative to demonstrating that cellular mechanisms are related to specific learned behaviors, studies linking neuroanatomical systems to learning and memory have been more straightforward. A primary advance in our understanding of the neural substrates of memory over the last century is the growing recognition that there are multiple kinds of learning and memory that rely on different neuroanatomical systems. In a classic description of these multiple memory systems (see Squire and Knowlton 2000; Chapter 58, this volume), the hipppocampal complex, amygdala, striatum, cerebellum, neocortex and reflex pathways have all been linked to specific types of learned behaviors. In short, changes with specific experience seem to be a component of most neural systems. Most prominently, the hippocampal complex has been identified as critical for learning that results in declarative, episodic or relational memory. In humans, this type of learning is generally characterized as expressed through explicit, often verbal, report. In contrast, learning some kinds of habits or skills is thought to involve the striatum. This type of learning is usually assessed through the facilitation of choices or motor actions, such as faster reaction times. The amygdala has been to be shown to be critical for learned fears, particularly as they are expressed through physiological measures. In summary, there is abundant evidence in humans and other animals that a subset of specific learned responses assessed in the laboratory requires unique neural mechanisms (Schacter and Tulving 1994; Squire and Knowlton 2000).

This simple characterization of memory systems suggests that it might be possible to identify the correspondence between specific expressions of learning and their neuranatomical substrates in certain circumstances. Although experimental situations can determine that different neural systems may function independently to support different types of learning, in practice multiple types of learning occur simultaneously. For example, in a fear conditioning paradigm in which a neutral stimulus is paired with an aversive event, the learned fear response to the neutral stimulus, as expressed with physiological measures, has been shown to be dependent on the amygdala (LaBar et al. 1995; LeDoux 1996). At the same time, explicit knowledge of the relationship between the neutral and aversive events, as expressed through verbal report, is suggested to be dependent on the hippocampal complex (Bechara et al. 1995).

Studies investigating even simple learned behaviors have shown that neural systems that can independently support learning may also interact in the expression of learning. Because of this, determining the unique neural mechanisms linked to any given learned behavior or response is not always so easy. Returning to fear learning, it has been shown that the conscious, explicit knowledge of the parameters of a fear conditioning paradigm, which requires the hippocampal complex for acquisition, is not always necessary for the physiological expression of learned fear (Ohman and Mineka 2001). However, this type of knowledge may be sufficient for fear learning (Phelps et al. 2001). It has been demonstrated that abstract knowledge of the parameters of fear conditioning results in a physiological expression of learned fear, even in the absence of the type of direct experience that is thought to underlie the amygdala's involvement in fear acquisition (LeDoux 1996). Simply knowing that a neutral stimulus predicts the possibility of an aversive event is enough to generate a fear response. This abstract knowledge of fear may not seem to require the amygdala for acquisition, but the amygdala does play a role in the physiological expression of this type of learned fear (Funayama *et al.* 2001). In other words, the amygdala may interact with hippocampal-dependent forms of representation in the expression of these learned fears. Although the amygdala and hippocampal complex have unique and independent contributions to fear learning, in many situations these multiple forms of representation may both contribute to the expression of this learning. The notion that multiple forms of representations can influence the expression of a single learned behavior or response can make it extremely difficult to determine the precise relationship between the expression of learning and its neuroanatomical substrates.

This task is further complicated by evidence suggesting that different memory systems might not only interact in the expression of learning, but also may compete during the acquisition of learning (for a review, see Poldrack and Packard 2003). For example, studies of skill and habit learning have suggested that the striatum plays an important role in pattern learning, particularly as it is expressed through implicit measures such as reaction time or choice behavior (e.g. Knowlton *et al.* 1996). When explicit, hippocampal-dependent knowledge of these patterns becomes available, this explicit knowledge can also contribute to the expression of this learning assessed through these implicit measures (Knowlton *et al.* 1994). However, this type of hippocampal-dependent learning may additionally affect the involvement of the striatum during acquisition. It has been suggested that these memory systems interact in a competitive manner so that as the involvement of the hippocampal memory system increases during learning, the relative involvement of a striatal-dependent system decreases (Poldrack *et al.* 2001). In other words, even though the measure of learning is similar, the neural systems involved in the acquisition of this learning and the form of neural representation driving its expression may vary.

The goal of studies examining the neural representation of learning is to understand the mechanisms underlying learned behaviors. As outlined in this chapter, there are a number of challenges in achieving this goal. However, this endeavor is necessary not only to provide insight into these mechanisms, but also to understand the nature of these behaviors. An understanding of the neural mechanisms highlights subtleties of learned behaviors and responses assessed outside the nervous systems that are not always apparent from assessments of behavior alone. A scientific understanding of the concept of learning requires the consideration of the multiple levels of analysis, and a concerted effort to understand how they are linked.

9

Integrative comments
Learning: Multiplicity of mechanisms

Steve E. Petersen

Introduction

Discussions among the individuals contributing to the concept of learning, reflected by the points of view in the position papers contributed to this volume, make a very interesting animal. If one goal of this volume was to examine commonalities, or lack thereof, across experimental traditions involved in the study of memory, the fact that it was incredibly difficult for us to agree on much of anything, and that the minimal agreements that were made were questioned by other contributors to this volume might justify the premise of the volume.

For example, we agree that 'prediction error' (see Dickinson, Chapter 7) was a useful concept across a broad range of learning conditions. This unanimity might be questioned by others in this volume who offer the counterexample of 'statistical learning', where many models do not include apparent error terms.

The lack of agreement extended even to arguments about whether it is fruitful to define learning at all. Rescorla (Chapter 6) found that such definitions were often not helpful and even obstructive, while Liz Phelps (Chapter 8) felt it absolutely necessary before preceding further.

The expressed purpose of this chapter, integrating across the four position papers, presented certain intractable problems. Rather than trying to achieve true integration, this brief chapter will try to provide a slightly different perspective, inspired in part by the perspectives and information from the other chapters, along with some of my own observations.

Human flexibility

Mammals in general, and humans in particular, possess an amazing flexibility in the way that they interact with the environment. Within seconds, we can change our response to a presented word from its definition to the letters that make up the word, depending on whether we are in a vocabulary or spelling test.

On a longer time scale, we can adjust our behavior based on the ongoing consequences of our social interactions. Over the course of our development, we can adjust our movements to the length of our arms or the distance between our eyes. All of these capabilities allow us to shape ourselves to many different environments and to changes in our environments.

In humans, more than in any other animal, this flexibility extends to modifying the environment itself, producing tools, books, buildings, languages and all of the cultural artifacts that make up the real environments of humankind. The presence of culture extends the dynamics of flexibility across generations; in essence, culture allows 'inheritance of acquired characteristics' as information is passed to our children and our children's children.

The remarkable dynamic range and complexity that underlie these abilities strongly mitigate against compact explanations. Nonetheless, some categorizations occur. Learning, the focus of this series of essays, addresses the flexibility that comes when experience modifies behavior with some persistence. The time scale over which such modifications can take place can be broad (from a single instance, to minutes, to days, or longer). The time scale of the persistence can have an equally broad range. It is therefore often difficult to distinguish what we feel comfortable labeling as learning (e.g. vocabulary) from 'developmental' effects (ability to control impulsivity) that occur on the same general time scale.

From a conceptual standpoint, it is possible that all of experience-dependent change occurs as the result of a single underlying mechanism, or type of mechanism. On the other hand, many reasons exist to argue against such a stance.

The ability to switch task sets from a vocabulary test to a spelling test, due to our immediate experience with instruction sets, has a very different set of properties from our ability to associate meanings with arbitrary utterances. This distinction above is easy to accept, but other distinctions are much less clear. For instance, is it clear that there are fundamentally separate mechanisms underlying the ability to throw a dart at a target (which most would clearly put in a learning category) and adjusting to a new eyeglass prescription (which does not feel as comfortable in the learning category). It is here that I think Rescorla's chapter provides important insight. Should we be arguing from a conceptual standpoint over whether understanding how we adapt to a new prescription is useful to someone interested in learning, or should we just go ahead and try to understand the mechanisms behind the myriad kinds of experience-dependent change?

To this end, I would like to argue that it is very likely that multiple mechanisms exist that underlie experience-dependent change that would qualify as learning or 'learning-like' at several levels of analysis. Because I am a cognitive neuroscientist, my arguments will focus on neural mechanisms, rather than information processing, or cognitive level explanations. The points may be less true at the information processing level of explanation (but frankly I do not think that to be the case).

Levels of explanation

Information from many different levels of analysis can be brought to bear on putative learning mechanisms. However, building understanding across levels for questions of learning, even more than other aspects of cognition, provides real challenges.

Considerable experimentation and theory exist at the level of behavior. Years of careful behavioral experimentation contributed to Dickinson's explication of important learning principles. His principles include associative strength, associability and prediction error. It is altogether plausible that each of these principles might be implemented in terms of multiple known neurobiological explanations.

If this is the case, then the concept of, for example, associative strength at the level of behavior might be more clearly elucidated when it is mapped to these multiple underlying sources. In other words, the parsing of the neural mechanisms may lead to a clearer understanding of the subcomponents of the behavioral manifestation. It also seems clear that we are some distance from this mapping. Dickinson, as have many others, relates associative strength to changes in synaptic efficiency in his chapter. Several putative neural mechanisms may contribute to synaptic efficiency. Long-term potentiation/depression (LTP/LTD) is the neurobiological mechanism most frequently associated with changes in synaptic efficiency. It is also very frequently studied in the hippocampus, a brain region clearly associated with aspects of memory. Thus, it seems reasonable to include LTP in discussions of associative strength.

However, the relationship of LTP in the medial temporal lobe to associative strength in behavior is tenuous at best. Beyond LTP, there are other mechanisms that may reflect persistent, experience-dependent change at the synapse (e.g. dendritic elaboration, axon retraction, etc.) that may also contribute to changes in synaptic transmission. LTP/LTD is also common in many other brain regions, conspicuously the cerebellum and the cortex. Each combination of mechanism and location will have slightly different contributions to changes in behavior. Thus, multiple forms of synaptic change in multiple locations may have to be combined to provide a satisfying explanation for associative strength measured in a particular set of behavioral conditions.

To take a broader view of learning and memory mechanisms, explanations above the cellular level, at the level of brain regions, also suggest multiple underlying mechanisms. As discussed extensively in Phelps' chapter, the association of different forms of learning with different anatomical systems has been a widely disseminated success story for the systems neuroscience of memory. The most well-discussed example, of course, is the dissociation produced by lesions of the medial temporal lobe. Such lesions seem to leave many forms of experience-dependent change intact, while producing clear deficits in declarative or relational memory. Less discussed, but equally clear, is that damage to other regions of the brain can produce specific deficits in experience-dependent changes as well. Prism adaptation, eye-blink conditioning, adaptive plasticity of the vestibulo-ocular reflex, for example, are all deficient when specific parts of the cerebellum are damaged (see, for example, Martin, et al. 1996). Other forms of experience-dependent change are associated with basal ganglia (habit formation) and priming (specific cortical areas).

Further, the systems level view afforded by imaging has entered another level of observation above the single brain region level. Several studies have shown that different regions of the brain are emphasized for skilled and unskilled versions of the same task (Poldrack 2000). For example, left frontal cortical regions decrease their contribution and insular regions increase their contribution to peformance of tasks following practice (Raichle et al. 1994).

Conclusion

There are many ways in which the nervous system can change through experience at many levels of scale. This includes putative multiple mechanisms at the synaptic, cellular, regional, systems and behavioral levels. One of the questions that was related to me when the 'Science of memory: concepts' project was initiated was whether there were a set of integrated concepts for memory. In the area of learning, it would be my contention that the positive aspect is that much is known about aspects of learning at many levels of analysis. However, the challenge for cognitive science is to incorporate information from across these levels of analysis in mutually beneficial ways to provide deeper understanding.

3

Coding and representation

While entitled to separate treatments, considering coding and representation together, as is done in this volume, makes perfect sense, particularly since, in this case, the medium might indeed be the message. The question of how information is coded and represented in brain and cognition is considered by many as the most crucial problem in the neurosciences. It is certainly a necessary condition for understanding how experience alters our knowledge, or, in other words, how memory is implemented in the biological world at multiple levels of analysis. In formal language, code refers to the expression of one language in another, whereas representation is an activated vector in neuronal coding space, or a map of event space in cognitive/neuronal space, or a mentally/ neuronally encoded model of the world that could potentially guide behavior. Discussion of coding and representation raises several fundamental issues that the coding and representational systems have to solve in order to be useful, such as mapping (how elements in one coding system are translated unequivocally into another coding system) and parsing (how distinctiveness of propositions is maintained). In the world of biological memory systems, additional questions surface, among them, are there multiple neuronal codes and why; how are such codes implemented in the neural hardware; and whether specific codes have evolved for the purpose of specific representations of cognitive goals, such as encoding and retrieval of procedural versus episodic knowledge.

Y.D.

10

Coding and representation: Time, space, history and beyond

Alessandro Treves

The concept of *coding* refers to the form in which a message is conveyed from an information source to a receiver, i.e. to the way it is *represented* in an arbitrary intermediate medium. Information theory describes, in the abstract language of mathematics, the transmission and storage of messages, e.g. in terms of the probabilities of different symbols or combinations of symbols. It is neutral with respect to the physical nature of the symbols themselves, be they letters written on parchment, phonemes carried by sound waves or the emission times of neuronal action potentials. The science of memory appropriates the full mathematical apparatus of information theory, but uses it in the framework of its own quest for the neurobiological mechanisms that allow, in the brain, the transmission and storage of messages.

The term *neural codes* also subliminally refers to the clever tricks devised by biological evolution to endow organic matter with the ability to convey messages; further implying, as in the expression '*cracking the neural code*' that Mother Nature, though intelligent, can always be outsmarted by brilliant researchers. Most investigators would not give a penny for the belief in intelligent design that the emphasis on nature's tricks may evoke, but appreciate such a connotation of mystery and discovery, and are happy to use it in their grant proposals. The term *representation* often carries, instead, a slight *cognitive* connotation, emphasizing what occurs inside the brain, in contrast to a purely 'black-box' behaviorist perspective. Such overtones will not be given further attention here: *coding* and *representation* will be considered as fully equivalent concepts.

As a message is conveyed from a source to a receiver, it can pass through the intermediate medium in a flash, or it can indulge in it for any length of time. The distinction between information transmission and storage is therefore fuzzy, from a purely mathematical point of view. The concepts of coding and representation apply to both. It is nevertheless useful, in the context of memory studies, to distinguish between reasonably stable information storage, realized for example in changes of synaptic efficacy, and information coded 'on-line' in neuronal activity, in close temporal proximity to the activity of the information source, be the latter external, e.g. a sensory stimulus, or internal, e.g. an item recollected from autobiographical memory. Neural activity can express somewhat more transient information storage, as in the selective patterns of activation maintained in working memory in the frontal lobes, so the distinction refers more to the substrate—the activity of neurons versus the efficacy of synapses, to be concrete—than to whether there is, strictly speaking, a memory component in the process under consideration. In this volume, ample attention is devoted to the forms in which information may be coded when it is stored in a stable manner, so this contribution will focus on its *on-line* coding and representation by means of neuronal activity.

r(t)

The simplest way in which a group of cells, a so-called 'population' of neurons, can convey information in their activity is by each and every one transmitting the same message. This, to a good approximation, is thought to be the case for the relatively small clusters of midbrain neurons releasing neuromodulators such as dopamine, serotonin or norepinephrine. Dopamine-releasing cells in the ventral tegmental area, for example, whose axonal projections innervate vast areas of the frontal lobes, the amygdala, nucleus accumbens and other 'limbic' structures, are thought to be all sending the same signal. The impulses of individual cells may occur at different times, but, given the relatively slow time course of their effect, the difference is irrelevant: it is only the average rate of release of dopamine from VTA (ventral tegmental area) cells, or their firing rate $r(t)$, that matters, a simple function of time. A similar simplicity applies to dopamine-releasing cells from the substantia nigra (pars compacta), which project to the striatum. The *content* of this signal has been interpreted, particularly in light of experiments in monkeys (Schultz *et al.* 1997), as related to reward expectation. Other interpretations have been advanced for the content of the messages conveyed by acetylcholine or norepinephrine release (Doya 2002; Yu and Dayan 2005). In each of these instances, the individual identity of the releasing neurons disappears in their mass action, and the single symbol used in such simple *chemical* codes can be taken to be just the average firing rate of neurons in the corresponding population.

r(x,t)

The use of the chemical diversity of neurotransmitters and their receptors is phylogenetically ancient, as testified by the evolutionary trees (cladograms) of their genetic codes. The next neural coding principle adopted by evolution seems to be the use of the spatial location of chemically (and electrically) identical neural elements to span a diversity of symbols. This more advanced principle operates in many peripheral sensory and motor systems across species. In the vertebrate retina, for example, identical ganglion cells convey different messages with their action potentials, as a function of their location on the retinal array. To the extent that, for a given cell, the exact timing of individual impulse can be neglected, in favor of a description in terms of short-time averaged firing rates (averaged, for example, over 10 ms or so), the activity of ganglion cells can be summarily described by a function $r(x,t)$ which depends solely on time and on space (the spatial location of each ganglion cell).

This type of coding, like chemical coding, does not in itself depend on any learning and memory process, and it can be hardwired or genetically programmed in the system. Spatial processing can be quite sophisticated, as in the dendro-dendritic subtractions hypothesized to take place in the fly lobula plate (Haag and Borst 2002). Mathematically, one can discuss to what extent spatially dependent codes are optimized to remove redundancies in the sensory world, as exemplified by the elegant 'ecological theory' of early visual processing (Atick 1992). Spatial codes (like chemical codes) are not memory codes *per se*, but they may be used to instruct the formation of memory representations in other cells, for example in the cortical cells that, directly or indirectly, receive the signals produced by the peripheral sensory systems.

$r_i(x,t)$

Memory-dependent representations are those in which the meaning of the action potentials emitted by a particular neuron is a *function of the activation history* of that neuron, synthetically denoted by the index i attached to the rate $r_i(x,t)$. In other words, the signal a cell conveys reflects its own experience of the world, encoded in long-term changes in the efficacies of the specific synapses which contribute to activate that cell. In this way, the diversity of symbols can grow enormously and match the number of neurons available in the population, even if their connectivity is random, or metrically organized but with insufficient spatial resolution to support very precise spatial codes. Memory-based codes cannot be hardwired, and they have to be established by learning and memory processes. They are the foundation of cortical processing mechanisms, both when embedded in clear topographic maps (Rolls 1992) and when topography is not evident (Redish *et al.* 2001).

An influential perspective on their utilization was produced by combining the general notions of associative plasticity and of cell assemblies (Hebb 1949) with the more detailed *codon* theory of David Marr (1971). The Hebb–Marr perspective has largely driven the development of the technology for large-scale multiple single-unit recording experiments (Wilson and McNaughton 1993) given that memory-based codes require each neuron to be listened to individually. Unfortunately, the very principle of memory-based diversity in the messages carried by individual neurons in the same population poses an inviolable bound on the insight that can ever be obtained with imaging techniques, such as functional magnetic resonance imaging (fMRI). The BOLD (blood oxygenation level-dependent) signal of fMRI reflects the average activity of many synapses (and of other neural components) and, independently of its poor temporal resolution, it cannot access the specific signals expressed by the activation of single cells. Still, imaging provides useful results on the gross aspects of cortical codes, similar in nature to the sociological analyses that can be derived from recording, in a large city, the average levels of noise produced, at every phase in the day, in each of its neighborhoods.

$\sigma(\{r_i\})$

The discussion so far has considered only explicitly neural representations, expressed in the activity of neurons. The science of memory includes, however, extremely useful approaches, which cannot yet be reduced to the neural level. Thus, in developmental psychology, it is known, for example, that inverted faces are not represented as belonging to the same category as other faces. Or, in studies of bilingualism, one can discuss, for example, the acquisition of the Japanese subject–object–verb word order by speakers of English. In general, one deals with internal representations (of behaviorally relevant objects, of a syntactic structure), which can be provisionally labeled by appropriately defined symbols σ, even though their relationship to the underlying neural activity variables $\{r_i\}$ is yet to be determined. The grand goal of elucidating this relationship is a fascinating challenge for cognitive neuroscience, and for the science of memory.

11

Coding and representation: The importance of mesoscale dynamics

Anthony R. McIntosh

The study of human memory is at the edge of a new frontier thanks largely to functional neuroimaging. Access to neurobiology can provide a critical link between psychological theories of memory and the concomitant physiology. Despite the promise, there remains a wide gap between our understanding of nervous system function and memory.

One reason for the lack of congruence is that the information processing in the brain is not explicitly considered when a psychological theory is constructed or tested. Information processing capabilities of the brain arise from brain anatomy and physiology. The anatomy endows an immense capacity for both information segregation and integration. The physiological attribute of response plasticity, where neural responses change as a function of stimulus intensity, significance and internal state, modifies the information as it is passed to different levels of the system. The distribution of information in the widely distributed neural circuits of the brain allows many parts of the brain to contribute to memory in its broadest psychological form. It is thus possible that many processes of coding of neural information will impact on memory. Memory is not the domain of particular systems in the brain, but of the brain as a whole. Memory is what the brain does.

Anatomical features

Neurons are linked to one another both locally and at a distance. The nervous system appears to be specialized for rapid transfer of signals. This means that a single change to the system is conveyed to several parts of the brain and that some of this will feed back onto the initial site. There are obvious extremes to just how connected a system can be, and the nervous system occupies some intermediate position. Local cell networks are highly interconnected, but not completely so, and this means that adjacent cells can have both common and unique connections. The term *semiconnected* was proposed to designate this particular property of local cell networks (McIntosh 2000). The networks themselves can be thought of as semiconnectors, especially in as much as their function, as discussed below, is not only to mediate the signal between different cerebral regions but also to modulate the signal, in keeping with the specific properties of different 'semiconnectors'.

The connections between local neural ensembles are sparser than the intra-ensemble connectivity. Estimates of the connections in the primate cortical visual system have suggested that somewhere between 30 and 40 per cent of all possible connections between cortical areas exist (Felleman and Van Essen 1991). Simulation studies show that this sparseness is a computational advantage in that it allows for a high degree of flexibility in responses at the system level even when the responses of individual units are fixed (Tononi et al. 1992). Additional analyses of the anatomical connections of large-scale networks in the mammalian cerebral cortex have demonstrated a number of distinct topological features that probably lead to systems with maximal capacity for both information segregation and integration (Sporns and Kotter 2004; Sporns and Zwi 2004).

Neural network theories of brain function have emphasized these two basic organizational principles: segregation and integration. At each level in a functional system, there is a segregation of information processing such that units within that level will tend to respond more to a particular aspect of a stimulus (e.g. movement or color). At the same time, the information is concurrently exchanged with other units that are anatomically connected, allowing first for units to affect one another and secondly for the information processed within separate units to be integrated.

It seems rather obvious but still worth stating that regions can only process information that they receive. Cells in the medulla tend not to respond to visual stimuli because they are not connected to visual structures. Anatomy determines whether a given ensemble is capable of contributing to a process.

Functional features

Long-term neural plasticity is detected in the brain following events that are not commonly considered as related to memory, such as neural damage. However, there is a type of neural plasticity that is more short lived and considered highly relevant to memory formation. Neurons can show a rapid shift in response to afferent stimulation that is dependent on the behavioral context in which they fire. This *transient response plasticity* has consistently been shown in the earliest parts of the nervous system, from single cells in isolated spinal cord preparations to primary sensory and motor structures.

The changes can occur within a few stimulus presentations and are probably a ubiquitous property of the central nervous system (Wolpaw 1997). Thus, one of the most important features rudimentary to cognitive operations, namely transient plasticity, can be observed in many parts of the brain.

Population and predictive coding

One consequence of the structural and functional properties of the brain is that adjacent neurons have similar response properties (e.g. orientation columns in primary visual cortex), whereas neurons slightly removed may possess overlapping, but not identical, response characteristics. These broad tuning curves are characteristic for most sensory system cells and for cells in motor cortices. The broad tuning curves result from anatomy, where cells share some similar and some unique connections. Interestingly, anatomy also ensures that response plasticity also has a graded distribution. This has important implications for the representational aspects of the brain. Rather than having each neuron code sharply for a single feature, the distributed response takes advantage of a division of labor across many neurons, enabling representations to come from the aggregate of neuronal ensembles.

Electrophysiological studies in motor and sensory cortices have provided some examples of aggregate operations achieved through population coding (Georgopoulos et al. 1986; Young and Yamane 1992). A different twist on identifying the biology of memory comes from looking at the capabilities of a single neuron or small group. Some of the basic ingredients necessary for cognitive processes such as attention, learning and memory are contained in all nervous tissue. Population coding is probably used for higher order cognitive functions, but on a larger scale than for sensory or motor functions. When neural populations interact with one another, these rudimentary functions combine to form an aggregate that represents cognitive processes. Cognitive operations are not localized in an area or network of regions, but rather emerge from dynamic network interactions that depend on the processing demands for a particular operation.

The anatomy and physiology of the brain produce a system with complex dynamics that are seldom considered in memory theory. However, the dynamics enabled by the anatomy and physiology of the brain are likely to be the most important consideration in the memory–brain link. The dynamics enable maximum use of brain tissue such that the same set of neurons can contribute to different mental operations depending on the status of other neuronal groups (McIntosh 2004). This 'neural context' is the first step in a change in thinking on how the brain underlies memory. Because of neural context, the same brain region can contribute to basic sensory processing and to conscious recollection depending on the pattern of interactions with its neighbors. Critical for the contextual dependency are the brain dynamics, where there are continuous changes in both the ensembles that are interacting and the behavior manifested.

It is important to realize that most brain dynamics are initiated from internal operations in the brain. Very little of the brain is actually exposed to the external world, meaning that the accuracy of our representation of the world must come from some model. This dilemma is encapsulated in the perspective of predictive coding (an idea that dates back to Helmholtz), and is the focus of much development in computer science and theoretical neurobiology (Dayan *et al.* 1995; Hinton and Dayan 1996). The basic idea is that the brain generates a model of the world from the sparse incoming information based on its own experience. A simple example of predictive coding in action is behavioral studies of change blindness, wherein subtle changes to a complex visual scene may not be recognized by the subject. Given the limited amount of information that can be transmitted by peripheral sense organs, the brain seems quickly to 'fill-in' a scene, freeing the input channels to process the most relevant information. This filling-in procedure is based on experience, a stored representation and a memory.

To restate, an important implication of the neural properties discussed here is that all processes in the brain have the capacity to lead to or modify memory. The brain seems particularly well adapted to encode and store information at all levels. It is tempting to say that memory in its highest form (e.g. episodic) is a derivative of the standard operations of the brain. While psychological theories tend to differentiate memory from nonmemory operations such as sensation and action, it is important to recognize that sensation, perception, attention and memory are intimately intertwined. The very acts of seeing, hearing and acting make use of the brain's capacity for memory. This is probably why, in typical circumstances, what forms the contents of our memory is not under intentional control. Indeed, those processes that facilitate memory (e.g. levels of processing) are essentially by-products of other cognitive operations.

Conclusion

I have made the argument that the ability of the brain to segregate and integrate information, to make use of population and predictive coding, makes for a system that is specialized for memory. The same mechanisms producing the large-scale dynamics that perceive a face, or hear a siren or symphony, are also those that give rise to memory. Such a general mechanism produces a formidable challenge for memory theory.

The difficult question for the science of memory is still how these neural codes and representations relate to the mental codes and representations that cognitive psychology has defined. To some it may seem somewhat dissatisfying simply to consider that the pattern of brain activity is the physical embodiment of cognition, but that, to this point, is what most data suggest. This could be taken to imply that if we were able to characterize all possible configurations of neural system interactions, and relate them to the cognitive operations they enable, we would be in a position to understand the brain–mind link.

Even if we could generate such a characterization, I doubt we would be closer to understanding as we do not have a good framework to link these two levels. It may be that our understanding of the brain and of the mind is not satisfactory to make this link—a likely scenario. The science of memory will require a substantial revision in the base concepts to characterize the brain–mind link. This is difficult to imagine, but consider the revolution in physics with the move from Aristotle to Newton to Einstein. Each of these changes led to entirely new concepts and new worldviews. For the science of memory, such a change will come from a more focused attempt to merge what we know about the brain with what we know about the psychological phenomena. It is certainly the case that studies of the neural basis of memory and psychological studies can proceed independently for some time. However, the conceptual change needed for the science of memory will require the unification of both research fields.

Acknowledgments

A.R.M. is supported by the Canadian Institutes for Health, Natural Sciences and Engineering Research Council and the J.S. McDonnell Foundation.

12

Coding and representation: Searching for a home in the brain

Endel Tulving

The idea that mental experience may leave residue in the soul, or mind, that allows later remembering of the experience is as old as recorded history, and probably older. The idea that this residue is physical, somewhere in the brain, is more recent, having been first proposed by Robert Hooke (1627–1703) who thought that memory is 'as much an Organ as the Eye, Ear, or the Nose', and that it has 'its situation somewhere near the Place where Nerves from the other Senses concur and meet' (Young 1965, p. 287).

The existence of this 'residue' with a remarkable staying power is now taken for granted, but much about it has remained baffling. How is it formed? What is its nature? What kind of thing, or entity or stuff is it? What is the relationship between the experience and its residue? What is the relationship between the residue and remembering that it enables? Where does the residue reside? Does every experience leave a residue? If not, then what determines which ones do and which ones do not? If yes, what kind of a place is it that can 'hold' an individual's untold experiences? Does the residue last forever? (Not many scientists believe this, but I think that some do.) Does it last at least as long as the individual is alive? These and related questions have been raised and debated, sometimes hotly debated, throughout the human intellectual history. At the present time, no one knows what the answers are, although we have undoubtedly made progress in getting a better grip on the questions.

The terms that have been used to refer to the memorially relevant components of the after-effects of experience have varied with the fashions of the times, the accumulated pertinent knowledge already available, and even the languages and dialects spoken by those who have thought deeply about the matter. A frequently used term is 'representation', another is 'coding'—as in the title of this section of the book. Other well-known terms are 'engram', 'memory image' and 'memory trace'. Each has its own connotations that vary from context to context and even from writer to writer, although the concept lying behind all these terms has been and continues to be relatively unambiguous.

Memory trace

A memory trace is the neural change that accompanies a mental experience at one time (time 1) whose retention, modified or otherwise, allows the individual later (at time 2) to have mental experiences of the kind that would not have been possible in the absence of the trace.

The critical ingredients of this definition are: (1) mental experience at time 1; (2) neural change; (3) retention of aspects of the change; (4) mental experience at time 2; and (5) the relationship between experiences at time 1 and time 2. The concept of memory trace ties together these features in an organized whole. Every single component is critical in the sense that its absence would be tantamount to the absence of the whole.

Some features of the definition may be worth emphasis, in order to minimize misunderstanding. First, the definition applies to cognitive memory, the kind of memory that has to do with mental experience. It has nothing to say about learning and memory in which mental experience of the kind that the definition refers to is missing. Thus, much of what has been written in the traditional literature on skill learning, conditioning, priming and simple forms of associative learning seems to have done perfectly well without invoking representation-like concepts of the mental type to which I refer here. All kinds of mental concepts, of course, were anathema to many psychologists during the heyday of behaviorism.

Secondly, the definition implies that not all but only some of the physiological/neural after-effects of an experience constitute the memorially significant 'residue', i.e. the memory trace. The question of which ones, and the whole issue of how to separate the wheat of the memory trace from the chaff of all sorts of neural activity that has nothing to do with memory, remains a challenging problem for the neurobiological side of the science of memory. The definition also assumes that the memory trace is a dynamic, changing, malleable entity (Dudai 2002; Nader 2003) rather than a 'fixed, lifeless' sort of thing that many cognitive psychologists came to look down upon, thanks to Sir Frederick Bartlett's well-known disdainful phrase.

Thirdly, the definition explicitly distinguishes between, and relates to each other, two kinds of entities: physical (neural change) and mental (experience), and thereby brushes on one of the central issues of our science: how does the mental arise out of the neural? Talking about mental experiences as separable from neuronal processes may be questioned by those who think that because mental experience depends on neuronal processes it must also be in some sense *reducible* to neuronal processes. Aside from the problem created by many meanings of the concept of reduction, the logic of this type of argument has always escaped me. At least for practical purposes—to get on with the 'business'—I find it more congenial to operate in a conceptual framework in which the mind depends on the brain but also has properties and capabilities that are different from those of the brain.

Fourthly, the definition reminds us that the memory trace is not just mere residue, or after-effect of a past experience, not just an incomplete record of what was. It is also a recipe, or a prescription, for the future. However, as it is usually only an impoverished record, it is also only an unreliable guide to what will happen in the future. What actually happens—what kind of a future experience it enables—depends not only on its properties at the time of attempted retrieval but also on the conditions prevailing at the time of retrieval. This was one of the deep insights of Richard Semon, the early and unappreciated prophet of memory, an insight that the subsequent experimental work by others has more than vindicated (Schacter 2001*a*).

Brain and mind

Fifthly, the definition of memory trace is given in terms of something happening in a physical object, the brain, and in that sense it is tempting to think of the trace also as a physical object, or physical entity. It is not. A definition of memory trace in terms of physical changes in the brain does not make the memory trace a physical entity itself. Memory trace is a change, and change is not an entity. It is a relationship (difference) between two things that are physical objects, the brain at time 1 ('immediately before' the experience) and time 2 ('immediately after' the experience), but the relationship itself is not a physical object. To illustrate: think of drawing a straight line. After you have drawn it, the line exists physically with all its properties. Then you grab the pencil again and make the same line a bit longer. After you have done it, the 'second' line exists physically with all its properties. The difference between the two does not exist anywhere other than in your mind. You can of course arrange for a comparison between them, by making a copy of the first line while it exists, and you can note their differences in length. However, the difference you note exists only in your mind, in physical reality there exist only two lines.

Sixthly, because there is no object or entity in the brain that can be said to *be* a particular memory trace (i.e. to represent a particular experience), it is in principle not possible to observe it as such, to identify it as such or to determine its properties as such. Memory trace, as defined, is something that makes something else possible, if and only if some other conditions are fulfilled at time 2. Since time 2 has not yet arrived, the relationship between the memory trace and the experience it yields is indeterminate. The situation is not unlike that of the relationship between an elementary particle's location and its momentum as described by Heisenberg in the 1920s.

Seventhly, the definition relates 'mental experience' to a physical happening (neural change). It is important to note that both experience and neural activity are part of the reality with which cognitive neuroscience deals. However, there is also a difference between them, one that many people get excited about. The difference is that the experience is real (only) from the first-person's point of view, whereas the neural events are real, at least in principle and increasingly so in actual scientific practice, from the third-person point of view. The 'subjectivity' of the first-person experience has traditionally been held as an obstacle to the study of such experience. That is not a problem, however. The only 'problem' is that the first-person experiences are not *directly* observable. Yet, like countless other things in the universe that scientists study, they are *indirectly* observable. In psychology, indirect observation has been successfully applied since day one. The most respectable and oldest part of experimental psychology, psychophysics, is all about indirect observation of 'subjective' experiences, and so is much about cognitive study of memory. The important criteria are not 'objectivity' and 'subjectivity'. The important criteria are the possibility of empirical validation and rejection of hypotheses, reliability and replicability of the empirical findings, and the coherence of the story (theory) that relates facts to one another in a way that would not be possible without science.

Eighthly, the definition reflects the basic assumption that memory trace, like any other concept, can be fully understood only in relation to other concepts. Here, the other concepts are experiencing something at time 1 (dealt with under the concept of *Encoding* in Section 6 of this volume), and experiencing something at time 2 (dealt with under the concepts of *Retrieval* and *Remembering* in Sections 10 and 11, respectively, of this volume).

Epilogue

In *Elements of Episodic Memory* (Tulving 1983) I talked about memory traces synonymously with engrams. I defined engram as the state of the memory system before and after the encoding of the event, as well by its position and relationship to other hypothetical concepts in GAPS, the general abstract processing system, which I proposed as the conceptual framework for studying episodic memory. The conceptualization of memory trace offered here is not greatly different from that of almost a quarter century ago. The main difference has to with the 'locality' of engrams. Then they resided in the 'memory system', now they have found a home in the brain. I think this is progress.

13

Integrative comments
Coding and representation: On appealing beliefs and paucity of data

Misha Tsodyks

Since the concept of memory representations is closely related to that of information, it is tempting to think of it in terms of the formal information theory developed by Shannon (1948). This theory considers the transmission of messages from sender to receiver via information channels. As a first step, the messages have to be encoded to acquire the form (representation) that can be transmitted via the channel (e.g. the famous Morse code with English characters encoded in sequences of dots and dashes for subsequent transmission by current pulses via electric wires) and ultimately restored by the receiver to their original meaning. The theory only deals with quantitative aspects of information, such as the minimal number of binary elements needed to faithfully represent a message, and not with the 'content' of the messages and their broader context. The mathematical apparatus of information theory allows one to analyze the optimal encoding that maximizes the speed of the transmission, and/or minimizes the errors resulting from channel noise.

In order to relate these ideas to biological memory, we have to define who is a sender and who is a receiver, what the messages in question are and how they are represented in the brain. The answer to the first question seems to be pretty straightforward—both the sender and the receiver is the organism or, more precisely, the brain. However, the receipt of the message, called in this context 'retrieval' (see Section 10 of this volume), is delayed in time for a period that can last from seconds to years. As pointed out in the contribution by Alessandro Treves (Chapter 10), this fact by itself does not fundamentally change the mathematical aspects of coding, even though one could argue that the required life span of the particular memory process plays a crucial role in selecting the corresponding representation (e.g. neural activity for short-term versus synaptic efficacies for long-term memory). Moreover, the long-lasting memory representations could undergo various transformations due to interactions with other information sources, as will be discussed in more detail below.

A more difficult question is what the messages are, in other words, what is it precisely that goes into the memory system of the brain and what is being retrieved from it. It appears to me that the answer to this seemingly innocent question strongly depends on the scientific tradition within which it is addressed. In behavioral sciences, it is the correct behavior in a certain situation that has to be acquired and eventually remembered. This approach, while being most consistent and solid, may appear, however, to be too mechanistic in light of all the variety and complexity of memory that is currently accessible to experimental studies (see Chapter 2, this volume, for a more elaborated discussion of this point). I would like here to consider briefly the suggestion, given within the tradition of cognitive sciences and expressed in Chapter 12 by Endel Tulving, that the 'messages' that are to be remembered are the 'mental experiences'. In other words, when the mental experience occurs, it results in a certain set of neuronal changes in the brain (serving as its representation) that can be retained until the time when the mental experience will be re-created, in full or in part.

Some of these representations could themselves depend on the previously acquired memories, as discussed in Chapter 11 by Anthony McIntosh. They could also come into interaction with other external and internal sources of information that is constantly being processed in the brain during the life span of the memory. This interaction among different representations formed over the life of the organism is an extremely important feature of memory, allowing the information to be represented and used in a way that is shaped by *context*, understood in the broadest possible meaning. As a result, information that is being retrieved always carries with it a train of acquired associations that, when accumulated, may make the re-created mental experience significantly different from the original one.

The aforementioned notion carries a lot of appeal, as it integrates in an attractive and natural way our introspective experiences—mental experiences, studied by cognitive psychologists—with the scientific knowledge acquired by generations of brain researchers about neuronal changes, or processes. Shall we thus conclude that this definition exhausts the issue of memory representations? As mentioned by Tulving, it leaves behind the kinds of learning and memory that do not necessarily involve explicit mental components, such as skill learning.

More fundamentally, however, this seemingly flawless construction may cause some unease in the adherers to yet another scientific tradition of empirical neuroscience. An implicit basic assumption in this tradition is that the functioning of the brain can be completely reduced to neuronal processes occurring in it, that encompass everything else (mental experience, emotions, self-awareness, etc.). In the framework of the discussion of coding and representations, one should assume thus that 'mental experiences' that Endel Tulving talks about are themselves 'represented' by some neuronal processes (e.g. spatiotemporal activity patterns in certain neuronal populations).

The picture that emerges is thus that of a *chain* of interacting neuronal transformations and encodings, resulting eventually in representations that can last for a life span of the memory process in question, albeit undergoing continuing context-dependent modifications as discussed above. Some of the initial representations in this chain are discussed in more details in Chapter 10 of this volume.

For example, think of an object, reflecting a light that hits the retina, that in turn sends electric impulses via the optic nerve to the brain, where after some amount of processing a certain activity pattern is emerging, that may lead to the emergence of the mental experience of 'seeing' this object. This activity pattern can itself cause other types of neuronal processes (e.g. modifications in neuronal connections) that can be retained for a period of time, and subsequently lead to the re-creation of this activity pattern or its modified version, that again may or may not lead to related mental experience. If other objects that are associated with the original one are observed, their representations can interact with each other, resulting in significant modifications in the activity patterns being re-created when the objects are viewed. For example, it can be reasonably assumed that the view of a Chinese character evokes vastly different activation patterns in the brain of a student of Chinese when seen for the first time and after years of studies. In other words, the neural representations should not be considered in separation, but as an interacting system that carries information about single memories, their context and history.

In this emerging framework, the concept of mental representations, even if useful for characterizing certain types of neuronal processes and relating them to particular cognitive phenomena, is not strictly speaking necessary for defining all the aspects of coding and representation in memory.

For the sake of intellectual clarity, I would like to argue that the above picture, even if implicitly shared by most neuroscientists, is largely based on common beliefs but not yet strongly supported by solid scientific knowledge, and may not even be free of some fundamental problems. First, despite great efforts, the relationship between neural processes and mental experiences is barely established. The strongest evidence in the primate of neural-over-mental comes from the experiments on sensory perception, where stimulation of certain brain areas was shown to bias perceptual decisions of monkeys (Cohen and Newsome 2004). In humans, we can cite largely anecdotal evidence, coming from patients undergoing neural surgery, that stimulating certain brain areas dramatically leads to the sense of 're-living' particular experiences from their lives (Penfield 1955). There is some evidence that points to delayed reactivation of some spatiotemporal activation patterns in the hippocampus (Wilson and McNaughton 1994), an area believed to be involved in episodic memory; however, it is not at all clear what if any role these reactivations play in memory. Recent funcional magnetic resonance imaging (fMRI) studies indicate that areas in the brain that respond to the view of various visual objects activate in a similar pattern when the subject is instructed to imagine seeing these objects (O'Craven and Kanwisher 2000)—a new promising research direction, but not directly addressing the causality relationship between mental and neuronal processes. It therefore appears to me that we are still light years away from having any reasonable characterization of the neuronal processes that could get even close in its richness to that obtained in cognitive sciences.

Moreover, from what we currently know after decades of experiments, there are myriads of ongoing neuronal changes occurring in the brain all the time, spanning the large range from the molecular via the cellular and the circuit to the brain-organ and whole-brain level. Some of these changes are probably irrelevant for representing information and are not unique to the brain, for example molecular processes that guarantee the energetic balance of the neurons. Yet others appear to be playing an important role unique for the brain, for example electric activity of the neurons, synaptic modifications and formation of new connections. Even if we succeed one day in empirically characterizing which ones of the neuronal changes are related to mental experiences and their memory representations, some as yet undiscovered novel theoretical principles will still surely be needed in order to understand the fundamental aspects of this relationship beyond statistical correlations. In the absence of these principles, the best we can now hope for is to have a 'translation table' between neuronal and cognitive processes (Dudai 1992), which by itself will not necessarily give us any deep understanding of the above-mentioned relationships.

We can thus see that attempts to define the notions of coding and representation as related to the science of memory, in a way that would be relevant for different scientific traditions, invariably confronts us with the most fundamental issues in science, such as the brain–mind relationship. It will be the task for the future generations of the scholars of memory to find out whether a unified definition of memory representations, that would be equally applicable to all the scientific traditions mentioned above, is possible. The history of science provides us with some remarkable examples when concepts that were initially thought of as being independent were reduced to one another thanks to progress in the corresponding theories. Such as, for example, when development of microscopic statistical physics resulted in the simple relationship between the temperature of matter (T) and the energy of its constituting elements (ε): $\varepsilon = n\dfrac{kT}{2}$. Energy itself was reduced to mass by Einstein in his special relativity theory by the most famous equation in science: $E = mc^2$. Modern neuroscience is yet to produce equally crucial breakthroughs, but it is still much younger than physics was at the time of these amazing developments.

4

Plasticity

Plasticity refers to the ability of an entity to undergo modification without immediate relaxation or disintegration. The founding fathers of the science of memory, such as James and Semon, were well aware that plasticity is actually a universal property of the biological stuff, which reaches some degree of perfection in the brain–world interaction. Konorsky deemed it to be one of the two meta-principles that underlie the operation of the nervous system: the first is reactivity, which is the capacity to be activated by stimulation of receptive organs; the second is plasticity, which is the capacity to change the reactive properties as a result of experience. This raises an interesting tension: the organism must retain its proper reactions in spite of changes in the world but, since the world is changing, ultimately the repertoire of potential reactions must also change. This dilemma illuminates two facets of plasticity, one is the ability to modify responses, the other is the ability to maintain homeostasis, i.e. maintain a steady state in face of change. Too many scholars of memory, excited by the first facet tend to forget the second. Whereas experimental psychologists and cognitive scientists focus on behavioral plasticity, their colleagues from the neuroscience community focus on circuit, cellular and, last but certainly not least, synaptic plasticity. The search for the translational rules of synaptic plasticity into behavioral plasticity, and vice versa, is a recurrent theme in the contemporary neuroscience literature, and provides an opportunity for a productive exchange among communities and levels of analysis in the science of memory.

Y.D.

14

Plasticity: New concepts, new challenges

John H. Byrne

Learning involves the induction of a change in the nervous system, whereas memory involves the persistence of that change. Plasticity is a very general term that is used to describe neuronal changes thought to be associated with learning and memory. Plasticity can be induced by intrinsic activity (e.g. spike activity) in a neuron, by extrinsic modulatory influences on a target neuron or by a combination of the two. These induction signals activate second messenger systems that modify the biochemical, biophysical and morphological parameters in one or more neuronal compartments (e.g. a synapse). The concept of plasticity is not restricted to memory, however. Plasticity is a concept also used to describe changes in the nervous system during development, aging and injury. These different domains of plasticity share some common underlying mechanisms including modulatory factors such as brain-derived neurotrophic factor (BDNF) and common signaling cascades (e.g. Carew *et al.* 1998). The concept of plasticity has been applied to memory since the work of Eugenio Tanzi in the 1890s, but it has continuously evolved and been refined. This chapter will briefly review, from this author's perspective, some relatively new concepts related to plasticity as well as the relationship between plasticity and memory.

Understanding plasticity is necessary, but not sufficient to understand memory

A great body of work over the past three decades has been devoted to understanding the ways in which neuronal properties are altered by learning and the ways in which those changes are maintained. An implicit assumption in these studies is that the understanding of plasticity will lead to an understanding of learning and memory. Indeed, this strategy has been successful for understanding several examples of learning and memory. It has been particularly successful for understanding relatively simple reflex systems that mediate procedural (nonexplicit) forms of memory in which the circuit is well understood.

In simple circuits, it is possible to relate directly a change in a neuronal property to learning and the maintenance of that change to memory. However, in many other examples of memory, particularly those involved in declarative (explicit) memory associated with the storage of information for facts and events, it is considerably less clear how the neuronal changes are induced, and, once induced, how the information is retrieved. This difficulty is due to a lack of understanding of the neural circuits that mediate these forms of memory. For example, how is the tri-synaptic loop in the hippocampus engaged during the acquisition of a memory, how does the hippocampal circuit engage cortical circuits and what specific circuits are engaged in different types of recall? Therefore, a major challenge for the future is to understand both the plasticity mechanism(s) and the neural circuit into which the plasticity mechanisms are embedded.

Plasticity is more than synaptic plasticity

The concept of plasticity as it applies to memory has most commonly come to mean alterations in the strength of synapses. Indeed, the search for the biological basis of learning and memory has led many of the twentieth century's leading neuroscientists to direct their efforts to investigating the synapse (Byrne 2001). For example, studies of learning and memory in the mammalian CNS have focused on elucidating the mechanisms that underlie long-term potentiation (LTP). Similarly, efforts to understand mechanisms underlying short- and long-term memory for behavioral sensitization of defensive withdrawal reflexes of *Aplysia* have focused primarily on investigating mechanisms supporting short- and long-term facilitation of the sensory–motor neuron synapse that underlies the reflex.

Although changes in synaptic strength are certainly ubiquitous, they are not the exclusive means for the expression of neuronal plasticity associated with learning and memory. For example, changes in synaptic strength in short- and long-term sensitization and classical conditioning in *Aplysia* occur in conjunction with an enhancement of excitability of the sensory neurons. In addition, changes in excitability of sensory neurons in the mollusc *Hermissenda* are produced by classical conditioning, and changes in excitability of a neuron in the central pattern-generating circuit mediating feeding behavior in *Aplysia* are produced by both operant conditioning and classical conditioning. These types of global changes in excitability have clear behavioral consequences as they can readily lead to an increase or decrease in the probability of a behavior being spontaneously initiated in the case of operant conditioning, or, in the case of classical conditioning, the ability of a stimulus to elicit a behavior. In vertebrates, classical conditioning of eye-blink reflexes produces changes in excitability of cortical neurons. Eye-blink conditioning also produces changes in the spike afterpotential of hippocampal pyramidal neurons. Finally, as described in their original report on LTP, Bliss and Lomo found that the expression of LTP itself was associated with enhanced excitability. Intrinsic and synaptic plasticity can co-exist and contribute to the formation and/or retention of the memory trace (for a review, see Brown *et al.* 2004).

Despite the growing body of evidence that plasticity in the form of apparent global changes in neuronal excitability is a mechanism for memory storage, theoretical neurobiologists have been slow to embrace changes in excitability as a memory mechanism. Their reluctance is due at least in part to the fact that such a mechanism potentially limits the information storage capacity of a memory system. For example, if each of a neuron's 10 000 synapses could be independently modified (e.g. the input or synapse specificity in some forms of LTP), a great amount of information could be stored. In contrast, if the plasticity mechanism was restricted to a change in a global property of a neuron such as excitability, considerably less information could be stored. Changes in excitability need not be cell wide, however. Restricted changes could occur in localized regions of dendrites and thus increase the potential information storage capabilities of this mechanism. One of the major challenges for the future is to examine further the extent to which the regulation of excitability is spatially localized and to determine the relative importance of excitability and localized synaptic plasticity to memory storage. The two mechanisms need not be mutually exclusive. Indeed, it will be interesting to examine whether the combination of the two is synergistic and provides for information storage capabilities greater than the linear sum of the two independent processes.

Plasticity has multiple temporal domains that can provide insights into the temporal domains of memory

Operationally, memory, as well as the plasticity mechanisms believed to underlie memory, have frequently been divided into two temporal domains, short term and long term. The working definition of these temporal domains relies in part on the underlying molecular mechanism. Short-term memory relies on plasticity mechanisms that require neither protein nor mRNA synthesis, and long-term memory requires both.

It has become increasingly clear from studies of a number of memory systems that this distinction is overly restrictive. There are many more than two, but probably a finite number of additional temporal domains of memory. For example, in *Aplysia*, an intermediate phase of memory exists with distinctive temporal characteristics and a unique molecular signature (Ghirardi *et al.* 1995; Sutton *et al.* 2001, 2002). The intermediate-phase memory for sensitization is expressed at times approximately 30 min to 3 h after the beginning of training. Like long-term memory, the induction of intermediate-term memory requires protein synthesis, but like short-term memory, intermediate-term memory does not require mRNA synthesis.

In addition to intermediate-phase memory, it is likely that *Aplysia* has different phases of long-term memory. For example, 24 h after training, synthesis of a number of proteins is increased. Some of these proteins are unaffected during and immediately after training (Barzilai *et al.* 1989; Noel *et al.* 1993). Yet blocking protein synthesis at times between 12 and 24 h after training does not block the underlying long-term synaptic facilitation at 24 h. These results suggest that the memory for sensitization that persists for times greater than 24 h may be dependent on the synthesis of proteins occurring at 24 h and may have a different molecular signature from the 24 h memory.

Recent studies of morphological correlates of long-term memory also indicate the presence of different temporal domains of long-term memory (Wainwright *et al.* 2002). For example, the long-term memory 1 day after the start of sensitization training is associated with synaptic facilitation and the *absence* of morphological correlates. In contrast, long-term memory 4 days after the start of sensitization training is associated with synaptic facilitation and the *presence* of morphological changes. These results indicate that long-term memory has different temporal domains that use different expression mechanisms. Given these results, a future challenge is to characterize more completely the repertoire of temporal domains of plasticity and understand the relationship between these temporal domains of plasticity and temporal domains of memory. By knowing the periods during which RNA, protein and morphological changes occur, interventions at those times could be used selectively to improve memory formation or to help remove memories associated with traumatic events.

Other challenges

In addition to understanding the aspects of plasticity described above, other relatively recently discovered aspects of plasticity and their relationship to memory need to be examined further. These characteristics and the issues surrounding them are as follows.

Plasticity at one site (neuron or synapse) is bidirectional and dependent on the temporal pattern of input

LTP in CNS neurons is produced by one pattern of input, whereas long-term depression (LTD) is produced by another. We need to know the extent to which a given learning paradigm induces LTP, LTD and combinations of LTP and LTD, and the extent to which the synaptic changes represent the memory.

Plasticity involves changes of multiple second-messenger systems within neurons that act synergistically

It has become increasingly clear that any one example of neuronal plasticity engages not one but multiple second-messenger systems in neurons. Some second-messenger systems are involved in a 'mediating' pathway. Others are involved in a 'modulatory' pathway that gates or regulates the mediating pathway (see *metaplasticity* below). However, the specific species of second messengers and kinases differ among different types of plasticity, even those having similar temporal domains. Given the diversity of signaling cascades in plasticity, we need to know the molecular logic by which different cascades are used for the different types of plasticity mechanisms.

Plasticity involves multiple types of cellular effector mechanisms

Voltage-gated membrane channels, ligand-gated membrane channels and neuronal structure are frequently implicated in the expression of neuronal plasticity, but it is likely that many other mechanisms will be identified. The role of a particular expression mechanism seems to vary at least in part with the temporal domain of the memory. However, we do not understand the molecular logic by which one expression mechanism is used preferentially for the storage of memory over another.

Plasticity is plastic (i.e. metaplasticity)

Modulatory transmitters (e.g. dopamine, BDNF) regulate the extent and the direction of plasticity in a neuron. Previous neuronal activity also regulates the ease with which synapses can undergo LTP versus LTD (BCM rule) (Brown *et al.* 2004). We need to know to what extent these metaplastic mechanisms are engaged in the normal operation of memory systems.

Plasticity is homeostatically regulated

Compensatory mechanisms exist to redistribute the weight of various presynaptic inputs to a postsynaptic target cell, while maintaining a consistent level of activity in the postsynaptic target (Turrigiano and Nelson 2000). This homeostatic regulation implies that whereas some synapses gain strength, some other synapses onto the same target cell lose strength. We need to know how this plasticity mechanism is used in memory systems and how a permanent memory becomes resistant to homeostatic regulation.

Plasticity can involve parameter-independent changes

All of the examples of plasticity discussed above involve changes in the biophysical, biochemical or morphological parameters of a neuron or synapse.

Although not examined extensively so far, there is growing appreciation emerging from the field of nonlinear dynamics that neuronal plasticity may be associated with stimulus-induced parameter-*independent* state transitions (Lechner *et al.* 1996). For example, a nonlinear dynamic system such as the gene network within a neuron or a network of nerve cells can have co-existing multiple stable states. Appropriate transient stimuli can perturb the network from one steady state to another and those transitions can be stable for indefinite periods of time. A challenge for the future is to identify the repertoire of such changes and the extent to which they contribute to different memory systems.

Acknowledgments

I thank Drs D. Baxter, L. Cleary and H. Shouval for their comments on an earlier draft of the manuscript. Supported by NIH grants MH 58321, NS 19895 and NS 38310.

15

Plasticity: A pragmatic compromise

Chris I. De Zeeuw

Plasticity is a widely used word in the field of learning and memory. Although there is no clear consensus among behaviourists, psychologists, cell physiologists and other major disciplines in neuroscience on the exact definition of plasticity, there are certainly trends emerging in the literature. Based on these trends, an attempt will be made to come up with a definition of plasticity. I will take a somewhat restrictive approach in that I will propose to use the word plasticity only for particular processes. On the other hand, the proposal for the definition of plasticity may not be as restrictive as it should have been in the eyes of some of our colleagues. The reason for this compromise is that there are good arguments for both narrowing and broadening the definition of plasticity. A narrow definition of plasticity may enhance the communication among scientists of various disciplines in the future, while a global definition will undoubtedly give more credit to the history of the word as presented in the literature and used by scientists of all these disciplines in the past.

The definition to be defended in this short communication is the following: plasticity is a *use-dependent, structural* change at the *cellular* level in the nervous system, which is necessary and possibly also *sufficient* to induce *long-lasting functional* changes that are usually *beneficial* for the organism. Below, I will explain my view on the words that are in italics in this definition.

Use dependent

Plasticity can be induced by particular synaptic and/or nonsynaptic inputs, and it can but does not need to depend on the source of these inputs; in other words, in some cases, use-dependent effects can be caused by an interaction of purely synaptic inputs, while in other cases hormonal effects or nonsynaptic release of neurotransmitters such as serotonin or noradrenalin play essential roles. Moreover, even when we restrict ourselves to use-dependent effects mediated only by synaptic inputs, it should be noted that these effects cannot only be caused by conjunctive pre- and postsynaptic activations, but also by presynaptic activities alone. While the literature is full of examples in which pre- and postsynaptic activities have to be combined to induce plasticity (for reviews, see Ito 2002; Malinow and Malenka 2002), only recently evidence has been obtained showing that plastic processes underlying learning and memory formation can in fact be located purely in the presynaptic terminal (Kushner *et al.* 2005). Thus, in particular cases, changing activities in the presynaptic terminal appear to be sufficient for both the induction and expression of plasticity.

Structural

The structures to be changed can include the quality, quantity and distribution of proteins such as ion channels, signaling molecules and kinases, as well as proteins directly involved in the formation of the shape of the cell such as microtubule-associated proteins. Interestingly, some of the molecules involved in learning and memory such as calmodulin kinase II (CaMKII) and protein kinase C may be involved in signaling processes mediating cell physiological effects such as long-term potentiation (LTP) and long-term depression (LTD) as well as direct structural changes (De Zeeuw *et al.* 1998; Elgersma *et al.* 2002; Ruiz-Canada *et al.* 2004). One of the major questions remaining to be answered is whether functional changes in plasticity can in fact occur without any change in synapses or spines at the morphological level. In this respect, it is important to note that structural changes can even occur temporarily in electrical synapses, resulting in altered plastic properties at the network level (Bullock *et al.* 2005). By proposing the definition given above, I assume that all physiological changes must be reflected at least at the molecular and in most cases probably also at the morphological level.

Cellular

Plasticity can be formed by both synaptic and nonsynaptic processes, and may not need to be restricted to neuronal processes. Thus, although the vast majority of plastic processes underlying learning and memory formation are probably mediated by changes in neuronal synapses, there are probably various other forms of plasticity that may also play a role in learning. One of these other forms may be mediated by changes in intrinsic excitability. Such changes have been observed in the cerebellar nuclei (Zhang and Linden 2003) as well as vestibular nuclei (Nelson *et al.* 2005), and may underlie particular aspects of, for example, eye-blink conditioning and adaptation of the vestibulo-ocular reflex (for a review, see De Zeeuw and Yeo 2005). Similarly, in the hippocampus, this form of neuronal plasticity could also be a cellular correlate of particular stages of declarative learning besides synaptic LTP (Xu *et al.* 2005). Moreover, apart from synaptic and nonsynaptic forms of plasticity in neurons, plastic processes in glia may play an instrumental and essential role in learning as well (for a review, see Allen and Barres 2005). Within the developing nervous system, astrocytes and Schwann cells actively help to promote synapse formation and function, and have even been implicated in synapse elimination, while in the adult brain, astrocytes respond to synaptic activity by releasing transmitters that modulate synaptic activity. The identity of the glial–neuronal signals and their precise significance will remain an important topic for investigations in the next decade.

Sufficient

One of the most difficult issues is the question as to whether single plastic processes are not only necessary but also sufficient for inducing learning and memory formation. Obviously one also needs the hardware plant to mediate learned responses, but apart from that necessity one might need additional secondary plastic responses within this hardware system to make the learning effective (for a review, see Martin *et al.* 2000). At present, it appears almost impossible to demonstrate that a primary change in a particular form of plasticity is by itself sufficient to induce learning. For example, even in relatively simple systems such as the mini-brain of the honeybee, it is difficult to show that a single plastic process can be sufficient for a particular aspect of the memory trace necessary for the foraging cycle (Menzel 2001, Chapter 63, this volume). The complexity of biological systems in general makes it rather unlikely that any plastic process stands on itself, yet data obtained with cell-specific mutants support the hypothesis that learning and memory formation can start initially at only one or a few essential plastic sites, which can be sufficient to trigger the remaining plastic processes downstream (see, for example, De Zeeuw *et al.* 1998).

Long-lasting functional

The plastic changes, which should ultimately affect the spike generation of the neuron involved or a neuron downstream, should last longer than control conditions in which no plastic change is induced. In other words, the plastic process should bring the neuron to another state that is relatively stable. How long such a stability will last can probably vary from milliseconds such as short-term plasticity in the Calyx of Held (von Gersdorff and Borst 2002) up to years such as occur for example after plastic processes necessary for long-term memory and/or developmental changes (Dumas 2005). In general, short-term forms of plasticity are probably mediated through homosynaptic mechanisms, while long-term forms of plasticity that lead to transcription and to synaptic growth usually require heterosynaptic processes (Bailey *et al.* 2005).

Beneficial

Not all secondary structural changes are plastic. Although the word plasticity is widely used for all sorts of changes secondary to neuronal damage (Woods *et al.* 2000), I propose only to do so when such a change can in principle be beneficial for the survival of the organism including both forms of plasticity directly involved in learning and memory and forms of compensatory recovery mechanisms following damage. If the word plasticity is used for all secondary structural changes, even when they hamper survival, one of its main characteristics, i.e. its potential positive effects, will be lost. Moreover, if we do not restrict ourselves in the use of the word plasticity, it will become a word without meaning. Thus, although it should be recognized that such an addition to the definition of plasticity presents a teleological argument, it will allow us to distinguish genuine forms of plasticity from negative or neutral changing processes such as noncompensatory secondary neuropathological events and aging.

Conclusion

The definition and explanation given above for the term plasticity provides on the one hand an open view including most forms of neuronal and glial plasticity, synaptic and nonsynaptic plasticity, as well as electrophysiological and devel-opmental plasticity, while on the other hand it proposes to restrict ourselves to cellular phenomena that have a potential positive impact on the survival of the organism. Thus, I propose to not use the term plasticity for learned behavior itself (but use it in fact for the cellular process that causes such a change) and not use plasticity for natural processes such as aging that occur automatically over time (while one could use it for secondary processes that can compensate for such a downward process). By choosing such a compromise, the field of learning and memory could enrich its language and enhance the communication both within in its domain and across its participating disciplines.

16

Plasticity: On the level

John T. Bruer

I will attempt to characterize how the concept of plasticity is used in psychology and neuroscience at levels of analysis ranging from the behavioral level to the molecular. Of special interest is how plasticity is understood and applied in memory research. In this discussion, I will refer to the behavioral level as the highest level of analysis and the molecular level as the lowest.

In neuroscientific and psychological contexts, plasticity is synonymous with change and contrasts with stability. Plasticity is used to describe changes in systems at all levels of analysis from the behavioral level (ethologists describe bird song as plastic) through the subcellular (neuroscientists investigate mechanisms of synaptic plasticity).

Plasticity is a descriptive term. It describes an experimentally established change, in which events and entities at one level of analysis cause a change at the same level of analysis (e.g. auditory experience causes changes in bird song) or at a lower level of analysis (e.g. monocular deprivation causes changes in ocular dominance columns).

Plasticity does not pre-suppose exogenous causes. Psychologists and neuroscientists speak of both developmental and experience-dependent plasticity. The first is assumed to arise from endogenous causes, the second from exogenous causes. Both lesions and pathology are discussed as causes of plasticity. There is no assumption that plastic changes to the system are adaptive. Changes in bird song or ocular dominance columns with atypical experience are plastic changes, but it is not clear that these changes in behavior or brain organization are adaptive for the organism.

Although plasticity is a descriptive term, it tends to occur in explanatory contexts. Scientists, like humans generally, seek explanations for change and are less interested in stasis. In 114 review articles on plasticity at various levels of analysis, the term 'plasticity' occurred 2711 times and 'mechanism' 1682 times—one occurrence of 'mechanism' for every 1.6 occurrences of 'plasticity'.

Plasticity occurs in explanatory contexts after a plastic phenomenon has been characterized experimentally. The best example of this is ocular dominance column plasticity. Clinically, it was well established that some types of abnormal visual experience in young animals, but not adults, rendered the young functionally blind. Hubel and Wiesel (1970) showed that the effects of experience on behavior are mediated by changes in brain structure. They established that monocular deprivation caused plastic changes in the organism at a higher level of analysis, ocular dominance columns in visual cortex. Hubel and Wiesel's 1970 paper is strictly descriptive, with some speculation about the clinical implications of ocular dominance plasticity. Stent (1973) provided an argument that this phenomenon might be explained at the synaptic level by appeal to Hebbian synapses and the associated learning rule (Hubel and Wiesel 2005). Attempts to explain ocular dominance column plasticity, as well as the temporal limitations of it, at the synaptic level have been one of the major enterprises within neuroscientific research. This model system has served to further our understanding of possible causal mechanisms responsible for ocular dominance plasticity.

A characterization of the plasticity concept

How might one characterize the plasticity concept in general? As a descriptive term, plasticity refers to an experimentally established change between entities at the same or lower levels of analysis, where the lower level entity, C_l, causes a measurable change at the same or lower level of analysis, E_m, $m \leq l$. In explanatory contexts, this causal relationship, $C_l \rightarrow E_m$, that establishes the existence of the plasticity phenomenon, appears as the explanandum, where one seeks a causal explanation of $C_l \rightarrow E_m$ at an even lower level of analysis, $C_l \rightarrow L_n \rightarrow E_m$, $n < m$.

Figure 16.1 shows examples of plasticity and their explanations at various levels of analysis. Solid straight arrows indicate the causal relationship establishing plasticity. Dashed straight arrows indicate other causal relationships involved in the experimental paradigm that are not the immediate targets for explanation. Curved dashed arrows indicate causal relationships that are hypothesized to explain the observed plasticity. For language, the plastic phenomenon is identified at the behavioral level and psychologists posit maturational changes in the central nervous system as an explanation for the phenomenon. For cortical plasticity, stimuli from the environment (behavioral level) cause changes to cortical structures. Ocular dominance plasticity, for example, is a special case of cortical plasticity, where visual experience causes measurable changes in ocular dominance columns. Explanations for the plasticity of cortical structures are sought at the synaptic level. For long-term potentiation (LTP) and other forms of synaptic plasticity, explanations are sought at the molecular level.

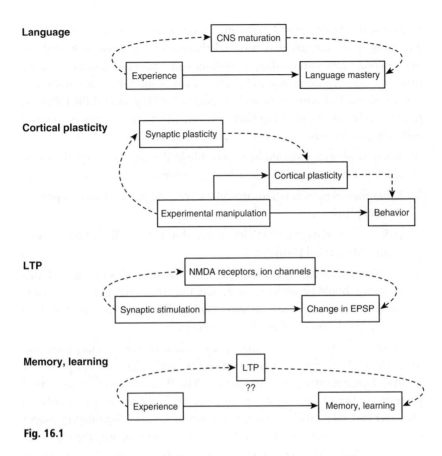

Fig. 16.1

Explaining plasticity

Plasticity as a descriptive term is reasonably straightforward. There is little debate, for example, that differences in timing and duration of language experience or monocular deprivation have an effect on ultimate language mastery or ocular dominance columns. Problems arise with explanations offered for these plastic phenomena. Does synaptic plasticity explain cortical plasticity? Does LTP, or other mechanisms of synaptic plasticity, explain the observed plastic changes in memory and behavior? How does one decide such questions?

As an example, consider the hypothesis that synaptic plasticity explains, or causes, cortical plasticity. Buonomano and Merzenich (1998) specifically addressed this hypothesis and provided experimental criteria that should be met to establish this causal link. Typically in these discussions, neuroscientists attempt to analyze causal claims using necessity–sufficiency accounts of causal relationships (Shors and Matzel 1997; Buonomano and Merzenich 1998). Assuming, in this context, that causal relationships can be adequately analyzed in terms of necessary and sufficient conditions, one must establish that synaptic plasticity is both a necessary and sufficient condition for the occurrence or cortical plasticity. Buonomano and Merzenich (1998) provided the following four criteria for establishing that synaptic plasticity is a necessary and sufficient condition for the occurrence of cortical plasticity:

1. Synaptic plasticity should be observable in the appropriate pathways in animals where cortical plasticity has been observed.

2. Experimental manipulations that block synaptic plasticity should prevent cortical plasticity.

3. Induction of synaptic plasticity *in vivo* should be sufficient to generate observable cortical plasticity.

4. The forms of synaptic plasticity and the learning rules that govern this plasticity should be sufficient to explain fully the experimental data using computer simulations that use only and faithfully represent experimentally established, biologically real forms of plasticity.

The first two criteria establish that synaptic plasticity is a necessary condition for cortical plasticity, i.e. they establish the truth of 'If cortical plasticity occurs, then synaptic plasticity occurs'. The first criterion requires that synaptic plasticity be observable retrospectively in the appropriate pathways whenever cortical plasticity occurs. The second criterion is logically equivalent to the first. The contra-positive of 'If cortical plasticity occurs, then synaptic plasticity occurs' is 'If synaptic plasticity does not occur, then cortical plasticity does not occur'. The second criterion is somewhat stronger in that it requires prospective evidence, where one blocks synaptic plasticity using, for example, genetic or pharmacological interventions. The third criterion establishes the truth of 'If synaptic plasticity occurs, then cortical plasticity occurs', i.e. that synaptic plasticity is sufficient for cortical plasticity. The fourth criterion is not properly part of a necessity–sufficiency account, but can be thought of as a completeness criterion. Our understanding of the causal link between synaptic and cortical plasticity should be sufficiently complete that it would be possible to write an experimentally faithful and biologically realistic computer simulation that accounts for all experimental data. Applying these criteria, Buonomano and Merzenich (1998) concluded that as of 1998 the claim that synaptic plasticity caused cortical plasticity remained an open hypothesis.

The status of this particular hypothesis might have changed since 1998. Nonetheless, the criteria Buonomano and Merzenich applied remain relevant to assessing the adequacy of other causal explanations of plastic phenomena.

It is easy to adapt their criteria to other hypotheses. For example, replace synaptic plasticity and cortical plasticity with CNS maturation and language performance. Or, more interestingly replace them with LTP and memory.

Shors and Matzel (1997) made this replacement and concluded that at least one form of synaptic plasticity, LTP, did not meet the criteria for providing a causal explanation of memory. To make a long argument very short, they documented instances where changes in memory occur without LTP and where LTP occurs without changes in memory, i.e. they documented that LTP is neither necessary nor sufficient for memory change. Part of the problem resides in ambiguities over the definition of LTP. Another difficulty arises with applying the third criterion. Genetic and pharmacological interventions to block LTP can have general, rather than specific, effects on the organism, making experimental interpretations difficult.

However, Shors and Matzel cite a more fundamental problem. They report that between 1974 and 1997, over 1300 articles appeared that had LTP in their title. Of these, fewer than 80 described any behavioral manipulation relevant to assessing changes in memory and that articles containing behavioral manipulations tended to provide evidence against the hypothesis that LTP is a memory mechanism. Thus, the final panel of Fig. 16.1 that posits LTP as a high level causal mechanism for learning and memory may represent more of a dogma of neuroscientific memory research than a hypothesis that is being rigorously tested.

Plasticity becomes a problematic concept across levels of analysis when in assessing explanations of plastic phenomena, we ignore the criteria the causal explanations should satisfy.

17

Integrative comments
Plasticity: more than memory

Edvard I. Moser

Plasticity is a broad concept used in a number of scientific disciplines. A search for scientific journals and books with 'plasticity' in their title gave a number of hits, but only a fraction of them were in neuroscience. Other titles were devoted to plasticity in evolutionary biology and ecology, where species are known to develop in response to their current environment (e.g. water snails adapt to lake or pond conditions), or in materials science and physics, where 'plasticity' refers to the property of materials to undergo irreversible changes of shape in response to applied forces (e.g. clay or wet chewing gum can be stretched to many times their original length). In these sister disciplines, 'plasticity' covers a variety of observable changes at the structural or functional level, often in global and general properties of the unit of study.

In neuroscience, 'plasticity' is an umbrella term that covers a wide diversity of processes and mechanisms involved in small-scale or large-scale remodeling of the nervous system. These processes include changes in morphology, internal dynamics and function. Most neuroscientists would add reversible modifications to the definition, although these are generally considered to show at least some degree of stability. Attempts to provide a clearer definition raise a number of issues. I shall discuss some of them, focusing on the disturbingly broad diversity of processes that could be described by 'plasticity', the implications of a broad definition for an integrative science of memory, possible restrictions of the concept, the difference between descriptive and explanatory uses, and the relationship of 'plasticity' to memory as studied at the behavioral level. Several of these issues are highlighted in the accompanying position chapters.

Plasticity is an umbrella term

'Plasticity' is more than memory. For a developmental neuroscientist, plasticity refers to the range of processes and mechanisms responsible for transforming

neurons and neuronal systems from early to more advanced stages of maturation. For a neuroscientist interested in regeneration, plasticity may characterize the wide range of processes that take place in the nervous system after
stress, injury or disease. In some behavioral studies, plasticity is used to
describe the global ability of nervous systems and organisms to undergo
changes in intrinsic organization or output in response to new environmental
demands.

Plasticity is a multilevel concept. Beginning at the molecular level, there is
abundant evidence for 'plasticity' in synapses, where the modification of an
existing protein or the synthesis of a new protein may be sufficient to influence significantly how the neuron interacts with its peer neurons. There is no
sharp distinction, however, between synaptic 'plasticity' and the general
dynamics of synaptic molecules. If phosphorylation of a protein is a typical
form of molecular plasticity, can the same be said about the hydrolysis of ATP?
If the answer is 'it depends', when are phosphorylation and hydrolysis exemplars of plasticity and when are they not? 'Plasticity' tends to be used only for
events that significantly outlast the inducing stimulus when the latter is
known, but there is no minimum duration for plasticity; the term is sometimes used for modifications that last only a few milliseconds. Most neuroscientists would reserve the term for instances where molecular events are
associated with remodeling at a higher level of analysis (changes in synaptic
potentials, changes in firing rate, or changes in memory), but whether such
links exist is not given *a priori*.

As indicated in Chapters 14 and 15 of this volume, plasticity is not limited
to synapses. When synapses are strengthened by long-term potentiation
(LTP), for example, there is often also an enhancement of the excitability of
the neuron (Bliss and Lømo 1973). Induction of long-term potentiation (LTP)
or long-term depression (LTD) is counteracted by homeostatic plasticity
mechanisms that prevent destabilization of the neuron or the neural network
(Turrigiano and Nelson 2000). Such mechanisms are often global, expressed
as changes in excitability or synapse numbers across the entire neuron. Under
some circumstances, neurons may be replaced entirely and newborn neurons
may be integrated into existing circuits to become fully functional (Ming and
Song 2005). Moving up yet another level, plasticity is expressed as changes in
structure and dynamics of neural networks and systems. Sensory representations, for example, are continuously modified by experience. The area of
cortex allocated to representing a particular peripheral input source may be
modified during learning or after removal of sensory input such as after
peripheral injury (Buonomano and Merzenich 1998). In song birds, entire

nuclei may wax and wane due to neurogenesis and neuronal death accompanying seasonal changes in song behavior (Nottebohm 2004). Finally, plasticity is used to describe changes in behavior or behavioral potential, such as the transition from language-general to language-specific sound perception in human infants (Werker and Tees 1999), or the calibration of auditory localization by visual input in developing barn owls (Knudsen and Knudsen 1985). Together, these examples illustrate that 'plasticity' is used at all levels of analysis in neuroscience, from molecules through networks to behavior. This broad range of mechanisms, across all analytical levels, is what is meant by 'plasticity'.

Plasticity has a number of phenotypes. First, plasticity can be both additive and subtractive. Synapses may be strengthened or weakened (Malenka and Bear 2004), synapses may be added or removed (Bailey and Chen 1983; Moser *et al.* 1994; Woolley *et al.* 2004), and neurons may appear or disappear (Nottebohm 2004; Ming and Song 2005). Secondly, plasticity may be short-lasting or long-lasting. The shortest modifications, such as paired-pulse inhibition, facilitation and post-tetanic potentiation, last from milliseconds to minutes (Zucker and Regehr 2002). Longer modifications such as LTP may last hours, days or more (Bliss and Lømo 1973; Martin *et al.* 2000; Malenka and Bear 2004). Thirdly, plasticity can be associative or nonassociative. Associative plasticity plays a key role during development (Debski and Cline 2002) and may be necessary for most types of long-term memory (Martin *et al.* 2000; Malenka and Bear 2004). Nonassociative plasticity is observed during habituation or sensitization in single reflex pathways (Pinsker *et al.* 1970). Fourthly, plasticity can be caused by exogenous as well as endogenous factors. While plasticity during learning is normally related to events that are external to the organism, developmental plasticity may rely more on endogenous signals, such as developmentally regulated expression of a signal molecule. Plasticity may also result from endogenous rhythms in the secretion of hormones such as the estrous cycle of adult female rats (Woolley *et al.* 1990). Finally, plasticity is not limited to neurons. Astrocytes, for example, promote synapse formation in developing animals and release transmitters that modulate synaptic activity in the mature nervous system (Allen and Barres 2005). The role of neuron–glia interations in memory formation is probably underestimated.

With these examples, I intended to show that plasticity is used to characterize a number of mechanisms at a number of analytical levels in widely different brain systems across all developmental stages. To reiterate, the term is an umbrella term for changes in neural structure and organization, physiological response patterns, representations, network dynamics, functional divisions and behavior, bearing little more in common than the fact that the system or parts of it undergo, or can undergo, a change following some identified or unidentified external or internal factor. This is an alarmingly broad definition.

What is outside the umbrella?

Although most neuroscientists have felt the need for an umbrella term to refer to the multitude of change mechanisms in the nervous system, the broad definition of plasticity naturally leads one to ask for a description of processes and mechanisms that do *not* count as plasticity. Such examples are hard to pinpoint. Most neuroscientists would not include the immediate effects of drugs or injuries in their definition of plasticity, nor would they adopt more slowly emerging changes that could directly be attributed to disease or aging. What is common to these outsiders is that they are not considered to be adaptive to the organism. The exclusion of negative changes is stated explicitly in Chapter 15 of this volume. However, as recognized by De Zeeuw, the use of a beneficial outcome as an inclusion criterion is problematic. First, we rarely know *a priori* which changes are adaptive and which are not. Injury and disease are accompanied by modifications that compensate for the initial harm, such as changes in gene expression, axonal or dendritic sprouting, or changes in representational boundaries. The distinction between disruptive and compensatory changes is particularly difficult in the case of aging and slowly developing diseases, where first- and second-order effects develop more or less in parallel. Secondly, a particular type of change may be adaptive in one context but disruptive in another. Reductions in synaptic number, for example, occur in a number of conditions. Synaptic density decreases following stress and disease (McEwen 2001) and social and environmental deprivation (Moser *et al.* 1994), but so does it after some types of learning, such as long-term habituation of the gill-withdrawal reflex in *Aplysia* (Bailey and Chen 1983). When is the loss of synaptic contacts detrimental and when is it adaptive (e.g. subserving learning)? We cannot know *a priori*. Similar doubts can be raised with respect to sprouting. Sprouting can lead to regeneration of function, but may also result in dysfunctional connections. Following injuries in the nervous system, the latter is prevented by the synthesis of myelin-associated proteins that inhibit outgrowth of axons (He and Koprivica 2004). Because we cannot tell without empirical investigation which changes are beneficial and which are not, teleological definitions of plasticity may not be useful after all. On the other hand, without such constraints, 'plasticity' becomes very similar to the common term 'change' or 'ability to change'. At best, 'plasticity' can be limited to changes that are 'potentially' adaptive to the organism, although this does not help for practical uses of the concept.

The relationship between plasticity and memory

'Plasticity' as defined so far is a descriptive term. As addressed by John Bruer in Chapter 16 of this volume, 'plasticity' is sometimes also used in explanatory contexts, particularly where observations at one level of analysis are 'explained' by observations at another level (usually a lower level). Because the concept includes a wide range of neural activity patterns correlated with an observed change in behavior, 'plasticity' is sometimes used as a reference to the underlying mechanisms, e.g. as an implicit 'explanation' of learning or functional recovery after a brain lesion. It is important to be aware that such uses of the concept are still descriptive; there is no implication in the concept about the particular mechanisms involved.

Although most neuroscientists might not use 'plasticity' in a strictly explanatory sense, the distinction between descriptive and explanatory uses introduced by John Bruer points to a more general problem related to explaining observations at higher levels of analysis (e.g. behavior or systems properties) by observations at lower levels (e.g. molecular or synaptic changes). The problem is illustrated by the classic question of whether LTP, one expression of plasticity, is a mechanism of memory, another expression of plasticity. A large body of research on the molecular mechanisms of LTP rests on the assumption that LTP has properties that overlap significantly with the cellular mechanisms necessary for encoding and storage of at least some types of memory. This assumption is supported by a number of interventions showing that treatments that interfere with LTP also interfere with learning (Martin *et al.* 2000). Although the evidence is almost exclusively correlative and animals have been reported to learn in the absence of LTP (Shors and Matzel 1997), LTP is generally thought to play some kind of necessary role in encoding and storage of memory (Martin *et al.* 2000). This does not imply, however, that the function of LTP is understood. A deeper appreciation of how LTP contributes to memory may require studies of how LTP is implemented in specific networks of the brain, and how changes in some synapses but not others alter the function of these particular networks. To do so, we must first understand the global computations and functions of the circuits in which LTP is embedded, as pointed out also by Byrne (Chapter 14, this volume). These computations and functions may vary from one circuit to another, implying that LTP has different roles in different systems (Ji *et al.* 2003; Thomas and Malenka 2003). Thus, although analyses of the molecular mechanisms of LTP are highly valuable for understanding synaptic transmission, a detailed description of these mechanisms is not sufficient for 'explaining' memory at the behavioral level.

Do we need 'plasticity'?

The science of memory needs some umbrella terms. Both small and large umbrellas may be needed. 'Plasticity' is certainly among the larger ones. The concept is convenient as a reference to a broad scope of modifications in the nervous system, but the current use of the concept is almost synonymous with the common terms 'change' or 'ability to change', and appears to include almost any type of modification in brain structure or function that outlasts the stimulus that triggered it. Considering that nearly all elements of the nervous system undergo some change over time, and that the inducing factors and the consequences of a particular change may not be known at the time when the change is referred to as an instance of plasticity, it is hard to separate out those changes that do *not* qualify as exemplars of the concept. 'Plasticity' is useful as a label for a wide repertoire of phenomena, but the definition is vague, its current use is variable and inconsistent, and the concept is in no way unique to neuroscience or the science of memory.

How does the broad use of 'plasticity' impact on the attempt to build up an integrated science of memory? Shall we abandon the concept? Neuroscientists may wish to use the term in some contexts for the same reason that they might not like to delete common-language concepts with equally broad and fuzzy definitions, such as 'change', 'stability', 'effect' or 'result'. Such concepts are useful as umbrella terms if we realize that they are vaguely defined descriptive entities. However, theories of memory should ultimately be based on more specific core concepts. For some purposes, 'plasticity' may be used in combination with other concepts, such as in 'synaptic plasticity' or 'Hebbian plasticity'. These terms are more restrictive. 'Synaptic plasticity' is a common label for short-term and long-term modifications at a certain location in the nervous system—the synapse—and 'Hebbian plasticity' refers to the subset of mechanisms by which synaptic strength is modified as a result of overlapping activity in presynaptic and postsynaptic neurons. For other purposes, a different but more specific term than 'plasticity' may be preferable (e.g. 'LTP', 'neurogenesis' or 'sprouting'). Used alone, 'plasticity' may give a false impression of precision and specificity. For a theory of science, it may be more appropriate to call a spade a spade.

5

Context

Context refers to the situation or circumstances in which an event takes place. The term can refer either to the external circumstances (such as the environment in which an event occurs) or to internal states (experiencing events after ingesting a particular drug or while in a happy mood). When the context refers to specific features of the environment, the term cue (or cues) is often used. For example, an event might be paired with a particular tone or color of light. The cue or context can distinguish one event from another in discrimination tasks, or it can provide a signal for a response, or it can provide a stimulus for retrieval of events. One research technique that provides insight into the operation of context in learning and memory is systematically to vary cues during both learning of information and later testing, such that the context in the two cases can vary from highly similar to dissimilar. The expectation from several fundamental principles (stimulus generalization, encoding specificity, transfer appropriate processing) is that performance should benefit to the extent that encoded context is similar during learning and testing. As such, the role of context and the power of cues play central roles in the study of learning and memory.

H.L.R.

18

Context: What's so special about it?

Michael S. Fanselow

The term context has a wide range of uses in psychology because behavior is strongly influenced by the circumstances or setting in which the behavior occurs. A kiss may be welcomed in some situations and completely taboo in others. The meaning of some words is determined by other words that surround them. Animal learning experiments too, must occur in a context. Thus the context is one determinant of behavior in Pavlovian conditioning experiments. In particular, contextual fear conditioning has emerged as one of the major tools for analyzing learning and memory. Despite the heavy use of contextual conditioning procedures and the frequent use of the term in papers, little effort has gone into providing a definition of this term. The purpose of this chapter is to develop a definition of what is meant by the term that relates to the history of research that has made the term so common today.

The prototypical Pavlovian conditioning experiment focuses on the conditional stimulus (CS) that acquires the ability to control behavior because of an exact temporal relationship with a biologically meaningful unconditional stimulus (US). For example, conditioning is expected to be best when there is a perfect dependent relationship such that the US always occurs with the CS and never at other times. However, Pavlovian researchers rapidly recognized that the conditioning apparatus itself gains significant ability to control behavior—it becomes a CS. This fact attracted little interest until conditioners discovered that conditioning to one CS was dependent on not only the relationship with the US but also the presence of other CSs. A major advance in conditioning theory occurred when Rescorla and Wagner (1972) provided a set of rules describing how multiple CSs interact with each other. If CSs interact, and the conditioning apparatus was a CS, then these apparatus cues should influence learning to the target CS. This realization gave rise to the modern interest in context conditioning. The terms apparatus cues, static cues and context cues were used interchangeably. They simply referred to the constellation of cues that were necessarily part of a conditioning experiment other than the two stimuli that were the emphasis of conditioning, the discrete CS and the US. Over the years, the term context seems to have become dominant and one rarely sees 'static' and 'apparatus' used. Therefore, I will refer to these CSs as context and to traditional explicit Pavlovian CSs as cues. Operationally, context was manipulated by changing the apparatus in which conditioning took place. Typically, multiple features are changed (shape, smell, lighting, background noise, location).

Much of the research during this period did not measure a conditional response (CR) to the context. Rather, it looked at how a context altered CRs to cues that were embedded in them. For the most part, that research showed that contexts affected conditioning to cues in much the same way as an additional cue would. It also showed that context played an absolutely critical role and was responsible for effects such as contingency devaluation (Dweck and Wagner 1970), US-pre-exposure deficits (Randich 1981), reinstatement after extinction (Bouton and Bolles 1979) and preference for signaled shock (Fanselow 1980a). Contexts did not only influence responding to CSs. They could also cause a conditional modulation of the unconditional response (UR), much like a traditional CS could. One important avenue of research this opened up was the realization that the context of drug taking provided a CS that was responsible for many of the effects of drug abuse such as opiate tolerance (Siegel 1976).

About the same time, it was found that the freezing response seen following a shock US in a fear conditioning experiment was actually a CR to the context and not a UR to shock (Fanselow 1980b). Following this realization, several studies of fear CRs such as freezing and analgesia used contexts in lieu of cues (e.g. Fanselow and Baackes 1982). In all of this research, the definition of context did not seem very important. Context was simply a stimulus. Operationally it could be manipulated by manipulating apparatus cues, and behaviorally it functioned much like any other CS.

If a context is just another stimulus, then there should be no fundamental differences between conditioning to cues and contexts, but analysis of a phenomenon that has come to be called the immediate shock deficit showed this not to be the case. Blanchard et al. (1976) reported that rats that received a shock immediately after being placed in a context did not reduce their activity. Rats given a few minutes to explore the environment first, however, showed a robust suppression of activity. They suggested that rats that did not have an opportunity to explore assumed that there were escape exits and they did not freeze because they were looking for these exits. This explanation suggested that giving a shock right after placement in the chamber affected expression, but not learning, of fear. I began a series of experiments to test this notion and came to the opposite conclusion (Fanselow 1986). The reason the rats failed to freeze when they received a shock immediately after placement in the chamber was that they failed to form an association between the context and shock. It was not that they expressed their fear with a behavior other than freezing; it was because they were not afraid. For example, rats that received an immediate shock did not interact with escape exits even when they were available. They not only did not freeze, they did not defecate. Follow-up experiments replicated this immediate shock deficit using several different indices of fear [e.g. passive avoidance and potentiated startle (Kiernan *et al.* 1995) and conditional analgesia (Fanselow *et al.* 1994)]. Finally, immediate shock does not cause the neuronal changes typically observed during conditioning, such as immediate early gene expression in the amygdala (Rosen *et al.* 1998) or the temporary decrease in neurogenesis in the dentate gyrus of the hippocampus generally observed with traditional contextual fear conditioning parameters (Pham *et al.* 2005).

Another finding of these early experiments was that freezing gradually increased as the interval between placement in the context and shock increased (Fig. 18.1). This suggests something fundamentally different about contexts and cues.

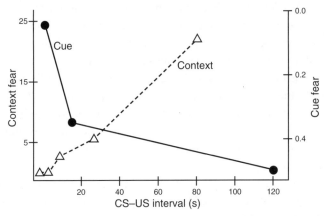

Fig. 18.1 Fear as a function of CS onset to US onset interval for a cued and contextual fear response in rats. The context data are percentage of time spent freezing (axis to the left) and are based on Fanselow (1986). The cued fear data are for a white noise CS and are based on Kamin (1965). Cued fear is presented in terms of suppression ratios where 0 represents maximal fear and 0.5 is no fear (axis to the right). The *y*-axis for suppression ratios was inverted so that the level of fear is a positive function for both axes. The cue was on continuously during the CS–US interval (delay conditioning) as that corresponds best with the context conditioning preparation. However, Kamin found virtually identical data when all groups had a 1.5 s CS (trace conditioning).

One of the standard rules of Pavlovian conditioning is that as the interval between onset of the CS and onset of the US increases, the magnitude of the CR decreases. While there is some debate as to whether conditioning is best with simultaneous onset of CS and US or if the onset of the US should be slightly delayed (Rescorla 1980), it is considered universal that CR perform- ance degrades as the interval between CS onset and US onset increases by anything more than a trivial interval. Importantly, Kamin (1965) showed that cued fear conditioning decreased when the CS–US interval increased from 1.5 to 15 s and decreased even further at 120 s. Kamin's data are also plotted on Fig. 18.1, which shows how conditioning with a cue and a context are inverse functions with respect to the CS–US interval. Cue and context conditioning differ at a very fundamental level.

This finding meant that there was something different about context and cue. One difference is that compared with a cue, contexts are made up of multiple features from several sensory modalities. To facilitate conditioning, cues are designed to be highly salient, but for the most part the features of a context are not. Additionally, unlike a cue, the features of a context typically have rather poor contiguity with shock. Some features (e.g. the shading in a particular corner) will only be experienced intermittently when the animal is exploring a particular location or attending to that feature. Thus individual features will receive multiple presentations and perhaps one of those presenta- tions will be contiguous with the US. Others will be available continuously (e.g. the odor) and those will have a long CS–US interval. So no feature will be in a good position to condition. Thus, I argued that to condition a context successfully, the set of features must be first integrated into a 'Gestalt'. This gestalt takes time to form because it requires exploration and assimilation of the features, and that integrative process results in the function shown in Fig. 18.1. Once this representation is formed, context can function as a stimulus and context conditioning can proceed.

Another set of differences between cue and context was how they responded to manipulations of brain function. Both hippocampal lesions and intracere- broventricular infusions of an N-methyl-D-aspartate (NMDA) receptor antag- onist selectively decreased context not cue fear (Kim et al. 1991; Kim and Fanselow 1992). Based on this, it was suggested that NMDA receptors within the hippocampus were responsible for forming the context representation.

So what is a context and is it somehow special? The context is a stimulus. Every stimulus modality has certain unique aspects. Obviously, auditory and visual cues are processed by dissociable neuroanatomy sculpted by evolution for each modality's specific function. The same is true of context. Neuroanatomically, the hippocampus receives some of the most highly processed and compressed multimodal information in the brain. Such a region would be ideally suited for forming memories about a context. Remember that you can only perceive a subset of features of a context at one point in time so the context gestalt must be retrieved by a small subset of cues. The ability to remember a complex stimulus when only a subset of the stimulus' features are available is called pattern completion, and the architecture of the hippocampus has long been recognized as well suited for the task of pattern completion (O'Reilly and McClelland 1994). From this perspective, the participation of the hippocampus in contextual memory makes perfect sense.

This chapter has emphasized what a context is as opposed to what a context does. A context can do all the things any other stimulus can. I mostly described research where a context acts as a direct elicitor of learned behavior. Contexts can also act as retrieval cues and can help disambiguate cues with multiple meanings. However, none of these properties uniquely define context as simple cues can do all of these things. It is also hazardous to define context in terms of any of these properties because the definition will tend to be circular. For example, saying X resolved ambiguity so it is a context because contexts disambiguate is circular. It also neglects the fact that simple cues can disambiguate too. The aspects that define a context are not what a context does; simple cues can do everything a context can. What defines a context are its unique set of stimulus properties, principally, that it is made up of many features from multiple modalities and these features have moment to moment variation because of exploration or shifts in attention.

19

Context: Mood, memory and the concept of context

Eric Eich

The concept of context has long been considered central to understanding memory. Sixty-plus years ago, John McGeoch observed that what has been learned in a particular physical setting or psychological state is most express-ible in that same situation. McGeogh also maintained that this principle of 'altered stimulating conditions' ranked alongside interference and inadequate set to remember as one of the three central causes of forgetting. Similar ideas are apparent in other classic contributions to the science of memory, includ-ing the drive-as-stimulus theories proposed by Clark Hull (in the 1940s) and Neal Miller (1950s), as well as in such contemporary (1980s) accounts as Gordon Bower's network model of emotions and Endel Tulving's encoding specificity principle (see Eich and Macaulay 2007 for references).

Today's literature on context and memory is vast and varied in scope as well as methods. Many studies have examined different subject species (ranging from marine mollusks to university undergraduates), retention tasks (fear condition-ing, autobiographical recollection and paired-associates learning, among many others), memory systems (procedural versus declarative, episodic versus semantic), and both external and internal contexts (physical environments, for instance, in contrast to pharmacological states). This diversity reflects not only the theoretical richness of the concept of context, as it applies to memory, but also the range of empirical problems that researchers in the area have addressed.

To clarify, consider *mood congruence*, *mood dependence* and *mood mediation*—three specific problems that, prism like, present different sides to the general question of how affective states, such as happiness and sadness, function as internal or experiential contexts for memory and cognition.

Mood congruence

Evidence from many sources suggests that people tend to perceive themselves, and the world around them, in a manner that is congruent with their current mood.

Thus, for example, happy people tend to tell happy stories, think well of others, generate positive associations to words, remember mostly pleasant events from their personal past and predict mostly good things for their future (Ellis and Moore 1999; Bower and Forgas 2000).

Over the past 25 years, explanations of mood congruence have gradually evolved from psychodynamic and conditioning approaches toward cognitive accounts, such as the concept of affect priming which Bower (1981) first formalized in his well-known network theory of emotion.

With accumulating empirical evidence, however, it has also become clear that while mood congruence is a robust and reliable phenomenon, it is not universal. In fact, in many circumstances, mood either has no effect or even has an incongruent effect on cognition. How are such divergent results to be understood?

The affect infusion model (AIM) proposed by Forgas (1995; Bower and Forgas 2000) offers an answer. The model implies, and the literature indicates, that mood congruence is unlikely to occur whenever a cognitive task can be performed via a simple, well-rehearsed direct access strategy or a highly motivated strategy. In these conditions, there is little need or opportunity for cognition to be influenced or 'infused' by affect. According to the AIM, it is more common for mood congruence to occur when individuals engage in substantive, constructive processing to integrate the available information with pre-existing and affectively primed knowledge structures. Consistent with this claim, several studies have shown that mood-congruent effects are magnified when people engage in constructive processing to compute judgments about peripheral rather than central conceptions of the self, atypical rather than typical characters, and complex rather than simple personal conflicts (Bower and Forgas 2000). As will be seen in the next section, the concept of affect infusion in general, and the idea of constructive processing in particular, may be keys to understanding not only mood congruence, but mood dependence as well.

Mood dependence

Are events that have been encoded in a certain state of affect or mood (such as sadness) more retrievable in the same mood than in a different one (such as happiness)? In other words, is memory mood dependent?

The question is straightforward and so, it would seem, is the answer. As noted elsewhere (Eich and Macaulay 2007), the existence of mood dependence is predicted or implied by many influential memory theories, including the classic and contemporary contributions cited in the opening paragraph. Moreover, the clinical literature is replete with conjectures implicating mood-dependent memory (MDM) as a causal factor in the memory deficits displayed by patients with alcoholic blackout, bipolar disorder, chronic depression, multiple personality and other psychiatric conditions (see Reus *et al.* 1979).

Though there are good reasons to believe that memory *should* be mood dependent, showing that it *is* has proved to be a nontrivial task. A succession of mostly positive results in the 1970s gave way to a string of largely negative outcomes in the 1980s. Consequently, memory theorists in the early 1990s were left to wonder whether MDM even exists as an empirical phenomenon, and whether the idea of affect or mood as a contextual cue for remembering buys anyone anything as a theoretical construct (Eich 1995*a*).

Today the outlook is more optimistic, as recent research has shown that it is possible to obtain clear and consistent evidence of mood dependence— provided that certain conditions are met. For instance, the likelihood of demonstrating MDM is increased by instilling moods that participants perceive to be reasonably strong, stable over time and emotionally real or sincere. Another key consideration is the manner in which memory is tested. By several accounts, mood dependence is more apt to obtain when retrieval is mediated by 'invisible' cues produced by the subject than by 'observable' cues provided by the experimenter (Bower and Forgas 2000). Just as the odds of finding MDM are improved by having subjects generate their own cues for retrieval, so, too are these prospects enhanced by having subjects generate the target events themselves. Thus, encoding tasks that place a premium on the active elaboration or construction of new information, rather than on the passive conservation of the information given, are more conducive to demonstrating mood dependence—and, for that matter, mood congruence (Forgas 1995). Owing to these developments, MDM has lost its reputation as a 'will-o'-the-wisp' phenomenon (Kihlstrom 1989), and the concept of mood as a contextual cue for remembering has won new support.

Mood mediation

The third issue of interest concerns the *mood mediation hypothesis*: the idea that memory impairments incurred in the transition from one physical environment to a different environment, or from one pharmacological state to another, are mediated by alterations in affect or mood. In essence, the hypothesis holds that both *place*-dependent memory (PDM) and *drug*-dependent memory (DDM) represent special—and rather subtle—cases of *mood*-dependent memory (MDM).

With respect to place dependence, the mood mediation hypothesis has already been applied with some success. A series of studies (Eich 1995*b*) showed that how well information transfers from one place to another depends not on how similar they *look*, but rather on how similar they *feel*. Thus, even when undergraduates encoded and retrieved target events in the same place (e.g. a scenic, sunny garden), the students' retention performance suffered if the mood they experienced during retrieval differed from the mood they had experienced during encoding. Conversely, a change in environment (e.g. moving from the garden to a drab, windowless office) produced no retention deficit if—whether by chance or by design—the subjects' mood at encoding matched their mood at retrieval. These results imply that PDM is occasionally—not invariably (Smith and Vela 2001)—mediated by alterations in affect or mood, and that data that seem on the surface to demonstrate *place* dependence may, at a deeper level, denote the presence of *mood* dependence.

With respect to DDM, the case for mood mediation is more circumstantial, and hence more circumspect. That said, close comparison of the DDM and MDM literatures reveals that several of the factors that regulate one phenomenon also regulate the other. For example, both effects are more likely to emerge when retrieval is mediated by subject-produced than it is mediated by experimenter-provided reminders or cues (Bower 1981). Also, evidence from several sources suggests that, much like MDM, the odds of demonstrating DDM are improved by having subjects generate not only the cues required for retrieving the target events, but also the target events themselves (Eich 1995*a*). Just as strong or intense moods are vital to MDM, so are substantial drug doses essential for finding DDM (Eich 1980). Thus, for instance, shifting from a mildly intoxicated state at encoding to a sober state at retrieval is no more likely to impair memory performance than, say, a shift from feeling 'slightly happy' to 'slightly sad'.

Though these parallels between DDM and MDM are consistent with the mood mediation hypothesis, they are clearly no substitute for direct, experimental tests (perhaps along the lines outlined in Eich and Macaulay 2007). However, it is also clear that the idea deserves a close, hard look. Memory theorists have been struggling for decades with the problem of how extrinsic or global contexts—pharmacological conditions, physical environments, emotional states and the like—affect learning and remembering (Davies and Thompson 1988; Roediger and Guynn 1996). Were it possible to show that three seemingly distinct phenomena—drug-dependent, place-dependent and mood-dependent memory—can be distilled into one (MDM), then the problem would immediately become more manageable, and ultimately more solvable.

20

Context: A reference for focal experience

Steven M. Smith

Context, most generally defined, is that which surrounds. Something can be bounded by time, by space, by circumstances and by meaning; hence, the terms *temporal context, environmental context, situational context* and *semantic context*. How *context* as a general concept should be defined is not clear because there are so many different types of context, including those mentioned above, as well as perceptual context, moods, story plots, tasks, drug states, and so on. Although unitary stimuli have sometimes been referred to as 'contexts', it is usually the case that contexts are composed of many constituents; contexts are constellations of elements. Contexts can vary in terms of how rapidly changing they are and, concomitantly, how many events and objects are subsumed by a context. Whereas the rapidly changing words of a sentence can serve as context for a single word, a novel can serve as context for thousands of sentences, and a period of one's life the context for many novels. Contexts can vary in terms of how *enmeshed* they are with the focal events for which they serve as context. Physical environments that fully engage people, such as control rooms or sports settings, may provide a high degree of contextual support for activities that take place there, encouraging a high degree of mesh with the environmental context, whereas the surrounding environment in which one carries on an involving phone call or videogame may have little, if any relation to one's focal activities.

Context acts as a reference for focal material, and can be used to give perspective, to disambiguate and to interpret. All stimuli can be coded relative to varying perspectives, and are therefore subject to multiple interpretations. Context bestows set, a preparedness to respond. Context-induced set can affect cognition at many levels, such as perceptual sets that influence what is seen or how distant an object seems, learning sets that can influence how new material is encoded, and mental sets that can become associated with problem solving when a series of similar problems are solved with the same algorithm or heuristic. 'Context' is an umbrella term that subsumes other types of knowledge structures that support specific focused information processing, and that have setting and referential functions, structures such as schemata, frames, tasks, plans or situations.

Memory is said to be *context-dependent* because experiences always occur within contexts, and memories of events depend upon the contexts in which those experiences occur. The influence of context can be seen both at encoding and retrieval. Events we experience can become bound to our surrounding contexts, and more so the more enmeshed are our activities with encoding contexts. Context can enable or activate memories of previously associated events, a phenomenon referred to as *contextual cuing*. Reinstatement of past contexts can cue memories of events experienced in those contexts, a phenomenon referred to as a *context reinstatement effect* (e.g. Smith 1979). A particular episodic memory is more reliably evoked by a context cue if fewer events are stored in memory in relation to that cue (Watkins and Watkins 1974). Context reinstatement effects can revive seemingly lost memories, and can be phenomenologically powerful experiences that seem to transport people into their personal pasts. The limits of such 'time travel' experiences, such as the degree of accurate and false memory triggered by contexts, or the recovery of memories that are temporally or physically proximal to one's original experience in a reinstated context, are not known. Context also can be used to verify memory, i.e. to monitor and attribute the source of retrieved knowledge and experiences, as in episodic recognition. Whereas contextual cuing involves retrieval of to-be-remembered material in response to contextual cues, *source monitoring* involves the reverse, i.e. retrieval of contextual information in response to to-be-remembered material.

Mental context, sometimes known as *functional* (as opposed to *nominal*) context, is the cognitive representation of an individual's context, i.e. context from the subject's perspective. Mental context is manipulable by an individual, and may or may not correspond to physically ambient stimuli. Put more simply, the context one imagines can be different from one's current physical context. Imagined mental contexts can be instantiated or activated, maintained and used without recourse to ambient environmental conditions during activities such as reminiscing about the past, daydreaming and prospective projection into future situations. Mental context reinstatement effects can occur when one imagines a previously experienced context associated with to-be-remembered material. When someone's mental context corresponds directly to the ambient environmental context, that mental context can be a combination of automatically and effortfully processed elements of the environment. Because self-generated contexts, as well as other conceptual activities, vie for the same limited pool of attentional resources that process one's immediate environment, ambient contextual stimuli can also be suppressed to conserve resources

(Glenberg 1997), and their influence supplanted by self-generated mental contexts. Therefore, the degree to which memories are context dependent (i.e. affected by nominal manipulations of the context) is inversely proportional to the degree of contextual suppression that occurs at encoding and at test (e.g. Smith and Vela 2001). That is, suppressed environments do not affect encoding and retrieval.

Two important aspects of the relationship between memory and context are *contextual integration* and *contextual binding*. Because contexts are comprised of multiple elements, those individual elements can vary in their degree of integration. Better integrated contexts, especially unitized ones, can be better memory cues. The way that the brain assembles and integrates contextual material is fundamentally important to understanding how contexts are instantiated, how they are maintained and stabilized over time, and how they are destabilized so that new contexts can be instantiated. Memory of an event can become bound to a context, resulting in contextual associations. Contextual binding is at the heart of the two major phenomena involving context and memory, namely contextual cuing and source monitoring.

Memories bounded by contexts vary in their degree of insularity. A person can be insensitive to interpretations of focal objects that involve inactive contexts. The degree of insularity ranges from insular mental objects bound to unique contexts, to completely decontextualized mental objects that need no contextual referents. *Decontextualized knowledge* can be accessed and used regardless of one's currently instantiated context. Knowledge can become decontextualized if it is retrieved and used in many varied contexts, because such experience leads to the ability to access the material regardless of one's retrieval context. At the other extreme, strongly context-dependent memories can be quite insular, i.e. inaccessible when context cues are not provided. This insularity may be understood by analogy; context can play the analogous role in human memory that is played by, for example, a carrier wave for a radio station. Signals that are coded in relation to a reproducible reference, such as a carrier wave, can only be recovered by reinstating the same referential information. A radio program cannot be heard if one is tuned to the wrong station. Likewise, contexts that differ from those that are encoded in association with unique experiences cannot provide access to memories of those experiences.

Contextual fluctuation refers to the changes in one's mental context with the passage of time, shifting of environments, new stimuli and the flow of consciousness. As time passes, the contents of one's mental context tend to change, as well. Thus, the relationship between clock time and contextual fluctuation is probabilistic. Slow contextual fluctuation can occur within rigid, unchanging mental states, and it is also possible for sudden shifts in one's mental context to occur when tasks, situations or environments are abruptly changed.

Other context-dependent memory phenomena include *interference reduction effects* (e.g. Bilodeau and Schlosberg 1951) and *multiple-learning-context effects* (e.g. Smith *et al.* 1978). When two sets of materials are learned in different contexts, rather than both learned in the same context, an interference reduction effect can be observed; recall of material learned in each context is better because of less interference from the other set of materials. Another reliable finding involving context and memory is that repeating to-be-learned material in multiple contexts, relative to repetitions in a single context, produces better retention, a multiple-learning-context effect. Interference reduction and multiple-learning-context effects, both of which separate learned material into different physical contexts, are the most robust effects to be found in controlled laboratory studies of incidental environmental context (Smith and Vela 2001). In both cases, the learning context acts as an organizational cue that subsequently can be used to facilitate recall of the learned material. In interference reduction, the context cue is more specific to each set of learned materials when each set has its own unique context cue; thus, when recalling one set of materials, a context cue does not evoke material from the potentially competing set of material. In multiple-learning-context effects, learned material becomes bound to more context cues when multiple learning contexts are used, resulting in more memory cues and, therefore, better recall.

The effects of context cues are relative, not absolute. The effects of context at learning can be *overshadowed* by more potent, controlling influences, resulting in the selective encoding of the more potent cues and a failure to encode contextual material. One such source of potent noncontextual cues can be semantic associations and relationships among to-be-remembered items. Even if context has been successfully encoded, the effects of context at test can also be nullified by the presence or use of more potent cues such as inter-item semantic associations, an *outshining* effect. The degree to which focal experiences mesh with one's context can determine how much influence context has over learning and remembering.

21

Integrative comments
Context: The concept in the human and animal memory domains

Mark E. Bouton

The concept of context, which Smith defines as 'that which surrounds', is clearly central to memory; perhaps like the context in a memory experiment, the concept is always lurking in the background. The three preceding chapters clearly indicate that context has a large number of meanings and applications in the science of memory. Yet an integration is not necessarily difficult. Through the lens of learning theory, it is possible to discern at least three fundamental uses of the concept. The first is the one emphasized by Fanselow in Chapter 18: the context is often a background stimulus that elicits behavior directly. For example, tolerance to a drug such as morphine is said to be 'context specific;' tolerance is lost, and overdose more likely, if a drug is taken in a context never associated with it (e.g. Siegel 2005). The context operates through its direct association with the drug (an unconditional stimulus, or US), which allows it to elicit a compensatory response that cancels the drug's effect. The context plays a similarly direct role in studies, such as the ones emphasized by Fanselow, in which rats associate an experimental chamber with footshock and therefore freeze in its presence. It might also play a similar role in eliciting the many 'automatic' habits and behaviors that are so much a part of human nature (e.g. Bargh and Chartrand 1999). In all of these cases, the influence of context is simple and direct. Despite some differences noted by Fanselow, it mainly operates like Pavlov's bell, a conditional stimulus (CS) that elicits behavior directly because of its own direct association with the US, or perhaps its direct association with the response.

A second role for context builds upon the first. Associations to a context can influence learning about, and/or judgments about, the significance of cues that occur in them. In classic work by Rescorla (e.g. Rescorla 1968), animals showed remarkable sensitivity not only to the probability of the US in the presence of the CS, but to the probability of the US in the *absence* of the

CS—the context in which the CS and US occur. Subjects given an equal number of CS–US pairings showed different levels of conditioned responding depending on how often the US was also presented when the CS was not on; when the two probabilities were equal, there was no conditional responding. Human contingency and causal judgments may proceed in a similar fashion; we judge an event to be a weak cause of a second event if the probability of the second event is already high (e.g. Baker *et al.* 2005). The same idea can be applied to trial-spacing effects: massed conditioning trials may yield inferior learning because they create a high overall expectancy of the US in the background. In these cases, the context seems to *compete* with the target stimulus, either because the CS and context ultimately have to share a limited amount of associative strength (e.g. Rescorla and Wagner 1972; Wagner 1981), or because a highly valued context suppresses performance to the CS (e.g. Gallistel and Gibbon 2000; Denniston *et al.* 2001). In either case, the context is once again directly associated with the US, but its effect is to influence learning about, or responses to, cues that are presented in it.

A third role for context is the one we infer when we change the context between learning and a retention test. In the animal laboratory, the apparatus can be changed after the animal learns something about the CS. Sometimes a context switch after conditioning reduces responding to the CS, although such a result actually occurs surprisingly rarely (e.g. Bouton 1993). Instead, context switches are far more disruptive after extinction, the retroactive interference paradigm in which responding declines when a CS is presented repeatedly alone, without the US, after conditioning. When the context is changed after extinction, extinction performance may be lost; the original response may be 'renewed'. This and other results suggest that extinction does not destroy the original learning, but instead engages new learning that is specific to the context in which it is learned (e.g. Bouton 2004). Since extinction is thought to be involved in many cognitive behavior therapies, the basic interdependence of context and extinction may have implications for clinical lapse and relapse (e.g. Bouton 2002).

Although I have argued that a context change after extinction causes a failure to retrieve what is learned in extinction, in principle, its effect can be understood in many ways. For example, the context may be a second cue in a cue–context configuration, and the change in context might merely hurt performance by causing generalization decrement. Alternatively, the context might enter into its own association with the US; for example, if conditioning occurs in context A and then extinction occurs in context B, the extinction context might theoretically become a conditioned inhibitor (e.g. Rescorla and Wagner 1972) and inhibit performance to the CS as long as the CS is presented in it.

In the 1980s, my students and I ran many experiments that tested these views, and in the end we found them wanting. The context was doing something different. It was as if the context was determining the current 'meaning' of the ambiguous CS, much as verbal context disambiguates the meaning of ambiguous words. Although the role of context seemed new and unusual here, we eventually recognized the similarity between it and the effects of 'occasion setters', a new sort of stimulus that contemporary research in other laboratories was investigating (e.g. Holland 1992). Occasion setters essentially select or activate a target CS's current association with the US; they do this in a hierarchical manner that is not reducible to their own direct association with the US. Research suggests that ordinary tone and light cues can acquire an occasion-setting function provided the experiment is run right. Generally speaking, for a tone or light CS to become an occasion setter, it must be less salient than the CS whose performance it disambiguates; otherwise it acquires its own association with the US (Holland 1989). In most animal memory experiments, the context is present for a long period of time, perhaps making it nonsalient through habituation. What I and others (e.g. Spear 1981) have identified as a retrieval effect of context appears analogous to Pavlovian occasion setting.

Although Fanselow would define context as a specific complex stimulus, that is not the universal view. Instead, as illustrated by what I have implied above, the context is often thought to be made up of whatever stimulus is in the background. Consistent with this approach, it is possible to make much sense of the literature on retroactive and proactive interference in animal learning by accepting a broad and inclusive definition of context (e.g. Bouton 1993). For example, the passage of time has effects that parallel those of changes of the environmental context. If time passes after extinction, one observes spontaneous recovery, which can be viewed as the renewal effect that occurs when the temporal context is changed. It has been fruitful to think not only of contexts provided by the apparatus in which conditioning (and extinction) occur, but also the organism's interoceptive state created by the ingestion of drugs, deprivation state and memory of recent events, in addition to the passage of time. When learning (or especially extinction) is conducted in the presence of any of these stimuli, it can be shown to be specific to that context. We do not know whether time or the interoceptive state caused by ingesting alcohol or a benzodiazepine is complex, but we do know they can have effects similar to those of apparatus contexts, because a change in of any of them can cause extinction to go away.

The sense of context as occasion setter or retrieval cue is probably the sense of context that is most widely considered in human memory. Memory for word lists is often inferior when the environmental context is changed between learning and testing (e.g. Godden and Baddeley 1975; Smith 1979). Also, as Eich and Smith have emphasized in Chapters 19 and 20, respectively, we also often speak of semantic context, mental context, and mood or emotion context in addition to the ones mentioned immediately above. Are these different from the contexts investigated in animal memory? I am mostly impressed by the parallels. One striking similarity between human and animal context switch effects is that it is often rather difficult to find them. A context switch after learning a word list often has no discernible impact on memory for words (e.g. Smith 1988) just as a context switch after conditioning often has little effect on responding to the CS. In the animal case, switching the context might not matter when the CS itself is such a potent cue for the US (in associative learning terms, the CS is a more valid predictor of the US); this is what Smith calls 'outshining'. The fact that the context becomes more important after extinction is also consistent with other parts of the human literature: context switch effects on memory are easier to detect in interference designs in which the participant learns a conflicting word list in a second phase (e.g. Smith 1988). Analogous to extinction, the second word list produces context-specific interference with memory for the first. It is as if memory is organized to encode the second thing learned as the conditional, context-dependent exception to the rule (e.g. Bouton 1994). The context becomes important when it can disambiguate. One of the most general facts about context as a retrieval cue is that it is important only to the extent that it affects encoding. Context affects memory retrieval only to the extent that it affects encoding or 'integration' of the context with the focal experience.

Do the three roles of context discussed above exhaust the context's influence on memory? Probably not. A context can influence how objects are perceived, and this will clearly influence their encoding (and thus the cues that will help retrieve them, as the encoding specificity principle implies). Context can also guide the current mental set, as in mood-congruent cognition, and this may also influence encoding. Contextual cues are also essential in defining the episodes in episodic memory and are the object of source monitoring. Does this make the context special? Many of us are ambivalent. Learning theorists have clearly done quite a lot with the concept without giving it a special status. The eliciting and competing stimulus is something that basically plays the same role as a blocking cue. As I noted earlier, even the retrieval/occasion setting function seems to be present in ordinary discrete CSs when they are given nonsalient status in ordinary compound conditioning experiments.

Yet there may be something more than this. Fanselow (Chapter 18) argues that the apparatus context his rats associate with shock is special in terms of its complexity; as Smith notes (Chapter 20), contexts are often a 'constellation' of cues. Contextual stimuli do appear to need to be 'unitized', with their elements being inter-associated, although this is theoretically true of any complex stimulus (e.g. McLaren and Mackintosh 2000). However, I do wonder whether the elements that make up the context necessarily compete with one another in the same way compounded stimuli are usually thought to. Maybe they do; although a context is presumably made up of a very large set of elements, the system probably finds a reliable and invariant subset of elements from which it can activate and retrieve the whole (e.g. McClelland and Rumelhart 1985; McLaren and Mackintosh 2000). This function—the 'stimulus selection' function that finds the most informative elements or stimuli—could easily be served by standard rules of cue competition; stimulus selection is what conditioning theories (e.g. Rescorla and Wagner 1972) are all about. However, contextual cues that define a unique memory episode may do something different. Here, the system seems to need to detect the variances between situations, rather than their invariances (e.g. Sherry and Schacter 1987). Compared with the contexts identified in conditioning experiments, cues that define a memory episode might have a different character after all.

6

Encoding

Encoding refers to initial registration or acquisition of information and is the necessary prerequisite to later memory performance of any sort. Any successful act of retrieval requires initial encoding and persistence of information in the nervous system. Although a critical stage, defining encoding precisely is difficult, because any separation between the end of the encoding stage and formation of the memory trace (or consolidation) is rather arbitrary. When does encoding end and persistence (sometimes called storage) begin? Sometimes encoding of an event is equated with its perception, which suffices as a verbal definition, but the operational measures of perception and memory are often quite similar. Research on encoding usually involves issues of initial acquisition of information and changes in the nervous system leading to persistence of the initial trace.

H.L.R.

22

Encoding: Models linking neural mechanisms to behavior

Michael E. Hasselmo

The discussion of memory concepts is useful, but ultimately verbal terms are insufficient for describing memory function. A full description of any physical system requires an effective mathematical theory. True understanding of memory mechanisms will ultimately require a rigorous framework, which will only partially map to current colloquial and scientific terms describing memory concepts. The mathematical description of memory function will be structured according to neural mechanisms and their role in behavioral action selection by an agent in an environment. This work is not complete, but I will describe examples in which neural models give an important perspective on the mechanism of encoding.

I define encoding as the neural mechanisms which form persistent representations of events for later retrieval. To address the neural mechanisms, the event being encoded should be defined in terms of neural activity. This neural activity includes an agent's sensory perception of the external state of its environment (e.g. features such as location, and visual and auditory stimuli), the agent's internal state of neural activity (e.g. plans, thoughts and mood) and sequences of neural activity induced by sequential states and proprioceptive feedback about actions. The encoded representations can be measured by their influence on subsequent memory-guided behavior, or by the reactivation of neural activity during retrieval which at least partly matches neural activity during encoding (e.g. reminiscence does not necessarily involve behavioral output).

The neural mechanisms of encoding form representations for different types of memory, including both working memory and episodic memory.

Working memory

The neural mechanisms for encoding of working memory include sensory input eliciting physiological activity in different brain regions, which persists after the sensory input has ceased. This activity can include depolarization or sustained spiking of individual neurons (Jensen and Lisman 2005; Fransen *et al.* 2002). For novel sensory stimuli, the sustained spiking of neurons could result from intrinsic mechanisms which are activated during synaptic input, and allow neurons to maintain the pattern of neural activity induced by sensory input (Fransen *et al.* 2002; Hasselmo and Stern 2006). If the sensory stimulus has been experienced previously, prior modification of synaptic connections allows reverberatory synaptic interactions to maintain spiking.

Episodic memory

The neural mechanisms for encoding of episodic memory include persistent changes in molecular structures directly or indirectly altering synaptic transmission between neurons, which are studied experimentally as phenomena such as long-term potentiation (LTP) or spike timing-dependent plasticity (STDP) (Levy and Steward 1983). Changes may also include persistent changes in the response of neuronal membrane conductances to synaptic input, thereby enhancing the likelihood of spiking or inhibition in response to a particular pattern of synaptic input. The induction of these long-lasting synaptic and cellular changes can be enhanced by the persistent spiking associated with working memory (Jensen and Lisman 2005). For example, most studies of LTP and STDP show changes in synaptic strength dependent upon repetitive conjunctions of pre- and postsynaptic activity (though single spiking events can cause synaptic change). The requirement of repeated spiking for synaptic modification in the hippocampus might be provided by intrinsic mechanisms for persistent spiking in the entorhinal cortex. The nature of encoding may differ considerably for different types of task demands. For example, item recognition based on familiarity could involve simple reductions in synaptic strength within a single region. In contrast, encoding for subsequent remembering requires recruitment of additional regions (Davachi and Wagner 2002) which form sequential associations between items and neural activity on the slower time scale of context (Hasselmo and Eichenbaum 2005).

Encoding and retrieval

On a physiological level, the neural processes of encoding and retrieval for episodic memory are somewhat incompatible. Encoding a new episodic memory requires strengthening of synapses without interference from activity induced by prior retrieval, whereas retrieval requires strong transmission across previously modified synapses. Interference can be reduced by separation of encoding and retrieval into interleaved periods of separate network function.

Within the hippocampus, encoding mechanisms such as LTP may predominate during specific time periods on a short time scale (Hasselmo *et al.* 2002), whereas during other short time periods physiological mechanisms of retrieval may predominate. These rapid shifts in dynamics between encoding and retrieval may occur during each cycle of the hippocampal theta rhythm (which usually has a frequency of about 7 Hz). These time scales are much shorter than the time scales of behavior.

The encoding periods described above contrast with the definition of an encoding period during an experiment. This is an experimentally defined behavioral time period during which subjects are predominantly forming new memories based on experimentally controlled input, in contrast to a separate experimentally defined testing period or retrieval period during which subjects use retrieval for memory-guided behavior based on prior encoding. The encoding period in experiments usually does not match the time scale of neural encoding. Similarly, the retrieval period of an experiment might involve multiple different retrieval phases. For example, during retrieval of a long list of words, individual words or sequences of words in the list may be retrieved in each retrieval phase of the theta cycle (50–60 ms) and then buffered in neocortical circuits for later generation of the response. Additional hippocampal retrieval may be suppressed or ignored during the time needed to generate the response. During a long delay between words being generated at a behavioral level, there might be many hippocampal theta cycles retrieving words which were already generated behaviorally, but which are rejected by prefrontal mechanisms for selecting responses.

A common fallacy to avoid is the notion that encoding and retrieval are completely separate processes or involve different neural substrates. The physical nature of episodic memory representations requires that the location of physical changes induced by encoding must be involved in at least part of the neural activity during retrieval. Retrieval activity can only be induced by the synapses or neurons which were modified during encoding, unless the locus of the memory has shifted due to reactivation processes during consolidation. Different supporting structures may separately supplement either encoding or retrieval, but the neural substrate for storage must be shared unless some consolidation process has shifted the substrate.

Encoding and consolidation

Encoding and consolidation processes work together to form lasting representations of events in the environment. Consolidation has been used to refer to at least two processes, including (1) the slow physical processes which continue after perception to enable temporary changes in activity and synaptic strength to become long lasting, and (2) the reactivation of neural activity at later times to allow an additional phase of induction of long-term synaptic change, both in the region where the representation was initially formed (e.g. the hippocampus) and in additional regions where the representation was not initially as strong (e.g. neocortical structures), but which receive spreading neural activity from the hippocampus. Encoding is difficult to separate from the first definition of consolidation, because the encoding event can induce cellular processes of molecular change with many different time scales (from seconds to days). However, encoding is distinct from the second definition of consolidation, because the spiking activity inducing the initial encoding will eventually cease (as working memory buffers are used for other purposes), and the start of a consolidation event can be defined as the later reinduction of activity in the population of neurons subserving the same neural representation.

Encoding and the second type of consolidation require very different dynamic properties of cortical circuits, as encoding is a function of neural activity induced by current experience (including sensory input), whereas consolidation is a function of neural activity induced from memory (e.g. spreading from the hippocampus). These different dynamic states may be regulated by the neuro-modulator acetylcholine (Hasselmo 1999). Acetylcholine causes physiological effects which enhance encoding, including enhancement of self-sustained spiking of individual neurons (Fransen et al. 2002), enhancement of the induction of LTP and reduction of interference through suppression of excita-tory transmission. The modulatory effects of acetylcholine last for many seconds or minutes and can result in enhanced memory performance during alert waking. However, the modulatory state of encoding cannot persist indef-initely, as consolidation appears to be necessary for effective memory func-tion. High acetylcholine levels suppress the excitatory feedback connections which appear to drive the reactivation of memories and the influence of hippocampus on neocortex. Lower levels of acetylcholine during quiet waking or slow wave sleep appear to allow appropriate dynamics for the consolidation of previously encoded information (Hasselmo 1999).

Encoding applies to all forms of memory, including both episodic and semantic memory. Semantic memory is currently believed to develop primarily from consolidation of neocortical representations based on reactivation of episodic representations in the hippocampus. However, semantic memories also appear to be formed even in individuals with severely impaired episodic memory (Vargha-Khadem et al. 1997), suggesting that encoding could directly alter and build representations for semantic memory.

Depth of processing

The nature of encoding depends upon the nature of the perceived event, including the modality of its perception, and the interaction of the perception with previously encoded representations. In particular, the interaction of persistent spiking with formation of long-lasting synaptic changes relates to cognitive evidence on encoding. On a cognitive level, encoding is described as depending upon the perception and comprehension of sensory input, and can be enhanced by strategies such as elaborative rehearsal of sensory features (Craik 2002b). All of these processes may involve working memory mechanisms dependent upon persistent spiking activity. Thus, the enhancement of encoding by depth of processing may depend upon activation of persistent spiking in specific cortical circuits. Evaluation of superficial sensory features (such as font or rhyming) does not enhance encoding for subsequent recall to the same extent as evaluation of semantic properties (Craik and Watkins 1973). This could occur because evaluation of sensory features involves spiking in sensory or motor cortices which have weaker processes of synaptic plasticity, and less connectivity with medial temporal lobe structures. This could underlie the lack of recall enhancement with rehearsal of superficial features. In contrast, association cortices in the temporal lobe involved with 'deep' processing of semantic features may be more plastic and may more directly activate components of the hippocampal formation to strengthen the episodic representations. Notably, verbal rehearsal does increase subsequent recognition performance (Davachi et al. 2001), consistent with a greater role of neocortical structures in recognition versus recall.

In summary, many neural mechanisms for encoding have been described, including both cellular processes and changes in network dynamics. Further experimental analysis and computational modeling will allow convergence toward a unified mathematical framework for describing encoding as a component of memory function.

23

Encoding: A cognitive perspective

Fergus I. M. Craik

The group of scientists given the task of defining and analyzing the concept of encoding at the Palisades meeting agreed that encoding refers to 'the set of processes involved in transforming external events and internal thoughts into both temporary and long-lasting neural representations'. This pithy definition raises an immediate host of questions, however, including: How are the 'cognitive' processes we experience during encoding related to the 'physiological' processes that are presumed to occur after the person's attention has turned to other matters? Are different encoding operations required for the optimal encoding of procedures, facts and events into different memory systems? What roles do both *attention* and *intention* play in the encoding process? What other factors affect encoding in a lawful fashion? What is the relationship of encoding to the later retrieval of the same event? What can we learn about encoding, storage and retrieval processes from clinical cases of impaired memory? Finally, can we construct a viable science of memory that must presumably give plausible accounts of the facts at the levels of experience, cognitive models, dynamic neural processes, biochemistry, pharmacology, etc., *and* provide mapping rules that connect these very disparate levels of description?

To provide some organization and coherence to these many different questions, and as a starting point for answering some of them, I will first describe the levels of processing (LOP) framework proposed by Craik and Lockhart (1972) and elaborated in later articles by Craik and Tulving (1975) and Craik (1983, 2002*b*). One major assumption embodied in the LOP perspective is that memory is not a separate faculty in either cognitive or neurological terms, but rather is one aspect of the overall cognitive system whose structures and processes are also involved in attention, perception, comprehension and action. Lockhart and I also stressed the idea (following Bartlett 1932) that human memory is an *activity* of mind, i.e. both encoding and retrieval processes are represented as dynamic patterns of neural firing.

Clearly there must also be structural changes in the nervous system to enable retention of learned information, but the only phases of memory and learning that have cognitive correlates are encoding and retrieval, and these appear to be neurophysiological processes rather than neuroanatomical structures. Just as perceiving reflects the dynamic interaction of processes invoked by the stimulus and processes associated with innate and learned schemas, so retrieval processes reflect the interaction of a stimulus (which may be a retrieval cue, a memory query, an environmental event or a transient thought) with pre-existing representations to give rise to the experience of recollection. We further suggested that the primary concerns of the cognitive system are perception and comprehension (as humans we need these abilities crucially to navigate the environment successfully and to know which aspects to approach and which to avoid), and that these processes of perception and comprehension also serve as 'memory encoding processes'. That is, there are no separate cognitive processes that constitute encoding; memory representations are created automatically in the course of perceiving and understanding the world around us.

The main line of evidence for this assertion comes from studies in which memory performance is assessed following either incidental or intentional learning. The experiments reported by Craik and Tulving (1975) in conjunction with those cited by Craik and Lockhart (1972) make it clear that memory performance, both qualitatively and quantitatively, reflects the processing operations that were carried out when the item or event was initially studied. In general, 'deeper' semantic processing is associated with higher levels of subsequent memory than is the relatively 'shallow' processing associated with sensory, structural or phonological processing. The effects are dramatically large. When single words were tested following positive answers to initial questions about case ('is the word in lower case?'), rhyme (e.g. 'does the word rhyme with BRAIN?') or meaning (e.g. 'does the word fit the sentence: The girl placed the—on the table?'), the probabilities of later recognition were 0.15, 0.48 and 0.81, respectively (Craik and Tulving 1975, Exp. 2). When the experiment was repeated under intentional learning conditions, so that participants knew there would be a later memory test, the corresponding recognition scores were 0.23, 0.59 and 0.81 (Craik and Tulving 1975, Exp. 9). It is worth stressing that the *same words* occurred in the three different conditions, counterbalanced over subjects: all that changed was the qualitative nature of the initial encoding, which increased memory by a factor of five from structural to semantic processing. The LOP effect can be obtained reliably in a single subject, and it has therefore proved useful in neuroimaging experiments on memory encoding (Kapur *et al.* 1994). One main conclusion from the Craik and Tulving studies was that intentionality is not necessary for good memory and learning; performance is a function of the type of encoding operation carried out initially, regardless of the original motivation for that processing. Of course, intention to learn material will typically boost performance, because the participant will carry out further processes such as rehearsal, organization, associative learning, and so on, but the point remains that later performance reflects the operations carried out during initial encoding, for whatever reason. Thus *intention* plays no special role in encoding, but *attention* is of the essence. It is not simply a question of 'paying attention', however; it is also necessary to specify both the amount of attentional resources devoted to processing an event and the qualitative nature of the processing operations involved.

Many experiments on human memory are carried out using verbal materials, and in this case deep processing implies retrieving the semantic/conceptual aspects of words, sentences or stories. However, deep processing can be carried out on any type of material; the general principle is that the new information is related conceptually to relevant pre-existing schematic knowledge. Thus familiar odors, pictures, melodies and actions are all well remembered if related to existing bases of meaning at the time of encoding. On the other hand, stimuli that lack an appropriate schematic knowledge base (e.g. words in an unknown foreign language, locations in a strange city, faces from a different racial group, snowflake patterns) are extremely difficult to remember.

Why exactly do deeper levels of processing result in higher levels of remembering? Our assumption is that schematic knowledge representations are highly organized and differentiated (like a well-ordered library), so that incoming events processed in terms of such knowledge bases will result in a processed record that is *distinctive* relative to many other encoded representations. At the time of remembering, the framework provided by schematic knowledge also facilitates efficient retrieval. A library analogy may again be helpful; if a new acquisition is 'encoded deeply' it will be shelved precisely in terms of its topic, author, date, etc., and the structure of the library catalog will later enable precise location of the book. If the new book was simply categorized in terms of its surface features ('blue cover, 8″ × 10″, weighs about a pound'), it would be stored with many similar items and be difficult or impossible to retrieve later. The ability to process deeply is thus a function of a person's *expertise* in some domain—it could be mathematics, French poetry, rock music, wine tasting, tennis or a multitude of other types of knowledge. Perceived information in the relevant domain will be analyzed and categorized precisely using existing schemas, and the new information added to these schemas. Distinctiveness is a function of the richness of analysis of the resulting analyzed differences between the present event and other similar stored events. An expert wine taster may identify a wine as being from a specific region of Burgundy and encode it as such, whereas another person may simply register 'a red wine with a slightly musty taste'. Successful retrieval of the event at some later time will again make use of available schemas and would thus enable correct recognition of the wine by the expert but not by the novice.

The LOP framework thus postulates no special 'store' or 'faculty' of memory—or even special memory processes. Encoding processes are simply those processing operations carried out primarily for the purposes of perceiving, understanding and acting; retrieval processes ('remembering') represent an attempt on the cognitive system's part to re-enact encoding processes as completely as possible. However, what happens in between the dynamic activities of encoding and retrieval? Presumably there must be some mechanism, some structural change, enabling the cognitive system to recapitulate (to some extent) the pattern of activity that occurred during initial encoding? My suggestion here (Craik 2002a) is that schematic knowledge representations are organized hierarchically, with specific instances (episodic events) represented at the branch terminals, and increasingly general, abstract, context-free knowledge represented as higher order nodes (see Fig. 23.1).

In the scheme shown in Fig. 23.1, there is no clearcut distinction between episodic and semantic memory—they are not different systems, but more simply levels of specificity in complex representations of knowledge. The scheme also renders unnecessary any suggestion that different types of encoding might be necessary to encode events into different memory stores or systems. By the present view, there *are* no different stores or systems, only different processing operations, representing sensory, phonological, visuospatial,

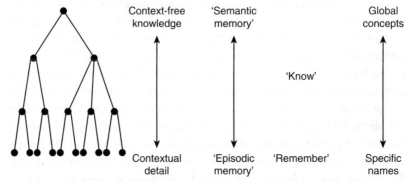

Fig. 23.1 A schematic model of knowledge representations. The suggested hierarchical organization with specific episodic records in lower nodes and general abstract knowledge occupying higher nodes. 'Remember' and 'Know' judgments reflect access to lower and higher nodes respectively.

conceptual or other types of information, which act to modify relevant existing representational schemes, in part by adding episodic records to appropriate representations. From this perspective, fleeting 'sensory memories' are not rapidly decaying traces but the ongoing processing of sensory information. Encoding 'into long-term memory' involves modification of representational systems, detectable later as recollection of the learning episode, as modifications of relevant knowledge or as more fluent processing of some perceptual–motor sequence observed in one of several 'implicit memory' tasks. Encoding for short-term or working memory involves ongoing processing activities as with sensory memories, but in this case the processing operations draw on more stable learned routines such as strings of articulation or visuospatial images (the articulatory loop and visuospatial sketchpad proposed by Baddeley and Hitch 1974). It also seems necessary to assume that processing in working memory involves long-term knowledge representations and makes use of their structure in order to deal with information as organized 'chunks' rather than as individual elements. This assumption of long-term memory involvement in working memory also explains the large increase in memory span for words if the words are presented as a meaningful sentence rather than as a random string. The ongoing processing activities that constitute working memory may draw on several different representational systems, resulting in a richly elaborated multidimensional experience. This appears to be the situation captured by Baddeley's (2000) recent suggestion of an 'episodic buffer'.

Encoding processes can be modified by a large number of factors. Some of these (such as expectations, set, goals and context) will bias processing towards relevant or salient aspects of the attended event. Other factors will reduce the amount of available attentional resources—dual-task situations, increased rate of presentation, fatigue, sleep deprivation, aging, intoxication and benzodiazepines are among the possibilities here. In these latter cases, the reduction in processing resources will result in encoding operations that are shallower, less elaborated and less effective in forging associative and organizational connections (see Fig. 23.2). In turn, these less efficient encoding operations are associated with lower levels of subsequent recollection.

This account of encoding processes has been couched in purely cognitive terms, but it has clear implications for corresponding neural activities. First, memory-encoding processes should be indistinguishable from the neural activities associated with attending, perceiving and comprehending. Secondly, the correlates of retrieval processes should overlap those occurring during encoding, in part at least. Thirdly, some neural activations may be specific to either encoding or retrieval; the HERA (hemispheric encoding/retrieval asymmetry) model proposed by Tulving and colleagues (1994) is one case in point.

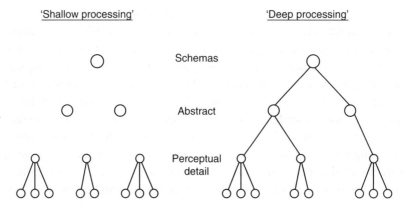

Fig. 23.2 A schematic model of knowledge representations. Deep semantic processing appears to entail integration of episodic records with pre-existing knowledge, whereas shallow processing lacks such integration.

Such process-specific activations may reflect control processes rather than the qualitative content of memories, however. Alternatively, the marked activation of the left inferior prefrontal gyrus observed during deep processing of verbal material (Kapur *et al.* 1994) may be associated with the retrieval of meaning from long-term conceptual representations ('semantic memory'). It is relevant to note that this left frontal activation occurs more strongly in verb generation (hear 'paper', say 'write') than in noun repetition (hear 'paper', say 'paper') in a purely word-processing context where memory encoding is not mentioned (Raichle *et al.* 1994). Yet when Tulving and colleagues (1994) followed these word-processing tasks with an unexpected recognition task 5 days later, recognition levels for noun repetition and verb generation were 0.26 and 0.50, respectively, again illustrating that intention to learn is unnecessary for effective encoding. It is also noteworthy that the left prefrontal activation associated with deep semantic processing is greatly attenuated when attention is divided during encoding (Shallice *et al.* 1994) and also in older adults (Grady *et al.* 1995); both cases are associated with a reduction in processing resources and with reduced levels of memory.

Finally, it is clear that a full account of memory encoding must include a host of neurophysiological processes that occur *after* cognitive processing has ceased. These neural activities constitute the processes of consolidation, discussed in the accompanying chapters by Hasselmo and Davachi. Consolidation has no apparent cognitive correlates, but various manipulations following cognitive encoding have been shown to affect subsequent recollection (Frankland and Bontempi 2005). Perhaps the most dramatic evidence for such post-perceptual effects comes from cases of amnesia following hippocampal damage. Such amnesic patients can perceive and comprehend normally, yet have little or no subsequent recollection (see Tulving 2001, for discussion). The relationships between the cognitive and neurobiological aspects of encoding thus provide a rich set of related research questions. What are the neural correlates of encoding at the cognitive level? What neurobiological mechanisms constitute the processes of consolidation, and do they have any cognitive or experiential counterparts? Finally, how do cognitive manipulations affect the nature and effectiveness of consolidation processes, and can such manipulations continue to influence consolidation *after* the event has been perceived, comprehended and dropped from conscious awareness?

24

Integrative comments
Encoding: The proof is still required

Lila Davachi

Encoding is an interesting concept in memory research because its existence can only be defined in terms of some other event occurring later in time. In other words, successful retrieval or recovery of a stimulus or event is the prima facie evidence that the stimulus or event was encoded. Thus, once retrieved, the fact that a memory was encoded becomes a truism. This means that, at present, the only means to measure encoding, whether it is at a cognitive level or a cellular level, is through assessments of what the organism is able to retrieve at some point in the future.

The fact that encoding can be assessed only indirectly is reflected in the work of Craik (Chapter 23) and Hasselmo (Chapter 22), who address the mechanisms of encoding at different levels of analysis. At a cognitive level, Craik describes the forms of attentional orientation (deep versus shallow processing) that reliably enhance encoding as measured by a later recognition or recall test. At the cellular level, Hasselmo describes neural encoding as including processes such as long-term potentiation (LTP). LTP also is measured not while it is being induced but, rather, at a later time point, as a potentiated response in a post-synaptic neuron to input from a pre-synaptic one based on the prior history (co-occurrence of spiking) between the two.

Although this work informs our understanding of encoding processes, it leaves underspecified both the cognitive and cellular mechanisms that determine whether an encoded event will be later recollected. This is because one could imagine that a stimulus could affect the same initial changes in a system (i.e. be encoded) but, due either to other factors taking place in the interim between encoding and retrieval or to factors influencing retrieval alone, this stimulus is not available for retrieval. Hence, it may have been encoded but we are not in a position to state that *unambiguously* since it was not retrieved. The hope for future work is that further specification of the encoding process itself will allow us to make claims about encoding disentangled from retrieval.

The overarching goal of this chapter is to highlight some ways in which encoding processes might be more precisely specified in terms of mechanisms operating at multiple levels of analysis. Towards that end, four points about encoding will be considered—how to define encoding and differentiate it from other related processes, how systems-level descriptions link cognitive and cellular accounts of encoding, how the medial temporal lobe (MTL) plays a critical role as an encoding system and, finally, how encoding into long-term memory as opposed to working memory might involve some similar and some distinct memory processes.

Definition and differentiation

The term 'encoding', as used by Craik, Hasselmo and myself in this chapter, refers to the processes (cognitive, systems, cellular and molecular) by which a stimulus or event leads to an alteration of the brain, allowing it to be later retrieved. The latter portion of the definition, however, must be expanded slightly to reflect the fact that there are many different forms of what has been termed 'retrieval'. In other words, depending on the nature of the change taking place in the brain at encoding, retrieval may be expressed in many different ways including increased facility with perception/attention (e.g. priming), motor output (e.g. skill learning) and in the conscious recovery of stimuli and events from our past (declarative memory). For the purposes of exposition, I will focus mainly on declarative or, more specifically, episodic memory encoding.

It might be fruitful to consider *when* encoding occurs as a means for differentiating it from other processes. Encoding for memory is distinct from the concept of perceptual 'coding' of a stimulus because presumably coding may or may not have any future consequences for conscious retrieval. Coding is more akin to a set of processes that support the perception of the stimulus itself, partitioning of items and context in a scene, and object recognition processes, among others (see section 3). Encoding into memory is conceptualized as distinct from perception as such, although, as was highlighted in both chapters by Craik and Hasselmo, perceptual processes are clearly components of memory-encoding processes. Encoding occurs during attention to and/or perception of a stimulus (internal or external) and may even persist for some time after attention has been drawn away from the stimulus or event. This persistence of processes supporting later retrieval will not be discussed further as it relates intimately to the concept of consolidation, considered elsewhere in this volume. However, an interesting conceptual issue is whether consolidation should be seen as a part of encoding or whether these are separable processes. If the latter, then one might ask when does encoding end and consolidation begin? I do not believe an answer to this question will ever be provided until we have more specific definitions and conceptualizations of what these two processes entail. I believe the increased specificity needed will be at the cellular and molecular level of description since ultimately the underlying mechanism of encoding is a physiological one. At present, most would agree, I think, that processes contributing to later retrieval occurring while the stimulus is being actively or consciously attended to will fall under 'encoding', while processes occurring once conscious attention is turned away from a stimulus will fall under 'consolidation'.

Systems-level descriptions link cognitive and cellular accounts of encoding

Much of what Craik and Hasselmo have described in their respective chapters is in agreement. Craik offers a description of encoding from a primarily cognitive perspective and Hasselmo describes the molecular and cellular changes that are thought to accompany the transformation of an experience into a longer lasting representation. However, there is a fundamental distinction between these different levels of analysis.

Craik provides elegant evidence to support the idea that memory encoding does not entail any additional cognitive processes above and beyond those involved in supporting perception, attention and comprehension. This conclusion is strongly supported by results from experiments designed to understand how attention to different features of a stimulus during encoding relates to later probability of retrieval. The results from this levels of processing (LOP) framework are crystal clear: the ability of an individual to retrieve information later in most types of recall and recognition tasks is a direct function of the individual's attentional orientation to the to-be-remembered item, with attention to 'shallow' or structural information leading to poorer memory retrieval than attention to 'deep' or semantic information. It is therefore concluded that 'memory encoding' is not a separate cognitive process, but rather is the result of these other cognitive processes and, as measured by recall and recognition tests, can be indirectly manipulated by the kind of cognitive process engaged in. In contrast, Hasselmo describes additional putative neural processes that might directly support encoding. These include persistent changes in molecular structures that directly or indirectly alter synaptic transmission between neurons and induce changes in membrane conductances to a particular pattern of synaptic input. Critically, these persistent changes are not necessary for perception, attention and comprehension at the time of encoding, and, thus, can be considered unique elements of encoding. If we can agree that the underlying mechanism of encoding is a set of molecular and cellular processes whose actions transform the participating connections in such a way as to allow later recovery of that same neural pattern, a crucial question is how these biological processes map onto the cognitive processes of encoding.

To answer this question, one could turn to a systems-level analysis and hypothesize, as many in the field of cognitive neuroscience do, that specific brain regions or networks of brain regions support different forms of neural encoding processes and, thus, different forms of memory encoding. Importantly, like the cellular processes described above, it is hypothesized that some systems (in particular the MTL system) may support mnemonic function independently from supporting other cognitive processes, such as attention and perception. On this view, a brain system dedicated to mnemonic processes does exist, perhaps linking the high-level cognitive processing with the cellular and molecular mechanisms described. Importantly, one could imagine at least two ways in which systems-level encoding may support different forms of memory. The first is that the cellular and molecular transformations underlying encoding may be distinct depending on *which* brain system is undergoing these changes. On the other hand, Hasselmo mentions that the cellular substrates themselves may be system general but that the brain region (or system) within which the changes are elicited may differentially impact the form of encoding (e.g. neocortical synaptic/cellular modification for priming and hippocampal synaptic/cellular modification for declarative memory) (see Chapter 22). Thus, from this viewpoint, the systems level may be distinguished from the cellular level in that different forms of encoding may depend on similar cellular changes occurring in distinct regions that differ in their anatomical input and local circuitry.

The MTL as an encoding system

The term encoding is most often applied to the transformation of a stimulus or event into a long-term memory trace. Evidence from neuropsychological, electrophysiological and imaging methodologies all converge on the finding that MTL mechanisms are primarily responsible for episodic encoding into long-term memory. Since the hallmark bilateral MTL resection performed on H.M. (Scoville and Milner 1957), much attention has focused on elucidating the critical role of the MTL, including the hippocampus, entorhinal, perirhinal and parahippocampal cortices, to memory formation and retrieval. H.M. and others with damage to the MTL exhibit a deficit in forming new declarative memories, with many perceptual and attentional capacities remaining relatively spared. These patients appear normal in that they can navigate their worlds, perceiving and attending to the external environment, and are even able to carry on simple conversations (suggesting that working memory operations are relatively intact). However, the neural encoding processes within the MTL that allow healthy individuals to form lasting representations of experienced events is lacking in these individuals. Indeed, the notion that the MTL is a critical locus underlying memory formation is grounded in the pattern of spared and impaired functions following damage to this region.

Evidence for the role for the MTL in the encoding of novel episodes into long-term memory has also emerged from functional neuroimaging studies that, on the whole, find that engagement of regions within the MTL during the encoding stage of a memory experiment is enhanced for events that are later retrieved. This has been termed the subsequent memory effect (Sandquist et al. 1980; Paller et al. 1987). These findings in healthy individuals dovetail with neuropsychological findings in demonstrating that the processes subserved by the MTL are important, and one might speculate, are *specific* to mnemonic processes such as encoding and retrieval.

Encoding into long-term versus working memory

Although I am focusing on encoding into long-term memory, encoding as a concept may be applied to shorter term forms of memory, such as working memory. Are these encoding operations distinct from those that support long-term memory? A definition of working memory is first needed before we can consider it in relation to long-term memory. 'Working memory' encompasses the processing of a stimulus beyond the initial perception of the item. In other words, as soon as a mental representation of the item is conceived, one that can be 'worked with' in some manner (rehearsed or manipulated), it can be said to have entered one's working memory space. Perhaps the most basic function of working memory is the maintenance of a stimulus once it has dropped from view (Goldman-Rakic 1987), and this process has been linked to a compelling cellular substrate of sustained neuronal firing during the delay period of a task that requires the bridging of a stimulus input (cue) to a response without an external stimulus in the intervening (delay) period. Thus, encoding into working memory seems to entail a translation of the perception of a stimulus into a pattern of neural activity that is sustainable over some seconds, probably via active rehearsal mechanisms. This concept, I believe, is distinct from the concept of encoding into long-term or intermediate-term memory, although they need not be considered entirely independent. In other words, encoding into working memory may be necessary for encoding into long-term memory, meaning that a transformation of a stimulus into an internal representation to which one is attending may be necessary, even if the item is not actively rehearsed, for it to be accessible to the changes that will allow it to become a long-term memory. In a way, this minimal entry stage into working memory could even be more akin to 'focal attention' (Cowan 1993) and/or a 'refresh' process (Johnson et al. 2005).

This is not in contradiction to the levels of processing (LOP) findings since encoding into working memory may be necessary for processing information at all levels. Indeed, the form of working memory operation may vary with the level of processing. From a cognitive perspective, shallow or structural processing of items may lead to a transformation of the item into a working memory space, with perhaps only the attended features entering focal attention. On the other hand, attention to phonological aspects of a stimulus might result in the item gaining access to internal rehearsal operations. Finally, attention to semantic or content information may require a 'working with' the representation that has now entered into this mental space. Thus, the cognitive operations that are differentially engaged in the LOP framework may differentially impact later memory retrieval via their recruitment of different component operations of a working memory system that may, ultimately, interface with the MTL differentially. Thus, encoding into working memory may be indirectly related but strongly correlated with encoding into long-term memory.

Levels of processing and differential access to MTL encoding mechanisms

Initial evidence for different levels of processing impacting upon different forms of later memory (e.g. item versus relational) via varying stages of 'working with' information comes from imaging studies showing that BOLD (blood oxygenation level-dependent) activation in brain regions known to be engaged during rote verbal rehearsal (i.e. left inferior frontal, parietal, supplementary motor area and cerebellum) display subsequent recognition memory effects for items that are rehearsed (Davachi *et al.* 2001; Blumenfeld and Ranganath 2006). This suggests that the engagement in working memory rehearsal mechanisms during an event might impact later recognition. Interestingly, during rote verbal rehearsal, subsequent memory effects were not seen in the hippocampus. On the other hand, attention to relational information (Cohen *et al.* 1999) during encoding, perhaps 'working with' representations, has been shown to correlate with increased activation in the hippocampus (Davachi and Wagner 2002) and this activation during encoding correlates specifically with later relational memory retrieval (Davachi *et al.* 2003; Kirwan and Stark 2004; Ranganath *et al.* 2004). Furthermore, activation in the MTL has been now consistently noted in tasks that are formally considered working memory tasks (Ranganath and D'Esposito 2001; Stern *et al.* 2001). These data taken together suggest that there may be different routes through which information becomes encoded, with cortical encoding mechanisms (e.g. simple refresh or rehearsal) having *some* impact on later recognition memory, while MTL encoding mechanisms (e.g. relational processing) are perhaps more strongly related to the probability of later recollection and or recall. Hasselmo provides a nice description of the potential distinct cellular changes that might support these different levels of encoding.

Conclusions

It is clear that a definition of encoding can be agreed upon by researchers such as Craik, Hasselmo and myself, with all approaching the concept in similar ways, but with each concentrating on a different level of analysis. That said, the concept of encoding at this stage suffers somewhat from the need for proof of encoding gathered during a later stage of retrieval. One desired goal would be to reveal the precise operations or mechanisms that we can confidently call 'encoding' irrespective of later retrieval. Indeed, the most likely candidate for this operation will be a synaptic or cellular mechanism that, when effected in distinct brain regions (neocortex and hippocampus) may result in the formation of distinct forms of later memory.

7

Working memory

Working memory is a discipline-specific concept: though we all rely heavily on this mental faculty in daily life, the concept beyond it had hardly been contemplated outside the professional cognitive circles. The emergence of the personal computer and the ensuing popularity of 'cache' and 'desktop' have rendered the concept popular, but only implicitly and in other names: many computer buffs discuss this concept without being aware of its role in their own memory. Working memory is that system that holds information in temporary storage during the planning and executing of a task, often in face of competing demands. It merges two major seemingly conflicting attributes: persistence and ephemerality. This is because, on the one hand, information in working memory relies on persistence of previously acquired knowledge, but on the other hand, it must phase out, or at least phase out of the focus of attention, on completion of the task, otherwise it could interfere with the subsequent task. It is noteworthy that working memory means something a bit different to cognitive investigators and to brain investigators, respectively. Some in the first tribe focus on working memory as a short-term memory process, or phase, in which information is processed before it enters the long-term 'store'. In contrast, most brain scientists consider it more like a dynamic desktop on which on-line information (sensory or mental) is combined with off-line information (memory) to permit performance. Hence for the cognitivist, working memory is linked to encoding and the formation of a new memory, whereas for the brainist it is linked to retrieval and the use of memory. These views are not mutually exclusive, they just emphasize how important is it to discuss the meaning and use of concepts and the terms that express these concepts in language.

Y.D.

25

Working memory: Signals in the brain

Wendy A. Suzuki

Working memory is a limited-capacity system for maintaining and manipulating information that underpins our capacity for a wide range of complex and flexible cognition, including language, the ability to perform mental arithmetic, playing chess, extemporaneous speech and planning for the future. The influential model proposed by Baddeley and Hitch (1974) has been very successful in providing an integrated account of working memory function in normal adults.

There are, however, a number of key issues that remain unaccounted for in this model. One of these issues concerns the relationship between working memory and long-term memory (Baddeley 2000). While early results suggested that working memory and long-term memory systems were functionally independent (Baddeley and Warrington 1970; Shallice and Warrington 1970), other theories have suggested a strong inter-relationship between the two (Atkinson and Shiffrin 1968). In support of the latter suggestion, findings from recent functional imaging studies suggest that the structures of the medial temporal lobe (MTL), a region strongly associated with long-term memory, may also play a key role in certain forms of working memory (Ranganath and D'Esposito 2001; Ranganath *et al.* 2005). However, this interpretation is difficult to differentiate from one in which the MTL's involvement in working memory is incidental to its primary role in long-term memory formation.

One way to start to differentiate between these possibilities is to examine the neurophysiological patterns of activity in these areas as animals perform various working memory tasks. If both the prefrontal cortex and MTL participate in the same way in working memory, then similar patterns of working memory-related neural activity should be observed across the two areas. Here I argue that findings from single-unit neurophysiological studies suggest a compromise between the two possibilities described above. Thus, while the neural activity in both the prefrontal cortex and the MTL can signal working memory, the substantially more prominent working memory signals seen in the prefrontal cortex suggests that this area ultimately makes a much stronger contribution to general working memory functions than the MTL.

Working memory signals in the prefrontal cortex

The classic task used to study visuospatial working memory in monkeys is the delayed response task. In the standard version of this task, a subject is shown the location of a preferred food that is then hidden from view. Following a delay period of several seconds, during which the subject must remember where the food has been placed, the subject is given the opportunity to retrieve the food. Circumscribed bilateral lesions limited to the region of the principle sulcus (area 46) in the monkey brain produce a devastating impairment on performance of this task (Pribram *et al.* 1952). Consistent with these findings, neurophysiological studies showed that neurons in the prefrontal cortex exhibit striking activity during the 'memory' delay period of the delayed response task (Fuster 1973).

The neural correlates of working memory have been examined in greater detail using an occulomotor version of the delayed response task (Funahashi *et al.* 1989). In this task, one of 4–16 possible visual target locations is cued and, after a short delay interval, the animal must make an eye movement to the location of that target. These studies not only confirmed the large proportion of prefrontal cells with striking delay activity, but also showed that prefrontal cells respond selectively to particular remembered target locations in the delay interval of this task (i.e. location-selective delay activity). This prominent delay activity that is selective for the to-be-remembered target location is widely believed to underlie spatial working memory in this task.

Working memory and the medial temporal lobe

In contrast to the severe deficit observed on the delayed response task after dorsolateral prefrontal lesions, large bilateral lesions of the MTL do not impair performance on this task with a short 10 s delay, but impairment is observed only when the memory demand of the task is taxed with increasing delay lengths (Zola-Morgan and Squire 1985). This finding led to the suggestion that while prefrontal cortex is important for short-term or immediate memory functions, MTL becomes critical only with longer delay intervals (but see Ranganath and Blumenfeld 2005 for an alternative view).

While delayed response tasks and their variants have not typically been used to probe the neural correlates of memory in the medial temporal lobe, operationally similar delayed match to sample tasks requiring short-term/working memory for objects have been used extensively. In these tasks, the animal is first presented with a to-be-remembered sample stimulus and, after a delay interval, a variable number of nonmatching test stimuli are presented. The trial ends with the repetition of the sample stimulus or match.

To perform this task, animals must retain in memory the sample stimulus and release a bar when it is repeated. Two key studies have described the memory signals in the prefrontal cortex and perirhinal cortex (areas 35 and 36 of the MTL studied by Miller *et al.* 1996) or entorhinal cortex (area 28 of the MTL studied by Suzuki *et al.* 1997) using the same version of the delayed match to sample task with multiple intervening test stimuli. These studies showed that neurons in the prefrontal, perirhinal and entorhinal cortices all exhibit some form of stimulus-selective delay activity during this task.

However, the pattern and magnitude of that delay activity differ in several ways across these areas. For example, many prefrontal neurons exhibit robust delay activity that is selective for the to-be-remembered sample stimulus. Moreover, this selective delay activity was maintained across multiple intervening test items to the end of the trial (e.g. 'bridging' delay activity). This suggests that prefrontal neurons maintain task-relevant information about the to-be-remembered sample stimulus on-line throughout the duration of the trial. In contrast, while perirhinal neurons maintain selective information about the sample stimulus during the immediately preceding delay, this selective delay activity is abolished by even a single intervening test item. Thus, perirhinal neurons do not provide a useful working memory signal for the performance of this task.

In contrast to perirhinal neurons, entorhinal neurons are more similar to those described in the prefrontal cortex, at least with respect to their prominent delay activity. For example, 35 and 56 percent of the cells in the entorhinal and prefrontal cortex, respectively, exhibited significant activity in the delay intervals compared with baseline activity. However, while 49 percent of the delay-active prefrontal neurons (or 28 percent of the total number of isolated cells) exhibited activity selective for the to-be-remembered sample stimulus, only 17 percent of the corresponding entorhinal cells (or 6 percent of the total number of isolated cells) exhibited selective delay activity. While these findings suggest a working memory signal exists in the entorhinal cortex, it is substantially less robust than the working memory signal observed in the prefrontal cortex.

If the majority of the entorhinal delay-active neurons are not stimulus selective, what are these cells signaling? Many of the nonselective entorhinal delay cells either increased or decreased their delay activity as a function of the delay interval, suggesting a role in the timing of the trial or possibly in coding the expectation of the upcoming reward.

Summary

While superficial similarities exist in the pattern of delay activity observed across the prefrontal cortex and MTL, a more detailed examination shows clear differences in the pattern and strength of their delay activity. Of the three areas examined, the prefrontal cortex exhibits the most robust working memory signal that persists over multiple intervening test items (i.e. bridging delay activity). In contrast, perirhinal neurons do not exhibit bridging delay activity, though selective activity during the immediately preceding delay interval is observed. A small number of cells in the entorhinal cortex show bridging delay activity, though the vast majority of entorhinal delay-active cells are not stimulus selective. Further studies will be needed to determine the specific role of this nonselective delay activity. These observations raise the important question of how best to define a working memory signal in behavioral neurophysiological studies. The findings so far suggest that not all patterns of delay activity are equivalent. Indeed, these kinds of neurophysiological descriptions, taken together with a detailed analysis of the behavioral/working memory demands of the task, may help establish a more detailed set of criteria to define the nature of working memory signals in the brain. This kind of information will complement the detailed knowledge we have about working memory functions from the human experimental psychology literature.

26

Working memory: Multiple models, multiple mechanisms

Alan Baddeley

Complex thought requires the manipulation of information, and such manipulation demands temporary storage. Working memory is the system that provides this. It is assumed to be limited in capacity, but flexible in operation.

One can distinguish between the general concept of working memory, and specific models such as the multicomponent model originally proposed by Baddeley and Hitch (1974). Models vary considerably in both their emphasis and the modeling style they adopt, which ranges from purely verbally expressed models such as that of Baddeley and Hitch (1974), through models using production system language (Kieras *et al.* 1999; Young and Lewis 1999) to more mathematically expressed models (Burgess and Hitch 1999; O'Reilly *et al.* 1999). Most models, however, have in common the assumption of some kind of attentionally limited executive control system, coupled with storage mechanisms that typically involve at least two subsystems, one verbal and the other visual spatial (for an overview, see Miyake and Shah 1999).

The Baddeley and Hitch (1974) model began by studying in some detail the verbal subsystem, termed the *phonological loop*, proposing that it is a temporary storage system that has evolved from mechanisms for speech perception and production. It is assumed to form the basis for the acquisition of language, and for the temporary maintenance of speech-based information. The system can be employed as an attentionally undemanding method of maintaining goals and guiding behavior (Baddeley *et al.* 2001*b*). It is domain specific rather than modality based, and can encode visually presented stimuli via a process of subvocal articulation into a phonological storage system, a system that is accessed directly by spoken language. It is also accessible by lip-read information, again indicating that it is not a simple auditory storage system.

Its visual equivalent is the *visuospatial sketchpad*, which is able to combine visual information such as shape and color with information on spatial location, and probably also kinesthetic and motor information. There is good evidence available on the separability of the visual or object-based system and its spatial counterpart, but less evidence on kinesthetic and motor codes (Smith and Jonides 1997). The function of the system is to reflect the environment, potentially allowing future actions, such as finding one's way from a hotel to the station, to be planned and optimized.

Working memory is assumed to be controlled by an attentionally limited component, the *central executive*. Two broad categories of control are assumed, based on the proposals of Norman and Shallice (1986). The first of these involves the control of action by habits and schemata that rely principally on environmental cues for the performance of routine and well-learned actions. However, when novel behavior is required, for example to resolve an impasse, a second system, the *supervisory attentional system* (SAS), is assumed to intervene to find a goal-orientated solution. Although somewhat homunculus like, the concept of an executive identifies a series of problems, which can then be systematically tackled, allowing the homunculus in due course to be replaced by a set of clearly specified processes.

More recently, a fourth component has been proposed (Baddeley 2000), namely the *episodic buffer*. This is assumed to comprise a limited capacity store, utilizing a multidimensional coding system. It serves the function of integrating information from the visuospatial and phonological subsystems, from sensory sources and from long-term memory. It is assumed to serve as a temporary storage system that allows information to be bound into multidimensional chunks (Miller 1956), serving as a workspace for complex thought that is accessible to conscious awareness (see Baddeley 2007 for further details).

Evidence on the neurobiological basis of working memory comes from patients with specific lesions and from functional brain imaging. The data are broadly consistent in identifying the storage component of the phonological loop as depending the left temporo-parietal cortex, with the rehearsal component dependent on Broca's area. The sketchpad depends principally on occipital, parietal and frontal regions, principally within the right hemisphere, whereas the central executive is heavily dependent on the operation of the frontal lobes (Smith and Jonides 1997; Henson 2001). Evidence on the episodic buffer is still sparse, but right frontal areas would appear likely to play a role (Prabhakaran *et al.* 2000).

The multicomponent model is broadly consistent with data from single unit recording in primates (Goldman-Rakic 1987). The initial findings of Pat Goldman-Rakic were of single-cell activation associated with storage of information regarding location. The relevant cells were principally frontal, suggesting an executive component in the task, which one would assume could also be detected in more posterior regions, by analogy with the human neuropsychological and neuroimaging data.

Although complex in detail, the basic concept of a multicomponent model has proved to be applicable to a wide range of practical issues ranging from language learning in children to cognitive decline in Alzheimer's disease (see Baddeley 2007).

27

Working memory:
What it is, and what it is not

Susan E. Gathercole

In cognitive psychology, the concept of working memory denotes a set of processes that support the temporary storage needs of complex cognitive activities; together, these constitute the working memory system. Functioning in concert, these components provide a flexible mental workspace that can be used to maintain and transform information, and that acts as a temporary bridge between externally and internally generated mental representations. The following sections identify some key features of working memory.

Working memory is not equivalent to short-term memory

Working memory is related to but distinguishable from short-term memory. Working memory is a hypothetical cognitive system that has been described in a number of distinct frameworks (e.g. Baddeley and Hitch 1974; Daneman and Carpenter 1980; Baddeley 2000; Cowan 2001). Short-term memory is a term that refers to memory activities such as immediate serial recall that require storage for relatively short periods of time. The short-term retention of verbal and visuospatial material is served by distinct storage components of working memory, termed the phonological loop and visuospatial sketchpad, respectively, in the influential Baddeley and Hitch model of working memory.

A second use of the term 'working memory' is to describe memory tasks such as reading span and listening span, that impose substantial loads on both storage and processing activities. Short-term memory and working memory are distinguished principally by whether or not they incorporate a significant concurrent processing element.

Working memory involves attention

Effective use of the working memory system, particularly under conditions of complex demands involving both storage and other processing activity, requires conscious attentional control. Temporary representations in working memory are subject to rapid decay and possibly interference unless the rememberer is engaged in active maintenance activities, which themselves require attention. Attention is diverted away from maintenance activities when other processing is required, leading, so it is postulated, to storage loss. Working memory is thus a highly fragile holding system, from which loss of information is typically catastrophic rather than gradual in nature. One specialized strategy for maintaining activated verbal representations is subvocal rehearsal; this process is under volitional control and acts to offset decay by re-activating phonological representations. Although the use of working memory requires attention in these respects, the detailed cognitive processes underlying its operation are not consciously controlled or available to conscious scrutiny. Retrieval of information from working memory is direct, and does not typically require conscious cue elaboration.

Working memory is limited in capacity

Mental arithmetic serves as a useful illustration both of a complex cognitive activity that requires working memory support, and of the capacity limitations on the system. Consider the task of calculating the product of two two-digit numbers without recourse to either pen and paper or a calculating device. The task involves (1) mental storage of the two numbers while (2) arithmetic rules are retrieved from long-term memory and applied, generating (3) partial solutions which must be stored while (iv) further calculations are made, and then (4) successfully integrated to yield the solution. It is working memory that provides the temporary storage medium for the representations generated at each of these steps, maintaining the representations while the learned mathematical rules are accessed and executed. Limits on working memory capacity are demonstrated by the fact that we are much less likely to be able to calculate accurately the product of three-digit than two-digit numbers, although the requisite mathematical knowledge is equivalent in the two cases. The limit is on the sheer amount of information that can be stored under the particular processing demands of the situation.

Although working memory is in this sense limited in capacity, this capacity cannot meaningfully be expressed as a unitary value, because there are multiple constraints on the operation of working memory. Any particular task will place specific demands on this system, so that performance will be limited only by relevant constraints. Thus, a verbal memory task will be limited by individual phonological but not visuospatial storage capacities, although both represent significant components of working memory. Working memory therefore has a functional rather than precise limit that is a product of the specific demands of the particular cognitive activity. A further reason why working memory capacity cannot be estimated from any single task is that memory activities typically also involve access to and support from knowledge that is not stored in the working memory system. There is, therefore, no such thing as a 'pure' working memory measure, although some tasks may be more effective at isolating particular working memory components from more permanent knowledge structures than others.

Working memory receives inputs from long-term memory

There are identifiable cognitive processes that are specific to the working memory system; these relate to the quality of storage and the persistence of temporary representations, and possibly to controlled attention. In practice, however, working memory operates in synchrony with other parts of the cognitive system, taking inputs from more permanent memory systems in a seamless manner that is not open to introspection. This is illustrated by the substantial benefit in immediate recall tasks to memory items that are words rather than nonwords, reflecting the use of primed lexical knowledge to reconstruct incomplete phonological representations stored in working memory, in a process of redintegration (i.e. the process in which reconstruction of memory is prompted by cues that are part of the response; Schweikert 1993).

Working memory provides inputs into long-term memory

The association between working memory and long-term memory is reciprocal: in addition to receiving inputs from long-term memory as described above, working memory itself acts as a conduit for the acquisition of more permanent knowledge representations. Two distinct learning pathways have been identified. First, temporary phonological storage in working memory of the unfamiliar phonological forms of new words contributes to learning of lexical phonology, via a process of gradual abstraction across repeated exposures to a new token (Baddeley et al. 1998). This is a primitive learning process that is most dominant at the early stages of learning a language when existing knowledge cannot be effectively bootstrapped to mediate learning, but can be used to support word learning in adulthood when required.

Secondly, the working memory system provides a more general limit on the ease of learning. In childhood, impairments of working memory are closely associated with poor academic progress in key scholastic domains such as reading and mathematics. Children with working memory impairments frequently fail to meet the working memory demands of many routine classroom activities such as following lengthy instructions, place-keeping in complex tasks and coping with combined processing and storage requirements (Gathercole *et al.* 2007). Working memory thus acts as a bottleneck for learning, preventing children from succeeding in the individual learning episodes which, if successful, will contribute to the incremental process of the acquisition in knowledge and skill.

28

Integrative comments
Working memory: The mind is richer than the models

Randall W. Engle

The term 'working memory' has gained wide use in psychology, brain research and artificial intelligence. The authors of the accompanying chapter in this section have discussed a selection of the different uses and attempted to define the term. It could be agreed at the outset that the uses of the term in some disciplines of the science of memory do not mean the same thing that is typically referred to as working memory by cognitive psychologists. First, many production system models of memory, based on the computer metaphor, assume that working memory holds the productions until they are implemented. This appears to be a technical term that is unlimited in capacity and we exclude that from our definition. Secondly, studies that use certain maze tasks in the rat sometimes describe their results as reflecting working memory. These procedures probably reflect long-term memory, not working memory, so we also exclude that use from our definition.

With these exclusions in mind, and in line with the authors of the accompanying chapters, I prefer to define working memory from a relatively lofty perspective so as to include as many other uses as possible, and agree with Baddeley's definition that 'Working memory is a limited capacity system for maintaining and manipulating information and it underpins the capacity for complex and flexible cognition'.

Additional points of agreement could be identified among the authors of the chapters in this section. First, that the monkey paradigms used by researchers in the Joaquin Fuster and Pat Goldman-Rakic tradition reflect one aspect of the working memory system as studied by those researchers who use human subjects. Specifically, the procedures reflect temporary maintenance of domain-specific information over a brief period of time in a form that is fragile and vulnerable to the consequences of distraction. Secondly, that there needs to be more interaction and discussion among researchers contributing to the animal and human literatures. Thirdly, that there seems to be general agreement about the nature of working memory and the relevant unanswered questions. There is, however, some debate about the elements of this hypothetical system. Baddeley has proposed a speech-based buffer, a visuospatial-based buffer, and an episodic buffer along with the central executive. I have proposed (as described below) that while speech-based and visuospatial-based coding are important, there are many other coding formats in other modalities (e.g. kinesthetic) that can be used for temporary storage.

Last but not least, the authors of the accompanying chapters seem to find considerable agreement about the role of volitional attention in working memory. All note the importance of actively maintaining information in an easily accessible and retrievable state, with the importance of the system being able to block or inhibit internally or externally generated representations from the limited contents of working memory.

My perspective on working memory

From the point of view I have developed over the years, working memory represents a system that serves to regulate the flow of mental elements into and out of a state in which those elements are highly active, possibly in conscious awareness, and capable of influencing thought, emotion and behavior. The system is most important under conditions with a high level of proactive interference or strongly prepotent behaviors counter to the current task goals. In fact, I have suggested that perhaps the system only comes into play under such conditions of heavy distraction or interference.

Types of formats in working memory

We can represent the world and our experience in it in many different formats, and the mental elements in working memory could be in any of those representational formats. The Baddeley model (Baddeley and Hitch 1974) proposes primarily two representational formats, one speech based and one based on visual and spatial formats. My view is that there are dozens of different formats, including the two proposed by Baddeley (Engle and Kane 2004). In fact, visual and spatial formats are clearly separable. For example, consider how I represent the keyboard on which I am typing this work. I have seen a keyboard many more times than I have typed on one, but if you show me a drawing of a keyboard with the letters missing and ask me where the 'l' key is located, I will make a movement with fingers on my right hand and then tell you the key to which I moved to type the 'l'. That coding may be spatial or motoric, but it is clearly not visual. (I could not draw the keyboard from memory without using hand movements.)

Likewise, if you have ever tried to teach a child to ride a bicycle, the process is almost impossible to convert into speech, despite the fact that we know the action very well; again, it is difficult to imagine that the representational code is visual or spatial. My sense is that I can clearly retrieve and maintain thought of a motor action in a code that is neither speech, visual or spatial. I would argue that the contents of working memory can be based on auditory, kinesthetic, gustatory and olfactory sensations, as well as compiled codes such as listening to complex music. Phonological and visuospatial codes are just the most convenient microscopes for psychologists to study the coding formats, but the human mind is less limited. In fact, I can conceive of nearly a dozen different distinguishable codes that might be subsumed under the category acoustic/auditory/articulatory/phonological/speech. In sum, there are as many different coding schemes for temporary storage as there are modes of thought.

Function of working memory

I propose that the primary purpose of the working memory system is to allow us to function in the face of proactive interference and highly prepotent behaviors that are counter to the task facing us at the moment. Much of the information we need to function in the world is automatically retrieved quickly enough from long-term memory to be useful in even the most pressing and complex cognition. The problem arises when the automatically retrieved information is not appropriate for the current task or when retrieval fails because of conflict among representations associated with the current retrieval cue (i.e. response competition). The effects that we generally attribute to short-term memory or working memory are probably found only under conditions of interference (see Crowder 1982). For example, Keppel and Underwood (1962) found that the much cited retention function in the Brown–Peterson short-term memory interference paradigm does not hold for the first or even the second trial in an experiment. It is only after interference has built up and there are intrusions from automatic retrieval that the prototypical Brown–Peterson effect of retention interval occurs. It is under those conditions that we need to do the mental work necessary to achieve and maintain rapid access to the most recent relevant information. I predict that effects such as phonemic similarity, articulatory suppression and other effects of short-term memory studies would also not be found over the first trials in an experiment.

What is the role of attention in working memory?

This is a key question to my view of working memory capacity. However, first, we need to distinguish several ways the term 'attention' is used. Posner's work (Posner and Petersen 1990; Fan et al. 2001) makes a distinction between *alerting*, *orienting* and *executive attention. Alerting* means becoming prepared that some important event is likely to occur soon and preparing to analyze and respond to that event. *Orienting* means selecting a part of our immediate experience where we expect that important event to occur. This could be a region in space, a particular auditory channel, etc. In the natural world, many different events capture our attention and lead to alerting and subsequent orienting. When we hear a loud noise, see a bright or flickering light, or hear a sick child crying in the night, our attention is captured, which serves to bring that event into our focus.

Nonetheless, there is clearly some level of control over whether that capture occurs and that is the province of *executive attention*; the ability to control the contents of focus in the service of the current task. The ability to resist capture of our focus is the most important limiting factor in working memory capacity. While there are potential individual differences in all aspects of the working memory system and in the three aspects of attention, the difference in executive attention capability is *the* critical factor reflected in the relationship between measures of working memory capacity and a huge range of real-world cognition (Engle and Kane 2004). We and others have invested heavily in studies of the relationship between measures of working memory capacity such as reading, operation and counting span, and measures of higher order cognition such as reading comprehension and complex reasoning or fluid intelligence. The findings are quite clear in showing that co-varying out individual differences in coding, rehearsal, domain-specific knowledge, processing speed, etc. does nothing to diminish the relationship (Engle *et al.* 1999; Conway *et al.* 2002; Turley-Ames and Whitfield 2003).

Some views of capacity limitations have been cast in terms of the number of items that could be maintained in the focus (Miller 1956; Cowan 2001). However, the view that capacity is limited by ability to control the contents of the focus through attention makes predictions quite different from a view that capacity is limited to X ± 2 items. Two studies (among many) make this point. Both tested subjects who were placed in the upper quartile (high spans) or lower quartile (low spans) on one or more measures of working memory capacity such as reading or operation span. Conway *et al.* (2001) had high and low spans perform a dichotic listening task in which subjects heard different lists of words to the two ears and repeated back the words presented to one of the ears. Unbeknownst to the subjects, their first name had been digitized and was inserted into the list presented to the nonattended ear. At the end of the session, subjects were asked whether they had noticed anything unusual in the nonattended ear. Our view that differences in working memory capacity reflect the ability to control capture of attention makes a rather counterintuitive prediction. High spans should be better able than low spans to reject the distracting information from the nonattended ear and therefore should be less likely to report hearing their name. That is exactly what Conway *et al.* (2001) found. While only 20 per cent of high spans reported hearing their name, 65 per cent of lows spans reported hearing their name.

Another study (Unsworth *et al.* 2004) tested high and low spans in the anti-saccade task, an even more primitive test of executive attention. Subjects fixated on a center cross on a computer monitor and there was an outlined box 11.33° to each side of the cross. After an irregular period, one of the boxes would flicker and this required an eye movement either to that box or to the box on the opposite side of the screen. In the pro-saccade condition, the saccade was to be made to the box. This condition is a prepotent and highly prepared response, which relies on millions of years of evolution to orient to things that afford movement. High and low spans should not differ in this condition and they did not. In the anti-saccade condition, however, subjects must go against the prepotent response tendency and immediately look at the nonflickering box on the opposite side of the screen. This tests the subjects' ability to resist attention capture and to implement the rules of the current task which are counter to highly prepared response tendency.

While both high and low spans made more errors in this task by occasionally looking toward the flickering box, low spans made many more errors than did high spans. In other words, individuals who recalled more items on the working memory task, in this case operation span, were less likely to have their attention captured in the anti-saccade task. This finding makes no sense from a view that working memory capacity is limited by either the number of items or by processing speed, but it makes perfect sense if that limitation reflects differences in the ability to control the contents of working memory.

One problem with this view is that executive attention is the most difficult aspect of attention to model in any substantial way because it seems homuncular in nature. However, cognitive control can be conceptualized in computational terms (O'Reilly *et al.* 1999) and it is becoming clear that this ability is mediated by brain circuits associated with the prefrontal cortex and the anterior cingulate, that dopamine is a principle neurotransmitter associated with cognitive control and that these abilities have strong genetic underpinnings, particularly the catechol-O-methyltransferase (COMT) gene, which is critical to the regulation of dopamine in the brain. We seem well on the way to mechanizing the homunculus.

While individual differences on measures of working memory capacity appear to reflect trait aspects of cognitive control, these measures also reflect moment-to-moment state aspects of this capability. For instance, life event stress (Klein and Boals 2001), stereotype threat (Schmader and Johns 2004) and fatigue all lead to reductions in working memory capacity that lead to reductions in performance on other cognitive tasks. Thus, we might best think of working memory capacity as a trait and a state variable, similar to anxiety, with profound effects on the control of thought, emotion, and behavior.

8

Consolidation

The concept of consolidation is an offshoot of the concepts of 'growth' and 'development'. It means that things must mature before they can fulfill their function properly. Specifically, in the science of memory, consolidation refers to the progressive post-encoding stabilization of the memory trace. The term itself is also used to refer to the memory phase(s) during which this stabilization takes place. During that phase, but not afterwards, the memory item is susceptible to amnestic agents. In the history of the science of memory, the identification of consolidation windows was taken to reinforce the paradigm that long-term memory resembles growth; bodies and organs gradually mature, so do memories. The application of the concept of consolidation to the biography of items in memory is not without its difficulties. Two types of doubt haunt the use of this concept recurrently. One, is the role of 'consolidation' indeed to stabilize the new information? An alternative view is that new information is encoded and 'stored' instantaneously, in which case the role of 'consolidation' might be only to facilitate future accessibility to the information, or to create new computational space for new memories to come. The second: does consolidation occur just once per item, or, alternatively, does the memory item reconsolidate each time it is reactivated? The aforementioned questions bear on important issues in the science of memory, including persistence and retrievability. It is noteworthy that the term consolidation is rarely used in the psychological literature, as opposed to its abundance in the neurobiological literature, but the concept is clearly alive in the psychological literature as well, though in disguise (i.e., retroactive interference).

Y.D.

29

Consolidation: Molecular restlessness

Alcino J. Silva

Science constantly changes the world around us, and it also shapes the world within. It was not so long ago that I used to think of my own memory as a hard drive full of pictures, events, emotions, History 101. In other words, I used to be a staunch believer in the consolidation dogma. According to this dogma, the senses bring the world to the brain and the brain consolidates the bits that it finds interesting, distressing and useful, etc. into a state that assures the stability, and most importantly the reliability of these memories. According to the strong version of the consolidation dogma, unreliable memories are like unrestricted cell growth in a tumor: however common, they both reflect the failings of biological systems caught between the imperfect compromises of evolution, the abuses of our environment and our own spotty genetic heritage. Here, I will share a personal view of memory consolidation that is neither fair nor balanced, but that illustrates the growing ambivalence towards this enormously influential idea: it was first proposed more than 100 years ago, and it continues to have a paradigmatic hold on memory research (McGaugh 2000). The criticisms described below do not target the gentler versions of this old horse of memory research (Nadel and Moscovitch 1997). These gentler versions, however, may push this hypothesis to safer grounds, therefore masking its predicaments and allowing it to survive well beyond its expiration date.

I came to the study of memory nearly two decades ago through the brave new world of molecular and cellular cognition. The little we knew about the biochemistry and physiology of memory fit comfortably within the gothic vision of the consolidation dogma. This dogma portrays memory as a Ludwigian palace that we spend a lifetime building, with dark and nebulous rooms for certain, but solid, firm, structured and brick-like reliable. This dogma saw the mechanisms of memory as processes that gradually cement new memories, bricks gradually added to our cognitive castles. For example, in the early 1990s, we demonstrated that the enzyme alpha-calmodulin kinase II (αCaMKII), which modifies proteins by phosphorylating them under the regulation of calcium, triggers synaptic plasticity and memory acquisition (Silva *et al.* 1992*a*,*b*). A few years later, our laboratory discovered that the ubiquitous regulator of the expression of genes, cAMP responsive element-binding protein (CREB), has a key role in stabilizing plasticity and memory (Bourtchuladze *et al.* 1994; Kida *et al.* 2002). Remarkably, pioneering physiological studies in *Aplysia* and neurogenetic analysis in *Drosophila*, as well as many other subsequently published studies, echoed these findings (reviewed in Silva *et al.* 1998). The consolidation dogma was so strong that very little attention was paid to the obvious transformative properties of these dynamic molecular and cellular processes.

The activation of αCaMKII, CREB and all of the other numerous molecules implicated in memory, the induction and stability of synaptic plasticity, as well as the circuit processes that support the representations of information in the brain (i.e. hippocampal place fields) are all highly dynamic and probabilistic in nature and they do not reflect the determinism and 'solidity' of the consolidation dogma. Nevertheless, we readily framed these observations within the dogma: the idea that memory has an initial labile stage (e.g. dependent on αCaMKII) that is followed by a second stage (memory consolidation) in which it is permanently etched in brain circuits. Indeed, products of CREB-dependent transcription were proposed to mediate neuronal growth that locked memories in neuronal networks (Bourtchuladze *et al.* 1994; Kida *et al.* 2002). Many of us ignored the psychological data that demonstrated the dynamic if not fickle, capricious and self-serving nature of memory. These well-documented psychological observations clearly contradicted the idea of memory as stable, reliable and objective (Schacter *et al.* 1998), but were consistent with an emerging biology that populated the science of memory with molecular, cellular and system mechanisms that were just as dynamic, and perhaps even fickle, as memories themselves.

For me, the beginning of the end of the consolidation dogma can be traced back to the publication in 2000 of two very influential papers: a lucid review by Susan Sara (Sara 2000), and a research paper by Karim Nader, Glenn Schafe and Joe LeDoux on memory 'reconsolidation' (Nader *et al.* 2000), another unfortunate term which I am sure will confuse unaware readers for years to come. Essentially, these and other papers, some dating back to the 1960s, argued that memories are actually undergoing 'consolidation-like processes' nearly every time they are recalled (hence, the term 're-consolidation'), and that interfering with consolidation mechanisms during recall weakens or even erases these memories. Discovering this nearly forgotten literature was a real shock to me and to many other memory researchers obfuscated by the consolidation dogma: how could a brief recall episode paired with blockers of consolidation mechanisms (i.e. protein synthesis inhibitors) disrupt a consolidated memory? Does recall really trigger a novel round of consolidation? And if so, what is the meaning of consolidation to start with? How can supposedly solid and stable memories be actually so fluid and seemingly plastic? The irony of the term 'reconsolidation' was not lost on many of us puzzled by these findings.

The reconsolidation findings contradicted so glaringly the predominant consolidation paradigm that they were met initially with considerable skepticism. Fortunately, Sheena Josselyn and Satoshi Kida, two post-doctoral fellows in our laboratory, overlooked my doubts, and decided to use a new state-of-the-art transgenic inducible system to test the possible role of CREB in memory 'reconsolidation' (Kida et al. 2002). I did not resist the idea too vigorously because I had become increasingly aware of memory's little betrayals, its blending of fact and fiction (Schacter et al. 1998). Sheena and Satoshi's persistence paid off: their results demonstrated that the very process of recall placed emotional memories into a labile state that required CREB for stability; interfering with CREB function specifically during recall disrupted memory (Kida et al. 2002). These and subsequent findings demonstrated that the molecular machinery that we thought fixed memories into a permanent state was also required for stabilizing memories every time they were recalled. How could something that was supposed to be so solid and reliable be fluid every time is used? If memory was this fluid, then how could we go on believing in the consolidation dogma? Amazingly, reconsolidation findings, which involve a large number of experiments in many forms of memory and in several species, have attracted a great deal of attention, not because of their obvious implications to mainstream concepts of memory, but as odd, curious and interesting phenomena in the circus of memory.

The decisive tipping point for me came with our studies of remote memory (Frankland et al. 2001; Frankland and Bontempi 2004). Until recently, molecular and cellular analysis of memory had been focused in many research groups on the early stages of hippocampal-dependent acquisition and processing. Little was known about the biological mechanisms that stabilize hippocampal-dependent memory over weeks, months and years. We all suspected that the neocortex, by virtue of its potentially large storage capacity, was involved, but beyond that little else was known. Studies from a couple of laboratories, including our own, uncovered direct evidence for the involvement of cortical networks in remote memory (e.g. Wiltgen et al. 2004). Importantly, in our studies of remote memory, we came across hints that this form of memory is not simply a cortical version of the earlier hippocampal-dependent memory. We noted in our mouse studies, for example, that remote (cortical) memories seemed more general, as if they were semantic versions of their earlier, more specific (episodic-like?) counterparts. It is as if the brain uses two different, but complementary memory processing and storage systems: a RAM-like hippocampal-based system optimized for fast acquisition and high content, and a neocortical system seemingly optimized for gradual extraction and integration of new information into previously formed knowledge structures (Wiltgen *et al*. 2004). These ideas and findings do not share much in common with the rigid views of memory purported by the consolidation dogma. Just as with the reconsolidation work, remote memory studies suggest a more dynamic and plastic view of memory.

In retrospect, the idea of consolidation has made important contributions to memory research, including the concept that memory has multiple distinct phases with unique molecular, cellular and behavioral properties (McGaugh 2000). Unfortunately, it may have also distracted research from a variety of pertinent and fascinating questions concerning the dynamic, constructive and metamorphic properties of memory. I believe that the persuasive power of the consolidation dogma and its hold on our imagination stems among others from a profound human need to trust our remembered pasts. Life is so fleeting, our best and most dear moments pass so quickly, that it is important for us to imagine memory as a dependable anchor to those moments, a bridge to times passed and to the ethos of our identity. Even now, as I complete this essay, I hesitate to tinge cherished memories, many undoubtedly fabricated by the rituals of repeated family recounting, with the shadowy uncertainty of memory's unreliability. However, science has the last word, and my view is that the weight of emerging evidence may be turning 'consolidation' into an historical note.

30

Consolidation: Challenging the traditional view

Joseph E. LeDoux

It has long been known that new memories must be stabilized or consolidated if they are to persist (McGaugh 2000). This concept began to take shape in the early days of experimental psychology when William James introduced the idea that memories are initially stored in a temporary form, primary memory, that over time is stabilized into a persistent form, secondary memory. Shortly thereafter, Muller and Pilzecker provided experimental evidence that temporary or short-term memory (STM) paves the way for long-term memory (LTM). The concept of consolidation is thus closely intertwined with the concepts of STM and LTM. The standard, and long-accepted, view is that STM is temporary and subject to disruption, while LTM, once consolidated, is persistent, stable and insensitive to disruption.

How do we know consolidation exists?

Consolidation is not something we subjectively experience or that has a distinct behavioral signature. As a result, the existence of consolidation is inferred rather than experienced or observed. Specifically, consolidation is inferred from the effects of manipulations that prevent the conversion of STM into LTM. Consolidation is thus typically defined in terms of STM, and STM is defined as the time when a memory can be disrupted, and thus prevented from being consolidated. Even if we ignore the circularity of the logic (consolidation being defined by STM and STM by consolidation), another major problem hampers a clear conception of consolidation, i.e. the term consolidation itself is used in different ways in the modern literature.

What are the different meanings of consolidation?

Consolidation has been used in at least three ways. In the verbal learning field, a field that follows directly from Muller and Pilzecker, and their forerunner, Ebbinghaus, consolidation is traditionally inferred from studies in which interference is produced by distracting information. In such studies, memory can be disrupted for seconds or at most minutes after learning. This brief store that is subject to distraction and interference is now often called working memory (WM), a term that helps to distinguish this from other uses of STM, as described below (see Chapter 28, this volume). WM involves both verbal and nonverbal modalities in humans, and various nonverbal modalities in animals, especially primates. At the neural level, WM is mediated by the prefrontal cortex. The creation of a long-lasting trace on the basis of WM, in contrast, most probably involves connections from the prefrontal cortex to the medial temporal lobe memory system.

A second meaning of consolidation refers to the fact that electrical stimulation of the brain or chemical treatment, especially with protein synthesis inhibitors, can disrupt the conversion of STM into LTM (Davis and Squire 1984; McGaugh 2000). Such studies are typically performed in animals due to the invasiveness of the procedures, but similar effects on memory occur in patients subjected to electroconvulsive shock therapy. STM, as revealed in this way, lasts minutes to several hours. This type of study has led to the view that newly synthesized proteins play a key role in the consolidation of STM into LTM, and that it takes several hours for this to occur. The term 'cellular/molecular consolidation' is used to refer to this protein synthesis process underlying the conversion of STM to LTM (Dudai and Morris 2000).

Studies of consolidation of STM into LTM at the molecular level typically involve aversive or appetitive conditioning tasks that induce implicit forms of memory. In implicit learning situations, STM and LTM are typically thought of as state changes within a single system. WM tasks, in contrast, are explicit memory tasks that depend on the prefrontal cortex for immediate or short-term processing and the medial temporal lobe system for LTM storage. Thus, in order to become an LTM, a brief WM must presumably undergo protein synthesis consolidation in the medial temporal lobe just as a STM must undergo consolidation in the brain system that forms the LTM. In other words, consolidation of a WM possibly involves a protein synthesis-*independent* process in the prefrontal cortex and a protein synthesis-dependent process in the medial temporal lobe. However, little research has explored biological transformation of WM into LTM.

The final meaning of consolidation also involves the conversion of a temporary memory into a persistent memory. In this case, though, the temporary memory is not a WM lasting a few seconds or minutes or an STM lasting several hours. Instead, the temporary memory is a consolidated LTM in the medial temporal lobe that, with time (months to years), comes to be less dependent on, and even independent of, the medial temporal lobe (Squire 1987). Thus, damage to the hippocampus, a major component of the medial temporal lobe memory system, initially results in the loss of explicit LTM but then later the same lesion has no effect. The standard view, though not all accept it (see Chapter 31, this volume), is that the memory moves from the hippocampus to the neocortex in the process of being fully consolidated (McClelland *et al.* 1995). This version of consolidation is called 'systems consolidation' since the memory is said to move from one system to another. Systems consolidation probably requires molecular consolidation first in the hippocampus and later the neocortex (Dudai and Morris 2000).

How did molecular consolidation become a dogma?

Each of the three meanings of consolidation, though related, deserves individual scrutiny. In the remainder of this chapter, I will focus on the conception of molecular consolidation and leave the two additional meanings for others (e.g. Chapter 31, this volume).

Over the past 40 years, the idea of molecular consolidation has grown from an observation about how memory can be disrupted to a dogma about how memories are formed and stabilized. In brief, the dogma is that when we learn about or encode some experience, the synapses in the brain involved in the learning/encoding are strengthened, and the pattern of connections so established either encompasses the memory or at least makes access to the memory possible. Initially, the memory involves unstable physiological/chemical processes that are subject to disruption until they are stabilized in the form of new synaptic connections that then make the memory persist. In Hebb's (1949) influential theory, the temporary traces was said to be due to electrophysiological activity (reverberating circuits) and the persistent trace to structural change. Subsequent studies showed that protein synthesis inhibition (1) had no effect on STM for several hours but prevented LTM and (2) was required for the growth and stabilization of new synapses. These and other observations have helped establish the view that LTM is essentially a process by which gene expression, leading to protein synthesis, converts temporary traces into persistent memories (Bailey *et al.* 1996). The temporary traces, contrary to Hebb's view, are, like LTM, thought to involve proteins, rather than just physiological activity. However, the proteins involved in maintaining STM, as opposed to LTM, pre-exist at the time of learning and do not require gene expression and new protein synthesis. They simply involve activation or phosphorylation.

Do we understand molecular consolidation?

A careful analysis of the logic of consolidation studies reveals that some of the conclusions may not be as solid as we think. In general, consolidation is thought of as something that takes place after learning or encoding. Almost all studies have used the so-called post-training paradigm (McGaugh 2000). This has the important advantage of ensuring the subject has learned and that the manipulation is only affecting storage. For example, a drug given before training could affect both acquisition and storage, but a drug given after training can only affect storage.

However, there are several problems with the way the post-training paradigm has been used (Rodrigues *et al.* 2004). First, in order to be sure of the role of the drug in consolidation (the conversions of STM to LTM), a test should always be used to show that STM is unaffected. Many consolidation studies have only measured LTM. This may be due to the strong influence of Hebb's idea that STM involves electrophysiological reverberation while LTM is chemical. However, now that we know that STM involves the phosphorylation of pre-existing proteins, it is possible that some consolidation effects are due to a chemical disruption of STM. A test of STM would easily determine this. Secondly, there are multiple waves of protein synthesis initiation after learning. A single post-training injection of an inhibitor may not always be enough. Multiple time points should be tested. Third, pre-training manipulations are also important. Suppose a drug given pre-training affects LTM but has no effect on STM. Also, suppose further, the same drug given post-training has no effect. By all standards, this pattern of results would be called a consolidation effect since LTM but not STM is affected. However, since post-training manipulations do not produce the effect, it would be a consolidation effect that can only be disrupted during training. Pre-training blockade of L-type voltage-gated calcium channels has this effect (Rodrigues *et al.* 2004), but a post-training test has not yet been reported. All of this suggests that much of our understanding of the particulars about the neurobiology of memory consolidation may not be as solid as we thought.

Is molecular consolidation the answer to memory storage?

While it is important to re-evaluate the role of various brain chemicals in consolidation, another important issue is whether the molecular consolidation dogma, as traditionally conceived, provides the correct framework for thinking about memory. That this needs to be asked has become apparent as a result of recent studies on the topic called 'reconsolidation'.

Shortly after it was discovered that consolidation after learning disrupts LTM but not STM, other studies showed that prevention after retrieval affects the ability of the memory to be subsequently retrieved (Sara 2000). This suggested that after retrieval, memory has to be restored, presumably through new protein synthesis, hence the term 'reconsolidation'. These findings did not fit with the emerging dogma that LTM involves the creation of new synaptic connections via protein synthesis since why would memory retrieval destabilize the new synaptic connections? The findings were thus ignored as the dogma developed.

In the late 1990s, reconsolidation was revitalized by Sara (2000). However, her studies used systemic injections. Around this time, my laboratory had successfully used local protein synthesis in the lateral amygdala to selectively disrupt LTM and spare STM of fear conditioning. We therefore decided to examine intra-amygdala blockade of protein synthesis after retrieval of the memory (Nader *et al.* 2000). STM was intact and LTM was impaired.

These new studies of reconsolidation were followed by many subsequent ones showing that post-reactivation treatment with protein synthesis inhibitors, and a variety of other compounds that disrupt intracellular signaling, can lead to an amnestic state (reviewed in Nader *et al.* 2000*b*; Alberini 2005; Dudai 2006).

Everyone agrees that a retrieved memory is not a carbon copy of the initial experience, and that during retrieval memories are updated. This is why one's memory of a crime can be influenced by reading a newspaper report. The key issue is what happens to the original memory during reactivation. Strong interpretation of the reconsolidation results suggests that the original memory is lost. A weaker version suggests that the original memory is changed. Future work will have to resolve this.

Conclusion

Consolidation has several meanings. This essay has emphasized molecular consolidation, and its implications for what memory is at the biological level. Research on reconsolidation has challenged the traditional view of molecular consolidation that posits that a memory is consolidated by protein synthesis after learning, and then persists in that form. Reconsolidation suggests that memories are restored each time they are retrieved. The main issue is whether the restorage is a new memory or a modification of the original memory. Some have suggested that the terms active and inactive memory might be better than STM/LTM or unconsolidated/consolidated memory (Lewis 1979; Nader *et al.* 2000; Dudai 2006). The active/inactive distinction has the advantage of being theoretically neutral and thus does not force research into paradigms, such as the post-training paradigm, that were designed with consolidation in mind.

31

Consolidation: The demise of the fixed trace

Lynn Nadel

The concept of memory consolidation, with a century-long history, has throughout its life buttressed a particular paradigm of memory research—the idea that experience leaves behind a distinctive trace, or engram, that has a discernible structure. Within this paradigm, consolidation is the process by which this engram is, over time, stabilized in final form. I will argue here that this notion of a fixed memory trace, and its strengthening during consolidation, now stands as a barrier to further progress in understanding the nature and underlying bases of memory.

Why an engram?

Lashley (1950) famously concluded that his search for an engram in the brain led him to the conclusion that learning simply was not possible. A possible solution to the problem raised by Lashley's work was provided by Hebb (1949) in his 'connec-tionist' theory of synaptic change, cell assembly formation and phase sequence activity. These postulated mechanisms presumed to show how an engram could be distributed within the brain, and how the full pattern of the memory trace could be activated by many different paths, or cell assemblies. Hebb's theory showed how a memory trace could exist, could avoid total disruption when damage occurred and could permit what we now call 'pattern completion'. It seemed, in other words, that Lashley searched in vain because he was looking for the wrong thing; and, that it still made sense to talk about a fixed memory trace.

Why consolidation

Within Hebb's formalism, consolidation was an essential part of the story. Experience triggered some short-term process, such as reverberation within cell assemblies, and over time this repetitive activity 'consolidated' structural changes that then subserved long-term memory. It is not accidental that the first wave of empirical research on consolidation occurred shortly after Hebb's speculations, and explicitly cited his inspiration. Hebb never addressed the question of why so much time was necessary to stabilize a memory trace. In his view, the consolidation period was quite brief, and in fact much of the work in the 1950s and 1960s reflected the assumption that consolidation lasted minutes rather than days or weeks.

Long-lasting consolidation

Work with amnesic patients, however, indicated that consolidation in at least some types of memory in humans lasted a lot longer than this. The argument went as follows: H.M. and other amnesic patients, with damage to the hippocampal system, seemed to have no problem with short-term memory lasting in the order of 10–20 s. Nor, it was argued, did they have a problem recalling quite old memories. Their problem consisted in an inability to consolidate information from short-term to long-term format, at least as regards explicit memory. Thus, it was concluded, the hippocampal system was not itself the place where engrams related to previous events were stored. Instead, consolidation was taken to reflect a long-term interaction between the hippocampal system and actual storage sites in the neocortex.

The engram was assumed to reside in multiple and disparate cortical sites, which could not readily communicate with each other at the time of initial encoding. The hippocampus, in this formulation, helped to 'bind' these neocortical sites together, making retrieval possible. With sufficient repetition over time (possibly during sleep), these cortical sites became directly connected and the intervention of the hippocampal system was no longer needed. At this point, consolidation was concluded and damage to the hippocampus should have no effect on retrieval of a memory. This view of consolidation, now termed the 'standard model' of systems consolidation (to be distinguished from synaptic consolidation, see Chapter 30, this volume), was spelled out by Squire et al. (1984), and adopted by many others since (e.g. Squire and Alvarez 1995; McClelland et al. 1996). One problem with this way of thinking is that the consolidation period began to lengthen as more precise methods for assessing recall of remote memories were developed. What originally seemed to last months or a few years stretched to a decade or two.

Multiple trace theory (MTT)

Partly in response to the absence of any plausible explanation for why it should take 10–20 years to 'consolidate' a memory, Moscovitch and I developed a different approach, which we termed 'multiple trace theory' (Nadel and Moscovitch 1997, 1998; Moscovitch et al. 2005). MTT started by assuming that within the domain of explicit memory one had to treat episodic and semantic memory separately, an assumption at odds with the standard model, which in most formulations treats these two kinds of memory the same way. MTT argued that the standard model essentially got it right with respect to semantic memory, but was wrong with respect to episodic memory. The normal retrieval of episode memories, we argued, always required the hippocampus. In the absence of this brain system, episode retrieval would be either absent or impoverished.

We suggested that episodes are comprised of various components, including objects, people, actions and the contexts within which these all occurred. The hippocampal system, we argued, represented the spatial context, and in so doing provided a scaffold to which objects, people and actions could be bound. The retrieval of an episode led to the strengthening of the hippocampal representation, through what we initially conceived of as a 'multiplication' of the underlying trace.

The central prediction of MTT

Perhaps the most direct prediction of MTT was that retrieval of a remote memory should activate the hippocampus, something that the standard model, in its initial formulation, denied. The advent of neuroimaging methods made it possible to test this prediction, which was robustly confirmed (Nadel *et al.* 2000; Ryan *et al.* 2001). Activation in the hippocampal system during remote retrievals has now been observed in numerous studies and is no longer debatable.

In the face of these data, the standard model had to evolve, one proposal being that hippocampal activation during remote retrievals reflected the fact that a new 'encoding' event was taking place. Thus, each time an old memory is retrieved from neocortex, it is, according to this view, re-entered into hippocampal circuits, and re-encoded. Exactly why this happens, and what consequences it has, were left unspecified. This omission is important for the following reason: the up-dated standard model supposes that when an individual without hippocampal function retrieves a remote memory, this memory is 'normal, i.e. it is as richly detailed and vivid as any remote memory an intact individual might retrieve. If this is the case, then it becomes difficult to understand what functional consequence the proposed hippocampal 're-encoding' has, since it seems to make no difference to the state of that memory later on.

Reconsolidation

At about this time, the phenomenon of 're-consolidation' re-emerged (e.g. Sara 2000; Nader 2003). It was shown that retrieving an already consolidated memory seemed to return it, at least temporarily, to a state of fragility. Reconsolidation sounds like re-encoding, which itself sounds like the very mechanisms suggested by multiple trace theory, and also by work several decades ago that had been largely ignored by the reigning consolidation paradigm (cf. Lewis 1979).

The paradigm sinks under its own weight

When one asks the simple question, what is 'reconsolidation' for, one comes to see that the entire 'fixed memory trace' paradigm that has guided thinking and research for more than 50 years has perhaps become a barrier to further progress. In my view, reconsolidation reflects the fact that it is important for traces of prior experience to be left open to modification by future events. Such traces are not only subject to passive processes such as decay (forgetting), and the active but indirect process of interference. They are also subject to meaningful transformation as a function of new experience. These transformations allow an organism to incorporate new experiences into existing knowledge structures, changing them in ways that are generally (but not always) adaptive. Recurrent 're-encoding', or 'reconsolidation', and the underlying instability they reveal, are signatures of this transformative capacity of memory systems.

By this view, there is no such thing as a fully consolidated and hence 'fixed' engram. As we suggested some years ago (Nadel and Wexler 1984), it is time to jettison this idea. We now have ample reasons to think that prior 'memories' are altered by subsequent events; perhaps the most prominent, but by no means the only, example lies in the work of Loftus and her colleagues (see also Chapter 55, this volume).

Steps to a new paradigm

If the traces of prior experience are as dynamic as this work implies, then how should we think about memory? Wexler and I suggested that the notion of 'knowledge' could be substituted for the concept of 'memory'. As a function of experience we obtain knowledge, which is represented in various brain systems. What we call a 'memory' is constructed from this knowledge as required. The hippocampal system, serving as a contextual binding device, plays a critical role in this construction process. It deals with a shifting database, creating memories that reflect not only some initial event, but also various experience-induced alterations in the knowledge bases that encode the elements of this event. By this analysis, there is one part of the system whose contents could remain relatively unchanged over time—the representation of context itself. When the representation of the context changes sufficiently, it would become the scaffold for an entirely different episode. Work on the mechanics of 're-mapping' within the domain of hippocampal 'place cell' system should shed some light on these critical processes (e.g. Moita *et al.* 2004).

Concluding comments

Few memory researchers, in private, defend the fixed memory trace paradigm. They know that memory is far more dynamic than our models have typically allowed. If we are to make further progress in understanding what goes on when we mentally re-visit the past, we must begin to build these dynamics into our models. I would argue that the surest way to do this is to step outside the reigning paradigm. This may strike some as a frightening prospect— abandoning the known in favor of the unknown is always a bit scary. However, we should not let fear of the unknown bind us to a way of thinking that increasingly appears to have reached a dead end. The way forward involves facing up to the complexity of memory and the processes involving the acquisition and constant transformation of knowledge as a function of experience. With the development of better methods to monitor these transformations will come a clearer understanding of how we 'store', 'consolidate' and 'retrieve' memories.

Acknowledgments

This thought piece benefited from years of collaboration with Morris Moscovitch and Lee Ryan, numerous discussions with Oliver Hardt, and papers written over the past 5–10 years by various authors. Space constraints do not permit referencing most of these works, many of which are consistent with the general thrust of what I am saying here. Due credit will, I hope, be attributed when these thoughts are translated into a more extensive paper in the not-too-distant future. I gratefully acknowledge the support of various funding agencies over the past several decades, including the McDonnell Foundation, the Flinn Foundation, the Arizona Alzheimer's Research Consortium and NINDS.

32

Integrative comments
Consolidation: From hypothesis to paradigm to concept

Susan J. Sara

The hypothesis

Consolidation started out as a simple hypothesis contending that memory formation takes place gradually over time after initial exposure to new information. The hypothesis was formulated from early clinical observations published by Ribot in the late nineteenth century, indicating that older memories are more resistant to traumatic interference than newly acquired ones. The obvious prediction of the hypothesis is that there should be a temporal gradient of efficacy of an amnestic event. This led to more careful analyses of clinical amnesias as well as the development of animal models of 'experimental amnesia'. From these early studies, the consolidation hypothesis rapidly emerged as a full-blown paradigm dominating memory research for over a century.

Indeed, once a paradigm is well entrenched, Thomas Kuhn has noted, it sets the problems to be solved and dictates experimental protocols aimed at 'bringing nature and theory into closer and closer agreement' (1962, p. 27). In Chapter 30 of this volume, Joseph LeDoux provides us with an overview of the several meanings of the term 'consolidation' as it has evolved over the years. It is implicit in his account that the concept has become inextricably linked to animal models of amnesia. In Chapter 31, Lynn Nadel has a more clinical view showing how the conceptual framework of the consolidation hypothesis was adapted to the evidence that amnesia gradients in humans can extend back in time for weeks, months or even years. In Chapter 29, Alcino Silva provides a view from the 'brave new world of molecular biology', noting that this world has yet to liberate itself from the throes of the 'consolidation dogma'. He laments that a fresh view of the neurobiology of memory compatible with the dynamic nature of the underlying molecular processes has not yet emerged. All three express, to varying degrees, dissatisfaction with the concept of consolidation and the role it has played in memory research for the past century.

From hypothesis to Paradigm

The overwhelming majority of animal experiments aimed at testing the consolidation hypothesis used a rapidly trained task, usually aversive, followed by a 'consolidation blocker'. Donald Hebb's and later John Eccles' assertion that propagating or recurrent impulses of a specific spatiotemporal pattern underlie initial memory made electroconvulsive shock the preferred amnestic treatment, since its impact would disrupt this patterned activity. Other treatments that interrupted normal brain activity such as hypoxia and hypothermia were also widely used to study the consolidation gradient. The efficacy of the treatment was assessed by behaviorally testing the animal, usually a rat, 24 or 48 h later. If the rat fails to avoid the place where it had the shock, then it is assumed that the animal had no memory for the previous aversive experience because the post-training treatment blocked time-dependent consolidation. Protein synthesis inhibitors were added to the plethora of amnestic agents, and they soon revealed two phases of memory consolidation as described by LeDoux in Chapter 30. (Squire and Davis 1982). This was an important step because it paved the way for a more hypothesis-driven neurobiological approach to the study of memory consolidation. The emerging field of molecular and cellular biology was rapidly providing new information about the intricate processes within the cell, governing new protein synthesis and providing tools, such as genetically modified mice, to evaluate their role in memory consolidation (Dudai 2004). Alcino Silva provides us with a lively account of his own personal adventures along this path.

Pitfalls and problems with experimental amnesia

One of the several problems inherent in experimental amnesia lies in the fact that the 'trace' can never be accessed directly. Strictly speaking, it is a hypothetical construct whose very existence is inferred from its retrieval and behavioral expression at the retention test. This was already underlined by William James, who said, 'the only proof of there being retention is that recall actually takes place'. In both animals and humans, memory retrieval and its behavioral expression can be influenced or modulated by many factors present in the immediate testing environment. Thus an investigator is on shaky logical grounds in asserting that a rat that freezes 40 per cent of the time during a test has less memory or a weaker trace than a rat that freezes 60 per cent of the time, no matter how robust the statistics may be. A more detailed analysis can be made for passive avoidance data, where step-through latency is usually taken for the retention index. Very often rats express 'amnestic' behavior as measured by the step through latency (which in most experiments terminates the test), but express excellent memory for the aversive experience in their post-step-through behavior of defecation, pilo-erection, shuttling back and forth between compartments or even freezing, behavior very different from that of a control group having received the amnesic agent but no the unconditioned stimulus (UCS; e.g. Sara *et al.* 1975). This argues for a multiple trace representation (see Chapter 31, this volume) and suggests that the retrieval process requires effective integration of the various attributes of the past experience, perhaps at multiple storage sites, in order to create the 'trace'.

These pitfalls and problems were recognized early on, with many experimenters going to heroic lengths to design experiments controlling for nonmnemonic factors in behavioral expression. Moreover, there were some serious challenges to the interpretations of the behavioral deficits in terms of prevention of trace consolidation, with investigators showing recovery from the amnestic effects of consolidation blockers by drugs (e.g. Sara and Remacle 1977) or reminders presented before retrieval (e.g. Miller and Springer 1973; Sara *et al.* 1975).

Others showed that consolidation blockers could produce amnesia for a well-established memory when it was reactivated, suggesting that memory 'reconsolidates'. This large body of reconsolidation literature benefited from a thorough and thoughtful review as early as 1979 by Donald Lewis. His conclusion at that time was that memory 'fixation' was very rapid—a matter of seconds, and that the extended retrograde amnesia gradient was due to the effect of the treatments on retrieval. Lewis was on the right track with his plea for focus on retrieval to understand memory processes, as I will argue later, but he may have been wrong about 'fixation' time. Rapid developments in molecular and cellular biology soon showed that intracellular cascades required for long-term plasticity underlying memory take place over hours.

Missed opportunities

In 1997, we found that an injection of an N-methyl-D-aspartate (NMDA) receptor antagonist after a successful daily trial on a radial maze made the rat amnestic when tested the next day. Lewis' idea of active memory being labile (Lewis 1979) furnished a conceptual framework for interpretation of these unexpected results. We designed a complete experiment and showed that a well-consolidated spatial memory, acquired over many days, reactivated by a single errorless trial, was dependent upon intact NMDA receptors to maintain stability (Przybyskawski and Sara 1997). We went on to investigate the role of beta-adrenergic receptors in this putative 'reconsolidation' process and showed that post-reactivation administration of the beta-adrenergic blocker propranolol induced amnesia in both an appetitive and an aversive task (Przybyskawski *et al.* 1999). So the phenomenon was neither drug nor task dependent.

Our new data merely confirmed and extended results obtained by many others nearly three decades earlier. Lewis (1979) had proposed, in light of the large amount of data already available in the 1970s, to replace the consolidation paradigm by a conceptual framework of *active* and *inactive* memory in *labile* and *stabile* states. Nevertheless, the data and Lewis' review were largely ignored. In light of this, I wrote an update review, arguing for a paradigm change, as its title suggests: Retrieval and reconsolidation: toward a neurobiology of remembering'. The fate of this review has been only a little better than that of Lewis'; oft-cited, ill-read, with no real impact on the prevailing paradigm. There has, nevertheless, been a surge of renewed interest in 're-consolidation' initiated by elegant experiments from the LeDoux laboratory (Chapter 30, this volume).

Unfortunately, in these and the many experiments inspired by this work, the preferred experimental approach remains that of amnesia. It is becoming increasingly evident as the literature grows that we are still stuck with the same old questions. Does the amnestic agent block consolidation, or now re-consolidation, or impair retrieval? Is the memory deficit permanent or is there spontaneous recovery or the possibility of recovering the memory by further treatments or reminders? It is evident that the same logical objection voiced by Weiskrantz (1966) years ago persists with this new 'reconsolidation' literature. He warned that experimental amnesia studies are fatally flawed from the outset, since it is not possible to prove the null hypothesis, i.e. the absence of a memory trace.

Alcino Silva's chapter poignantly recounts another missed opportunity, by asserting that the 'highly dynamic and probabilistic nature' of the cellular and molecular processes underlying memory precludes a rigid, static conception of a consolidated memory trace. This emerging field should have given rise to new theories of memory formation compatible with the new biology. However, the consolidation paradigm was so deeply entrenched in the thinking of many investigators that the experiments continued to be designed to compel nature to conform to theory. Amnesia continues to be the preferred experimental approach, albeit with targeted knock-outs and sophisticated pharmacological tools. Moreover, behavioral analysis has been further impoverished with the almost universal adoption of the conditioned fear protocol. The research is now devoted to applying the latest conceptual and technological updates in our knowledge in neurobiology to the experimental examination of memory consolidation within the existing paradigm. The paradigm has, indeed, become an 'object for further articulation and specification under new or more stringent conditions' in true Kuhnian fashion (Kuhn 1962, p 23).

A third window of opportunity for disengaging the consolidation hypothesis from experimental amnesia was opened when clinical investigators realized that amnesia gradients could last for weeks, months or even years. However, then 'systems consolidation' was invented to accommodate the data (Squire *et al.* 1984). This slow consolidation hypothesis during which the memory gradually becomes independent of the hippocampus was derived from human clinical studies, but supporting evidence has come from animal studies. Lesions to the hippocampus induce amnesia for recent but not remote memories. Lynn Nadel (and see Chapter 31, this volume) later pointed to the inadequacies of the concept of systems consolidation to account for these extended amnesia gradients, proposing in its place the multiple trace theory, as he outlines in his chapter.

A new look at systems consolidation

If 'systems consolidation' refers to neuronal activity occurring off-line, in regions not necessarily engaged in the early stages of memory formation, then there are very interesting new lines of research in full blossom. Gygory Buszaki (1989) proposed a two-stage model of memory consolidation that fit well with the clinical picture of disengagement of the hippocampus over time. Briefly, the idea is that the hippocampus is engaged during acquisition; later off-line, high frequency bursts of activity, known as ripples, occur during slow wave sleep (SWS). This activity would reinforce hippocampal–cortical networks underlying the memory. Development of neuronal ensemble recording techniques has made it possible to test this notion. Recording activity from a whole population of neighboring neurons suggested that cells that fire together during exploratory behavior are reactivated and tend to fire together during subsequent SWS (McNaughton 1998). It remains to be demonstrated that this 'replay' or reactivation is indeed related to memory. Interestingly, we have recently found that noradrenergic neurons of the locus coeruleus, usually quiescent during sleep, are transiently activated during a limited time window during SWS in rats after learning. Networks engaged in replay during this time would be likely to be reinforced through facilitation of synaptic plasticity by noradrenaline (Yeshenko and Sara 2007). The off-line delayed activation of the noradrenergic system after learning fits with our earlier studies showing a nonlinear amnesia function obtained when rats were treated with a beta-adrenergic antagonist after learning or after memory reactivation (Roullet and Sara 1998).

A wide range of imaging techniques, noninvasive in human subjects or *ex vivo* in animals are contributing to a new look at the notion of systems consolidation. The division between cellular and systems consolidation might break down with these new approaches. The group of Robert Jaffard were early pioneers in using ex vivo methods in rodents to illustrate spatiotemporal dynamics of long term-memory consolidation (Bontempi et al. 1996). Alcino Silva's group has delineated the temporal dynamics of specific molecular and cellular mechanisms involved in consolidation of remote memories in specific cortical regions (Wiltgen et al. 2004).

From paradigm to concept

The multiple trace theory puts the focus on the retrieval aspect of memory, which is an essential step in breaking out of the consolidation paradigm. Norman Spear was an early champion of the notion that memory consolidation could not be considered independently of retrieval (e.g. Spear 1973). Along with Endel Tulving, they have promoted the idea that retrieval occurs as a result of integration of incoming change in environmental information with the 'memory network' driven by that information (Tulving and Thomson 1973). It follows from this that retrieval will lead to the formation of new memories made upon the background of a prior experience. It is thus inconceivable that new memory can be acquired independently of retrieval of past experience, in that it is memory of the past which organizes and provides meaning to the present. Embracing such a view would serve to neutralize much of the consolidation/reconsolidation polemics discussed above.

Where does this leave consolidation as a concept in the science of memory? I, for one, am not ready to throw the baby out with the bath water. Consolidation is no longer a hypothesis; no student of memory would deny that information processing takes place off-line after a learning experience and that the processes are complex, and occur at the molecular, cellular, synaptic and network levels in the brain. There is enough evidence now so that consolidation has earned its status of concept in memory research. However, it is absolutely essential that memory research and theorizing no longer depend so heavily on amnestic patients and animal models of amnesia. Continuing advances in imaging from molecular to systems level can provide a spatiotemporal map of brain activity during learning, off-line consolidation and retrieval, to provide a major complement to clinical and experimental amnesia studies. Then, just as the demarcation of cellular and systems consolidation is breaking down, we should see a breakdown of the delineation between consolidation, retrieval and reconsolidation. Each time a memory is retrieved, it is integrated into ongoing perceptual and emotional experiences and becomes part of a new memory. Keeping this in mind, the concept of consolidation still remains an essential part of the whole memory process. Current research is reinforcing the view that consolidation is dynamic ongoing process that allows a living organism to continually update information to organize adaptive behavior.

Acknowledgments

I thank Alcino Silva, Lynn Nadel and Joe LeDoux for intensive discussion in preparation for the writing of this chapter. Due to space limits, many important contributors, especially those scores of investigators of the 1960s and 1970s, have not been cited. Donald Lewis' 1979 review should be obligatory reading for any student of memory who wants to know more about earlier controversies and challenges to the consolidation paradigm.

9

Persistence

Persistence is a core concept in the science of memory, but until quite recently has only seldom been explicitly included in the terminology of this discipline. Rather, an alternative term has been commonly used, 'storage', which is a misguided metaphor, of the type quite abundant in the science of memory. Persistence is continual existence, and in the science of memory it refers to an essential attribute of memory, which is the retention over time of the information learned. The similarity of that information to the original event or fact notwithstanding, the main point is that encoding induces a change in knowledge, which persists over time, and is potentially capable of modifying behavior when the relevant knowledge is retrieved. Since the brain is a biological construct, and biological material is characterized by a massive turnover of its components, persistence of memory invokes a classic philosophical problem, which is dubbed in metaphysics as 'The Ship of Theseus'. The ship of the mythical Greek hero was placed on display in Athens and, with time, parts of it were replaced, one by one, till none of the original remained. Is this still the same ship? The biological stuff that encodes memory is likely to suffer the same fate as the mythical ship, and some evidence indicates that this may occur on a time scale much shorter than the life span of some memory items—so how come the information still persists over time? It is left for the science of memory to unveil how this happens.

Y.D.

33

Persistence: Necessary, but not sufficient

Howard Eichenbaum

Persistence is an essential and defining feature of memory. Most simply stated, if a change in neural representation or behavioral expression does not persist, we do not call it memory. We instead would call it merely a 'response' to the stimulus that evoked neural activity or behavior. At the same time, persistence is not sufficient for a neural or behavioral memory to be retrieved or revealed. There are many instances, a few examples of which will be described below, where an established memory fails to be revealed, yet its existence can subsequently be demonstrated by extended efforts. In these instances, we are compelled to conclude that the memory persisted but, for reasons discussed below, could not be accessed. My goal here is to characterize persistence both by what it does for memory and by what it does not do for our ability to remember.

Persistence is a necessary feature of memory

To say that persistence is a necessary feature of memory is an understatement. Persistence is a general and defining property of any kind of 'memory'; it is almost a synonym for memory. Persistence is not special to neural systems or to learning and memory. It can be defined as any lasting modification of structure or process consequent to experience, and this definition is applicable in a broad variety of biological systems, e.g. injury and immunity, and in nonbiological systems, e.g. plastic materials, and many more situations. As applied to memory, *persistence is the temporal extension of a modification in neural representation or behavior resulting from experience.*

Within this definition, the persistence of a neural representation refers to a lasting firing pattern of neurons or a lasting change in the pattern or magnitude of response to a specific stimulus or associated with a specific behavior. The persistence of behavior refers to lasting behaviors or a change in behavioral responses to a stimulus or complex aspects (e.g. sequencing) of behavioral patterns. A central operational problem in measuring persistence is that neural representations are not readily observed, but this does not mean they do not persist. Some have challenged the usefulness of the concept of persistence for memory representations that are not, or cannot, be observed in behavior (see Chapters 34 and 35, this volume). In my view, this criticism misses a central aspect of memory as an internal representation that is only, and only sometimes, expressed in overt behavior.

The persistence feature of memory is used operationally to define an effect upon memory in many experimental paradigms. Consider, for example, the widely used delayed nonmatch to sample task. In this test, initially a sample stimulus is presented, followed by a blank delay period during which the sample is not present. Then the subject must select a new stimulus in preference to the sample in a choice test, thereby demonstrating memory for the sample. The strength and persistence of memory is measured by varying the delay period, and measuring performance across longer delays compared with that after a very brief delay. This task is commonly used to assess the effects of selective brain lesions, drugs, molecular genetic manipulations or other interventions on memory. Typically normal subjects exhibit a decline in choice test performance as the delay is lengthened, and this decline is considered a reflection of the normal rate of forgetting. When the intervention results in a more rapid decline than observed in normal animals, it is generally concluded that the intervention interferes with memory by decreasing its persistence. In contrast, any effect that is not dependent on the delay, i.e. that is observed at the briefest delay and is equivalent across delays, is considered to reflect interference with perception, motivation or cognition, as opposed to memory. Similarly 'delay-dependent' changes in performance are used to define a selective effect on memory in a diverse array of discrimination, maze learning and other kinds of tasks.

Persistence is also used to define memory in paradigms that observe changes in neural activity that may underlie memory. For example, persistence is a defining feature of the changes in responsiveness observed at the synaptic and cellular level resulting from strong activation in long-term potentiation (LTP) and long-term depression (LTD). A change in field potential or cellular responsiveness that is persistent over many minutes or hours is identified as the putative trace of a memory mechanism. Conversely, changes that do not last are not considered candidates for a memory mechanism. In studies that examine single neuron activity patterns in behaving animals, persistent activity in the absence of a prior activating stimulus (e.g. during the delay period in a delayed nonmatch to sample task) and suppression or enhancement of responses to stimulus repetition (e.g. during the choice phase of that task) are taken as reflecting a neural representation that persists in memory.

Persistence also distinguishes theoretically distinct forms of memory. The duration of susceptibility to drugs or brain damage is used to distinguish effects on distinct stages of memory, including immediate memory, short-term memory, consolidation and long-term memory.

Persistence, combined with specificity of a neural representation or behavioral response, is sufficient to support some forms of memory. As far back as Aristotle (350 BC), it has been recognized that a persisting representation of a previous stimulus or event may support a template matching process that underlies the sense of familiarity even in the absence of recollective experience. Persistence may also support implicit memory, including forms of procedural and emotional memory (see below).

Mere persistence is not sufficient for remembering

There are (at least) two fundamental features of memory, only one of which is persistence. William James (1890) wrote, 'Memory being thus altogether conditioned on brain paths, its excellence in a given individual will depend partly on the *number* and partly on the *persistence* of these paths' (p. 659, *italics added*). James viewed the persistence of memory as innately determined, albeit variable with age and across individuals, and he concluded that persistence was not modifiable by experience or training. He emphasized the number of brain paths as a critical determinant of memory. 'In mental terms, the more other facts a fact is associated with in the mind, the better possession of it our memory retains'. James argued that the 'secret of a good memory' is forming diverse and multiple associations with every fact we care to retain. Modern research has confirmed that our ability to remember depends in part on a cellular persistence mechanism and in part on the size and organization of the network of persistent associations in which a memory resides.

Therefore, persistence is not a sufficient condition for memory. Modern cognitive neuroscience has clarified that different types of memory depend as much on the nature of their expression and associative structure as they do on persistence *per se*. Declarative memory is defined by retrieval conditions and relies on a rich network of associations among memories. Procedural learning is defined by overt behavioral responses and relies on associations between stimuli and actions. Emotional memory is defined by engaging affective responses and relies on associations between stimuli and rewards or punishments. We might say that modern cognitive neuroscience has elaborated James' concept of 'number' of paths, and specified that memory is dependent on the elaborateness of the associational network and on the structure of representations within each memory system (Eichenbaum and Cohen 2001).

There are a few examples worth mentioning to drive the point home that a memory can be persistent even if it is not revealed in behavior. For example, in the phenomenon of experimental extinction, animals once trained to produce a conditioned response can lose the response if presented repeatedly with the conditioning stimulus alone (Pavlov 1927). It appears that the original learning has not persisted because the conditioned response has ceased to occur. However, in many situations, brief retraining (or merely time passing) can result in reappearance of the conditioned response. So, had the original trace lost its persistence? No, some sort of internal representation no doubt persisted. However, as has been shown in conditioning, extinction does not eliminate the memory of the initial learning. It suppresses or overwrites the persisting trace with additional learning, such that the former conditioning stimulus now predicts the absence of the former reinforcer. The absence of a behavioral response is insufficient to support the conclusion that persistence of the initial internal trace is lost. Rather, the persistence of the existing trace can be demonstrated by its indirect effects on new learning or spontaneous recovery of the response.

Another example comes from a former controversy about the nature of amnesia. Early studies on the amnesic patient H.M. indicated that his memory for pictures (as well as many other things) faded abnormally rapidly (Scoville and Milner 1957), i.e. his memories apparently failed to persist. Yet, Warrington and Weiskrantz (1968) demonstrated that H.M.'s memory for pictures could be revealed in his ability to identify partial drawings of common objects based on prior exposure to successively more complete fragmented drawings. They argued that H.M.'s memory did in fact persist, but was not accessible by normal retrieval through conscious recall. We now understand that the difference in success in retrieving memories through recall or naming of partial pictures reflects the impairment of a conscious recall system contrasted with intact performance of a perceptual recognition system (Tulving and Schacter 1990). The point is that persistence within one system was not sufficient for remembering. We had to consider the nature of different kinds of memory traces and the systems that support them.

Consider also an occasion when you met someone who was very familiar but you could not recall who they are or why you knew them. Probably a conversation ensued in which some key clue was offered and suddenly you recalled many details about the person. This situation reflects the persistence of a perceptual trace that is sufficient to support the sense of familiarity and, at the same time, the initial failure of access to a separate associative network that contains many factual and episodic details. Remembering depends on both the persistence of traces and the number of access routes to the details, just as James described it.

Finally, persistence as an important concept in memory research tends to divide along disciplinary boundaries. Molecular and cellular biologists focus on the mechanism of persistence over relatively short periods (Dudai 2002b), whereas much of cognitive neuroscience is focused on the expression of memory and its underlying associative structure. I suspect the importance of persistence as a central concept will rely on a merging of these disparate foci.

34

Persistence: Discrepancies between behaviors and brains

Richard F. Thompson

Persistence is an essential property of memory. Indeed if memories did not persist at all, there would be no memories. Persistence as a property of memory can be operationally defined in terms of measurements. In this sense, it is not a concept but merely a measured property that might represent the concept in the practical world. However, complications arise in such measurements. To take an example at random, consider the Morris water maze, which is a paradigm widely used to quantify spatial learning and memory in rodents. Under some conditions, animals with altered nervous systems (e.g. knock-out or transgenic mice, animals that sustained targeted brain lesions) show little improvement in performance over training (no memory persistence), but in later probe trials show preference for the hidden platform quadrant (memory persistence), and vice versa (e.g. Goodlett *et al.* 1992; Nolan *et al.* 2003).

Habituation provides a simple example of the problem of measurement of the persistence of memory. When measuring, for example, limb flexion in a preparation with a severed spinal cord ('spinal preparation'), after a sufficient number of stimulus trials the behavioral response is completely absent (habituated), yet intracellular recording from the relevant spinal motor neurons shows that the stimulus still evokes excitatory postsynaptic potentials (EPSPs) but they are now below spike (or neural 'firing') threshold (Spencer *et al.* 1966). By one measure habituation is complete (persistence), but by another measure it is not (no persistence). Even at the behavioral level, there are complications. Habituated responses recover fully over time. Habituation does not persist. Yet if repeated habituation and recovery sessions are given, habituation occurs successively more rapidly—some underlying neural process has persisted, otherwise there would be no savings (Thompson and Spencer 1966).

Experimental extinction provides a clear example. In classical conditioning, extinction training involves presenting the conditioned stimulus (CS) in the absence of the unconditional stimulus (US) until the behavioral conditional response (CR) no longer occurs. By this behavioral measure, the memory does not persist—it no longer exists. However, as Pavlov showed so many years ago, and many have verified in many paradigms and protocols afterwards, spontaneous recovery and very rapid reacquisition ('saving') both indicate that the memory for the conditioned response does still exist (Pavlov 1927; Scavio and Thompson 1979).

In my view, the most important achievement in the past many years in the study of memory is the realization that there are several different forms or types of memory that engage different brain systems. We contributed to this with our discovery that the cerebellum is the essential structure for acquisition and initial memory for aversive delay classical conditioning of discrete reflexive responses (e.g. eye-blink, limb flexion, etc.). Indeed, evidence strongly supports the view that the memory traces for eye-blink conditioning is formed and stored in the interpositus nucleus of the cerebellum, that the mechanism involves the growth of new excitatory synaptic terminals, and that the cerebellar cortex facilitates learning and provides adaptive timing of the response (see Christian and Thompson 2003).

The rapid relearning of CRs must mean that some trace of the memory exists in the brain but it has been difficult to find. There is some preliminary evidence for persistence of neuronal storage for eye-blink conditioning in the cerebellum following extinction training. Gould and Steinmetz (1996) recorded neuronal activity in both the cerebellar interpositus nucleus and in the cerebellar cortex (lobule HVI) over the course of extinction training. Neuronal unit activity recorded from the interpositus nucleus extinguished in exact correspondence with the behavioral eye-blink conditioned response. However, learning-induced changes in neuronal activity of Purkinje neurons in cerebellar cortex persisted throughout extinction and were present when the behavior CR was completely extinguished. This does not necessarily mean, of course, that no neuronal trace persisted in the interpositus, only that it was not detected by measurement of action potentials. Subthreshold synaptic potentials could still of course exist.

In the absence of extinction training, CRs exist for long periods of time with little or no forgetting. Thus, the memory for eye-blink conditioning persists without any decrement at all for a period of 1 month and with some decrement for more than 6 months, a long period in the life of a rabbit (Coffin and Woodruff-Pak 1993; Christian and Thompson 2005).

Interestingly, in the trace conditioning procedure where a period of no stimulation intervenes between CS offset and US onset, the hippocampus is also necessary for acquisition and initial retention but the hippocampus, at least, is not necessary for long-term (1 month) retention. The behavioral trace

CR itself is retained almost perfectly but the essential brain systems change (Kim *et al.* 1995). Studies with humans by Clark and Squire (e.g. 1998) support the conclusion that trace eye-blink conditioning is an elementary example of declarative memory. The time-limited dependence on the hippocampus seems true of declarative memory in general. In terms of measurement of memory, recordings from the hippocampus show no sign of persistence but the behavior does. Hence memory-related brain changes that seem not to persist, do persist, but in a different version and location.

It is clear that declarative memories may be malleable, as shown in the work of Loftus and others with humans (see Chapter 55, this volume) and in the studies of 'reconsolidation' in the animal literature (see Chapter 32, this volume). Perhaps one reason for this, in hippocampal-dependent memories, is the 'transfer' of memory from the hippocampus to other structures, that may be accompanied by alterations in the manifestation of persistence and hence possibly provides an opportunity for alterations in the original information. In any event, for procedural tasks (e.g. delay conditioning), the memories and their brain substrates remain unchanged and relatively permanent, whereas in declarative tasks the brain substrates appear to change over time and the memories are perhaps more subject to change.

35

Integrative comments
Persistence: In search of
molecular persistence

John E. Lisman

In their accompanying contributions in this volume, Eichenbaum and Thompson nicely illustrate a difficult aspect of memory investigation: using behavioral methods it is not possible to determine whether a memory is persistent. Since the successful recall of a memory requires both specific recall processes and the persistence of the memory to be recalled, failure to retrieve can always be attributed to failure of the retrieval process. One might argue that control experiments with other memories could verify the intactness of the retrieval system. Unfortunately, there would remain the possibility that retrieval failure was specific to particular memories. Indeed, Eichenbaum's citation of James nicely illustrates how retrieval depends on the number of associations with the item to be recalled. If these associations become too sparse, the memory, though there, will not be retrievable. We can conclude that behavior is not a good method for studying persistence.

However, why should we restrict ourselves to behavioral assays? In answering this question, let us consider another, artificial memory system. Over centuries humans have stored their memories in books by making marks on paper. One can study the persistence of this mechanism behaviorally by asking a student to retrieve information from a book. If the student fails, it could be because the persistence mechanism has failed or it could be because the student cannot find the index or does not know the language. The reason for the student's failure can be simply assessed: if one opens the book and the ink has completely faded, one can verify that what has failed is the persistence mechanism itself. Similarly, the persistence of brain memories will become possible to measure once we know its mechanisms.

Correlation versus causality

As emphasized by Thompson (Chapter 34, this volume), one of the major accomplishments of memory research has been the demonstration of different memory processes and stores. However, this research has not yet identified the mechanism of persistence for any type of memory. In the case of working memory, it has been suggested that what persists is the firing of neurons within an assembly (Fuster 1997). There is now a substantial body of experimental work showing that such firing of neurons occurs during working memory tasks. Such correlation is not, however, sufficient to demonstrate causality. What is needed are precise methods to interfere with this firing in a defined network. If the hypothesis is correct, behavioral access to the memory will cease at the moment the activity is stopped. The recent development of new methodologies suggests how such critical experiments might be done. Artificial ion channels that rapidly hyperpolarize neurons when illuminated have been developed (Banghart *et al.* 2004). It would be impressive if the cessation of firing caused by activation of such channels would abolish the persistence of the working memory, as measured behaviorally.

However, even here there is unexpected complexity. Suppose that when one turns the light off, the depolarization recovers and the firing starts again? One would have to conclude that persistent firing resulted from some other mechanism. In this case, we would conclude that persistent firing is not actually the mechanism of persistence, but rather an 'expression mechanism' of some other mechanism actually responsible for persistence. This example illustrates an important point: to demonstrate that one has interfered with the persistence mechanism itself, one must show that interfering with the putative persistence mechanism produces an *irreversible* loss of a preceding memory item.

These issues relate directly to some surprising findings regarding the mechanism of working memory. Until recently it was thought that the persistent firing during a working memory task was most likely to be due to synaptic reverberation in a recurrent circuit (Hebbian reverberation) (Wang 2001). According to this idea, firing is the essential mechanism of persistence: the firing of neurons at one moment in time triggers, through recurrent connections among cells of the neuronal assembly, the firing at subsequent moments. Because there are now cases where groups of cells in a network are highly innervated by recurrent connections, it is widely thought that Hebbian reverberation is the persistence mechanism of working memory. Recent work, however, suggests an alternative. This work shows that neurons in the entorhinal cortex have a mechanism for producing persistent firing that is intrinsic to individual neurons and hence does not depend on recurrent synaptic input to the neuron (Egorov *et al.* 2002). Strong transient input to these cells (such as occurs when a memory is introduced) produces a persistent afterdepolarization that then triggers persistent firing. If the cell is briefly hyperpolarized by current injection, firing will stop. However, when the current injection is terminated, the afterdepolarization will return and trigger new firing. Thus, interfering with firing does not produce an irreversible disruption of this form of working memory. It can be concluded that firing itself is not the mechanism of persistence, but rather an expression of the processes that produce depolarization. What then is the mechanism of persistence? This remains to be determined. It appears to be some biochemical change in the channels that produce the after depolarization.

Long-term memory

In the study of long-term forms of memory, efforts have focused on synaptic modifications as a likely candidate. These can be bidirectional. Thus synaptic connections are strengthened by long-term potentiation (LTP) and weakened by long-term depression (LTD). According to this view, we would expect to find the persistence mechanism at the synapse itself. The synapse might change through modulatory mechanisms such as enhancement of release of neurotransmitter or the enhancement of the postsynaptic channels that are sensitive to the neurotransmitter. Alternatively, structural mechanism might change the size of the synapse or add or delete synaptic contacts altogether.

There is now substantial evidence for all the types of synaptic changes described above. Moreover at synapses in area CA1 of the hippocampus (the most studied model), all these changes can be inhibited by blockers of the *N*-methyl-D-aspartate (NMDA) glutamate receptor channel. These blockers also inhibit memory, as measured behaviorally (Morris 2003). However, what does this tell us about the mechanism of persistence? How do we know whether these changes are actually the mechanism of persistence or simply the expression of a deeper mechanism?

One possibility is that the enzyme calcium/calmodulin protein kinase type II (CaMKII, an enzyme that modifies proteins by adding phosphoryl groups and is regulated by calcium) is responsible for persistence. We know that blocking this enzyme, like blocking NMDA channels, interferes with both the modulatory and structural changes associated with LTP (Lisman *et al.* 2002). Moreover, artificial introduction of active CaMKII can enhance synaptic transmission. Furthermore, memory processes, as measured behaviorally, are inhibited. Importantly, changes in the phosphorylation state of CaMKII and the synapse content of CaMKII persist long after induction, making these into candidate mechanisms for what underlies LTP. Finally, theoretical calculations indicate that the autophosphorylation processes of CaMKII (i.e. processes in which the CaMKII phosphorylates CaMKII) could make it a stable information storage device capable of holding information for up to many years (Miller *et al.* 2005). However, the role of persistent CaMKII activity in the persistence of LTP remains unproven. As discussed in Section 7 on working memory, the most critical experiment for establishing a role in persistence is to interfere transiently with a molecule and show that the memory (or at least LTP, which is assumed to model some facets of it) goes away irreversibly. Experiments of this kind are needed to evaluate the role of CaMKII in the persistence process of long-term memory.

Molecular basis of persistence

Although specific hypotheses regarding molecules that subserve memory have been proposed, it is often argued that there is no need for memory molecules when it comes to the long-term memory and its encoding by structural changes. Many believe that while particular enzymes, such as CaMKII, may be responsible for persistence during early stages of memory, eventually memory becomes encoded by growth processes that enlarge the synapse or allow altogether new synaptic connections to form. It is then argued that such growth processes are themselves stable and that no molecular mechanism need be sought. However, anyone who has watched neurons in culture will have seen just how unstable neuronal and synaptic structure can be. It therefore follows that there must be special processes that underlie stable structures and these must be explainable in molecular terms. In summary, I argue that there must be memory molecules that have a special ability for stable information storage.

What is arguable is the time constant of stability. At one extreme, one could argue that the molecule itself must store information stably for a human lifetime. Alternatively, one might suppose that a network 'attractor' state could refresh memories, perhaps during sleep (Wittenberg and Tsien 2002). In this case, the stability of the molecular memory need only be on the same order as the time between reactivations of the attractor.

Concluding remarks

My view is that once memory molecules responsible for persistence are identified, the investigation of persistence can be put on a solid footing. It will be possible to separate persistence from retrieval processes by direct biochemical tests. In Alzheimer's disease, it remains unclear whether memory failure is due to problems with retrieval, encoding or persistence mechanisms. Once persistence mechanisms are known, it will become possible to determine whether deficits in persistence contribute to this disease.

10

Retrieval

Retrieval refers to accessing stored information. The learning and memory process can be conceptualized in three overlapping stages of encoding (also called acquisition, or learning), storage (retention, or persistence over time) and retrieval (access to, reactivation of or reconstruction of internal traces). On any occasion when accurate remembering occurs, all three stages in the learning and memory process must be intact, but cases of forgetting can arise because of problems at any stage or combination of stages. At least some (and perhaps many) cases of forgetting can be attributed to retrieval failure, when knowledge available in memory cannot be accessed or retrieved with a particular set of cues at a particular time. Retrieval cannot be considered as a separate stage by itself, because whether an event can be retrieved depends on how it was encoded, as well as the cues present in the test environment when retrieval is requested. In neurobiological accounts, retrieval is often considered as reactivation of latent traces that guide behavior; in more cognitive accounts, the retrieval process is considered a constructive (or reconstructive) attempt to recapture past events based on stored information, particular cues and general knowledge. The reconstructive process weaves together these strands of information to form a coherent memory to correspond to events of the past, although the verdicality of retrieval is a frequently studied topic. At least in humans, various states of awareness may be associated with different forms of retrieval.

H.L.R

36

Retrieval: Molecular mechanisms

J. David Sweatt

Molecular mechanisms of memory retrieval are virtually unexplored experimentally, and this makes for quite a challenge in conceptualizing the molecular basis of retrieval. This consideration leads me to think that it is useful to go back to first principles, and integrate them with the few available experimental data directly relevant to molecular mechanisms of retrieval. By bringing together things that we know from first principles with the few things that we know from extant experimental results, hopefully we will be able to synthesize a few conclusions to guide our thinking at this early stage of the game. The following is an attempt at a preliminary synthesis of this sort.

I will organize this brief chapter as follows. First, I will review four basic and greatly simplified sets of observations, that have been already published and which are relevant as a foundation for making some conclusions about how molecular mechanisms of retrieval might operate. Then I will proceed to some deductions, conclusions and speculations about the molecular basis of retrieval and where the future might lie in this untapped area of molecular neurobiology.

Some things we know

First, we should consider the impact of retrieval on the molecular basis of storage *per se*. As Yadin Dudai (2002*a*) has stated 'Retrieval is not merely a passive readout of information, it also is an experience; therefore, once retrieved *the engram is unlikely to remain exactly the same*'. This is a valid and compelling point not only from a cognitive perspective but also from a molecular perspective. The molecular mechanisms of retrieval probably directly impinge upon the molecular basis of storing the engram.

Secondly, we know from molecular studies of retrieval that retrieval triggers large-magnitude molecular changes in the brain (see Zhang *et al.* 2005 for a recent example). The molecular changes triggered by retrieval are of a large enough magnitude, and involve a sufficiently high number of neurons, to be able to be directly measured biochemically. For example, protein kinase phosphorylation, transcription factor activation and altered gene expression have been demonstrated to occur in the CNS when recall is triggered in an animal. These changes are measurable biochemically using various molecular markers, and are manifest as a result of an animal receiving environmental signals that trigger memory retrieval. Thus, in contrast to what might be our pre-conceived notion, i.e. that retrieval in molecular terms is mundane and pedestrian, retrieval itself is a fairly momentous event at the molecular level. Interestingly, many of these *retrieval*-associated molecular changes involve the same molecular pathways that are activated when memory is *consolidated*. Below I will speculate about a possible basis for a need for similar molecular mechanisms to operate in both consolidation and retrieval.

Thirdly, Susan Sara, Joe LeDoux, Karim Nader, Yadin Dudai and others have demonstrated that retrieval triggers a process of *re-consolidation* in many forms of memory (see Alberini 2005 for a recent review). Again in several instances, the molecular processes of reconsolidation are similar to the molecular processes of the original consolidation, although this is not always the case. This observation tells us that the molecular mechanisms subserving the engram are neither constant nor immutable. In many cases, triggering retrieval precipitates a necessity for re-instantiating the molecular mechanisms of storage.

Fourthly, from a biochemical perspective, we are able to make at least one conclusion about the fundamental chemical nature of the information storage process. As has been described in greater detail in a prior publication from my research group (Roberson and Sweatt 1999), we are able to deduce that a certain, specific type of chemical reaction must be involved in memory maintenance. This reaction has the following general form:

$$X + X^* \rightarrow X^* + X^*$$

In this equation, X^* is an activated form of X, capable of catalyzing conversion of another molecule of X to X^*. This formula describes a self-perpetuating chemical reaction, which allows a molecule to pass along its acquired characteristics to a successor molecule. This is the only type of biochemical reaction capable of sustaining itself in the face of protein turnover. It is the essential biochemical reaction of the engram. Known examples of this type of reaction include: epigenetic mechanism such as histone acetylation and DNA methylation; prion autoconversion; and transcription factor autoregulation.[1] Therefore, when we discuss a retrieval mechanism impinging upon a biochemical storage mechanism, we know that the retrieval mechanism must perturb at least one chemical reaction of this form.

Some preliminary conclusions we can make

The four ideas and observations described above allow us to make three general conclusions about molecular mechanisms of retrieval. These conclusions specifically apply in those forms of memory where reconsolidation is necessary.[2] I will state two conclusions first, and then discuss them briefly. I will then proceed to a third, much more speculative conclusion as well.

Conclusion 1. The molecules of retrieval 'touch' the molecules of storage, rendering them labile.

Conclusion 2. Retrieval disrupts a self-perpetuating, robust molecular mechanism of storage. We can conclude this because self-perpetuating reactions are requisite for very long-lasting memory storage, and the fact that retrieval can cause a loss of a pre-existing memory means that the self-perpetuating feedback loop must have been broken.

The first two conclusions may seem mundane at first glance, but in my opinion are quite exciting from a biochemical perspective. Disrupting a self-perpetuating chemical reaction is no small feat. Powerful molecular processes must be at work in order to be able to accomplish the termination of a self-reinforcing chemical reaction. By way of illustration, useful analogies are stopping a nuclear chain reaction, or de-differentiating a differentiated cell.

Moreover, the disruption must be subtle enough to allow the self-perpetuating reaction to re-establish itself, perhaps even in a slightly modified form, as appropriate. I say this because the process of re-consolidation, as described above, implies a re-instantiation of the engram. I speculate that this attribute

---

[1] In brief, these are specific known examples of biochemical reactions that are capable of catalyzing themselves. Thus, prions in the 'scrapie' conformation catalyze the conversion of other 'normal' prion protein molecules into the 'scrapie' conformation. Similarly, an activating transcription factor, once expressed, may bind upstream of its own gene in the genome, stimulating and perpetuating its own expression. Epigenetic modifications such as DNA methylation and histone acetylation/methylation can also regenerate themselves through mechanisms still under investigation. For more details on these processes, see Roberson and Sweatt 1999; Levenson and Sweatt 2005; Sweatt 2003, Chapter 12, this volume.

[2] This statement is not necessarily true for reconsolidation-independent forms of memory, if they exist. However, at present, it is not clear whether, indeed, all forms of memory might require reconsolidation after retrieval.

may be the reason why highly similar but distinct molecular mechanisms are involved in both memory consolidation and reconsolidation. The reconsolidation mechanism must put the storage mechanism back in place in either an identical or similar state.

Conclusion 3. These self-perpetuating mechanisms, which are impacted by retrieval, are likely to be those that we refer to at present as *epigenetic.*

The third speculation, invoking epigenetics as a key mechanism in storage that is impacted by retrieval, is likely to introduce a new term unfamiliar to many neuroscientists. Classically, the term epigenetics refers to a set of heritable and self-perpetuating modifications to DNA, DNA-associated proteins such as histones, or specific cytoplasmic proteins, that carry information in a heritable fashion through cell division (for a review, see Levenson and Sweatt 2005). These modifications frequently take the form of either methylation of DNA or modifications to histones including acetylation, phosphorylation, methylation or ubiquitylation, that result in the expression of specific patterns of gene expression. Epigenetic marking of the genome in metazoans is associated with the developmental processes of determination and differentiation whereby totipotent stem cells are induced to become a terminally differentiated tissue of a specific type, e.g. a neuron or a liver cell. Thus, epigenetic marking of the genome can be considered a persistent form of cellular memory, whereby terminally differentiated cells store information concerning their phenotype.

Why is it necessary at this point to introduce epigenetics specifically? Recent discoveries have indicated that the nervous system has co-opted this ancient form of cellular memory to subserve induction of synaptic plasticity and formation of long-term memory in general. Therefore, we are able to speculate that when the retrieval signal impinges upon the molecular basis of the engram, it impinges specifically upon one of a set of mechanisms that we currently refer to as 'epigenetic'. As epigenetic mechanisms in the adult nervous system become more precisely defined, this may allow us entrée into hypothesizing specific molecular mechanisms that may be necessary for retrieval to impact these specific storage processes.

Summary

Overall then, I conclude that molecular mechanisms involved in retrieval must be able to impinge directly upon the molecular basis of the engram, simultaneously triggering a re-activation of many of the same molecular changes involved in establishing the engram initially. Something very interesting is happening at the molecular level with retrieval—there seems to exist a specific mechanism capable of halting or erasing a chain reaction, but re-starting it in a plastic form that may end up being slightly different. A mechanism that is capable of accomplishing this is quite mysterious to me based on present knowledge. Nevertheless, having hopefully deduced its existence, the mechanism should be amenable to experimental investigation in the near future.

Acknowledgments

I wish to thank Yadin Dudai, Joe LeDoux, Endel Tulving, Roddy Roediger, Kathleen McDermott and Courtney Miller for helpful discussions and suggestions. The work in my laboratory is supported by funding from the National Institutes of Health and the American Health Assistance Foundation.

37

Retrieval: Properties and effects

Norman E. Spear

The concept of retrieval must accommodate memories acquired by animals and nonverbal humans as well as conventional verbal memories of adult humans, if not memories associated with the immune system, magnets and plants. This breadth is accommodated in my favorite definition of retrieval '... to access residue of past experience and (in some cases) convert it into conscious experience (Roediger 2000, p. 57)', when the qualifier, 'in some cases', is applied. An alternative way of stating it is '...the process through which separable attributes of a memory become active with the potential to influence contemporary behavior' (modified from Spear and Riccio 1994, p. 16). Such a general view can accommodate basic features of memory retrieval in both humans and animals.

I find it hard to discuss retrieval without considering its properties, and to me the properties of interest are empirically drawn relationships with other concepts. This leads to a set of assertions about relationships that define retrieval in terms of what it is, does and yields for the process of memory.

Especially in tests with animals, retrieval has been a useful concept primarily for dealing with memories that are 'forgotten' relative to their state when originally acquired, i.e. inaccessible due to conventional sources of forgetting such as a long interval between learning and test, associative interference or invasive sources such as an amnestic treatment (e.g. inhibition of protein synthesis, electroconvulsive shock, concussion, neurochemical malfunction or even brain damage). In such cases, a retrieval process is assumed when environmental or neurochemical circumstances nevertheless provoke behavioral manifestations of the previously inaccessible memory, a result seen in literally hundreds of experiments, including such extreme sources of forgetting as induced by huge hippocampal lesions after memory acquisition (de Hoz *et al.* 2004).

Is the retrieval process for inaccessible memories the same regardless of how the memory became inaccessible? There might seem to be little chance that the fate of a memory's expression would be similar after, say, a long interval or inhibition of protein synthesis, but that is what the evidence suggests so far (e.g. Spear and Riccio 1994; Sara 2000; Millin *et al.* 2001). Although implicit memory was discovered by promoting memory retrieval in humans with antero-grade amnesia due to chronic brain damage (Warrington and Weiskrantz 1970), and tests of state-dependent retention in humans have exploited retrieval deficits by chemical, emotional or environmental events (Eich 1980), it is probably no surprise that a more broad range of forgetting sources has been studied with animals than with humans.

Yet understanding of memory retrieval has in some ways been advanced more fully by tests with human infants carried out by Carolyn Rovee-Collier, Harlene Hayne and others than by any other means (for reviews of the facts of memory retrieval studied with developing humans or animals, see, for example, Spear and Riccio 1994; Rovee-Collier, Hayne and Columbo 2001; Hildreth-Bearce and Rovee-Collier 2006). It is notable that tests of memory retrieval in early development have provided a partial solution to the paradox of infantile amnesia. The paradox is that despite the older child's or adult's failure to remember their infancy, experience during infancy can drastically affect later behavior. The resolution is that infantile amnesia largely reflects memory retrieval failure that can be alleviated by reactivation experiences. The other aspect of the resolution, unrelated to memory retrieval, is that effects of early experience can be mediated by epigenetic mechanisms not usually viewed as involving memory, i.e. gene activation or suppression (e.g. Weaver *et al.* 2004).

Apparent properties of retrieval

Retrieval includes elaboration and reconstruction, but not always

The idea that retrieval is inherently an elaborative and reconstructive process has been developed usefully since discussed by Neisser (1967). It has helped understanding of memory malleability generally and resolution of false memories, and encouraged a profitable link between processes of memory retrieval and perception (Roediger 2000). Yet it seems unlikely that retrieval always requires elaboration and reconstruction. Perception itself is frequently considered to be direct, completely without elaboration and reconstruction (Gibson 1979). Also, in memory retrieval by adult humans, reconstruction or straightforward reproduction can prevail depending on circumstances at the time of memory retrieval (Hasher and Griffin 1978). Although retrieval is subject to selection processes such as inhibition, as incorporated in influential theories of human memory (Anderson 2003; Hasher *et al.* 1999), retrieval simply seems too rapid for substantial elaboration or reconstruction, at least in instances such as recognition by mechanisms of familiarity or fluency, conditioned associations or well-learned motor responses.

Retrieval can be stimulated and promoted by simple re-presentation of events associated (directly or indirectly) with the target memory

For humans, this strategy has been applied with particular success in studies of human infants by Rovee-Collier and her colleagues, mentioned earlier, leading to a variety of insights about the ontogeny of memory processes (Rovee-Collier *et al.* 2001). Re-presentation of neurochemical events associated with the critical episode or those that generally promote cognition has been applied in a similar strategy to stimulate retrieval in animals and simultaneously understand neurobiological control of memory processes (for reviews, see Spear and Riccio 1994; Sara 2000). However straightforward this recipe for retrieval may appear, it is often difficult to accomplish in practice without inadvertently affecting attention, perception or motivation.

Retrieval increases vulnerability of a memory to its modification, including strengthening

Retrieval-induced vulnerability of a memory has become increasingly accepted and employed to analytical advantage in more general considerations of memory, including normal and abnormal memory in animals and humans. Circumstances known to induce retrieval of an inaccessible memory not only alleviate the forgetting, but can modify the memory in accord with contemporary environmental events. They also may change subsequent rate of forgetting the modified memory. Instances of memory retrieval strengthen subsequent retention in proportion to their number (e.g. Hildreth-Bearce and Rovee-Collier 2006).

Neural processes at the time of memory storage, often said to induce 'consolidation', occur in modified form when the memory is retrieved. Neurochemical effects associated with initial memory storage and subsequent retrieval have made this quite clear (Sara 2000; Nader *et al.* 2003). It seems unlikely, however, that neural processes at storage and retrieval are identical. There is at best a weak correlation between rate of initial learning (storage) and efficacy at retention (retrieval). In humans, for example, this is the case in normal as well as brain-damaged people and for tasks engaging automatic processing or implicit memory (Spear and Mueller 1984).

Characteristics of recently reactivated and recently acquired memories

Reactivated and recently acquired memories are similarly susceptible to treatments that induce forgetting or strengthen the memory. There are two related issues. The first is whether the relationship between a recently acquired and reactivated memory depends on how the memory became inaccessible, i.e. the source of forgetting. Although phenomena of memory retrieval have seemed strikingly similar for different sources of forgetting—from an innocuous retention interval to the most invasive amnestic treatment—relative strength of recently acquired and reactivated memories may be an exception: whereas memories forgotten due to retention interval are made stronger by reactivation (e.g. Miller *et al.* 1991), those forgotten due to amnestic treatment seem weaker after reactivation than when recently acquired (Spear and Riccio 1994). The second issue is whether a reactivated memory is represented in brain separately from the previously stored memory or merely replaces the older one. Research will eventually reveal whether a reactivated memory is merely the same as the original (and so, 'reconsolidated'; Nader 2003) or is new and separate from the original memory, and how these two versions differ functionally.

Retrieval of memory for an episode that has become encoded differently from during memory acquisition

Among others, the encoding-specificity theory of Tulving, the leader in ideas and evidence relevant to retrieval, expects retrieval failure if one's encoding of an episode changes between acquisition of an episodic memory and its retrieval. Such a change in encoding is likely when, for instance, one develops from infancy to adulthood. Neisser (1962, pp. 62–69; 1967, pp. 289–290) articulated well the basic feature of this subset of theories of infantile amnesia—that a change in cognitive operations or processes between infancy and adulthood interferes with recall of the events of infancy. This interpretation of infantile amnesia has a significant history: only one of Freud's explanations for infantile amnesia involved repression, whereas he was adamant about allowing that adults may be impaired in recalling events of childhood because their representation of reality is so disparate from that used as an infant. This interpretation also has contemporary significance for understanding the retrieval of memories of infancy in humans (Hayne 2004). Although 'age-specific encoding' often implies a deficiency of infancy, it can in some cases yield more effective learning in infants than older animals (e.g. Spear *et al.* 1994), and laborious tests of the effects of the most obvious encoding change in humans—language development (and accompanying changes in brain)—have yielded surprising insight into its effects on retrieval of specific memories of infancy (Hayne 2004).

Comment

It is unclear whether others agree with the significance—or even the reality—of the above properties. However, not many would deny the importance of the topic. Probably most of us agree with Roediger (2000) that '…retrieval is the key process to understanding human memory (p. 52)', and I would add that it is also a key to understanding the neurobiological basis of memory generally.

38

Retrieval: On its essence and related concepts

John M. Gardiner

In my experimental tradition, retrieval is usually defined in terms of the utilization of information in memory and it is commonly contrasted with encoding. In the *Oxford Handbook of Memory*, for example, Brown and Craik (2000, p. 93) gave the following definitions: '*Encoding*, therefore, refers to the process of acquiring information or placing it into memory, whereas *retrieval* refers to the process of recovering previously encoded information'. Sutherland (1996, p. 400) defined retrieval as: 'The accessing and recovery of information from memory, whether in an organism or in a computer'. Such definitions are widely accepted and have aroused little or no controversy. Thus, the concept of retrieval is firmly rooted in cognitive information processing terms and it depends crucially on stage and storage (or temporal and spatial) metaphors of memory (Roediger 1980) and on the analogy between mind and computer. Retrieval, by this view, essentially entails the coming together of information that is available at the present with information that has been acquired at some time in the past.

The contrast between retrieval and encoding, however, is perhaps drawn too sharply in the way that these concepts are usually defined. Encoding entails retrieval. Retrieval entails encoding. The way new events are encoded, and the way new knowledge is acquired, is heavily dependent on previous experiences, the retrieval of which determines how a new event or new information is perceived and interpreted. Subsequent retrieval of this information from memory in and of itself creates new mental events and experiences—however similar they might be to the original ones—which are in turn encoded. Cognitively, encoding and retrieval involve continually interchangeable, constructive and reconstructive processes; and they involve complex interactions between semantic, episodic and working memory systems and between information processing components within each of those systems.

Operationally, the concept of retrieval implies the use of experimental manipulations that separate hypothetical retrieval processes from processes at the encoding and storage stages of memory that precede them temporally. One common technique is to have such manipulations occur only at the time of retrieval, which, given appropriate comparisons across encoding and storage conditions that have been held constant, allows the attribution of any differences in memory performance to the differences in retrieval conditions. The concept of *retrieval cue* refers to specific information in the environment that affects the retrieval of information from memory, either beneficially, in facilitating access to information that might not otherwise be recovered, or adversely, by decreasing access to information that otherwise might be recovered (Slamecka 1968).

It has long been known that retrieval itself may also have either beneficial or adverse effects on subsequent retrieval. Successful retrieval, and even some unsuccessful retrieval attempts (Gardiner *et al.* 1973), can increase the likelihood of retrieval on a later occasion. Retrieval can also decrease the likelihood of the subsequent retrieval of related information (Brown 1968), a phenomenon that has been called retrieval-induced forgetting and which has been attributed to retrieval inhibition.

Without the concept of retrieval, there is no distinction between the availability and accessibility of information (Tulving and Pearlstone 1966), and so whatever information is available in memory has by the same token to be accessible. Failure in retrieval implies that information may be available in memory but not accessible. Success in retrieval, from episodic if not semantic memory, depends heavily on the partial reinstatement of the information and conditions prevailing at the time of encoding, as stipulated by the principles of encoding specificity and transfer-appropriate processing. Observations of memory are always relative to, and determined by, a given set of retrieval conditions.

It is important to appreciate that the concept of retrieval refers to the environment prevailing at the time memory is engaged, not just to a class of hypothetical information processes. It also refers to the internal as well as to the external environment. The external retrieval environment ranges from the time and general location to much more specific environmental features. The internal retrieval environment includes all organismic activity that might potentially influence, or reflect, retrieval, including physiological, emotional and other conscious mental states. Many aspects of the environment can potentially influence retrieval and hence, in the broadest sense, function as retrieval cues including, for example, the reinstatement at retrieval of drug-induced states that were present at encoding.

Conscious mental states associated with retrieval have been particularly important in my own work and require additional concepts. One additional concept is that of *retrieval volition* (Richardson-Klavehn *et al.* 1996), which refers to a distinction between voluntary and involuntary retrieval strategies with respect to retrieval from episodic memory (as in comparisons between explicit and implicit tests), though retrieval from semantic memory may also be voluntary or involuntary. These retrieval strategies are mindful acts of will. Retrieval volition is related to the concept of *retrieval mode* (Tulving 1983), but retrieval mode refers to the cognitive system as a whole being set for episodic memory and for the processing of incoming stimuli and mental experiences as potential cues for episodic retrieval.

Another additional concept, which might be simply called 'memory awareness', refers to mental states such as *remembering* and *knowing* when defined, respectively, as expressions of autonoetic and noetic consciousness (Tulving 1985). These mental states are primarily consequences, or products, of retrieval, not determinants of it, though the feedback they provide may influence subsequent retrieval attempts. Retrieval is not necessarily accompanied by experiences of remembering or knowing, of course, and it may sometimes give rise to other experiences such as those of perceptual fluency. Memory awareness (and memory unawareness) is independent of retrieval volition, in the sense that these mental states may occur regardless of conscious intention. Memory awareness matters because what counts personally and socially is not the veridicality of whatever information is retrieved from memory but one's belief (or disbelief) in its veridicality, and the uses to which it is then put. The science of memory is also a science of mind and consciousness.

In that respect, the concept of *retrieval monitoring* (Koriat and Goldsmith 1996*b*) is also important for fully understanding the concept of retrieval. Retrieval monitoring refers to the evaluation of whatever information is retrieved with respect to its correspondence with whatever information was sought. Decisions made on the basis of retrieval monitoring include decisions as to whether or not to report the information that has been retrieved and whether or not to continue to attempt retrieval. Retrieval monitoring, like retrieval volition, refers to aspects of the conscious control of the task, whatever that happens to be, but it is concerned with decision processes following retrieval rather than with the conscious strategies prevailing at the time of retrieval.

There are yet other concepts that have been closely associated with the concept of retrieval and which, therefore, further broaden our understanding of it, such as those entailed in the distinction between consciously controlled and automatic processes (Hasher and Zacks 1979). Retrieval can involve a great deal of conscious control, as in the more protracted problem-solving retrieval attempts that sometimes characterize remembering in autobiographical memory. However, even in autobiographical memory retrieval can seem to be automatic and to occur in the absence of any act of will, as when some stimulus unwittingly brings to mind experiences from one's past—sometimes vividly so, as in the famous Proustian example from the taste of a madeleine cake.

Some of these different retrieval concepts have been conflated for theoretical purposes. For example, automatic and consciously controlled retrieval processes have been identified with memorial states of awareness, knowing and remembering, on the assumption that knowing is automatic and remembering is consciously controlled (Jacoby 1991). These assumptions map different kinds of concepts on to each other, so changing their meaning in subtle but significant ways. Such conceptual conflation is not, of course, uncommon in theory development and may even be necessary to it. However, conceptual conflation may impede theoretical progress as well as advance it, not least because of confusion from the use of concepts that may mean rather different things to different theorists. For similar reasons, use of the same terms to refer both to memory awareness and to hypothetical retrieval processes (as has commonly been done with terms such as remembering, recollection, and familiarity) is unfortunate because that too can create conceptual confusion.

Thus, the concept of retrieval, from my perspective, refers to information processing at a particular temporal stage of memory, namely that at which memory is made use of, and to the environment prevailing at that time, which includes the mental environment. The concept of retrieval therefore seems absolutely fundamental to the science of memory. Arguably, it is the key concept, as encoding and storing information in memory are irrelevant if the information is never accessed or used (Roediger 2000). Other concepts that are essential to the broader meaning of the concept of retrieval include those of retrieval cue, retrieval volition, retrieval mode, memory awareness and retrieval monitoring.

39

Integrative comments
Retrieval: Varieties and puzzles

Kathleen B. McDermott

In the Introduction to *Memory, Amnesia, and the Hippocampal System*, Cohen and Eichenbaum (1993) remark that 'Memory is a big word, encompassing a host of different capacities mediated by functionally distinct components or subsystems that collectively produce the performances we call memory' (p. 16). One of the tenets of the present remarks is that the same could be said of retrieval. That retrieval is a big word can be demonstrated by considering a collection of behaviors that could—at least arguably—be classified as demonstrating retrieval. One can retrieve from sensory memory, short-term memory, working memory, semantic memory, episodic memory and procedural memory. Priming is a form of retrieval. Given the broad nature of retrieval, it seems pertinent to step back and consider its definition and the core concepts surrounding retrieval.

What is retrieval?

Retrieval is a concept intuitively familiar but with an elusive definition. It may be helpful to begin by considering a few definitions offered in the literature. Crowder (1976) refers to retrieval as being 'the extraction of information . . . when it is needed' (p. 2); Dudai (2002*a*) refers to the 'actualization of learned information', (p. 221). In his concept chapter in this volume (Chapter 38), Gardiner refers to retrieval as 'the utilization of information in memory'.

Note that these definitions do not invoke the concept of re-experiencing one's past in the vivid way that is the focus of much writing about the concept. This feeling of mental time travel to the past is indeed a part of retrieval, but the specific term applied to this concept is *remembering* (see the chapters on Remembering in Section 11 of this volume). The distinction between these two concepts can be seen in Spear's (Chapter 37, this volume) favorite definition of retrieval, put forth by Roediger (2000): 'to access residue of past experience and (in some cases) convert it into conscious experience' (p. 57).

Rather, the definition of retrieval under consideration here is very broad: the utilization or access of past experience. Retrieval can be manifested by nonhuman animals, by infants and even by the immune system (see Chapter 37 of this volume for discussion), although arguably none of these systems can remember (Tulving 1985). That retrieval has a molecular basis is a fact not much discussed or considered in most of the experimental literature on retrieval, but as Sweatt's intriguing concept chapter (Chapter 36) points out, the field may not be too far away from signs of progress on questions surrounding molecular mechanisms underlying retrieval. I do wonder whether retrieval *experience* in the phenomenological sense will ever be amenable to study at the molecular level; this seems to me to be an important question, as the vivid recollective experience that can accompany retrieval, or remembering, seems to be one of the most fascinating aspects of its character.

Fundamental concepts and related issues

Most introductory chapters on human memory contain discussion of the three phases of memory, often depicted in linear fashion: encoding → storage → retrieval. Hence, retrieval is often defined as the end-point that follows encoding. The separation of these three phases dates back at least to Köhler (1947) and Melton (1963; see Crowder 1976 for discussion). Gardiner makes the very interesting point that a problem with this conceptualization is that this linear view encourages one to lose sight of the fact that any retrieval event is also an encoding event, and any encoding event involves some elements of retrieval. Retrieval is a collection of processes. Some of these processes overlap with those used in encoding, and this point is made clearly in the behavioral, functional neuroimaging and animal literatures (and by all three contributors to this section). That encoding/retrieval interactions can be explored at the molecular level is quite interesting. Although it takes a bit of effort for me to conceptualize an integrated literature that considers retrieval at levels from behavior to molecules, I find the possibility fascinating.

As pointed out by all the concept chapters in this section, a fundamental aspect of retrieval from long-term memory is that the context during a retrieval episode can have a large influence. That retrieval cues are important is a fundamental tenet of such principles as transfer appropriate processing (Morris *et al.* 1977) and the encoding specificity principle (Tulving and Thompson 1973) and was at least mentioned in earlier works, too (e.g. McGeoch 1932). In general, retrieval will benefit to the extent that the processes invoked during the retrieval phase match those invoked during encoding.

Consideration of the intertwining of encoding and retrieval leads quite naturally to a consideration of *reconsolidation*. Briefly, the idea is that because every retrieval event is also an encoding event, a new phase of consolidation can follow retrieval (see Section 8 on consolidation in this volume). Further, the idea of reconsolidation is that the recently retrieved memory can become temporarily labile once retrieval has taken place (Nader *et al.* 2000). This finding has links to the literature within experimental psychology on reconstructive memory (e.g. Bartlett 1932; Loftus and Palmer 1974).

Despite difficulties disentangling encoding and retrieval, it is nonetheless possible (and quite profitable) to attempt to hold two phases of the learning and memory process constant and manipulate only features of the third phase. Hence, an examination of retrieval factors typically involves holding encoding and storage constant and examining the influence of retrieval environment. One implication, though, of the intermingling of encoding and retrieval is that encoding and retrieval interact; hence, the most complete understanding of memory will come only after one can observe and understand the interactions.

Note that the focus here (and in the concept chapters) tends to be on the relationship between retrieval and encoding. This is, at least, the focus of psychological experimentation, as encoding and retrieval are the only two stages amenable to much psychological control (and indeed retrieval is the only stage in which observable behavior is often possible). Storage is a phase that seems best suited to studies at the molecular level (or at least quite difficult to study within the tradition of experimental psychology).

In addition to the fundamental distinction between retrieval and remembering, an additional critical distinction is between availability and accessibility (Tulving and Pearlstone 1966). Information available in the system has been encoded and stored and could, in theory, be retrieved, whereas accessible information is that which is indeed retrieved at a given point in time. Within the animal learning literature, this distinction has strong ties to the concept of spontaneous recovery after extinction, whereby information that at once may seem 'lost' (or not accessible) is at a later time manifested; hence, it was available all along, but not accessible at a prior time (see Chapter 37).

An interesting point of consideration is whether humans need to go into 'retrieval mode' in order to remember episodes from the past. The idea here, forwarded largely by Tulving, is that one needs consciously to turn one's attention towards the past in order to retrieve (Tulving 1983). My intuition is that retrieval mode is not, in fact, necessary, as we all have the experience of having a full-blown retrieval episode occurring seemingly out of nowhere. Tulving's solution to this dilemma is that one may be able to be in retrieval mode without knowing it, but this situation is one I have trouble grasping.

A different but related concept is that of monitoring or the control processes we bring on line to determine whether our retrieval search has been successful or whether further searches are needed. The difference between retrieval mode and retrieval monitoring can sometimes become hazy, but one way of thinking about them is that retrieval mode is a proactive set that can be adopted to facilitate retrieval, whereas retrieval monitoring is a more reactive process that operates on the initial information grasped during the retrieval attempt. Other distinctions that are critical in understanding retrieval include concepts of automatic and controlled processes.

One final point addressed within the chapters in this section is the idea that retrieval is reconstructive, i.e. retrieval is not a passive readout of the encoding episode; rather, the episode is reconstructed through bits and pieces (Neisser 1967). Spear's point of view diverges a bit here in that he believes that fast retrieval episodes suggest that sometimes retrieval can be rather direct, without reconstruction.

Two potential obstacles to a truly integrative approach to the study of retrieval come readily to mind. First, the broadness of the concept of retrieval leads to the concern that researchers across disciplines might not truly be studying the same concept. As noted by Gardiner, even researchers within a relatively narrow field (e.g. human experimental psychology) can have trouble agreeing upon a core set of terms and definitions. A second issue, but not an insurmountable one, is that certain aspects of retrieval are much more amenable to study within a certain discipline than others. To study vivid recollection (i.e. remembering) with humans is relatively straightforward: one can ask other people what they recollect. On the other hand, studying such a concept at the molecular level or within pre-verbal humans or nonhuman animals offers a much greater challenge.

A small selection of interesting puzzles with respect to retrieval

This section is focused on interesting puzzles with respect to retrieval that were not addressed in the other chapters and that—in my view—have not yet been resolved. The focus here is on retrieval from long-term memory in humans. One such question regards the classic question of whether word list studies are adequately capturing the richness of memory we experience in everyday life (i.e. autobiographical memory). There are strong reasons to use word lists to gain understanding of memory (Tulving 1983, p. 146); nonetheless, I suspect these studies are missing some core processes fundamental to retrieval as most laypeople would consider it.

One such process might have to do with the relationship of the self to memory. It is becoming increasingly clear that there are neural changes that accompany thoughts of oneself relative to a well-known other (Kelley *et al.* 2002). Also, most remembering in the rich sense we would tend to consider in lay terms indeed seems subjectively to involve the self in a way that memory for a word list studied 30 min previously may well not.

Another puzzle, alluded to previously, arises with respect to the necessity of retrieval mode for retrieval to occur. Do we have to turn attention actively toward the past in order to become open to the possibility of remembering? In addition, Tulving (2002) has argued that retrieval mode is essentially one aspect of a larger system designed for mental time travel, or chronesthesia.

One other very interesting puzzle, not touched upon by the following articles, arises from the neuroimaging literature. Some of the brain regions that appear to be most clearly linked to retrieval have been virtually unanticipated from the neuropsychological literature. For example, regions in anterior prefrontal cortex, lateral and medial parietal cortices are all found to be more active during successful retrieval attempts than when such attempts fail (e.g. McDermott *et al.* 2000). What processes must these regions be contributing if lesions tend not to produce profound memory deficits?

Retrieval: a (very) key concept in memory

I believe the three contributors to this concept piece will agree with me that retrieval is absolutely a key concept to the understanding of memory. Endel Tulving has said 'The key process in memory is retrieval' (Tulving 1991), and Roediger (2000) provided an entire chapter defending this argument. Let me end with a quote from Crowder's *Principles of Learning and Memory* (1976), in which he suggested that encoding is 'a waste of time unless there is appropriate access to the stored material at the moment of truth' (p. 353). Hence, retrieval seems to me to be as integral a concept to the topic of memory as there can be.

Acknowledgments

I am appreciative of the enlightening (albeit perhaps too harmonious!) discussion with John Gardiner and Skip Spear at the Science of Memory meeting in Pallisades, NY; regrettably, Dave Sweatt was forced to cancel the trip at the last minute due to a hurricane but kindly agreed to participate in the written endeavor, nonetheless. I am also grateful to the attendees of my weekly lab meetings (Jason Chan, Shawn Christ, Sean Kang, Jeff Karpicke, Jes Logan, Karl Szpunar and Franklin Zaromb) for an interesting discussion of the concept chapters.

11

Remembering

Remembering, as a general term, refers to retrieval of events from the past. The term is used in many different senses in ordinary language. However, scientists often adopt a commonly used term for a special purpose. Endel Tulving proposed such a special use for *remembering*, to refer to the special ability mentally to travel back in time and to re-experience events from the past. The contrast term is *knowing*, which does not convey the sense of re-experiencing the past. Thus, a person might know she went to France as a child (though not remember the experience), but if she went to Paris 3 months ago she can probably vividly remember many experiences that occurred during the trip (as well as knowing that the trip occurred). Remembering and knowing are thus hypothesized to represent two fundamentally different ways of accessing the past, with the former being personal and often vivid and the latter being impersonal and nearly from a third-person perspective. One might know one visited Paris as a child just as one knows that Benjamin Franklin visited Paris – there is no warm tingle of recollection of personally experienced events in either case. Tulving proposed that only humans can *remember*, in this special sense of the term, and debate swirls both around whether this hypothesis is true and whether the distinction between remembering and knowing is scientifically useful.

H.L.R

40

Remembering: Defining and measuring

Andrew P. Yonelinas

The term remembering is used to describe memory for a variety of different types of information and skills (e.g. remembering where you left your keys, remembering that the capital of Canada is Ottawa or remembering how to ride a bike). However, in the scientific literature on memory, it is used in a more restricted way such that it refers to the retrieval of information about a previous event or episode (e.g. Tulving 1984). By its very nature, remembering a previous event relies on the retrieval of associative information. Simply retrieving an item such as a word, image, color, concept or idea is not sufficient for remembering. Rather, the item must be associated with something else such as another item, or a temporal, physical or mental context, that links it to a previous unique event (Yonelinas 2001).

The act of remembering necessarily involves an attribution or decision process, in the sense that retrieved information must be assembled and judged to be a memory for a specific event (see also Chapter 42, this volume). Retrieving an association, or even a complex set of associations (e.g. a daydream), is not sufficient for remembering. Rather the retrieved information must be judged to be a consequence of a specific event. The attribution process may be automatic, as when some cue triggers a vivid memory for a past event, or it may involve an effortful and time-consuming inferential process, as when trying to remember how to return to one's hotel room.

In order to understand the concept of remembering, it is essential to understand how it is operationalized and used in the scientific community. Because the experience of remembering is not directly observable by others, remembering lends itself only indirectly to scientific study. However, various convergent methods have been developed to measure remembering, and considerable progress has already been made in understanding its functional characteristics and neural underpinnings (for reviews, see Aggleton and Brown 1999; Yonelinas 2002).

Essential in measuring remembering is separating it from other forms of memory such as familiarity. For example, an object or person might be recognized on the basis of recollection, or, when recollection fails, on the basis that the item is perceived as familiar (e.g. Mandler 1980). Familiarity differs from recollection in the sense that it reflects quantitative memory strength information about an item, rather than qualitative or associative information about an event. In order to separate recollection from familiarity one approach is to use associative (or relational) recognition tests in which subjects must retrieve some specified qualitative information about a particular study event (e.g. Was it in list 1 or list 2? Where was it located? Was it paired with this item?) (see Jacoby 1991). An alternative approach is to rely on a subjective report method in which subjects are instructed to indicate when they remember qualitative information about a previous event, or whether they recognize items on some other basis such as familiarity or guessing (the 'remember/know' procedure of Tulving 1984; Gardiner 1988). Finally, confidence responses (or response bias manipulations) can be used to plot receiver operating characteristics (ROCs) in order to quantify the contribution of remembering to recognition (Yonelinas 1994; for a comparison of these various methods, see Yonelinas 2002).

Because there is no single defining feature of remembering, it can only be fully understood by examining it from various different perspectives. Moreover, because all measurement methods make critical assumptions that can at times be violated, it is essential to seek convergence across multiple measurement methods. For example, subjective reports can be notoriously susceptible to individual biases in the sense that whether an item is treated as having been remembered will depend on several factors such as how the term is understood by the subject, the subject's willingness to provide such a report and the specific retrieval conditions (e.g. Baddeley *et al.* 2001*a*; Bodner and Lindsay 2003). Without other more objective methods to verify these subjective reports of remembering (e.g. using associative recognition tests), these methods cannot serve as the basis for a mature science of memory.

Tests of associative recognition are less susceptible to subjective report biases, but they too can provide distorted views of remembering. For example, they can be too restrictive in the sense that subjects may remember aspects of the study event that do not support the discrimination required by the test (e.g. in a test of object location, subjects may remember having seen the object, but may be unable to remember where it was). Alternatively, associative tests can be too inclusive in the sense that accurate associative discriminations can be made even when remembering fails. For example, in a test of temporal order, subjects may find the object to be very familiar, and thus might correctly infer that it was presented in the most recent study list. Moreover, whether a test requires the retrieval of associative information depends on the remember's past experience with the particular test materials, as well as the manner in which they process the incoming stimuli (e.g. see Cohen *et al.* 1997; Yonelinas *et al.* 1999). For example, a string of letters may be treated as a set of associations between separate parts or as a single word, depending on whether the individual has experience with that particular word, and whether they are processing it as a word or as separate components. Thus, accurate performance on associative tests cannot serve as a litmus test for remembering.

Another approach is to use ROC methods to separate the contribution of remembering from familiarity-based recognition responses, but this method too relies on important assumptions that can sometimes be violated (Yonelinas 2002). One can, and should, design experiments to avoid or reduce these potential problems. However, because one can never be sure whether a method's assumptions have been met, only a convergent operations approach can ensure that our understanding of remembering is not biased by a specific measurement method.

Several properties that are often associated with remembering have not been included in the current definition because they appear to be accidental rather than necessary conditions of remembering. For example, the 'self' is sometimes said to play a critical role in remembering in the sense that it is always 'I' who remembers things about 'my' past. Although this is certainly true—it makes little sense to expect that I might experience someone else's memories—it does not seem that a sense of self is intimately involved in all forms of remembering (e.g. remembering that an object was presented in a particular context), so it does not appear to be an essential property of remembering.

Remembering is sometimes said to be more controlled or more flexible than other forms of memory. This appears to be true, but both control and flexibility seem to arise because remembering provides associative information rather than item information, and because the use of recollection is not obligatory, but involves an attribution or decision process. Remembering is also sometimes associated with the intention to retrieve. Although the intention to remember may increase the likelihood of successfully retrieving information, remembering can occur without the intention to remember. Recollection is sometimes said to be more accurate than other forms of memory. Because recollection involves associative information about a specific event, it can be considered to provide more detailed information about what actually happened at some point in time, and thus it may be more accurate than a simple strength-based form of memory such as familiarity. However, as the product of an attribution process, there is no reason to expect remembered information to be perfectly accurate. Moreover, if we grant that perception can be in error, as it certainly can be, it follows that memory for that perception can also be inaccurate.

Finally, some may be tempted to define remembering in such a way that it depends on the ability to report verbally on the subjective experience of retrieving information about a prior event (i.e. making a remember compared with a known response). However, the inability to communicate a remember response, in nonhuman animals, or in nonlinguistic or pre-linguistic human subjects, cannot be treated as evidence that these individuals do not remember. It may be the case that a nonlinguistic individual does not have the experience of remembering, but alternatively it may be that they are simply not able to communicate that experience verbally. If an individual can make use of the remember/know method, then one can use that method to infer that they do remember. If they cannot use that method then various other methods, such as the associative recognition and ROC methods, can be used to serve exactly the same purpose (see, for example, Yonelinas 2002; Fortin et al. 2004).

41

Remembering: A process and a state

Martin A. Conway

Remembering is a process and a state. The process is one of constructing from different sources of knowledge a mental representation that will come to be experienced by the rememberer as a memory. The state is a state of conscious awareness distinguished by a specific type of mental content and a particular *cognitive feeling*. The cognitive feeling of remembering is what Tulving (1985) called *autonoetic consciousness* or, interchangeably, *recollective experience* (for a review, see Gardiner and Richardson-Klavehn 1999). Together the mental content and the recollective experience constitute the experience of remembering. On some occasions there may also be some conscious awareness of parts of the construction process itself. When this occurs, the rememberer may have an experience of creating or discovering a memory, and this feeling and the mental content with which it is associated precede the experience of remembering proper. It is important to note that mental 'states' which can be consciously experienced are conceptualized here as being the end-points or output of processes that precede them. Such processes and states can be separated cognitively and biologically. A strong conjecture here is that it is never possible to be consciously aware of processes but only ever of their outputs into mental states. Thus, we can be consciuosly aware of memories and other types of knowledge retrieved from long-term memory but we cannot be consciously aware of the *processes* of retrieval.

The process of remembering

The process of remembering is complex and nonconscious (only outputs from the process can enter conscious awareness). It can be initiated and sustained intentionally or it can occur spontaneously, or at least in a way that appears spontaneous (to the rememberer). It may feature the discovery of knowledge long thought 'forgotten' or even of knowledge the rememberer did not know they possessed. It may be effortful and extended in time or it may occur rapidly and sometimes intrusively in a way that is outside conscious control.

These, and other qualities, of the processes of remembering can be subsumed under the term *retrieval*. Retrieval has a cyclic and iterative problem-solving aspect to it, first commented on in detail by Norman and Bobrow (1979) and subsequently developed by others (for a review, see Conway 2005).

In Fig. 41.1, retrieval always commences with a cue. A cue is a mental representation. It can be of anything and its origin or source may be external, internal or some combination of these. All cues cause activation of knowledge in long-term memory. Control processes can channel activation by elaborating a cue and using the elaborated cue to cause further, more focused, patterns of activation in the knowledge base. Cue elaboration can be conscious or nonconscious, intentional or unintentional, and is most likely to occur when a cue activates goal-relevant knowledge. In Fig. 41.1, two sets of control processes are shown. One set, termed the *working self* in Fig. 41.1, is centrally involved in goal processing. The other set, termed *executive processes* in Fig. 41.1, is conceived of as more routine 'house-keeping' processes (for a more detailed account of control processing in retrieval, see Conway and Pleydell-Pearce 2000; Conway 2005). Within this general scheme of control processing, two types of retrieval have been studied: *direct retrieval* and *generative retrieval*.

Direct retrieval occurs when a cue causes a pattern of activation in the knowledge base that could, if it entered conscious awareness, be experienced as a memory. Perhaps the most famous instance of direct retrieval is in Proust's (1925/1981) account of how the taste of a madeleine cake brought back a flood of detailed memories of childhood (see too Salaman 1970). Current findings indicate that direct retrieval occurs in about one-third of retrieval attempts (at least under laboratory conditions). The most striking cases of direct retrieval are to be found in the psychological illness of post-traumatic stress disorder (PTSD). In PTSD, a highly specific cue in the trauma experience, this could be a sensory–perceptual detail, feeling, thought or some combination of these, comes to act in a partly generalized way as a powerful cue for direct retrieval of the trauma memory (see Ehlers *et al.* 2004). Intrusive memories in PTSD are, of course, abnormal and destabilizing. More generally, it may be that cues which cause patterns of activations that have the potential to become memories without additional processing occur fairly frequently, perhaps many times a day. Clearly, if these were all to enter conscious awareness, then remembering would become incapacitating (as it is in PTSD) and other cognitive tasks could not be performed efficiently. Control processes act to prioritize which memories can come to mind and when. In general, control processes keep memories out of conscious awareness when tasks that do not require remembering are in operation, and this is probably most of the time. Neuroanatomically this may be evident in inhibitory control originating from neural networks in the

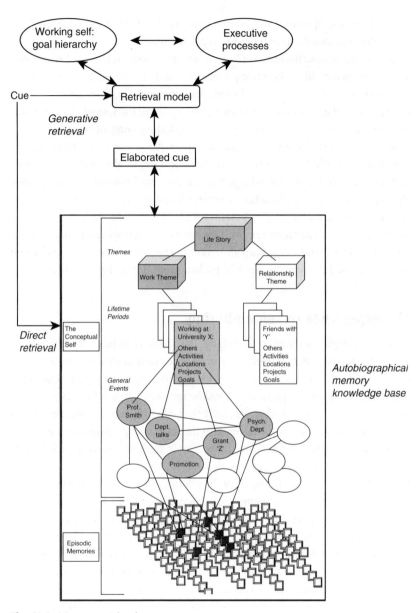

Fig. 41.1 Memory retrieval processes.

frontal lobes and operating on posterior networks located in the medial temporal lobes and/or accessed through hippocampal circuits.

In contrast, generative retrieval features the intentional retrieval of memories. This involves a cyclic or iterative process in which a cue is elaborated until an appropriate pattern of activated knowledge can enter conscious awareness and be experienced as a memory. In generative retrieval, the knowledge base may be accessed repeatedly and outputs evaluated by control processes until centrally generated constraints are satisfied. A person asked to recall, for example, a specific happy event from childhood might elaborate the cue into 'holidays' and probe the knowledge base for relevant knowledge. Perhaps they then recall a childhood holiday or several holidays. This information must now be elaborated further to retrieve a single episode with the required characteristics. Generative retrieval is observed when we introspect on our own memories, when we recall shared experiences with others, and when memory is used strategically for self disclosures to particular audiences.

The experience of remembering

Figure 41.1 depicts a complex knowledge base which can be probed by cues to set up patterns of activations that may become memories. However, for remembering to occur, certain types of knowledge have to be activated. What is critical here is the activation of *episodic memories*. Episodic memories are highly specific representations of short time-slices of experience, they often but by no means always come to mind in the form visual images, they generate emotions and moods and they are always recollectively experienced (see Tulving 1972; and for more recent treatments, see Wheeler *et al.* 1997; Conway 2005). Recollective experience is the sense of the self in the past and it is the feeling that allows us to experience our memories as memories. Earlier, Proust's account of an instance of direct retrieval was described, but what is often overlooked in this account is that Proust prior to the moment of direct retrieval could in fact recall his childhood but did not have recollective experience for what he could recall. The effect of the cue (the taste of the madeleine cake) suddenly allowed him to remember his childhood,i.e. to recall episodic memories and have recollective experience or autonoetic consciousness for the memories. This example illustrates that it is possible to remember without recollective exeperience but, when this occurs, the conscious experience of remembering, and perhaps the specificty of a memory, is strikingly different from remembering accompanied by recollective experience.

Thus, in the earlier example, simply remembering a holiday at, for example, a particular seaside resort will not lead to the experience of remembering.

This is because no episodic memories have entered conscious awareness and, instead, only conceptual knowledge about a past experience is in awareness. Recall of conceptual, generic or schematic knowledge about one's life often features in remembering, and it may be that this is the preferred level of entry into the knowledge base, perhaps because it delivers the optimum amount of information for the minimal amount of cognitive effort. Interestingly, conceptual knowledge about one's life is often preserved, to some extent, in amnesic patients who otherwise cannot recall episodic memories, suggesting that conceptual knowledge and episodic memories may be stored in different brain regions. To return to the example then, once the rememberer recalls a specific episode, e.g. 'learning to swim in a large rock pool', with the associated imagery and feelings that form episodic memories, then recollective experience will be triggered and the experience or state of remembering will occur.

One final question raised by this account of remembering is: are recollective experience and episodic memories uniquely human? Tulving (2005) strongly argues the case that episodic memory is phylogenetically a late developing memory system that is indeed uniqely human. It follows from this that recollective experience, the conscious experience of epsiodic memories, must also be a uniquely human experience. In striking contrast, Conway (2005) proposes that episodic memories serve the function of keeping track of progressing with short-term goal processing, i.e. what has taken place in the preceding few minutes and hours. Because of this, it is hypothesized that episodic memory is a species-wide memory adaptation and therefore a phylogenerically old memory system. It is suggested that a more recent development is that of a phylogenetically younger memory system of conceptual knowledge and it is this that is uniquely human. Future work will no doubt determine which of these rather sharply defined positions is correct.

Acknowledgments

The author was supported by the award of a Professorial Fellowship from the Economic and Social Research Council (ESRC), RES-051-27-0127 of the UK and he thanks the ESRC for this support. Communications should be addressed to Martin A. Conway, The Leeds Memory Group, Institute of Psychological Sciences, The University of Leeds, Leeds, LS2 9JT, or by E-mail to: M.A.Conway@leeds.ac.uk.

42

Remembering: Metacognitive monitoring and control processes

Asher Koriat

The recent upsurge of interest in memory accuracy and distortion has brought about a change in the dominant metaphor of memory—from a storehouse metaphor in which memory is assessed primarily in terms of the quantity of information that is retained and remembered (Roediger 1980) to a correspondence metaphor in which memory is evaluated in terms of its fit with past events (Koriat and Goldsmith 1996a). The correspondence conception has been inspired by many real-life phenomena, and is apparent in such varied topics and paradigms as eyewitness testimony, autobiographical memory, spatial memory, memory distortions and fabrications, false memory, memory illusions and schema-based errors (see Koriat et al. 2000).

The correspondence conception has spawned a more active view of the rememberer than that implied by the storehouse conception. Remembering is seen as an intentional, goal-directed attempt to reconstruct a memorial representation from a variety of pieces of information that come to mind, negotiating between different considerations in attempting to arrive at a faithful account of previously encountered events (Schacter et al. 1998; Koriat 2000). The notion of remembering has been extended to include a variety of *metacognitive processes* that mediate accurate memory performance, including source monitoring, the monitoring of one's own knowledge and performance, and self-controlled decisional processes used to avoid memory errors or to escape illusions of familiarity (Jacoby et al. 1989; Koriat and Goldsmith 1996b; Johnson 1997). A consideration of these processes, in turn, engendered a concern with the *phenomenal qualities* of recollective experience (Koriat 2007), qualities which attracted little interest in traditional quantity-oriented memory research. No longer mere epiphenomena, these qualities are seen as an integral component of the process of remembering (e.g. Johnson 1997; Schacter et al. 1998) and, in particular, as diagnostic clues for distinguishing genuine from false memories (e.g. Conway et al. 1996). Indeed, various subjective qualities of remembering have been examined in connection with reality and source monitoring, autobiographical memories, false recall, post-event misinformation, flashbulb memories and eyewitness testimony. The assumption is that the quality of phenomenal experience may be critical in leading the rememberer to identify the source of a memory and accept it as true, and hence may play a critical role in mediating memory accuracy.

Monitoring and control processes operate throughout the various phases of remembering. They are involved in deciding whether to initiate a memory search, what type of search and retrieval process to use, when to terminate the retrieval process and whether or not to report the retrieved information, as well as at what level of precision or coarseness to convey it. Such processes are integral components of the overall remembering process, influencing its course and the quality of its products. Traditional memory research generally avoided addressing person-controlled memory processes, perhaps because the operation of these processes was seen to conflict with the desire to achieve strict experimental control.

Consider, for example, a person on the witness stand who has sworn to 'tell the whole truth and nothing but the truth'. To meet this oath, the person must monitor the accuracy of information that comes to mind before deciding whether to report it or not. Performance is generally consistent with a simple model (Koriat and Goldsmith 1996b; Goldsmith *et al.* 2002) in which remember-ers first assess the probability that a candidate response is correct (monitoring) and then volunteer it only if its assessed probability of being correct passes a pre-set criterion. Otherwise, if there is a coarser grained answer whose assessed–probability–correct passes the criterion, this coarser answer will be provided (*control of grain size*). If not, the item will be withheld entirely (*control of report option*). The dynamics that guides the control processes is an *accuracy–informativeness trade-off*. Assuming that monitoring is relatively accurate, setting a higher report criterion results in a higher proportion of correct answers out of those reported (i.e. *output-bound accuracy*; see Koriat and Goldsmith 1996b), but the increase in accuracy generally comes at the cost of reduced informativeness—fewer items of information may be volun-teered (*report option*), and those that are volunteered tend to be less precise (*grain size*). Thus, the rememberer must weigh the competing incentives for accuracy and informativeness in order to arrive at the appropriate control policy for a particular memory situation. Several findings support this model. First, participants place complete faith in their subjective feelings (the within-participant correlation between the tendency to report an answer and subjective confidence in its correctness averaged over 0.95!), and do so even when subjective confidence is quite undiagnostic of accuracy (Koriat and Goldsmith 1996b). Secondly, participants strategically adapt their control policy to fit differing priorities for memory accuracy and quantity, adopting a stricter report criterion when accuracy incentives are stronger. Thirdly, the control over memory reporting generally allows participants to boost the accuracy of what they report, and even more so as the incentive for accuracy increases. Finally, the improved accuracy generally comes at the expense of memory quantity performance, but the extent of the quantity–accuracy trade-off depends critically on monitoring effectiveness, i.e. on the extent to which the person's confidence judgments discriminate between correct and incorrect answers. This implies that eyewitnesses cannot 'tell the whole truth' and also 'tell nothing but the truth', except in the extreme case when the subjective monitoring of the correctness of their answers is perfect.

In addition to report option, rememberers can boost accuracy by regulating the grain size of their report, for example reporting 'late in the afternoon' (which is more likely to be correct) rather than 'at 16:30' (Goldsmith *et al.* 2002, 2005). Neisser (1988) observed that in free-narrative memory reporting, participants tend to provide answers at a level of generality at which they are 'not likely to be mistaken'. Of course, more coarsely grained answers, while more likely to be correct, are also less informative. When participants are allowed to control the grain size of their report, they do so in a strategic manner, sacrificing informativeness (precision) for the sake of accuracy when their subjective confidence in the more precise-informative answer is low, and taking into account the relative payoffs for accuracy and informativeness (Goldsmith *et al.* 2002, 2005).

Of course, whether the remembering occurs in legal settings or in more mundane everyday situations in which people recount their memories to others, there are certainly other functional goals beyond accuracy that guide the remembering process. For example, people may generally strive to recall accurately, but in some cases the desire to make a good impression, to be entertaining or self-consistent may be more important (e.g. Neisser 1996; Conway 2005). Such goals presumably interact with—and may sometimes over-ride—the goal of accuracy.

How do people monitor the veracity of their memories? Several cues have been discussed in the metacognitive literature, such as the ease with which information comes to mind (Koriat 2007). In the source-monitoring framework (Johnson 1997), phenomenal cues such as vividness and perceptual detail are assumed to support reality monitoring. In the attributional approach to memory (e.g. Jacoby *et al.* 1989), illusions of memory are seen to result from the misattribution of fluent processing to the past. Others have proposed more specific mechanisms for screening out false memories (e.g. Dodson and Schacter 2002; Brainerd *et al.* 2003). At the same time, there is increasing interest in strategic processes that prevent false information from coming to mind in the first place (e.g. Jacoby *et al.* 2005) rather than by screening out false memories after they come to mind.

The consideration of the monitoring and control processes that operate in remembering can shed new light on many memory phenomena and raise new questions. Among these is the observation that although memory quantity performance decreases over time, memory accuracy performance can sometimes be quite stable, possibly because people strategically increase the coarseness of the information that they report as the retention interval increases (Goldsmith *et al.* 2005).

I have argued that the emerging accuracy-oriented conception of remembering leads to a greater concern with (1) the active role of the rememberer in guiding the process of remembering, in accordance with personal and situational goals; (2) the mechanisms that contribute to memory accuracy and distortion; and (3) the role of subjective experience and phenomenal cues. It should be noted, however, that any act of deliberate remembering also involves automatic activations of memories and a complex interplay between top-down and bottom-up processes (Koriat 2000). Furthermore, remembering can also occur involuntarily, with memories emerging spontaneously and unexpectedly into consciousness, sometimes even against one's own will, as with post-traumatic memories. Such nondeliberate memories also fall under the concept of remembering because of their phenomenological qualities.

Are the metacognitive monitoring and control processes emphasized in this chapter uniquely human? Although some rudimentary aspects of accuracy-oriented metacognitive regulation may be found in some animals (Smith *et al.* 2003), this is still an open question that deserves further scrutiny (Goldsmith and Koriat 2003).

Acknowledgment

This chapter is the product of discussion with Morris Goldsmith, and reflects our shared views on this topic.

43

Integrative comments
Remembering: A controversy and a challenge

Suparna Rajaram

The concept of 'remembering' is at once accessible and controversial. Remembering is a cognitive ability that lay persons can report they use and scientists report they can measure. The former's understanding of this concept, however, is not always in accord with the explanations of the latter. The controversy surrounding this concept pertains to one of definition— whether to include the properties of behavior as well as of the mind.

It is worthwhile to establish first what remembering is not. An act of retrieval in and of itself does not imply remembering. In some circumstances, past events influence current behavior, but such transfer (see Chapter 48, this volume) can often occur without an awareness of a relationship between the past and present events. This is not remembering. In some other circumstances, we might retrieve pieces of knowledge (the Taj Mahal is in Agra) without either ever having visited Agra or remembering where one learned this information. Alternatively, we might recognize a colleague we met at a conference but neither the colleague's name nor the conference where we met comes to mind. The sense of knowing in the first case or the sense of familiarity in the second case is not remembering. The expression of habits and skills is also not remembering because these acts of retrieval do not require access to specific episodes. In fact, they are carried out most successfully when repeated episodes of practice accumulate and distill to produce habits and skills. There is likely to be general agreement with the assertion that none of these instances constitutes remembering.

The concept of remembering is perhaps best considered as a collective expression of the following features—content, process, state, accuracy, goals and functions. The concept contributors—Conway, Koriat and Yonelinas— evaluate the relevance of several of these features. An assessment of these features can help reveal the significance of each in defining the concept of remembering and determine how widely we can apply it.

To be begin with, remembering implies that there is *content*—or episodes—to remember. Episodes can consist of internal events, as Ebbinghaus (1885/1913/1964/pp. 1–2) noted, 'mental states of every kind—sensation, feelings, ideas—which were at one time present in consciousness and then have disappeared from it, have not with their disappearance ceased to exist ... they continue to exist, stored up, so to speak, in the memory ...'. Episodes can also consist of external events such as vacations, conferences, meetings, dinners, a visit to the museum, and so on.

There is now general agreement that remembering implies that an organism's responses should meet the '*what–where–when*' criteria. We should be able to observe evidence that an organism exhibits memory for 'what' happened, 'where' it happened and 'when' it happened. Access to these three criteria converts an act of retrieval from merely knowing that a particular event belongs to the past to remembering that event as it unfolded in the past. The application of the 'what–where–when' criteria can help us distinguish between remembering and other forms of memory such as knowing and familiarity.

Next, remembering can be thought of as an *act* or a *process* where the process of recollecting past episodes can be either deliberate or involuntary. To use Ebbinghaus' words again,

> ... In a first group of cases we can call back into consciousness by an exertion of the will directed to this purpose the seemingly lost states ... that is, we can produce them voluntarily ... a second group of cases this survival is even more striking. Often, even after years, mental states once present in consciousness return to it with apparent spontaneity and without any act of the will; that is, they are produced involuntarily ... in the majority of the cases we recognize the returned mental state as one that has already been experienced; that is, we remember it (Ebbinghaus 1885/1913/1964/pp. 1–2).

The contributors to this section seem to be in agreement as far as the deliberate/involuntary distinction is concerned but they differ somewhat in their specification of these processes. The descriptions of the involuntary process do not appear to be very different—direct access to episodes (Conway), remembering without intention (Yonelinas) and nondeliberate memories (Koriat)—but the description of the deliberate process suggests some differences—monitoring and regulation (Koriat), attribution (Koriat and Yonelinas), activation of associative information and controlled processing (Yonelinas) and generative retrieval (Conway). The notions of monitoring, regulation and generative retrieval imply the involvement of subjective awareness, or properties of the mind, more explicitly than the rest. Nevertheless, two related points are worth noting here; awareness is not necessary for voluntary processing and a retrieval process that begins as a deliberate one could switch to direct retrieval, or vice versa, depending on several factors such as the availability of cues.

Remembering can also be a *state*. As a cognitive state, remembering is said to involve the re-experiencing of a past event. This feature implies conscious awareness of being engaged in the act of recollection. Humans are remarkably good at being able to report different states of conscious awareness such as remembering and knowing, even in experimental contexts (Tulving 1985; Gardiner 1988; Rajaram 1993). This sense also seems to be closest to the way many investigators who study nonmemory phenomena might define remembering.

Remembering as a cognitive state also implies involvement of a sense of self, as famously noted by William James, 'Memory requires more than mere dating of a fact in the past. It must be dated in my past. In other words, I must think that I directly experienced its occurrence. It must have that "warmth and intimacy" ... as characterizing all experiences "appropriated" by the thinker as his own' (James 1890/1998, p. 650). Finally, re-experiencing also implies a subjective sense of time that differentiates the past event from its present experience. In Tulving's conceptualization of episodic memory—and remembering as an expression of this memory—the self, subjective experience and mental time travel are critical, defining features (Tulving 2002). These features go well beyond the 'what–when–where' criteria discussed earlier and raise important questions about the applicability of this more inclusive definition across species.

The contributors generally agree in their assessment of 'content' and 'process' as critical features of remembering even though their positions differ in some of the elaborations of these features. However, they diverge in their evaluation of 'state' as a critical feature of remembering. This point of departure reflects the relative significance the contributors attach to behavioral versus mental properties in defining the concept. For example, Koriat's view of monitoring and control processes is predicated on the ideas of 'the role of subjective experience' and 'the active role of the rememberer' (Chapter 42) and Conway's view centers on 'recollective experience' and on situating 'the sense of the self in the past' (Chapter 41). However, Yonelinas (Chapter 40) does not consider the involvement of the self as 'a necessary condition' for remembering, or as being 'intimately involved' in it. In another comparison, Conway considers the subjective experience of content as belonging to one's own past to be important for distinguishing the experience of remembering from retrieval in general. However, Yonelinas places comparatively less emphasis on the use of subjective experience, citing its susceptibility to individual biases and to changes in experimental conditions.

As a related concern, it is important to evaluate accuracy as a defining criterion of remembering. Subjective reports are not universally considered to be a relevant feature of remembering (or at least of episodic memory) because the subjective feeling of remembering can occasionally be inaccurate (Eichenbaum *et al.* 2005). In contrast, others argue that subjective experience with its metacognitive properties can often help screen false memories (Koriat). Furthermore, functional goals that guide the remembering process such as projecting a certain self-image can sometimes interfere with the goal of achieving accuracy (Koriat); a decline in accuracy under these circumstances does not strip remembering of its other defining properties. In other words, accuracy itself is not considered by all to be the litmus test for including or excluding a defining feature, especially if it typically leads to accurate responses as is the case with subjective reports. Accuracy can also falter when other approaches that tap into other putative processes are used (Yonelinas), or when the grain size for accuracy is modulated (Koriat), or even when evaluating specific details about 'where' and 'when' a past event occurred (de Kort *et al.* 2005).

Subjective states can serve as a subtle but important diagnostic criterion of remembering in many instances because they differ in striking ways from other, related indices of memory. For example, subjective reports of memory are severely impaired in anterograde amnesia even when confidence judgments about memory—a generally reliable and useful method—are preserved (Rajaram *et al.* 2002). In this way, subjective reports can provide information about remembering when other approaches might fail to do so.

Others have emphasized the role of subjective experience and the involvement of the self because these features are seen as being intimately tied to an important functional goal—mental time travel to the past and the future (Suddendorf and Corballis 1997; Tulving 2002). These subjective properties are deemed critical for being able to use personal past experience in shaping and pursuing one's own future goals.

The content (what–where–when) and process of remembering can be evaluated largely based on behavioral criteria. However, experiential features— subjective experience, the sense of self and mental time travel—clearly are included in the definition properties of the mind, and bring with them different implications for how goals and functions are served by the cognitive act of remembering.

The key features discussed here—content, process, state, accuracy, goals and functions—allow us to compare the applicability of the concept of remembering across different levels of analysis. What features of the definition would enable investigations of this concept across different species? There is increasing consensus that the content—'what–where–when'—criteria for remembering can be successfully met not only by humans but also by animals such as birds and rodents (Clayton and Dickinson 1998; Eichenbaum *et al.* 2005; Chapter 62, this volume). The issue becomes complicated when the features of conscious experience and the sense of self are included in the concept of remembering. These features are difficult to assess in nonhuman species because communication of conscious experience depends on language. In light of this, Clayton and Dickinson (1998) have coined the term 'episodic-like memory' to describe the impressive retention of 'what–where–when' details exhibited by scrub-jays in food caching behavior. The inherent problems in evaluating the 'state' criterion in nonhumans has also led to in-depth discussions on the relevance of this criterion and the functions (such as future planning) it might serve (Clayton *et al.* 2003; Tulving 2005).

The concept contributors differ in their views on the application of various criteria in nonhuman species. Yonelinas (Chapter 40) rejects the state criterion as being necessary for the assessment of remembering in nonhumans and suggests that other methods can elicit the same information about remembering as do subjective reports. Koriat (Chapter 42) evaluates the process criterion (monitoring and metacognitive evaluation) that is critical for his definition and seems as yet uncertain whether nonhumans demonstrate the operation of this critical criterion adequately. Conway (Chapter 41) believes that remembering is a cross-species adaptation that serves to fulfill short-term goals. In his view, humans and nonhumans critically differ not in the ability to remember but in possessing conceptual knowledge, and it is the presence of such knowledge that allows humans to develop long-term goals. In this sense, the views of Conway and those of Tulving (2002) diverge on the role of remembering in subserving long-term functions.

In light of these complexities associated with the concept of remembering, can we apply it uniformly across human and nonhuman species? One possibility is that we can reject those criteria that do not apply across species and retain only those that generalize. Evidence that some nonhuman species show conjoint retrieval of what–where–when details makes the content criterion a prime one to retain. By this definition, animals remember past episodes.

Is it necessary then to include the sense of 'I was there' in the definition, the sense of vividly re-experiencing the event at a different time and in a different place, consciously regulating the metacognitive processes that enable mental travel back to that event, or using past experiences purposefully to plan long-term future goals? In short, is it necessary to take into account conscious experience that accompanies remembering? The answer may lie in the reality that remembering usually involves subjective experience in humans. People readily engage in this experience and consistently report it (Rajaram and Roediger 1997). If conscious awareness is a universal human experience, then does it not make sense to ask why humans have this experience when they remember the past and what purpose it might serve in the world?

The problem confronting us can then be summarized as follows. We do not know whether nonhumans have conscious experience, but we do know that they exhibit other important properties of remembering. Therefore, it is not useful to reject the possibility that animals can remember. In the spirit of Clayton and Dickinson's ideas, nonhumans exhibit a remember-like phenomenon. Conversely, humans occasionally make errors in their use of subjective experience but they also rely on it and use it effectively to recollect the past. Therefore, it is not useful to reject the relevance of phenomenology in the definition simply because we cannot detect its presence in nonhumans. A resolution of this seeming impasse would help us understand memory phenomena that involve both behavioral and mental components. For this reason, the challenge inherent in resolving this state of affairs makes remembering a central concept in the science of memory.

12

Transfer

Transfer refers to the effects of experience on one task to learning or performance of a second (criterial) task. Transfer must be considered relative to an appropriate control condition in which the initial task of interest is not practiced prior to performance on the criterial task. If the first task enhances performance on the second task relative to the control condition, then the situation is one of positive transfer; conversely, if the first task impairs performance of the second task, negative transfer has occurred. Of course, a particular task can have positive transfer for some criterial tasks and negative transfer for others. The term *transfer of training* is often used when learning is intentional and two tasks are directly compared so as to study the influence of one on the other. The broader term transfer may also refer to higher order cognitive skills (e.g. as in analogical transfer, in which the effect of learning to solve a problem that requires a particular rule is examined on an analogous problem (with different surface features) to ascertain whether the original solution involved rule learning that can be applied in a different context. The logic of transfer designs is also used in studies in which learning may not be intentional (such as studies of implicit learning or implicit memory). The concept of transfer has its origins in educational research (does learning one type of subject confer benefits to learning a different subject?) and also plays a great role in other settings where learning of new skills is critically important (such as training of particular skills in industry or the military). In general, transfer from one task to another seems greatest to the extent that component processes in the two tasks overlap.

H.L.R.

44

Transfer: Its transfer into neurobiology

Yadin Dudai

The use of the term *transfer*, in its meaning as the contribution of experience on one task to subsequent performance on a different task, is uncommon in the contemporary neurobiological literature. This is particularly the case in the cellular and molecular literature. The concept, however, is alive and kicking, albeit implicitly. Hence similarly to Moliere's bourgeois gentleman, who suddenly realized that he had been speaking prose for 40 years without ever knowing it, even molecular neuroscientists might ultimately realize that they have been studying transfer, though in disguise. This should not come as a surprise, as some authors argue that *transfer* is a central concept in the science of memory (Chapter 46, this volume).

As a matter of fact, the absence of the term 'transfer' from much of the discussion of the neural bases of memory epitomizes the distinction between a term and a concept: the latter exists and could even be quite influential before a specific term to express it has been designated or adapted in the particular discipline. Since in the science of memory, 'transfer' is used extensively in the behavioral and cognitive level of analysis, there is no reason why it should not be adapted for use, when appropriate, by neurobiologists who have never used it so far. However, it is not the terminology that counts, it is the concept itself and its repercussions in designing experiments, analyzing their outcomes and construction of models. Therefore, molecular and cellular neuroscientists might benefit from transferring 'transfer' into their discourse.

The concept of *transfer* implies that experience alters long-term internal representations in addition to those that directly subserve performance on the type of task that had been selected by the experimenter to start with. It may also be taken to connote metaplasticity—the plasticity of neural plasticity, meaning that the capacity of a neuronal system to undergo plastic changes is a function of its history.

In biological terms, transfer could be accounted for by assuming that either (1) the same brain loci of plasticity that subserve the original task (OT) also subserve additional type(s) of tasks (AT); or (2) global plasticity circuits (e.g. attention, emotion) that are engaged in experience-dependent modifications of AT come to modify internal representations of OT as well; or (3) the circuits that encode AT are modified as a consequence of subsequent integration of the modified representation of AT into more global structures of knowledge in the brain, so that they come to modify OT. The neurobiology of memory deals with all three cases.

Interdependence of plasticity over multisynaptic domains

It becomes apparent that use-dependent alterations in synaptic plasticity are not necessarily confined to the specific synapses that are being used. Furthermore, plasticity in an individual synapse is a function of previous activity not only in that specific synapse but also in other synapses on the same cell, which may encode different bits of information. This seems to be a consequence of the mechanisms of long-term plasticity, which involve a delicate interplay among synapses and their cell body.

A noteworthy example is provided by the processes which are dubbed 'synaptic tagging' and 'capture' (Frey and Morris 1997; Martin *et al.* 1997; Young and Nguyen 2005). In brief, the current textbook account is that for the 'teaching' stimulus to trigger long-term synaptic plasticity, it must set off molecular mechanisms both in the synapse and in the cell body that feeds that synapse. In the process, the activated synapse is labeled, or 'tagged', by modification of synaptic proteins and/or reorganization of such proteins. This results in a new synaptic configuration, and could also attract plasticity molecules from other parts of the nerve cell. The synapse itself contains a molecular apparatus capable of synthesizing proteins on location on the basis of messages (messenger RNA molecules, mRNA) that are delivered from the nucleus of the nerve cell. The output of the nucleus itself is also altered by the intracellular signaling cascades that were activated by the teaching stimulus. This synapse–cell body dialogue reinforces the tagging of the activated synapse, resulting in an enduring change in synaptic function. Since tagged synapses attract plasticity proteins from their cell body, and since the nerve cell controls many synapses, even synapses that are tagged by activity that by itself is insufficient to induce an enduring change in the synapse, can benefit from strong preceding activation in remote synapses on the same cell. This is because the strongly activated synapses trigger the generation in the cell body of effective levels of new mRNA and plasticity molecules, which are subsequently captured by the tagged weakly activated synapses.

In sum, synapses are hence tuned to each others' history. This synaptic inter-dependence might subserve the encoding of context and generalization. In a distributed system, in which synapses on the same cell may subserve different instances or even types of behavioral tasks, it might also subserve transfer-like processes.

Activation of global plasticity circuits

Rather simplistically (but useful heuristically), one could depict systems that subserve learning and memory as composed of two major types of elements: those that encode the specific information of a memory item, and those that perform operations that are either permissive or obligatory for the encoding of memory items. Whereas the first elements encode the specific content of the event (e.g. distinct target and source input), the latter subserve more general information and computations (e.g. an emotional or arousal state that reinforces the encoding of the specific information). Because in the processes of encoding and consolidation (see below), the general purpose systems are activated and modulated, it is plausible to assume that they also affect brain circuits that are not directly related to the specific information about the target item. Hence experience on one task could result in alteration in performance on a subsequently different task, i.e. *bona fide* transfer. Postulated general purpose learning systems are the amygdalar complex, the hippocampal formation and frontal circuits. For example, in addition to its role in encoding specific emotional information, the amygdalar complex is assumed to modify widespread brain circuits (McGaugh 2004). Indeed there is evidence that stressful experience induces long-term changes in the neuronal circuitry of amygdala, hippocampus and prefrontal cortex (Radley and Morrison 2005). Such experience also results in altered performance of rats on subsequent tasks (e.g. Vyas and Chttarji 2004). Another type of postulated general purpose systems are long-range central neuromodulatory systems, such as the nigrostriatal, mesolimbic and mesocortical dopaminergic systems or the basal forebrain cholinergic system. These widespread systems alter global brain states and, therefore, upon activation in one learning situation, might influence subsequent encoding or retrieval in a different situation, generating again a transfer of training effect.

Integration of modified representations into global knowledge structures in the brain

It is noteworthy that the concept of *consolidation* is relevant to *transfer*. This was already hinted at above, but deserves further elaboration. Inherent to the concept of *consolidation*, and particularly to that of system consolidation (Dudai 2004), is the notion that memory encoding does not come to an end upon termination of the relevant experience with the target stimulus, but rather proceeds afterwards, culminating in a stabilized trace. In the course of this process, the newly acquired information is postulated to integrate with existing bodies of knowledge in the brain, resulting not only in the long-term representation of the new information, but also in alteration of existing knowledge. According to the system consolidation model of declarative memory (ibid), during the first days and weeks after encoding, the hippocampal formation becomes dispensable for the persistence and expression of the newly acquired information, relegating these roles to the neocortex. In addition, there is also gradual strengthening of cortico-cortical links (e.g. Takashima *et al.* 2006). Given that, depiction of the encoding of an event as resulting solely in memory of that same event is bound to be rather simplistic. Rather, it is likely that system consolidation, by inducing additional associations, results in subsequent alteration in performance to cues different from those presented in the encoding phase. This mechanism engenders the potential for broad transfer. Though system consolidation is commonly ascribed only to declarative memory, time-dependent trace migration may also occur in procedural tasks (Kassardjian *et al.* 2005). This raises the question to what extent transfer of training in skill tasks, including in situations in which transfer can be exploited for rehabilitation of brain-damaged patients, is contributed by system consolidation-like processes.

The aforementioned types of biological processes and mechanisms demonstrate that the concept of *transfer* emerges in the neurobiology of memory even in situations in which the term 'transfer' is not employed. This happens because the concept, not the term, is inherent in the conceptual framework of memory: experience has far-reaching effects on distributed neuronal networks; its effects are unlikely to honor the task distinctions made by brain scientists. Having said that, it is now for the experimenter to determine, in each case, the particular brain mechanisms involved, and the extent or domain specificity of transfer. Healy (Chapter 47, this volume) points to cases of both generality of transfer and extreme specificity.

The almost unbearable lightness of shoving subjects into magnets ensures that transfer, not only transfer of training but also analogical transfer, is bound to gain popularity even among brain scientists who have never heard of it. However, even before the avalanche of brain maps spills into the literature on transfer, brain scientists can still practically benefit from noting the concept. A simple example illustrates the point. In molecular neurobiology, batteries of behavioral tests are routinely used to determine plasticity and memory in mutant mice (Crawley and Paylor 1997). Does the order of tests affect the performance on each of them? If this is the case, the outcome of the tests should be considered more carefully. This might complicate the life of those who erroneously consider behavioral tests to be simple assays—but at the same time might make them happy: could they be on the road to the molecular biology of transfer?

45

Transfer: Analysis in rats and other species

E.J. Capaldi

Transfer phenomena have long been of critical importance in setting the agenda in animal learning. Commonly, transfer has been investigated by reinforcing in a transfer phase stimuli, response or both different from those reinforced in an initial training phase. Recently, theorizing has been heavily influenced by combining these conventional transfer procedures with shifts to novel contexts (see especially Bouton 1993). Another major way of studying transfer in the study of animal learning is to employ a shift from one reward schedule (pre-shift schedule) to another (post-shift schedule). In the pre-shift phase, all trials may be rewarded (consistent reward or CRF) or only some trials may be rewarded (partial reward or PRF). Often in the post-shift phase, extinction is employed, with all trials being nonrewarded. Less frequently, shifts in magnitude of reward may occur.

The decline in vigor of responding that occurs in extinction has been explained in one of three general ways: Excitatory associations learned in acquisition are unlearned in extinction (e.g. Rescorla and Wagner 1972); excitatory associations learned in acquisition are opposed by inhibitory ones learned in extinction (e.g. Bouton 1993); or a discrimination is formed between stimuli signaling reward in acquisition and stimuli signaling nonreward in extinction (e.g. Capaldi 1994a).

Among phenomena unfavorable to the unlearning view is the rapid reacquisition that normally occurs following extinction (Napier et al. 1992). Nor is rapid reacquisition favorable to an inhibitory view: reacquisition cannot rapidly decrease inhibition. To understand why rapid reacquisition, as well as a variety of other extinction phenomena, favor a memory discrimination view, it will be helpful initially to consider performance under an acquisition schedule in which rewarded and nonrewarded trials alternate, an SA schedule.

Under the SA schedule, responding may come to be more vigorous on rewarded than on nonreward trials, a phenomenon called single alternation patterning (SAP). SAP has been obtained when the interval between trials was as long as 20 min (Capaldi and Stanley 1963) or 24 h (Jobe et al. 1977). These and other findings (see, for example, Jobe *et al.* 1977) suggest that under the SA schedule, the memory of the prior reward event signals current nonreward (respond weakly) and the memory of the prior nonrewarded event signals current reward (respond vigorously). In this view, extinction is rapid following CRF training because the memory of reward that comes to signal reward in acquisition is readily discriminable from the memory of nonreward that signals nonreward in extinction. Reacquisition is rapid because in extinction the memory of nonreward replaces the memory of reward, thus allowing the memory of reward to retain much of its previously acquired excitatory capacity. Resistance to extinction may be increased by PRF training relative to CRF training (the partial reward extinction effect or PREE) because under the PRF schedule, memories of nonreward may become signals for reward in acquisition, those memories promoting vigorous responding when they or similar memories are retrieved in extinction.

The major body of evidence supporting the present view is supplied by mature rats in the instrumental learning situation, a situation in which obtaining reward depends on responding. Recently, supporting evidence has been obtained in a Pavlovian situation, one in which responding occurred to a tone presented prior to food reward (Capaldi *et al.* 2005; Miller and Capaldi 2007). Miller (1999), in an unpublished Master's thesis, employed a great variety of acquisition schedules in which humans predicted verbally which of two figures (a circle or a square) would appear on the right side of a computer screen following the appearance of a triangle on the left side. In all three situations, similar findings were obtained. For example, in all three, SAP occurred. Also, in all three, the specific sequence in which events were presented in acquisition influenced extinction differently following limited and extensive training. Since no other animal learning model can explain these training level sequence findings, they will be emphasized here.

In the panel below, two 50 per cent schedules are shown, one in which only one nonrewarded (N) trial precedes a rewarded (R) trial (one N schedule) and one in which four N trials precede an R trial (four N schedule). The schedules shown were employed in a Pavlovian situation. In that situation, as in the instrumental situation and the human 'guessing' situation, the one N schedule produced the greater resistance to extinction following limited training, but less resistance to extinction following extended training (see Miller and Capaldi 2007). This is explained below.

	Trial number							
Schedule	1	2	3	4	5	6	7	8
One N	N	R	N	R	N	R	N	R
Four N	R	N	N	N	N	R	R	R

Considerable evidence indicates that rats are capable of discriminating between the memory produced by a single N trial and memories produced by two or more N trials in succession. In extinction, memories corresponding to long strings or N trials may occur. Thus it is clear that if memories associated with one and four N trials were equally excitatory, then later in extinction more vigorous responding would be produced by the four N schedule than by the one N schedule. This is indeed what occurs following very considerable acquisition training, enough to render the memories of one N and four N equally strong (i.e. asymptotic) signals for reward. Following a limited number of acquisition trials, reward would be signaled more strongly by the memory of one N than by the memory of four N because the memory of one N is retrieved on rewarded trials more often (4 to 1). Following limited training, the one N schedule produces greater resistance to extinction than the four N schedule. How a wide a variety of schedules in which percentage and sequences of reward influence extinction as a function of acquisition training level is considered elsewhere (e.g. Capaldi 1994*a*, *b*).

One way to indicate that the present approach to transfer phenomena has greater explanatory scope than other animal learning models is to apply it to a highly consistent body of findings that have not been otherwise explained. These findings are instrumental learning data for infant and adult rats (summarized in Amsel 1992) and for fish (e.g. Gonzalez *et al.* 1974). Amsel (1992) concedes that his frustration view cannot explain the infant rat data (see p. 174) and he made no attempt to explain the fish data. These fish and rat data are of importance not only for evaluating learning models but because they suggest that a major change occurring in ontogeny and in phylogeny is an increasing capacity to discriminate among memories produced by reward events.

Three phenomena examined in fish, infant rats (about 10 days of age), young rats (about 20–25 days of age) and mature rats (over, say, 30 days of age) are SAP, the magnitude of reward extinction effect (MREE) and the successive negative contrast effect (SNCE). The MREE consists in more rapid extinction following a large than following a small magnitude of CRF. An SNCE occurs when a shift from a large magnitude of CRF to a small magnitude of CRF produces poorer performance to small reward than in a control group trained under a small magnitude of CRF only. Findings are as follows. SAP occurs in fish, infant rats and, of course, in mature rats. In acquisition, fish and rats of all ages respond more vigorously to a larger magnitude of CRF than to a smaller magnitude. Mature rats show both an MREE and an SNCE. Fish continue for many trials to respond vigorously when shifted from a large to small reward and thus show neither an MREE nor an SNCE.

Infant and very young rats respond like fish and thus do not show an MREE before 20 days of age and an SNCE before 25 days of age.

The effects of training fish, 14-day-old rats, 20-day-old rats and mature rats under large and small reward are shown in Fig. 45.1. S^L represents the memory of large reward, S^S the memory of small reward, S^{N1} the memory of a single nonreward and S^{N2} the memory of two successive nonrewards. Memories corresponding to four, five, etc. nonrewards are not shown in Fig. 45.1. The solid lines above S^L show how strongly S^L signals reward when training occurs under large reward, and the solid line above S^S how strongly S^S signals reward when training occurs under small reward, higher lines indicating stronger signal capacity and thus more vigorous responding. The lines extending from S^L to S^S indicate how strongly signal capacity generalizes from these memories to other memories. In constructing Fig. 45.1, animals were assumed to differ in one respect and one respect only, i.e. how well they discriminated between memories: the better the discrimination, the larger the separation between memories in the figure. For example, S^L and S^S are separated by a greater distance in, for example, 14-day-old rats than in fish.

Of the three sorts of discrimination considered, SAP is relatively easy involving S^L versus S^{N1} or S^S versus S^{N1}. Not surprisingly, perhaps, SAP is better for large reward (S^L versus S^{N1}) than for small reward (S^S versus S^{N1}) and SAP occurs even in fish. A difficult discrimination is between S^L and S^S. Thus, as shown in Fig. 45.1, excitation in fish and 14-day-old rats is greater at S^S when it generalized from S^L than when training occurs directly at S^S. At 20 days of age, generalized excitation from S^L and directly acquired excitation at S^S are about equal, and so an SNCE does not occur. In mature rats, an SNCE occurs easily because generalized excitation at S^S from S^L is less than that acquired directly at S^S. Stimuli occurring in extinction, S^{N1}, S^{N2}, etc. acquire more generalized excitation from S^L than from S^S in fish and 14-day-old rats. Thus, in these animals, the opposite of an MREE occurs. In 20-day-old rats, memories occurring in extinction, particularly later in extinction, receive slightly less generalized excitation from S^L than from S^S and so a small MREE is obtained. In mature rats, the extinction memories receive much less generalized excitation from S^L than from S^S, producing a large MREE.

Figure 45.1 can be used to explain many other findings that have been obtained in fish, and infant, young and mature rats. One such is easily explained. Amsel (1992) reports that the younger the rat, the greater the resistance to extinction. The reason why is immediately obvious in Fig. 45.1. Memories that occur later in extinction, S^{N4}, S^{N5}, etc. receive less generalized excitation from either S^L or S^S as rats become older.

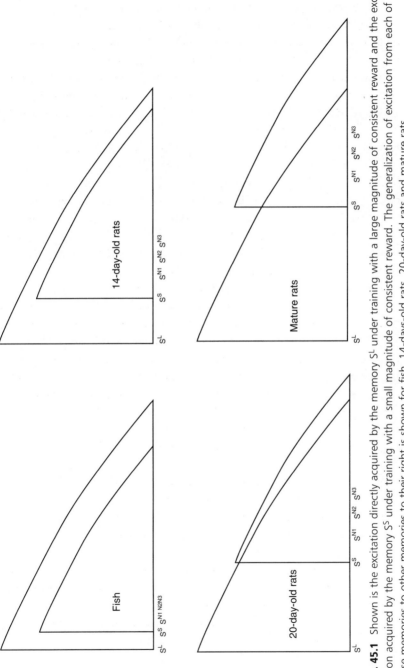

Fig. 45.1 Shown is the excitation directly acquired by the memory S^L under training with a large magnitude of consistent reward and the excitation acquired by the memory S^S under training with a small magnitude of consistent reward. The generalization of excitation from each of these memories to other memories to their right is shown for fish, 14-days-old rats, 20-day-old rats, and mature rats.

46

Transfer: Rediscovering a central concept

Mark A. McDaniel

Transfer is the most central concept in learning and memory. This is not an *a priori* position designed to create controversy, even though for many at the Science of Memory meeting transfer was viewed as a dusty 'retro-concept'. The claim is based upon consideration of the multifaceted role of the concept in our science of learning and memory, a role that has taken on a much richer mantle than many appreciate. First, in several senses, transfer has deep historical roots as a phenomenon that merits study in its own right. Secondly, in contemporary memory theory, transfer has become a fundamental explanatory construct. Thirdly, transfer is the *sine qua non* paradigm for informing the core question of what is learned. Fourthly, transfer is a concept at the heart of evaluation. Fifthly, transfer is the primary target for training and instruction. I next develop each of these themes.

Transfer as a phenomenon

The conditions under which transfer occur and the processes that underlie transfer are core issues in the psychology of learning that transcend a hundred years of paradigm shifts. Working from an educational perspective, early in the twentieth century, Thorndike and Woodworth (1901a) developed the common elements theory of transfer that remains influential in contemporary work (see McDaniel and Schlager 1990). Within the tradition of Gestalt psychology, Katona (1940) conducted a rich series of studies focusing on the issue of transfer and the kind of learning that fostered transfer. Researchers in the verbal learning tradition spawned complex transfer paradigms that became the prototype by which human learning and memory was studied (e.g. the AB–AC transfer paradigm) and from which standard underpinnings of forgetting theory originated (e.g. proactive and retroactive interference). In the contemporary cognitive arena, transfer remains a central phenomenon that is heavily investigated in the problem solving and skill learning (see Chapter 47, this volume) literatures.

More generally, it is possible to subsume all our empirical inquiry in the behavior of learning and memory as the study of transfer. The organism is provided with an experience or set of experiences and we observe subsequent behavior under another particular set of conditions. The observed behaviors reflect transfer from the original experience to the criterial conditions. Even in the standard memory paradigm, memory performances are indices of the extent to which processes engaged during study are able to transfer to the memory task.

Transfer as explanatory construct

Possibly the most widely invoked explanation of memory performance in the current literature hinges on the concept of transfer. The 'transfer-appropriate processing' (TAP) principle holds that memory performance is a function of the degree to which the learning activity stimulates processing that is appropriate for the memory test. TAP has been shown to be more important than the level or the quality of processing in determining memory performance on given memory tasks. For instance, semantic processing produces better memory performance than nonsemantic processing for memory tests for which semantic information is useful. In contrast, nonsemantic processing produces better memory performance than semantic processing for memory tests that require nonsemantic information (Morris *et al.* 1977). Thus, the mnemonic benefit of an encoding activity hinges directly on the extent to which the processing engaged at encoding transfers to the memory test administered.

TAP confers a unifying explanation for the dissociations between explicit and implicit tests of memory. The nature of these dissociations captured a remarkable amount of attention and theoretical creativity from memory researchers. These dissociations showed that stimulus presentation formats and processing activities that consistently produced superior performance on standard measures of memory (e.g. recall and recognition) had no effect or reverse effects on implicit measures of memory (e.g. word stem completion, priming). TAP provides a ready explanation. Explicit tests generally rely on conceptually driven processing, whereas many implicit tests generally rely on data-driven processing. Consequently, conceptually based encoding or processing activities transfer well to explicit memory tests, whereas perceptual encoding transfers well to implicit tests (Roediger *et al.* 1989).

I believe that failure to consider the dynamics of TAP has led to misguided testing practices in education. Multiple choice tests are ubiquitous in education, and these are tests that rely on recognition. Basic laboratory work indicates that processing of individual item information (e.g. details) but not relational information (organization) transfers readily to recognition tests

(Einstein and Hunt 1980). Consequently, time-consuming organizational study activities that students use and that may be recommended by instructors (such as outlining) probably do not provide expected performance benefits on recognition tests administered by instructors (thereby possibly discouraging rich study activities). Consistent with this claim, in an experiment conducted by an undergraduate honors student in my laboratory (Matt Hanson), students who generated outlines for material in a textbook chapter performed no better on a typical multiple choice test given a week later than students who simply read the chapter once.

A similar observation is pertinent for the content targeted on classroom tests. Thomas and McDaniel (in press) have shown that study activities that are not transfer appropriate for a given test penalize performance relative to reading alone. This situation perfectly reflects that experienced by the son of a colleague. In his high school history class, the instructor required students to engage in an integrative study activity (with the compelling acronym PERSIA) that fostered analysis of political, economic, religious and scientific dimensions of a culture. To assess learning, the instructor administered a multiple choice on details of the culture. Unwittingly, performance on the test was an index of TAP more than it was an assessment of the consequence of the rich study strategies encouraged.

Transfer: a window into what is learned

Perhaps the most fundamental issue identified by the cognitive paradigm shift in learning is to identify the mental representations that accrue from learning—this is the issue of what is learned, and it dominates the modern animal learning literature as well as the human concept learning literature. At the heart of this enterprise is the analysis of transfer performance. Transfer tasks are *sine qua non* in informing and revealing what is learned. The linchpins of cognitive theories of concept learning are based on seminal use of transfer tasks in assessing learning of single-attribute concepts such as 'red figures' or 'square shapes'. After training on a particular solution (e.g. any circle or square that is 'red'), the subject was given one of two transfer tasks (Kendler and Kendler 1962). In one task, the subject learned a new solution in which the defining attribute was another color (the reversal shift task). In another transfer task, the subject learned a new solution in which the defining attribute provided somewhat overlapping classifications to those learned with the prior solution (any blue or red square). By showing more positive transfer to the reversal shift transfer task than the other transfer task in humans (but not for nonhuman animals), abstraction and rule learning (color is the relevant dimension) were implicated as the basis of what is learned in categorization tasks (rather than stimulus–response associations).

The current paradigm in concept learning involves transferring subjects to categorize nontrained instances after learning to categorize a set of training instances. This transfer paradigm provides the data that have largely carried the enterprise of legislating and informing our prominent views of what it means to acquire a concept. More recently, the paradigm has been extended to evaluate what is learned when people acquire experience about the relationships between continuous inputs and continuous outputs (i.e. functional relationships). In these paradigms, learners are shown a range of input–output pairings (e.g. particular amounts of a substance ingested with corresponding values of anxiety experienced). After learning to predict the output value associated with a range of input values, learners are transferred to stimulus values outside the training range. The patterns of performance on these extrapolation transfer tasks provide decisive information about what has been learned (see McDaniel and Busemeyer 2005).

Transfer as evaluation

A science of learning must address how to assess competence and expertise, because expertise is the target end-point of learning. The primary gauge of expertise is transfer performance. Expertise is assumed to be dependent on the acquisition of abstract schemata that summarize, organize and penetrate to critical aspects of the domain that are not evident from surface features. Such abstract schemata that underlie expertise are revealed by superior and qualitatively different transfer behaviors: superior transfer to novel problems in a domain, different kinds of information used as foundation for transfer and buffering from negative transfer effects of misleading analogs (see Novick 1988). Thus, transfer is a core concept in evaluation and understanding of expertise.

Transfer as an educational objective

From an educational standpoint, a commonly cited failing is that students are not able to transfer what they have learned in the classroom to the real-world work settings. How to train to promote transfer is the most fundamental challenge of education, and thereby becomes a core concept in considering application of the science of memory.

In summary, the concept of transfer plays an intimate role at every conceptual level the science of memory engages: phenomenon of study, central explanatory construct in memory theory, primary window into the fundamental issue of what is learned and an objective for sound training. What could be more important?

47

Transfer: Specificity and generality

Alice F. Healy

In the science of memory, there have been several different uses of the term 'transfer', but it has typically referred to the effect of training one activity on training or performance of another. Thus, in studying transfer, two activities are normally investigated; let us refer to them as activities A and B. In assessing transfer, we examine the extent to which training activity A influences activity B.

In his classic article on the 'transfer and retroaction surface', Osgood (1949) pointed out that transfer has usually been studied under learning, whereas 'retroaction' has usually been studied under forgetting. Nevertheless, the two constructs of transfer and retroaction can be viewed as complementary. In assessing retroaction, we examine the extent to which activity B influences retention of activity A. The similarities between the stimuli and responses comprising activities A and B are crucial in determining the direction and extent of both transfer and retroaction. In fact, Osgood argued that the same empirical laws of similarity apply to both constructs.

On account of this correspondence between the concepts of transfer and retroaction, it might be thought that the concept of transfer is not unique in the science of memory because it can be understood fully in terms of the concept of retroaction, so that our understanding of the principles underlying forgetting will be sufficient for our understanding of the principles underlying transfer. However, recent research has revealed situations leading to no forgetting but a complete lack of transfer, implying that the conditions promoting optimal retention do not correspond with those promoting optimal transfer.

To illustrate this crucial aspect of the relationship between retention and transfer, let us consider two recent experiments. The first (Healy *et al.* 2006, Experiment 1) involved a speeded response task, in which subjects saw on a computer screen a clock face display with a central start position surrounded by a circle of digits. A target digit was displayed above the start position, and subjects used a computer mouse to move a cursor from the start position to the location of the digit along the circumference of the clock face.

The task was made more difficult by reprogramming the computer mouse to introduce stimulus–response incompatibilities. Three reprogrammed mouse conditions were used: either only horizontal movements were reversed, only vertical movements were reversed, or both horizontal and vertical movements were reversed. Subjects were trained in one condition for five blocks of 80 trials and then returned 1 week later for training in a second session in the same or another condition for another five blocks of trials. As shown in the top panel of Fig. 47.1, comparisons of performance on the first and fifth blocks of session 1 showed a large decrease in movement time (the time to move from the start position to the target location), demonstrating learning of this skill. Comparisons of performance on the fifth block of session 1 and the first block of session 2 also showed a small but significant decrease in movement time for those subjects who were in the same condition in both sessions, reflecting perfect retention and dissipation of fatigue across the 1 week delay. However, for those subjects who were in different conditions in the two sessions, there was actually a trend for movement time on the first block of session 2 to increase relative to that on the first block of session 1. Although subjects learned much during training in session 1, they could not transfer the skill they learned to training on a new condition in session 2.

The second experiment (Healy et al. 2005b, Experiment 2) involved a time production task in which subjects were trained to produce time intervals expressed in arbitrary units. Subjects were not told how long a unit was, but they learned how to produce intervals by feedback on each response. Subjects practiced this task under one of two conditions. In the control condition, they performed no secondary task, whereas in the difficult condition, they performed a secondary task in which they counted backwards through the alphabet by threes (e.g. s to p, etc.). Subjects were trained in one condition for six blocks of six trials, and then returned 1 week later for training in the same or the other condition for another six blocks of trials. Performance was measured in terms of the proportional absolute error (|produced interval – specified interval|/specified interval). Comparing performance on the first and sixth blocks of session 1 showed that subjects improved their skill of time production (see the bottom panel of Fig. 47.1). Also, comparing performance on the sixth block of session 1 and the first block of session 2 revealed no decrement in performance when subjects were in the same condition in both sessions, thus showing perfect skill retention. However, when subjects were in different conditions in the two sessions, performance did suffer across sessions, so that, in fact, performance in the first block of session 2 was comparable with that in the first block of session 1. Thus, again, there was perfect retention but no transfer of this skill from one condition to another,

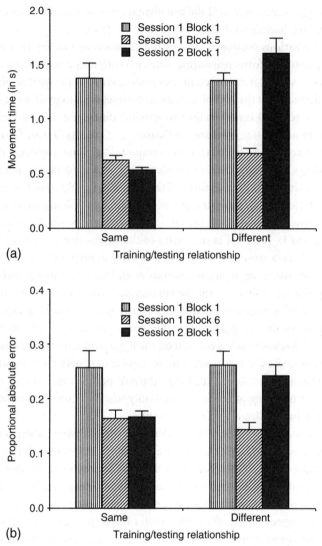

Fig. 47.1 (A) Response movement time (in s) as a function of the relationship between training and testing in reprogrammed mouse conditions for session 1 block 1, session 1 block 5 and session 2 block 1. From Healy *et al.* 2006 (Experiment 1). (B) Proportional absolute error as a function of the relationship between training and testing in time production conditions for session 1 block 1, session 1 block 6 and session 2 block 1. From Healy *et al.* 2005*b* (Experiment 2).

even though the required skill did not change; instead the only change was in the secondary, background task.

There are various possible operational definitions of transfer. One measure compares initial performance during activity B with initial performance during activity A. A second measure compares performance at the start of activity B with performance at the end of activity A, both when activity B is the same as activity A (retention) and when the two activities differ (transfer). A third popular measure of transfer compares the learning of activity B with the original learning of activity A (savings). However, no matter how transfer is defined, these findings, like many others in the literature, can be understood in terms of a set of relatively simple, straightforward theoretical principles and models.

According to the principles, transfer is optimal when training (activity A) and testing (activity B) match. By the *encoding specificity principle* (Tulving and Thomson 1973), retrieval is successful to the extent that the encoding cues and operations correspond with those available at retrieval. By the *transfer-appropriate processing principle* (Morris *et al.* 1977; McDaniel *et al.* 1978), performance depends more on the correspondence between the processing occurring during acquisition and that occurring during testing than on the level of processing during acquisition. By the *procedural reinstatement principle* (Healy *et al.* 2005a), which is focused on the long-term retention of knowledge and skills, procedural information is more durable than declarative information. Following Kolers and Roediger (1984), durable performance lacks generality because performance at test is optimal only when the procedures acquired during training are duplicated during testing.

Likewise, according to the models, transfer occurs only when there is a match in elements between the first and second activities. Thorndike (1906) was the first to propose this theory of 'identical elements', with stimulus–response associations as elements. Singley and Anderson (1989) proposed a more recent version of this theory, with production rules as elements.

The high degree of specificity of transfer implied by these principles and models and found in the research described here needs to be tempered with an acknowledgment of the generality of transfer found in other studies [e.g. Harlow's learning sets (1949)], so that a distinction should be made between specificity and generality of transfer. An expansion of the procedural reinstatement principle provides a working hypothesis about when there will be specificity or generality of transfer. Specificity (i.e. limited transfer) may occur for tasks based primarily on procedural information or skill, whereas generality (i.e. robust transfer) may occur for tasks based primarily on declarative information or facts. Another recent experiment has shown just how powerful transfer can be for such a task (Kole and Healy 2006, Experiment 3). In this experiment, subjects learned 144 facts, 12 facts each about 12 unfamiliar people or 12 unfamiliar countries. Experimental subjects were given prior training to associate each unfamiliar item with a familiar individual (e.g. a friend or relative); control subjects were given no prior association training. All subjects were given three rounds of fact learning followed by a cued recognition test. The proportion of correct responses on the test for experimental subjects who had been trained to associate the unfamiliar items with familiar individuals (0.643) was more than twice as high as that for control subjects who had not received such association training (0.308), and this advantage for mediated learning was essentially as large for learning facts about countries (which are conceptually unrelated to the familiar individuals) as for learning facts about other people. Also, prior knowledge about familiar individuals aided learning facts about unfamiliar individuals even though the facts were unlikely to be true about the familiar individuals with whom they were associated.

Based on the combined findings from these recent studies, the following hypothesis summarizes both the relationship between retention and transfer and the conditions yielding specificity or generality of transfer: for skill learning, retention is strong but transfer is limited, whereas, for fact learning, retention is poor but transfer is robust.

Acknowledgments

The research discussed here was supported in part by Army Research Institute Contract DASW01-03-K-0002 and Army Research Office Grant W9112NF-05-1-0153 to the University of Colorado. I am indebted to Lyle Bourne and Erica Wohldmann for insightful discussions concerning this chapter.

48

Integrative comments
Transfer: The ubiquitous concept

Henry L. Roediger III

Transfer refers to the effect of practice on one task to learning another task performed at a later time. Every case of new learning in any organism represents an instance of transfer, in the sense that past experiences may make the new learning easier or harder. No act of learning and memory occurs in a vacuum; new learning always reflects transfer of past habits and knowledge already acquired.

The simplest measure of transfer involves a criterial task of some type (called task B here for convenience). At issue is how some prior task might affect later performance on the criterial task, relative to a control group that has been given no training or training thought to be irrelevant to B (to control for general practice effects). One group of subjects might initially practice task A, a second group task C, and a third group may either receive no training or training on an irrelevant task. The results might show that, relative to learning of task B by the control group, subjects who had practiced task A performed better on task B, whereas those who had practiced task C performed worse. These outcomes would then represent cases of positive and negative transfer from tasks A and C, respectively. Of course, the logic of transfer of training designs, as they are called, hinges critically on the control group accurately representing a neutral point.

These elementary definitions in the preceding paragraph (and more complex variations) were once well known to every student of experimental psychology, even at the undergraduate level. Textbooks devoted both to experimental psychology and to human learning and memory routinely had at least one chapter devoted solely to transfer, or to transfer and the related concept of retroaction (e.g. Woodworth 1938). However, some time during the 1970s the topic of transfer fell out, both out of textbooks and, to some degree, out of the research literature. In retrospect, this seems quite surprising because all studies of learning and memory can be considered studies of transfer, as all the authors of chapters in this section note in one way or another.

Unlike other fundamental concepts considered in this volume (e.g. forgetting), the definition of transfer and designs to study the topic are not the subject of hot debate. Rather, the issue at hand is more the application of the concept across wide ranges of the field. As Dudai (Chapter 44, this volume) notes, transfer is never explicitly discussed by contemporary neurobiologists, although they implicitly use the logic of transfer designs in their research. Students of animal learning and behavior avowedly study transfer, and Capaldi (Chapter 45, this volume) notes that one of the great discoveries in animal learning behavior—that behavior persists during extinction training (with no rewards given) much longer if prior training had occurred with a partial schedule of reinforcement than with a continuous schedule of reinforcement—is based on a transfer design. Stated differently, the partial reinforcement extinction effect refers to the fact that partial schedules of reinforcement transfer better to extinction schedules than do continuous schedules of reinforcement. Of course, the study of many other central topics discovered in studies of animal learning, such as stimulus generalization, also depend explicitly upon transfer designs.

Healy (Chapter 47, this volume) is concerned with another critical dimension of transfer, its generality or specificity. Her new research reviewed here shows cases of remarkable specificity of transfer, agreeing with other findings in various literatures on the topic, from studies of reading and memory (see Kolers and Roediger 1984) to those of problem solving and reasoning (e.g. Gick and Holyoak 1980). The aim of education is to train for broad transfer, where students will leave their classes and go into the world able to apply their training to many different classes of problem. However, anecdotal complaints from the business world about students who cannot apply what they know, as well as considerable laboratory evidence (Chapter 47, this volume), shows that transfer is often narrow rather than broad. This specificity of transfer is a critical issue in psychology, in education and in many other domains (e.g. training for tasks in the military and in industry). McDaniel (Chapter 46, this volume) is not being overly exuberant when he writes that 'Transfer is the most central concept in learning and memory'. All research on learning and memory involves transfer; all tasks we perform every day are transfer tasks; all acts of retrieval are the transfer of learning from one situation to a new situation in which retrieval is provoked by cues and the subject's retrieval set (or mode), often induced through instructions.

Transfer effects have always been considered critical to education, and the explicit study of transfer of learning can be traced to educational issues debated at the turn of the twentieth century (and beliefs held long before that). Many educators believed in the concept of formal discipline, the idea that learning to memorize sets of material in one domain would practice some general skill and make learning of other types of material easier. Formal discipline was once a firmly held principle of educational practice and encouraged an emphasis on memorization as a skill. The concept has waxed and waned in popularity over the years, but never seems to quite lose its grip, despite largely negative evidence for its efficacy. I memorized Edgar Allan Poe's *The Raven* as a freshman in high school so that I could both write it and recite it, assured by my English teacher that this exercise would help me learn other subjects such as Latin and algebra more easily. Although one can point to studies here and there showing positive effects (e.g. Winch 1908), the literature mostly shows that such ideas are wrong. William James (1890) reported experiments in his famous textbook that led him to call formal discipline into question (Volume I, p. 666), and Thorndike and Woodworth (1901*a,b,c*) conducted numerous studies of transfer that called the concept into question. In *Educational Psychology: Briefer Course*, Thorndike thundered against the accepted idea of formal discipline: 'By doubling a boy's reasoning power in arithmetical problems we do not double it for formal grammar or chess or economic history or theories of evolution' (1914, p. 268).

One absolutely secure phenomenon somewhat related to that of formal discipline is learning-to-learn, shown in many tasks. If people are given the same experimental task (e.g. learning successive lists of paired associates with different pairs in each list), they get better over lists. Because the content across lists does not overlap, the subjects are learning general skills in how to learn the list (e.g. Postman and Schwartz 1964). However, learning-to-learn differs from formal discipline in that subjects become better on practicing the same task, not in transferring the general skill to other, dissimilar tasks (as would be required for a strict form of formal discipline). As Healy (Chapter 47, this volume) notes, even one task that seems to have great *a priori* similarity to another task can fail to provide positive transfer to that task.

Can any theoretical approaches account for positive and negative transfer across a variety of domains? At some broad level, almost all theories of transfer have something in common with Thorndike's theory of identical elements, which was advanced in his works already cited (Thorndike and Woodworth 1901*a,b,c*; Thorndike 1914). The general form of Thorndike's argument is that tasks can be considered as composed of elements (either its contents or processes) and that positive transfer will occur if elements from a first task (A) overlap with those in a second task (B). (The control task used is designed to have no elements in common.) If a first task (C) has elements that conflict with those of the second (B) task, then negative transfer results, because subjects must overcome the competition between elements.

Critics pounced on Thorndike's ideas for two basic reasons: elements of tasks are hard to define, and the relationship between elements of two tasks need not be one of literal identity; similarity of task components can lead to positive transfer. Both criticisms are accurate, although they differ in their severity. The second can be overcome by changing *identity* to *similarity* of elements, but the first—defining elements—is most difficult. Within the context of a particular task, such as paired-associate learning, it is possible to use task analysis to define components. McGuire (1961) argued (and showed) that paired-associate learning involved three component processes (response learning; stimulus discrimination; and associative hook-up, or associating stimuli to responses appropriately). Osgood (1949) proposed his 'transfer and retroaction surface' as a means to account for paradoxical findings of positive and negative transfer, but wholly in the domain of paired-associate learning. No one has attempted to generalize his arguments to more complex forms of transfer, such as those reported by Healy (Chapter 47, this volume) or Kolers and Perkins (1975), to take but two examples.

The idea of transfer-appropriate processing (a phrase coined by Morris *et al.* 1977) and advocated by McDaniel (Chapter 46, this volume), among many others, put the emphasis on types of processing instead of (or in addition to) the contents of memory traces (considered as elements or features). Briefly, according to the transfer-appropriate processing approach, performance on a test of memory (of whatever sort) will be enhanced when processing operations required during the test phase recapitulate those required during an encoding or study phase. This idea encompasses mental operations as well as mental contents as determinants of transfer, and is illustrated by findings in tasks such as rereading transformed text (Kolers 1975) or naming fragmented pictures or words (Roediger *et al.* 1989), tasks that measure retention indirectly.

The transfer-appropriate processing approach is able to encompass many findings in the cognitive memory literature in a general way, but suffers from certain difficulties. A major one is that there is no generally accepted catalog of types of processing [although Roediger *et al.* (1989) argued that perceptual and conceptual processing could be considered two important types]. A related difficulty, because of the inability to define features or processing crisply, is that all these approaches run the risk of circularity. When an experimental result fails to show the expected form of transfer, the theorist can appeal to having misidentified the relevant elements, features or type of processing (for discussion of this issue, see Roediger *et al.* 2002). Clearly much theoretical work remains in order to understand transfer effects properly. Osgood's (1949) theory is perhaps the most heroic, but is applicable to a limited domain (and debated even within that domain; see Hall 1971, pp. 375–385).

Transfer studies make another important point that might be called 'the relativity of remembering', using the term *remembering* in its generic, nontechnical sense (of 'memory performance'). Many different tests and assessments of memory are possible, even in laboratory settings; there is no acid 'test of memory'. When multiple valid measures of memory are examined as a function of various independent variables, they often reveal that performance across measures is uncorrelated. *Relativity of remembering* refers to this fact that the outcome of an experiment is relative, depending on the particular memory test used and the relationship between the study or encoding conditions and the test conditions. For example, studying words (e.g. *eagle*) in one study condition (e.g. judging whether a word belongs to a semantic category such as birds) may have a large positive effect relative to another encoding condition (making rhyme judgments about words; does the word rhyme with *legal*?) on a later recall or recognition test for the words. This outcome constitutes the standard levels-of-processing effect (Craik and Tulving 1975). However, after the same study conditions, the opposite outcome may occur on a memory test that measures recognition of rhyming words from the study list (did a word that rhymed with *beagle* occur in the list?), because the test requiring knowledge of rhymes overlaps more with the information encoded in the rhyming condition at study (Morris *et al.* 1977). Finally, on other tests that use phonemic retrieval cues, no effects of encoding condition have been observed (Fisher and Craik 1977). The same generally null results from varying phonemic and semantic processing during study occur on perceptual implicit memory tests such as identification of briefly presented words (Jacoby and Dallas 1981) or completion of word-stems or word-fragments with the first word coming to mind (Roediger *et al.* 1992).

The bottom line is that several different tests, all of which indubitably assess some form of memory, show completely different patterns of performance as a function of the type of study processing. Such dissociations are of interest to those studying memory, but often seem to be considered as exceptions to some general rule (of parallel results across tests). However, Kolers and Roediger (1984) argued that such dissociations are really the rule, not the exception, in transfer designs. The reason much research rarely uncovers such differences is that most experiments examine a single measure of retention. Whole careers are built on studying one measure (whether fear conditioning, or free recall, or the Morris water maze, or passive step-down avoidance) and assuming that the principles emerging from these studies are general ones, applying to all forms of memory. For example, what is known about episodic memory from neuroimaging experiments is almost entirely derived from studies of yes/no recognition memory.

The assumption that underlies such single measure experiments—that all memory measures correlate and measure some quantity such as 'strength of memory—is surely wrong. Perhaps the most systematic study illuminating the relativity of remembering was conducted by Challis et al. (1996), who crossed five encoding conditions in which words were studied with various tasks and instructions with six different conditions employing a variety of memory tests (with a different group of subjects receiving each test). The details of the study (using a 5 × 6 design!) are rather complex. However, the tests involved a variety of standard memory tests (both explicit and implicit) used in many laboratory paradigms. The fascinating results from the experiment showed radically different patterns of performance across tests, i.e. the tests differed markedly among themselves in revealing effects of past experiences afforded by the prior encoding conditions. Although the results of Challis et al. used many tests, practically every experiment using just two or three rather different memory tasks shows the same complexity between encoding and testing conditions. The standard outcome is an interaction, and this fact severely undermines the common assumption that memories vary in some straight-forward quantitative fashion, often referred to as 'memory strength', because such strength theories predict a uniformity of results across tests. Tests may be differentially sensitive to strength, by this view, but the ordering of conditions should not change. Yet clearly it does.

To conclude, if a researcher claims that 'variable X has a positive effect on memory', you can be almost certain the claim is untrue. The claimant really means 'Our study has shown that variable X has a positive effect on a particular measure of memory'. We can be almost certain that if some other perfectly valid measure were used, either no effect, a different effect or even the opposite effect would have been obtained. Transfer studies clearly undercut the idea of unitary notions of memory by revealing dissociations among tests and, consequently, the multiplicity of forms of retention. Ideas such as transfer-appropriate processing provide some understanding of these puzzling facts, although clearly much theoretical work to expand these ideas is needed. Transfer is the fundamental concept for understanding the science of memory.

13

Inhibition

Inhibition refers to situations when some factor causes performance on a memory task to fall below some neutral baseline or control condition. (When a factor creates an improvement in performance relative to the control condition, the corresponding term is facilitation.) However, this neutral definition of inhibition is not the sense that causes its inclusion here as a key concept. Rather, many researchers refer to a process of inhibition that impairs responding (behavioral inhibition) or that keeps unwanted memories from clogging the mind when some desired information is sought (cognitive inhibition). Some researchers have argued that inhibition is critical for successful performance in many memory tasks; for example, if in looking for a parked car, one were forced to retrieve simultaneously all prior places in which one had parked. Inhibition can be observed and studied in many different paradigms, and the concept is a central one. However, the mechanisms used to explain inhibitory effects differ across situations.

H.L.R.

49

Inhibition: Diversity of cortical functions

György Buzsáki

Summary

Learning and memory require that specific information is represented by specific coalitions of cell assemblies. In addition to principal cells, the cortex contains diverse classes of interneurons that selectively and discriminately innervate various parts of principal cells and each other. The hypothesized 'goal' of the daunting connectionist schemes of interneurons is to provide maximum functional complexity. Interneurons provide *autonomy and independence to neighboring principal cells* but at the same time also offer useful *temporal coordination*. The functional diversity of principal cells is enhanced by the domain-specific actions of GABAergic interneurons, which can dynamically alter the qualities of the principal cells. The balance between excitation and inhibition is often accomplished by *oscillations*. Thus, the cerebral cortex is not only a complex system with complicated interactions among identical constituents but it has developed a diverse system of components as well. Compromise with the inhibition-assisted process impairs both the learning process and recall.

Homeostatic dynamics in the brain can only be maintained if the excitatory forces are balanced by equally effective inhibitory forces. The required inhibition in the cerebral cortex is provided by specialized classes of inhibitory neurons. If only excitatory cells were present in the brain, neurons could not create form or order or secure some autonomy for themselves. Such autonomy of principal cells and cell assemblies is secured by the inhibitory system that can flexibly segregate neuronal coalitions, mechanisms fundamental to all cortical operations, and critical to mechanisms of learning and memory. Inhibition-mediated segregation allows that only specific information is learned and memorized, and that the same assemblies are mobilized in the recall process.

Inhibitory networks generate nonlinear effects

The most basic functions accomplished by neuronal networks are pattern completion and pattern separation, functions related to *integration and differentiation*. Separation of inputs in a network with only excitatory connections is not possible. However, with inhibitory connections, the competing cell assemblies and even neighboring excitatory neurons can be functionally isolated, and excitatory paths re-routed by the traffic-controlling ability of coordinated interneuron groups (Fig. 49.1). The specific firing patterns of principal cells in a network thus depend on the temporal and spatial distribution of inhibition. As a result, in response to the same input, the same network can produce a different output pattern at different times, depending on the state of inhibition. The coordinated inhibition ensures that excitatory activity *recruits the right number of neurons in the right temporal window* and that excitation spreads in the *right direction*. None of these important features can be achieved by principal cells alone. The balanced partnership between excitatory and inhibitory neurons ensures an overall homeostatic regulation of global firing rates of neurons over extended territories of the cortex, yet, this balance allows for dramatic increases of local excitability in short time windows, necessary for sending messages and modifying network connections. Balance and feedback control are also essential principles for oscillations, and interneuron networks are the backbone of many brain oscillators (Buzsaki and Chrobak 1995).

Interneurons multiply the computational ability of principal cells

Brain systems with 'simple' computational demands evolved only a few neurons types. For example, the thalamus, basal ganglia or the cerebellum, systems that can support only nonconscious memories, possess a low degree of variability in their neuron types. In contrast, cortical structures have evolved not only five principal cell types but numerous classes of GABAergic inhibitory interneurons as well (Freund and Buzsaki 1996). Every surface domain of cortical principal cells is under the specific control of a unique interneuron class. This is a clever way of multiplying the functional repertoire of principal cells, using mostly local interneuron wiring. Adding more interneurons of the same type linearly increases the network's combinatorial properties. Adding novel interneuron types to the old network, even if in very small numbers, offers a nonlinear expansion of qualitatively different possibilities.

The extensive computational capacity of a single principal cell is seldom utilized at once. Furthermore, principal cells with a large or small dendritic

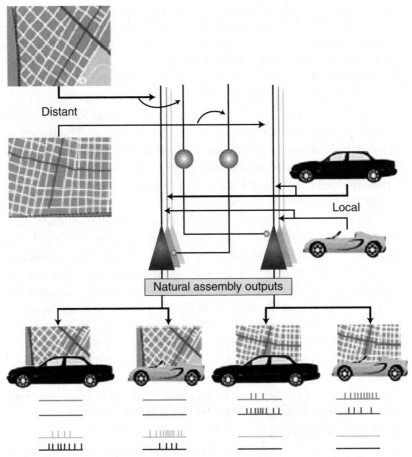

Fig. 49.1 Interneuron network-mediated inhibition allows for grouping and segregation of memory representations. Coordinated inhibition ensures that excitatory activity recruits the right number of principal neurons (blue) in the right temporal window, and that excitation spreads along the appropriate trajectory. Input from distant cues in one environment (e.g. city part) activates a set of interneurons (represented here by a single neuron, red) which, in turn, prevents the activity of assemblies representing other environments. Variations in local cues (e.g. from the car) selectively adjust the activity level of the chosen assembly members (right). (From Buzsáki, G. (2005). Similar is different in hippocampal networks. *Science* **309**: 568–69. Reprinted with permission from the American Association for the Advancement of Science.)

arbor or neurons with similar geometry but different distribution of ion channels generate a different output in response to the same input. Dividing the full computational power of principal cells into numerous subroutines that can be flexibly used according to momentary needs is an enormous advantage; this important service is provided with ease by the interneuron system. Interneurons can functionally 'eliminate' a dendritic segment or a whole dendrite, selectively inactivate Ca^{2+} channels, or segregate dendrites from the soma or the soma from the axon. In effect, such actions of interneurons are *functionally equivalent to replacing a principal cell with a morphologically different type*. The division of labor and, consequently, the multiplexed output of principal cells are brought about by a diverse group of interneurons (Freund and Buzsaki 1996; Somogyi *et al.* 1998).

In their relationship to the principal cells, three major interneuron families are recognized. The first and largest family of interneurons, basket cells and chandelier cells, controls the spiking output of principal cells by providing perisomatic inhibition. Interneurons of the second family target specific dendritic domains of principal cells. Every known excitatory pathway in the cortex has a matching family of interneurons. Several additional subclasses seek out two or more overlapping or nonoverlapping dendritic regions, and yet other subclasses innervate the somata and nearby dendrites with similar probability. Because the different domains of principal cells have different functional dynamics, interneurons innervating those specific domains adapted their kinetic properties to match their targets. Not surprisingly, members of the dendrite-targeting interneuron family display the largest variability.

In addition to affecting the activity of principal cells, interneurons also innervate each other by an elaborate scheme and affect each other's biophysical properties. An important subgroup with at least some overlap with the dendrite-targeting family contains a special set of interneurons whose axon trees span two or more anatomical regions and some axon collaterals cross the hemispheric midline and/or innervate subcortical structures, hence the term 'long-range' interneuron. Such widely projecting, long-range neurons are rare but, in light of the functional importance of small-world graphs, their role must be absolutely critical. They provide the *necessary conduit for synchronizing distantly operating oscillators* and allow for *coherent timing* of a large number of neurons that are not connected directly with each other. The third distinct family of interneurons has the distinguishing characteristics that their axons completely avoid principal cells and contact exclusively other interneurons. With perhaps 20 or more distinguished interneuron types in the cerebral cortex, the complexity of their wiring must be enormous, although the critical details are not yet known (Somogyi *et al.* 1998).

The advantage of varying the surface domain innervation of the principal cells by the different interneuron classes becomes especially clear when temporal dynamics are also included. For example, basket cells respond with decreasing efficacy when stimulated by high frequency inputs because of their 'depressing' input synapses. In contrast, several types of dendrite-targeting interneurons fail to generate spike output when driven at low frequency and require several pulses before they begin to discharge because their input synapses are of the facilitatory type. The consequence of such dynamics is easy to visualize. When a pyramidal neuron discharges at a low rate, it activates almost exclusively its perisomatic interneurons. On the other hand, at a higher discharge rate, the somatic inhibition decreases and inhibition is shifted to the dendritic domain. Time *is thus transformed into subcellular space*, due to the frequency filtering behavior of synapses.

The interneuron system as a distributed clock

Despite its multifarious wiring, the *principal cell system alone cannot carry out any useful computation*. It is the inhibitory neuronal network, when coupled to the principal cells, that provides the flexibility needed for the complex operations of the brain. *Balance of opposing forces*, such as excitation and inhibition, often *gives rise to rhythmic behavior*. Providing rhythm-based timing to the principal cells at multiple time scales is one of the most important roles of interneurons. Once a collective oscillatory pattern arises, it constrains *the timing freedom of its members* and decreases the windows of opportunity for the principal cells to discharge: principal cells, therefore, get synchronized. Synchronization by oscillation occurs at multiple time scales, according to the large numbers of oscillators at various frequencies, covering time epochs from tens of seconds to milliseconds. The duration of the oscillation, in turn, regulates the length of messages that can be transmitted as well as the spatial extent of neuronal pools involved. Through oscillations, the interneuron system allows the principal cells in the cerebral cortex to function at multiple temporal and spatial levels (Buzsaki and Draguhn 2004). The essence of cortical function is that the result of local computation is transmitted to distant groups. Conversely, large-scale cortical activity constrains local computation. This bidirectionality is a fundamental aspect of global cortical computation. Only systems with such regenerative and self-organized (spontaneous) activity can give rise to conscious behaviors, including declarative memories.

50

Inhibition: Attentional regulation of cognition

Lynn Hasher

The term 'inhibition' has played a role in psychology and physiology since at least the mid-nineteenth century (Smith 1992). Then, as now, some used the term loosely, others tied it to operations, or to physiology (or both). Indeed, many saw inhibition as an essential process for education, mental health and moral behavior (Smith 1992, Chapter 7). Many of the great names (e.g. Morgan, Freud, Ribot, James and Wundt) associated with the origins of psychology commented on, relied on and/or criticized notions of inhibition (see Diamond et al. 1963, Chapter 8). In today's light, some of the early meanings attributed to inhibition are insulting (e.g. to women) and wrong headed, others however (e.g. Morgan 1891, pp. 459–461) are congruent with the concept of inhibition proposed by Hasher and Zacks in 1988 (see also Hasher et al. 1999; 2007).

A fundamental assumption in the view of Hasher and Zacks, a fundamental assumption is that familiar stimuli activate their representations automatically—with or without awareness—and that this massive activation (and its spread to associated representations) can and must be downregulated in order for organized behavior to achieve an individual's long- and short-term goals. This downregulation is accomplished by *inhibitory* mechanisms that operate in the service of goals.

Familiar stimuli are present in both the immediate environment and in the world of thought. Individuals are presumed, in this framework, to differ minimally in activation processes, but to differ greatly in the efficiency of inhibition—or in the ability to downregulate activation. People with generally poor inhibitory abilities will have difficulty ignoring concurrent distraction, as well as difficulty in stopping thoughts and actions that were recently relevant, but that no longer are. As well, they may have difficulty stopping thoughts tied to anticipation of events in the near future, i.e. individuals (and groups of individuals) with poor or inefficient inhibitory mechanisms will have particular difficulty living in the moment and satisfying immediate goals because their thoughts and actions are rather more under the control of the excitation triggered by environmental stimuli and recent and future thoughts and events than under the control of their own goals.

Lapses in inhibitory regulation have a number of consequences. For one, they create high levels of distractibility, resulting in slowed and error-prone behavior. Lapses enable the production of strong but momentarily incorrect responses, as well as poor retrieval of specific events. Poor retrieval of details is the consequence of *two* inhibitory-based problems. The first occurs at encoding when poor inhibitory regulation creates memory representations (or bundles) that are cluttered with irrelevant along with relevant information. The problem created for retrieval is that searching through a cluttered memory trace results in slower and less accurate performance than does searching though an uncluttered trace. Inhibition plays a second role at retrieval. Because any cue can retrieve more than one memory representation, inhibition must suppress any nonrelevant representations that come to mind in order to conduct a search through the relevant memory bundle. That is, the downregulation enabled by inhibition is required for choice in memory retrieval (as it is in any other situation with competing options). Poor suppression at retrieval thus slows choice between activated sets of representations and, should that process be successful, poor suppression will also slow search within a selected memory bundle that contains nonrelevant representations.

On these bases, one might think that people with poor inhibitory abilities should have a great deal of difficulty achieving their goals and coping with the intellectual and social demands of their world—and some may indeed have such problems. However, it is also possible that the absence of strong inhibition can set the stage for aspects of preserved and possibly even superior cognition. For example, people who do not filter out irrelevant information during encoding will learn about that 'irrelevant' information tacitly and may be able to use that knowledge subsequently (e.g. Rowe *et al.* 2006). Also, greater creativity may be in part a result of reduced inhibitory regulation.

This viewpoint predicts (or postdicts) a number of reliable findings in the aging literature, including slowing, reduced working memory performance, differences in patterns of comprehension, reduced access to details about the past, poor control over strong responses, among others (see Winocur and Hasher 2002, for similarities and differences in inhibition between older humans and nonhuman animals). It is important to note with respect to human aging that not all differences between normal younger and healthy older adults (or any other groups with reduced inhibitory efficiency) should be attributed to inhibition because at least some differences may well be tied to differences in individuals' or groups' goals and values (e.g. May *et al.* 2005).

Healthy older adults are not the only individuals with reduced inhibitory regulation; those with mild cognitive impairment may show even greater problems, as may those with dementia. Depressed individuals and perhaps individuals with schizophrenia, with attention deficit disorder and those operating under high levels of stress may also have inhibitory deficits. Of course, there will be individual differences in the 'normal' young adult population as well. Recent neuroimaging studies with both younger and older adults have shown a relationship between the ability to suppress activation to irrelevant stimuli and the ability to remember the targets (Gazzaley *et al.* 2005).

Some have suggested that the gold standard for demonstrating inhibition is evidence of below baseline activation (where baselines vary with tasks). Such findings have been reported in both neuroimaging and behavioral studies (May and Hasher 1998; Gazzaley *et al.* 2005). It is worth noting, however, that to be effective, inhibition need not reduce activated representations to such a level, it merely needs to dampen the activation accorded to familiar or recent representations. It is this dampening that probably permits the selection of a goal-related representation in thought (or action), changes in the current contents of consciousness, the creation of boundaries between events and, ultimately, goal-driven behavior.

At a conceptual level, it is unclear whether or not there is one type of inhibition, or multiple types, each with different underlying determinants and with different age and individual difference trajectories. For example, the ability to regulate strong responses (termed *restraint* control by Hasher and Zacks, often referred to simply as 'inhibition' by others) may or may not be mediated by the same factors that underlie the ability to ignore concurrent distraction (termed *access* control) and both of these may or may not be different from the inhibition required to stop processing one topic (or to create an event boundary) and so to start another (termed *deletion* control; all terms from Hasher *et al.* 1998). All of these may or may not be different from the inhibition entailed in paradigms used by Anderson and Bjork (1994). The three mechanisms proposed by Hasher *et al.* are conceptually useful but may or may not prove to be separable at either a behavioral or a neural level.

With respect to the issue of tying behavior to underlying physiology, those connections are highly desirable now, as they were in the last century (Dodge 1926), and perhaps the goal is more attainable as well (Gazzaley *et al.* 2005). In addition to neuroimaging and animal model studies, another approach to understanding the underlying physiology is to explore performance on tasks requiring inhibitory control at peak versus off-peak times of day, on the assumption that excitatory processes are invariant across waking hours but inhibitory processes are not (Hasher *et al.* 2005). What the underlying physiology might be is currently unclear, but some evidence suggests a focus on frontal function and on neurotransmitters that are particularly critical for frontal function and likely pathways from frontal to other regions in the brain.

No good (or bad) concept is without its critics and, in this, the concept of inhibition is in excellent company, for example with such concepts as automaticity and capacity. Included among contemporary—and nineteenth and twentieth century—criticisms of the construct of inhibition are issues such as whether or not a particular task necessitates inhibition as an explanation and the lack of a direct connection from behavior to underlying physiology.

At a purely conceptual level, inhibition is a mechanism that stops ongoing activity or that reduces the activation of one or more competitors for thought and action, thereby enabling the selection of those consistent with goals. Like many of our forebears (see Smith 1992), we view inhibition as a general attentional mechanism impacting on intellectual life broadly, ranging from memory, to choice and decision making, to language comprehension, and to creativity and problem solving. In this conception, inhibition is a seen as a cognitive primitive that underlies individual, age and other group differences in the more commonly studied mechanisms of working memory and speed (see Hasher *et al.* 2007). As such, it may prove to be the (or a) key mechanism underlying general intelligence. When behavior is driven by excitation unmodulated by inhibitory control, people are likely to rely on implicitly acquired and expressed knowledge or on well-practiced behavior patterns and highly accessible constructs. Inhibition sets the stage for coherent behavior that is largely under the control of goals, rather than behavior that is under the control of passing stimuli and thoughts.

Acknowledgments

The conceptual work underlying this chapter was done in full collaboration with Rose Zacks. Because of conference limitations, she is not listed as a co-author. Considerable debt is owed as well to Cynthia May at the College of Charleston and Cindy Lustig at the University of Michigan. Many ideas were sharpened because of their questions. The work was supported by a grant from the US National Institute on Aging, R 37 AG 04306.

51

Inhibition: Manifestations in long-term memory

Michael C. Anderson

Many of the concepts discussed in this volume are concerned with mechanisms that enable or enhance memory. To see memory only through the lens of facilitatory mechanisms, however, is to miss a class of processes vital to its proper functioning: inhibition. Inhibition refers to a mechanism that acts upon a memory trace to induce a potentially reversible and graded change in its state, making the trace less accessible. At first blush, the idea of a process that impairs memory might seem odd, because forgetting is considered undesirable by most people. More often than people realize, however, having good memory for a prior experience is not what we want. We are frequently confronted with intrusive remindings that undermine performance on some task or that otherwise distract us. Sometimes, these remindings are unpleasant—memories of trauma or loss, or of events that make us sad, anxious or embarrassed. Other times, our motives for controlling unwanted memories may be utilitarian, as when we simply need to ensure that only the most current knowledge is accessed (e.g. today's parking spot, and not yesterday's). When unwanted memories intrude into mind, some means of reducing their accessibility becomes desirable (Bjork 1989; Anderson 2003).

In this chapter, I discuss the idea that inhibition functions to regulate the accessibility of unwanted traces in memory. The first section reviews key theoretical attributes of inhibition, and the functions that it serves. I then illustrate these attributes and functions with examples from research on the role of inhibitory control in forgetting.

The concept of inhibition

The previous definition points to four important attributes of inhibition. First, the term inhibition implies a mechanism external to a memory trace that acts upon it. The term does not refer to just any process that changes a memory; it excludes, for example, changes in the structural integrity of a memory that were not induced by an external process (e.g. memory decay). Secondly, inhibition modifies the state of a trace. This claim implies (1) that independent of its associative connections to other traces, a memory has a state of excitation that influences its accessibility, and (2) that that state can be altered by inhibition in a graded fashion. Thirdly, the reduction in activity renders the trace less accessible, impairing recall. Finally, the change in a memory's activation state is often thought to be reversible, so that a memory can regain some of its accessibility. This reversibility contrasts with permanent changes (e.g. unlearning) that might affect the structural integrity of the memory.

Most inhibition theorists also believe that inhibition achieves at least one of two computational functions: resolving competition between representations or processing structures, or stopping a process. Thus, when multiple responses are activated by a cue, or a process needs to be disengaged, inhibition limits the influence of undesired representations. These ideas are clearly reflected in work on memory control, to which I turn next.

The role of inhibition in memory control

The foregoing properties and functions of inhibition are well illustrated through work on how people control unwanted memories. In my work, for example, I have argued that people control unwanted memories by recruiting inhibitory mechanisms similar to those used to control overt action (Anderson 2003). By this view, memory control is an instance of response override, in which one must stop a strong habitual response to a stimulus due to situational demands. For example, each of us has reflexively tried to catch a falling object. If the object is a cactus, however, this reflex needs to be stopped to prevent a painful outcome. The ability to override habitual responses is thought to be supported by inhibition. If inhibition is central to stopping action, might it also be engaged to control internal 'actions', such as retrieval?

We have examined inhibition in two memory situations likely to require response override: the need for selection during retrieval and the need to stop retrieval itself. In both cases, overriding unwanted memories appears to impair memory in a manner consistent with inhibition. I discuss these two situations in turn.

Inhibition in selective retrieval

The role of inhibition in selective retrieval can be illustrated through the phenomenon of retrieval-induced forgetting. A central problem during retrieval is how we access a target trace when the cues guiding retrieval are related to many memories. A century of research shows that storing similar competing traces in memory impedes retrieval, and increases the chances of a retrieval error (for a review of this literature, see Anderson and Neely 1996). While calling a friend, you may dial their old telephone number by mistake or, while leaving work, you may accidentally walk to yesterday's parking spot. Such intrusions are at best distracting and, at worst, dangerous. According to the response override view, memory intrusions trigger control mechanisms that inhibit the unwanted trace. If inhibition persists, it may be detected by examining later recall of the distracting trace. Thus, this view makes a counter-intuitive prediction: the very act of remembering should cause forgetting. This predicted effect has been referred to as *retrieval-induced forgetting* (Anderson *et al.* 1994). Retrieval-induced forgetting has been found in a broad range of circumstances, including the retrieval of facts, semantic memories, word meanings, autobiographical memories and eyewitness memory (for reviews, see Levy and Anderson 2002; Anderson 2003).

The impaired recall of unpracticed items implies an active process that increases forgetting for competing items, beyond what would be expected by the passage of time. However, the enhanced forgetting does not by itself imply that inhibition was at work because there are many ways that recall can be impaired without inhibition (Anderson and Bjork 1994). The claim that inhibition underlies retrieval-induced forgetting amounts to the specific claim that the memory traces of the affected items have been reduced in their activation by an activation-reducing process that functions to overcome interference, and that memory impairment derives from this change in state.

Several properties of retrieval-induced forgetting specifically favor inhibition, however, and illustrate the concept outlined at the outset of this chapter. For example, retrieval-induced forgetting exhibits (1) *interference dependence*—retrieval only impairs related traces if they interfere with retrieval, consistent with the idea that inhibition resolves competition (Anderson *et al.* 1994); (2) *retrieval-specificity*—other forms of practice that do not require recall (e.g. extra study) do not impair competitors, showing that inhibition only occurs when intrusive memories need to be overridden (Anderson *et al.* 2000); and (3) *cue independence*—impairment generalizes to novel final test cues unrelated to those used for retrieval practice (e.g. Anderson and Spellman 1995). Retrieval-induced forgetting also occurs on tests of item accessibility, including item recognition and lexical decision (Veling and van Knippenberg 2004), confirming that impairment reflects a change in the state of the affected item. Finally, retrieval-induced forgetting has been found to recover after 24 h (MacLeod and Macrae 2001), suggesting that in at least some cases, impairment reflects a reversible change in state (however, see Anderson and Spellman 1995; Anderson 2003, for an alternative perspective on why inhibition may not recover with time). Together, these findings show that retrieval engages inhibition to overcome interference from competing memories, rendering them less accessible generally (for a review, see Anderson 2003), illustrating the core concept of inhibition.

Inhibition in memory stopping

A second situation likely to engage response override is the need to stop retrieval. So, for instance, upon confronting a reminder to an unpleasant memory, we may engage inhibition to stop retrieval, preventing the reminder from eliciting the memory. Can the mechanisms that stop reflexive responses be engaged to override retrieval? To study this, we put people in a situation in which they repeatedly confronted a reminder to a recently encoded memory, and asked them to attend to the reminder while willfully excluding the associated memory from consciousness. Afterwards, we asked subjects to recall the memories that they had previously kept out of awareness. Interestingly, the repeated presentations of reminders during the prior no-think phase not only failed to improve people's later retention of the associated memory—as one might ordinarily expect reminders to do—it impaired performance compared with performance on baseline items that were learned initially, but for which no reminders were presented in the interim. Thus, excluding an unwanted memory from awareness leads to a memory deficit for the avoided trace, and the properties of this deficit are consistent with inhibition (Anderson and Green 2001).

Recent findings confirm that the brain mechanisms underlying this type of memory inhibition are related to the ability to override reflexive responses. Suppressing unwanted memories recruits the dorsolateral prefrontal cortex, a brain region associated with inhibiting prepotent responses; this suppression reduces activation in the hippocampus, a structure associated with declarative memory (Anderson *et al.* 2004). Importantly, the engagement of frontal cortex and the modulation of hippocampal activation predict the amount of memory impairment for suppressed items. Whether the forgetting produced by suppression reflects the direct or indirect consequences of neuronal inhibition remains to be established, although the impairment is clearly related to modulation of brain activity at the systemic level. The capacity to inhibit unwanted memories may help people regulate consciousness of unpleasant or intrusive memories.

Concluding remarks

Taken together, the findings on memory inhibition suggest that many of our experiences of forgetting are produced by an inhibition process that regulates the accessibility of memory traces. When a memory interferes with retrieval or is otherwise unwanted, inhibition can be engaged to alter that memory's state of activation, rendering it less accessible when later desired. Although we have discussed inhibition in memory retrieval and retrieval stopping, many other phenomena may also be produced in whole or in part by inhibition, including the classic concept of retroactive interference (for a review, see Anderson and Neely 1996), part-set cuing inhibition and output interference (see Bauml 1996, 1998; Bauml and Aslan 2004, for evidence concerning the role of inhibition in these phenomena). If correct, this view suggests a new perspective on forgetting that contrasts with the passive view that has prevailed in psychology for much of its history—a new perspective that emphasizes the role of control processes in regulating the accessibility of our knowledge and of experience to accommodate the need for focused, goal-directed cognitive activity.

52

Inhibition: Elusive or illusion?

Colin M. MacLeod

'... the arrest of the function of a structure or organ, by the action upon it of another, while the power to execute those functions is still retained, and can be manifested as soon as the restraining power is lifted'

(*Brunton 1883*)

What do we mean by 'inhibition' in the year 2007? Quite possibly, we mean very much what Brunton meant 124 years ago. When we discover that history already contains the current view, it is quite common to express disappointment that there has been no progress, but this is not at all a necessary conclusion. In fact, our understanding of the concept of inhibition has grown very considerably over the past century and a quarter, particularly in the realm of neuroscience, but also in the study of cognition. The interested reader should consult two excellent books on the history of the concept—Diamond *et al.* (1963) and Smith (1992).

Start vectors

This brief chapter considers several issues critically connected to the concept of inhibition. To begin, however, it is important to indicate two 'start vectors'. First, this chapter takes as absolute fact that there is inhibition at the level of the brain and nervous system, based on the vast neuroscientific literature that has developed since Sherrington (1906). It is also accepted that we can stop motor actions (see, for example, Logan and Cowan 1984), a phenomenon widely called inhibition, although the term has a different meaning there than its neuroscientific cognate, and a more neutral term such as 'restraint' or '(executive) control' might be preferable. So the questions considered here relate to the concept of inhibition as invoked to explain memory at the psychological, cognitive or behavioral level—inhibition at the level of thought, not action (cf. Breese 1899).

A second start vector is also important to identify explicitly. No matter what one's position on the utility of the concept of inhibition in understanding cognition, it does not strengthen the argument to invoke the concept of neural inhibition. The two operate at fundamentally different levels of analysis. Nor is either a unitary entity: Cohen (1993), for example, identified four distinct subtypes of neural inhibition, each involving a variety of neural components. Certainly different ideas are conveyed by different uses of the term in the study of cognition. True, neural and behavioral inhibition both refer to a suppressed event, but that is where the analogy ends, and any kind of direct mapping seems very unlikely. Indeed, reserving 'inhibition' for the neural event and another term such as 'suppression' for the cognitive event, if it can be shown to occur, would be preferable. Put simply, a 'domain general' central concept does not seem plausible.

What might cognitive inhibition mean?

According to the *Oxford English Dictionary*, there are four senses of *inhibition*. Two relate to societal or legal prohibition. Interestingly, the other two relate *separately* to the physiological and psychological senses of the term, consistent with the present claim that these two senses are distinct. The defining elements of cognitive inhibition appear to be two—mental withholding and reduced performance. The latter is directly measurable as reduced response likelihood or lengthened response latency, given a suitable neutral baseline or control condition against which to make the comparison. However, the former is an inference from performance. Inhibition is not an outcome; it is a theory about the cause of that outcome. Note that Brunton's emphasis on the function returning to 'full strength' once inhibition is lifted is only sometimes woven into the definition.

As argued elsewhere (MacLeod *et al.* 2003), even the measurement of reduced performance is not without considerable challenges. The choice of a neutral baseline is rarely straightforward or unanimously agreed upon. Great care must also be taken not to equate reduced performance reflexively with inhibition: inhibition is only one possible mechanism that might contribute to or cause that reduction. The crucial questions then become: How are we to determine whether inhibition was involved? What are the defining features of cognitive inhibition?

Defining criteria for cognitive inhibition

Unfortunately, no 'litmus test' exists or is likely to appear, so we must rely on multiple co-occurring symptoms to support a diagnosis of cognitive inhibition. There are only two that have been proposed as specifically filling this role.

The first has been used in attention research but not yet in memory research. This is a kind of dissociation criterion wherein a pattern reverses from a benefit to a cost. [The cost/benefit terminology is borrowed (e.g. Jonides and Mack 1984) and is recommended as admirably agnostic with respect to process or mechanism.] Thus, in the phenomenon of inhibition of return, a cue appears at one of two spatial locations where a soon-to-follow target could appear. Although over trials the cue is not actually predictive of the location of the subsequent target, if the time between cue and target is brief, the cue provides a benefit in response time to a target at the same location. However, that benefit switches to a cost if the time between cue and target is lengthened. The received view is that when the delay is longer we inhibit the cued location, thereby slowing detection of the target should it appear there. The experimental conditions are unchanged except for the cue–target lag, so this reversal could serve as a marker for inhibition, although other explanations exist.

The second criterion, in contrast, is unique to the memory literature, and has been championed by Anderson and Green (2001). The logic is that if a memory is truly inhibited by some operation on a representation, then other operations on that same representation should also reveal evidence of that inhibition. Anderson and Green had people try not to think of a previously studied word when provided with a cue that had been studied with that word. They found that this led to poorer recall of the target word than was the case without having tried not to recall it. This outcome could be seen as suggesting inhibition—but in fact does not rule out simple interference. However, the target word was also harder to recall to a (related) cue that had not been studied, suggesting that the target word itself, not just the particular studied association, was suppressed by the act of not thinking about it. Anderson and colleagues have cited this pattern as strong evidence for inhibition in memory (although its replicability has been questioned, see Bulevich et al. 2006).

These two are worthy efforts in terms of trying to diagnose true instances of inhibition, but more criteria are needed. (Of course, inhibition is not alone in this predicament; other cognitive mechanisms certainly warrant greater definition.) To differentiate inhibition-based from non-inhibition based memory situations will require considerably more work and ingenuity. In so doing, the hope must be that the coherence of the concept will be considered as well, given that at present inhibition can mean quite different things to different memory researchers.

Plausible alternatives to inhibition

What process(es) might cause a cognitive task to slow down or to become more error prone? Inhibition of a component of the response, such as the representation upon which it relies, is certainly a candidate. However, discriminating inhibition from interference will continue to be a most difficult problem. So interference—being drawn to an alternative other than the nominally correct alternative—is also a candidate. The term 'interference' is also problematic, though, sometimes being used to refer to an observed phenomenon and sometimes to a possible explanation of the phenomenon. The crux of the problem was well laid out by Klein and Taylor (1994, p. 146) who said:

> Unlike in the neural sciences, however, where inhibitory mechanisms can be observed in the hardware, in cognitive models inhibition must be inferred on the basis of overt behavior. As such, there is a danger of circularity whereby investigators attribute interference effects to inhibition and subsequently define inhibition on the basis of behavioral interference. For this reason, the terms inhibition and interference are often confused.

In any given situation where inhibition is proposed as a possible account, other possible accounts are certainly available. These other possibilities vary, so a proponent of the idea of cognitive inhibition might argue that one of its virtues is its breadth. However, a critic could just as readily maintain that because inhibition means quite different things to different researchers, the apparent 'value added' of breadth is illusory and actually has considerable potential to create confusion. If those favoring inhibition accounts had to divide inhibition into subtypes, it might actually be better to abandon the umbrella term altogether, focusing instead on these subtypes as distinct processes.

MacLeod *et al.* (2003) argued, following several other investigators, that a viable alternative account to widespread inhibition in cognition could actually be more directly memory-based. Under this account, it is routine, even automatic, to retrieve continuously from memory information relevant to the present situation. Ordinarily, such retrieval is advantageous—a benefit—helping to narrow options and speed the decision regarding what to do. However, sometimes, retrieved information will conflict with the present situation, slowing processing and producing a cost. Although such costs could be seen as inhibition, they need not be: they are instead the joint product of automatic memory retrieval and consequent conflict resolution. Such an account works well in many situations that otherwise might seem to demand an inhibitory explanation.

Conclusion

The position put forth here is that we do not have strong evidence of inhibition in memory. There may be inhibitory processes in memory, but we simply do not know yet, and better indices are required. The existence of neural inhibition is seen as a different phenomenon. In the nervous system, it is the balance of excitation and inhibition that determines neural computation and ultimately behavior. It is therefore most likely that even if we can identify true cognitive inhibition, such inhibition will also rely on the balance of neural inhibition and excitation, and will not be uniquely related to neural inhibition. Under this view, the existence of inhibition in the nervous system in no way speaks to the likelihood or character of inhibition in behavior, any more than the existence of neural excitation necessitates a counterpart in cognition.

53

Integrative comments
Inhibition: An essential and contentious concept

Robert A. Bjork

In a 1989 essay on 'Retrieval inhibition as an adaptive mechanism in human memory', I argued that inhibitory processes played little or no role in then-current theories of human memory (Bjork 1989). I viewed that fact as puzzling— given that inhibitory processes had long been acknowledged by brain and behavioral scientists to be critical at the neural, sensory, attentional and motor levels, and in the ontogeny of brain development. Towards explaining *why* inhibition seemed out of favor as an explanatory concept, I suggested that two aspects of the prevailing research zeitgeist played a role:

> First, notions of inhibition or suppression in human memory have an unappealing association to certain poorly understood clinical phenomena, such as repression. Second, the information-processing approach, grounded as it is in the computer metaphor, leads us to think in term of processes like storing, scanning, grouping, erasing, and so forth. Notions like inhibition, suppression, unlearning, and spontaneous recovery are not easily compatible with the computer metaphor (p. 310).

My own history of research on directed forgetting, tracing back to my graduate-school days, illustrates the influence of such factors. I spent the first 15–20 years saying and writing that research on directed forgetting was important *not* because it had anything to do with clinical phenomena, such as repression, but because it could shed light on how our memories are kept current, how rehearsal and encoding resources are allocated and how competing items are segregated and differentiated in memory. During what MacLeod (1998), in a remarkable review of the literature, has referred to as the 'golden age' of research on directed forgetting (1968–1974) that began with a paper by Bjork *et al.* (1968), I attempted to explain directed forgetting findings via noninhibitory processes such as selective rehearsal and set differentiation. It took an accumulation of directed forgetting findings that proved hard to interpret without reference to inhibition, especially those reported by Geiselman *et al.* (1983), to convince me that retrieval inhibition played a key role in directed forgetting.

Historical perspective on the reluctance to postulate inhibition

Taking a broader historical view, however, the hesitancy to postulate inhibitory mechanisms in learning and memory theories clearly pre-dates the emergence of computer metaphor and the information processing approach. In fact, concerns about the necessity of assuming inhibitory processes go back to the early decades of controlled research on human and animal learning and memory. In the experimental and theoretical analysis of extinction phenomena, for example, questions and debates arose that are very reminiscent of present-day issues that have emerged in the context of blocking versus suppression accounts of retrieval-induced forgetting phenomena (cf. Chapters 51 and 52, this volume). In research on conditioning, for example, explanations of extinction in terms of inhibitory processes (e.g. Pavlov 1927; Hull 1951) did battle with interference explanations (e.g. Guthrie 1935) that asserted, in essence, that extinction is merely the learning of a new response to the old conditional stimulus.

Aside from whether inhibition or interference accounts of extinction could provide a better account of extinction phenomena, reviews from that period clearly reflect the hesitancy to postulate inhibitory processes. In referring to Pavlov's appeal to inhibitory mechanisms in accounting for extinction effects, for example, Woodworth and Schlosberg (1954) say 'Pavlov's rather speculative ideas of what goes on in the brain may be of little importance. Some psychologists go so far as to reject the concept of inhibition, although it seems to be a necessary—and respectable—concept in physiology' (p. 559). Later, in discussing the reaction of the field to Pavlov's interpretation of disinhibition, they comment that 'It is not surprising that psychologists who disliked inhibition regarded this suggestion as adding insult to injury' (p. 561). It became common, in fact, and for mostly good reasons, to avoid using the term *inhibition* in labeling empirical effects. In Osgood's (1953) experimental psychology textbook, for example, he provided the following caution in a preamble to his discussion of transfer and retroaction:

> Although the term 'retroactive facilitation' is commonly and acceptably used for positive retroaction, the term 'retroactive inhibition' has unfortunately been applied when negative retroaction is found. What is referred to here is simply an observed

decrement in performance, not a process—the decrement may or may not be due to some inhibitory process—so henceforth we shall use the more neutral term, retroactive interference (p. 520).

Why, historically, has there been a reluctance to postulate inhibitory mechanisms? Beyond any unsavory association to poorly understood clinical dynamics, or any effect of the computer metaphor, I think two other factors may play a role. One is parsimony: If effects can be explained in terms of cognitive processes that are better understood, such as selective rehearsal, then why appeal to inhibitory mechanisms, which are more poorly understood? A related consideration has to do with our subjective experience. We all have the conscious experience of selecting some items to rehearse, or encode or retrieve, but inhibitory processes are not accompanied by the same volitional and conscious experience. Even in cases where inhibitory effects are powerful and undeniable, such as in dichotic listening, when attending to one ear is accompanied by a gating of input from the other ear, what is available to consciousness is the decision to allocate attention to a given ear and the processing of input from that ear, not inhibitory operations that suppress input from the other ear.

Inhibition in the current research zeitgeist

At the end of my 1989 essay, I predicted that in the 'near future' there would be consensus that inhibitory processes play a critical role in the overall functioning of human memory. I made that prediction, in part, because I thought the combination of two developments—the emergence of new techniques to examine neural dynamics in the human brain, and the emergence of neural/connectionist modeling—would lead researchers towards theories that incorporated inhibitory processes. That proved to be a good prediction—at least as indexed by books devoted to the role of inhibition that appeared shortly thereafter (e.g. Smith 1992; Dagenbach and Carr 1994; Dempster and Brainerd 1995); by the subsequent proliferation of the word 'inhibition' in the titles of articles; and by the keen interest in experimental tasks thought to instigate inhibitory processes, such as the retrieval-induced forgetting, think/no-think and directed forgetting tasks—but concerns about the necessity of assuming inhibitory processes have been resurrected, too, as exemplified by Colin MacLeod's essay in this volume (Chapter 52).

Comments and perspective on the present essays

In the sections that follow, I comment—in the context of the splendid essays by Michael Anderson, György Buzáski, Lynn Hasher and Colin MacLeod—on the definition of inhibition; the adaptive nature of inhibitory mechanisms; and what I see as the remaining key issues and points of contention.

Defining inhibition

MacLeod cites Brunton's (1983) definition of inhibition, repeated below, and Anderson provides a useful and detailed characterization of the attributes of inhibition that goes beyond, but is consistent with, Brunton's definition:

> ... the arrest of the function of a structure or organ, by the action upon it of another, while the power to execute those functions is still retained, and can be manifested as soon as the restraining power is lifted (Brunton 1883).

I endorse that definition, but with respect to *retrieval* inhibition, I have tended to adopt an empirical, rather than conceptual, definition—one that focuses on the impairment of the *recall* of inhibited memory representations. One result that implicates retrieval inhibition is a violation of what might be called the 'law of forgetting', i.e. when something that is not recallable after a shorter delay becomes recallable at a longer delay. An example of such an effect is when the earlier learned of two competing memory representations becomes more recallable, in absolute terms, as time passes. Such 'regression' effects (Bjork 1978) are common in both motor and verbal learning, they occur on time scales ranging from seconds to months and years, and they occur across species (for a review, see Bjork 2001). A second result that implicates retrieval inhibition is when something becomes nonrecallable, but remains at full strength by other measures (e.g. when an instruction to forget impairs subsequent recall of the to-be-forgotten materials, but not the subsequent recognition or relearning of those materials). Again, such effects are very general and appear in research on animal learning as well as human learning. As Bouton (e.g. 1994) and Rescorla (e.g. 2001) have emphasized, based on research with animals, new associations do not overwrite or destroy old associations, and post-treatment 'return of fear', which is common in the clinical treatment of phobias (see Lang *et al.* 1999), is an especially salient example that the same is true for humans as well.

Inhibition as an adaptive mechanism

A thread running through the essays by Anderson, Buzsaki and Hasher is that inhibitory processes play a key and adaptive role in how our brains function and in how we contend with the learning, memory, decision and emotional challenges that are part of living, learning and managing ourselves. Buzsaki (Chapter 49), in remarkably few words, provides a clear and compelling description of how inhibitory networks and inhibitory interneurons multiply and refine the computational power of principal cells. That 'brain systems with "simple" computational demands', such as the basal ganglia, thalamus or cerebellum, are characterized by only a few neuron types, whereas systems that support conscious memory functioning are characterized not only by five principal cell types, but also by 'numerous classes' of inhibitory neurons, is an interesting and provocative aspect of the brain's structure. Speculatively— perhaps *too* speculatively on my part—that property of the brain's neural organization seems to link to Hasher's argument (Chapter 50) that familiar stimuli 'activate their representations automatically' and that in many circumstances 'this activation (and its spread to associated representations) can and must be downregulated in order for organized behavior to achieve an individual's long- and short-term goals'. The basic idea is that such downregulation is accomplished by 'inhibitory mechanisms that operate in the service of goals'.

The emphasis, in Hasher's treatment, is on attentional control and the ability to have one's thoughts and actions be guided by goals and plans, not by the activation triggered by environmental stimuli. Individuals, in her view, who have poor inhibitory abilities will also have difficulty 'in stopping thoughts and actions that were recently relevant, but no longer are'. Such a stopping function maps to one of the two adaptive functions Anderson (Chapter 51) attributes to inhibition, the other being to resolve competition in the use of our memories, but the emphasis is a bit different in Anderson's and Hasher's frameworks. Anderson's emphasis is on 'memory stopping', i.e. on stopping the retrieval of information that is stored in memory, but, when recalled, is a source of emotional discomfort or 'undermines performance on some task', whereas Hasher's emphasis is on inhibiting activations that are stimulus driven, automatic and perhaps unaccompanied by awareness.

With respect to resolving competition among items in memory, Anderson argues that selective retrieval, i.e. selecting one target item from memory from among competitors, engages an inhibitory mechanism to suppress the competing items and, thereby, enhances access to the target representation. This suppression, though, can persist and result in *retrieval-induced forgetting* of nontarget items (Anderson *et al.* 1994) should the recall of those items be required. Anderson and Spellman (1995) have argued that selective retrieval has properties that are parallel to selective attention; in both cases, inhibitory mechanisms act to enhance access to the external or internal target by suppressing competition from unattended external or internal nontargets. Bjork *et al.* (1998) have pushed that argument further by suggesting that such a selection-plus-suppression mechanism may be '*the* primary solution in the functional architecture of the human as an information-processing device to the problem of avoiding interference and competition at various levels of cognitive processing … in a broad range of motor and cognitive activities, *selecting* appears to involve *inhibiting*' (p. 133).

In my own case, I have argued that retrieval inhibition is a uniquely human and adaptive solution to the problem of keeping one's memory current. In contrast to man-made memory devices, in which—without special precautions—the storage of new information replaces or erases old information, learning and using new information (such as a new home phone number) does not destroy the representation of the information it replaces, but, rather, renders it nonre-callable over time. The old phone number (or street address, maiden name, locker number, etc.) remains in memory, can often be recognized and—should it again become relevant—can be relearned with great rapidity and savings.

Remaining issues and points of contention

In his current essay, and in an earlier review (MacLeod *et al.* 2003), MacLeod provides a broad critique of the readiness of today's researchers to attribute various empirical findings to inhibitory mechanisms. The central arguments reiterate and update arguments that emerged decades ago in accounting for phenomena such as extinction and retroactive interference. With respect to his two 'start vectors'—that there is (1) no denying inhibition at the neural/brain level, but that (2) the evidence of such inhibition cannot, by itself, be offered as evidence of inhibition at the cognitive level—I believe there can be no serious disagreement. Nor should there be any disagreement with his reiteration of the time-honored caution in discussions of inhibition versus interference: 'inhibition is not an outcome; it is a theory about the cause of the outcome' (Chapter 52, this volume).

At the risk of oversimplifying MacLeod's arguments, I interpret his critique as making two main points: first, that attributing some empirical effect to inhibition (versus some alternative process) requires meeting rigorous criteria and, second, that alternative interference-based explanations must be ruled out before inhibition is inferred. With respect to the first point, he suggests that we need evidence of dissociations analogous to those that have implicated inhibition in research on attention, such as the changing effects of a pre-cue in research on inhibition of return. I believe that results of this general kind already exist. In A–B, A–D paired-associate list-learning experiments, for example, one type of evidence supporting the response-set-suppression hypothesis (Postman *et al.* 1968) is that the retroactive effects of list two on list one are greater than the proactive effects of list one on list two, given a short retention interval, but the converse is true at a long delay—consistent with the proposal that B responses are suppressed during A–D learning, but then recover.

A recent finding from research on retrieval-induced forgetting can also, in my view, be seen as a kind of dissociation that implicates inhibition.

Items that are most recallable when tested [e.g. by virtue of being the strongest associates to a category cue (Anderson *et al.* 1994) or by virtue of their valence (Storm *et al.* 2005)] turn out to be the most subject to retrieval-induced forgetting. This result, which is one of three properties of retrieval-induced forgetting Anderson cites as favoring inhibition, is especially difficult to accommodate from within a blocking interpretation. The recent finding that retrieval success is not necessary for retrieval-induced forgetting to happen (Storm *et al.* 2006) also poses a problem for blocking theories, given that no competitor is strengthened when retrieval practice fails. Such a result, however, is readily interpretable in terms of a suppression mechanism.

There is an implicit—and subtle—assumption in MacLeod's analysis that seems to be widely held and needs to be examined. The assumption is that a kind of theoretical pecking order is justified; Noninhibitory ideas are to be preferred, unless totally untenable, and the burden of proof is on inhibition theorists. That is, before an inhibition interpretation is supported, interference mechanisms must be refuted, but the converse requirement is never made for interference interpretations. This subtle assumption, which may be justified via a kind of Bayesian prior-odds reasoning, constitutes another reflection of the reluctance to assume inhibitory processes.

Finally, even if the evidence of inhibition is considered convincing, a key question remains: Is inhibition a by-product of other activities, such as selective retrieval or selective attention, or does what might be termed 'pure' inhibition also characterize human cognition? Stated in the context of Anderson and Green's (2001) think/no-think paradigm, can we respond to instructions not to think of a target item in a direct, unmediated, way that inhibits subsequent access to the target, or can such suppression only be achieved via, say, active retrieval of arbitrary nontarget items? For the foreseeable future, this question will play a central and contentious role in research on, and discussion of, the role of inhibition in memory and cognition.

14

Forgetting

Forgetting is the loss of learned information over time. In general, the forgetting curve, or the function relating performance on a task from time since learning it, is negatively accelerated, with greatest forgetting occurring soon after learning and more gradual loss later. In most modern treatments of the subject, there is no assumption that forgetting necessarily reflects complete loss of stored information; rather, the problem may be loss of access to stored information because of a shift in context between learning and testing, or other reasons. Another definition of forgetting is the inability to retrieve information at a certain point in time that could be retrieved at a previous time. Some studies have shown dramatic recoveries of seemingly forgotten information when appropriate cues are provided to aid retrieval. Of course, the possibility that forgetting is at least partly due to decay or other types of change of the memory trace is quite plausible and is in fact assumed by most neurobiological theories of forgetting. Mechanisms discussed in theories of forgetting include changes in the nature of the memory trace, interference from earlier and later experiences, change in context between learning and testing, and insufficient or inappropriate retrieval cues.

H.L.R.

14

Forgetting

54

Forgetting: Once again, it's all about representations

Michael Davis

The term 'forgetting' is often used in different ways, which makes it an inherently difficult concept to study in a rigorous way. One use of the term is to describe the theoretical possibility that refers to a total erasure of the original memory that cannot be recalled, no matter what techniques are used to aid recall. I will call this the 'strong form of forgetting'. The other use of the term is to describe a failure of retrieval which, in essence, refers to all of the other instances where a memory may still exist, but, for whatever reason, cannot be retrieved.

Regarding the strong form of forgetting, the problem is that the only way to determine definitely if a memory is forgotten because of a total erasure of the original memory substrate is to examine an extremely simple neural circuit which can reveal all of the cellular and molecular events that occur when a memory is formed and then to show that all of these events have gone back to their original state at the time when the memory is not retrieved. I say *all of the* cellular and molecular events have to return to their original state because it is conceivable that any residue of change might be enough of a substrate to allow some sort of retrieval or saving, given clever enough experiments designed to bring out the original memory. Only when all the cellular and molecular events that occur when a memory is formed return to their original state would I say this would be evidence for true forgetting.

This strong version of the definition of forgetting could equally apply to short-term versus long-term memory. For example, imagine a very simple organism where short-term memory, defined as a change in synaptic strength, was mediated by phosphorylation of a single protein at a single site, and no other changes were observed. If this site was later dephosphorylated so that the protein returned to exactly its state prior to formation of short-term memory, I would call this an example of the strong form of forgetting. If a long-term memory in this simple organism resulted in the formation of a new synapse, and nothing more, then the loss of this extra synapse would return the system back in its entirety to that measured prior to memory formation and I would call this the strong form of forgetting. The obvious problem with this strong definition is that it is presently impossible to make these kinds of measurements on any organism, and so we still cannot be sure that forgetting actually occurs, given these criteria. Moreover, because in a slightly more complex organism we may never be able to make these measurements, I assert that the concept of this strong form of forgetting is not useful scientifically, because it probably can never be proven.

Another way to look at the strong form of forgetting would be with respect to dementias associated with cell loss. Basically, if all the cells in a complex network that stored a particular memory finally die, then I would consider this to be forgetting, because there would no longer be any substrate to allow for subsequent retrieval. I watched my mother gradually lose her memory over the last 10 years of her life. I used to test her when I saw her and asked her where her mother was born. Even though she no longer knew who I was, as best as I could tell, she would confidently say: Dearborn, Michigan. By the time she was 90, she no longer could remember even this very dear memory and her MRI showed there were no cortical cells left. So, I would say this would be an example of the strong form of forgetting. However, other than studying why cells die and how to prevent them from dying, this definition of forgetting becomes sort of trivial and self-evident, so again not very useful for the study of memory.

This leaves us with the second use of the term forgetting that deals with 'retrieval failure', a term I favor because it instantly invites the possibility of multiple mechanisms to account for an empirical phenomenon, namely one where a memory is absent, incomplete, inaccurate or even false. Moreover, this is more or less how most people regard forgetting and jibes with their personal experience (I cannot come up with his name right now). Numerous mechanisms have been used to explain such instances of retrieval failure, such as repression, interference, extinction, context, response competition, unlearning, pattern completion failure, as well as the strong form of forgetting, namely a full erasure of the original memory. So, this is a better term because it encompasses a larger number of possible, and researchable, mechanisms and does not have the connotation of an erasure of the original memory, although it does not exclude this as a possible mechanism. Also, it is clear there is a rich and very important literature looking at all of these mechanisms with respect to memory retrieval. My position is that it would be much better to view this literature in terms of factors involved in memory retrieval, or perhaps remembering, which are not necessarily identical concepts, rather than mechanisms of forgetting. However, implicit in this position is the idea that memories may never be 'forgotten' in the strong sense of the term, but only inaccessible, as a result of one or more of these mechanisms. However, this also seems not to be very satisfactory because it would seem useful for a brain not to remember everything it ever learned, given that this could lead to more retrieval failure based on interference mechanisms.

For example, if I travel a lot and stay in lots of hotels, I may at some time 'forget' the room number of the hotel where I am staying on a particular night. This would be forgetting during temporary long-term working memory and would probably be an example of retrieval failure because it is likely I could retrieve my room number with priming, recognition tests, etc. (i.e. if I was taken to the floor of my room I might well be able to figure out where my room was, based on the proximity of the elevator or other cues). However, if one makes the assumption, and it is only that, that the room number of every hotel I have ever stayed in during my life was never put into long-term memory, but only in some kind of temporary memory buffer accessible more or less during the time of my stay in the hotel and not much beyond that, then I think it is not useful to say that 'I forgot the room number of the hotel I stayed in 30 years ago', using the strong definition of forgetting. Furthermore, I do not think it is useful to say that 'I fail to retrieve the room number of the hotel I stayed in 30 years ago' because this implies the long-term memory was laid down in the first place, which I also think is unlikely, i.e. I would not like to say I have forgotten those room numbers or even that I fail to retrieve them. Instead, I would say I do not retrieve them now because those temporary working memories purposely were never consolidated into long-term memory.

So, where does this leave us? To those of us interested in memory and forgetting, I think it is critical first to ask: what are the possible sources of forgetting in the model of learning we are looking at. Could it be explained by a total erasure of the original memory, a partial erasure that would be enough to prevent retrieval permanently because it would have degraded the original pattern of the memory to such an extent that it can never be retrieved, a temporary retrieval failure that could be retrieved at some later time or with some other cues, or because the memory was never put into some form of long-term storage. Perhaps by always asking these questions we might be able to design better experiments to try to answer these somewhat different questions.

55

Forgetting: The fate of once learned, but "forgotten" material

Elizabeth F. Loftus

Sometimes an experience is stored in memory, and later becomes difficult, if not virtually impossible, to remember. We can only speculate about whether it is ever completely gone from the memory into which it was once stored.

A different situation arises, however, when an experience is stored in a person's memory, and later the person is exposed to some erroneous and contradictory fact. Assume that it too is stored in memory and that the post-event contradictory detail is all that the individual can now remember no matter how hard he or she tries. So, for example, a person sees a car go through a red light but later hears another witness call the light 'green'. Assume our witness embraces the misinformation and is now confident that he or she saw a green light. A fundamental question, then is, 'What happened to the original memory for the red light?' (Loftus and Loftus 1980).

A major issue that has been debated is whether misinformation actually impairs a person's ability to remember event details. Put another way, are memory traces actually altered by post-event misinformation? There are several ways in which misinformation could impair the ability to remember event details. First, misinformation could cause 'trace impairment', i.e. it could update or alter the previously formed memory. New information could combine with earlier traces actually to change the representation. A second way in which misinformation could impair event memory is through 'retrieval impairment', i.e. misinformation may not alter the original memory trace but may simply make it less accessible. (Morton *et al.* 1985). Impairment of some sort is implied by either the trace impairment or retrieval impairment mechanisms. Trace impairment implies real forgetting, however.

Some theorists have rejected the notion that misinformation impairs the ability to remember event details (McCloskey and Zaragoza 1985). They claim there is no impairment of either type in this type of situation, either trace or retrieval. Michael McCloskey and Maria Zaragoza disagreed with the idea that the misinformation effect was due to recoding processes or updating of previously stored memories, or that the misinformation effect arose because the older memory was rendered less accessible through a mechanism of inhibition or suppression. McCloskey and Zaragoza argued instead that the misinformation does not affect memory at all. Misinformation merely influences the reports of subjects who never encoded (or do not recall) the original event. Instead of guessing at the time of test, these subjects would be lured into 'guessing' the misinformation item. Misinformation effects could also be obtained if subjects remember both sources of information but select the misleading information because they conclude it must be correct. While these investigators did not observe a misinformation effect with what they called the 'modified test', subsequent investigators would (for a review, see Ayres and Reder 1998).

Several lines of experimental evidence were offered to support the notion that misinformation occasionally does impair the ability to remember original details. First, there are studies using tests that do not permit the misinformation option. Say a subject originally saw a stop sign but it was later referred to as a yield sign. Suppose we now give the subject a test that does not permit the selection of the yield sign (e.g. choose between a stop sign and a no parking sign). If the misinformation impaired memory for the stop sign, then the misinformed subjects would be less able to recover the stop sign (assuming memory impairment had occurred). If there is no memory impairment due to misinformation, then misled subjects would be expected to be as accurate as control subjects on a test of this type. Although some studies do show equal performance, there are several published demonstrations of deficits in performance with this restrictive type of test. One study presented pre-school children with stories followed by misinformation, and found impairment (Ceci et al. 1987). Another study presented adult subjects with visual scenes (e.g. nature scenes including ponds, flowers and mountains), and then provided similar visual scenes as post-event information. Subjects who received misinformation were less able to discriminate the original scene from novel distractors (Chandler 1991).

A second line of work supportive of a memory impairment interpretation involves the use of a yes/no test (Belli 1989). Robert Belli showed subjects a simulated crime, and then fed them some misinformation on a post-event narrative that they read under a pretense. Finally subjects were presented with a series of statements, each dealing with a critical event item. Subjects said 'yes' if they saw the item in the slides, and 'no' otherwise. Compared with memories for control items, there was a large reduction in accurate memory for the items about which subjects had received misinformation. The large reduction was not offset by the small improvement in memory (e.g. lower false alarm rate) for completely novel items.

Ayres and Reder (1998) reviewed the various theoretical perspectives that have been used to account for misinformation and its influence on original memories. They concluded that an activation-based semantic network model of memory was most useful in terms of its ability to account for the various and sometimes conflicting results in the literature; and they proposed it as a useful guide for planning for future research in the area.

Another way to think about the issue of whether misinformation impairs a person's ability to remember a previous event is to focus not so much on whether the earlier trace has been altered or degraded but on whether the retrieval cue becomes less effective. Wixted (2005) has referred to this problem as 'cue overload'. He argues that forgetting can involve trade degradation but also that cue overload effects are very real, as has been shown in numerous laboratory studies (e.g. studies involving proactive interference or list length effects, to name a few). Misinformation could be impairing memory performance by effectively increasing cue overload. Since cue overload is such a well-established principle, it seems likely that decrements in memory performance would occur by impairing access to the original information.

The debate over the fate of original memories may not have settled the issue of whether original memories are ever truly destroyed, as this was impossible to prove definitively. However, it did heighten appreciation for the different ways by which people come to report a misinformation item as their memory (Loftus and Hoffman 1989). Sometimes this appears to occur because they have no original memory, either because it was never storied or because it has faded away. Sometimes this occurs because of a conscious deliberation (e.g. I thought I saw a green light, but the other witness says red, so I'll say red.). Sometimes it appears as if the original event memories have been impaired in the process of contemplating misinformation.

For the sake of historical perspective, it is worth noting that much of the debate about the fate of previously stored memory traces after exposure to misinformation is reminiscent of the debates that occurred a half century ago under the rubric of 'interference theory' (see Roediger 1996). Back then, many researchers were less interested in examining distortions that permeated memory reports than in whether interfering material produced unlearning of prior material or whether it merely added to response competition that resulted in the appearance of 'forgetting'. By the early 1970s, interference theory, once wildly exciting to memory scientists, was becoming less important in the literature, when the first of the hundreds of misinformation studies began to be published. The new misinformation studies were similar in some ways to the earlier 'interference' studies in that both involved exposure to later material that reduced memory for earlier material. Both paradigms led to extensive discussion of the fate of the earlier material after exposure to later material. However, the misinformation studies often involved situations where new details were constructed in memory, as a result of misinformation, that were never explicitly mentioned.

The study of misinformation effects has had a 30 year history (Loftus 2005), and continues to be studied today. However, research specifically on the issue of the fate of original memories wound down in the 1990s, perhaps because of the enormous challenge of ever being able to prove that the memory trace was truly altered, distorted or gone. Alternatively, perhaps it was because researchers found it of sufficient interest that the memory reports of subjects could be so readily altered that they focused more on the behavior itself and its implications. At this stage, the whole topic of the fate of previously stored memory traces is still, to many, a fascinating and unresolved issue that is ripe for further investigation.

56

Forgetting: Its role in the science of memory

David C. Rubin

Forgetting is a key concept in the study of memory; it is what concerns people most. Remembering goes unnoticed, only forgetting draws attention. Thus researchers need to maintain forgetting as part of their vocabulary and use it to communicate their work to the public. Forgetting provides a window on memory processes, on why some experiences are lost more easily than others. However, my question is not whether forgetting is a useful concept in general, but whether forgetting is a useful concept in the science of memory. I will argue that it is not an especially useful in terms of what it denotes, but that what it connotes needs to be kept.

There are two ways to consider the concept forgetting. The first is in relation to other concepts; the second is in what we know about forgetting in particular. According to the framework of this book, concepts are mental representations that are always linked to other concepts, all of which are ultimately expressed in language. The key concepts of this book to which forgetting is most closely linked are remembering, retrieval, encoding, learning, memory, consolidation and inhibition. I begin by describing these relationships.

In colloquial terms, forgetting is the opposite of remembering, though in the science of memory remembering may have a more specialized meaning. What one cannot remember, one has forgotten. Both are processes that are measured at a particular time in a particular context. Remembering or forgetting here and now does not guarantee a similar behavior in other contexts, as noted by Tulving and Pearlstone (1966). Successful retrieval is what happens when you do not show forgetting. Failing to retrieve is forgetting, which may be remedied by additional retrieval attempts or a change in the retrieval context. Therefore, forgetting, remembering, and retrieval are conceptual variants of each other in that forgetting can be defined as not remembering, or failed retrieval.

A definitional prerequisite for forgetting is that one has encoded or learned something and so could later have a memory for it. Thus, the concepts of encoding, learning and memory are central to the concept of forgetting. Encoding must take place for there to be a memory. Learning is a process that results in the product of 'having' a memory. Under this view, memory is reification; process turned into product. Thus memories share properties with most other products, or things, including that they tend to have a single location. One can focus on either the process or the product, but not both at the same time. Researchers who stress one tend to have theoretical difficulties with those who stress the other. The product view is clear at the level of a natural language metaphor; it is easy to understand William James' attic in which things are placed and later retrieved. In contrast, some find the process view difficult to understand even when presented by good writers who have used it to make widely recognized empirical advances (e.g. Gibson 1966; Skinner 1974; Watkins 1990). When I was in graduate school, learning was something studied by Skinnerians who did not like putting things into the head, or perhaps they just felt that bird brains had no room to store memories given the evolutionary requirement of reducing weight for flight. Memory was something studied by cognitive psychologists who liked filling the expansive human mind with data structures of the kind computer science was inventing at the time (Rubin 1988). Many of these cognitive psychologists were reformed 'verbal learners' who traced their intellectual heritage back to Ebbinghaus's (1885/1964) book titled, *Memory*, rather than Bartlett's (1932) process oriented book titled, *Remembering*.

I prefer process, in part because it emphasizes the interaction of the organism with the environment, whereas structure emphasizes the memory as a thing located inside the organism. Either view is fine for the relatively constant environment of the laboratory, but process seems better suited for the richer and more varied environment of the world where the match between the context at encoding and context at retrieval (i.e. encoding specificity; Tulving and Thompson 1973) can vary more and where the environment can play a greater role in what is forgotten. For instance, if a building in which you spent time is destroyed or if a friend dies, then there are memories that you could have remembered by visiting the building or interacting with the friend that will now be forgotten because the context and cues for recall are lost. As Proust notes, 'The past is hidden somewhere outside the realm, beyond the reach of intellect, in some material object (in the sensation which that material object will give us) ... As for that object, it depends on chance whether we come upon it or not before we ourselves must die' (1913/2000, p. 55).

In any case, you can show you have a memory only by remembering something that you learned. Operationally, the demonstration of encoding, learning, memory, remembering, retrieval and not-forgetting are the same: an organism did not know something at time 1, was exposed to it at time 2, and displayed that it knew it by some test at time 3. Variations at time 2 would be interpreted in terms of encoding or learning; variations at time 3 in terms of remembering, retrieval or forgetting. However, in all cases, behavior at time 3 is the only evidence that there was encoding, learning, memory remembering, retrieval and forgetting. If there was another exposure to and test at time 4, a learning curve could be plotted or the effects of spaced practice studied. Alternatively, if at time 4 there was only another test, a retention function could be plotted. Thus, in terms of what they really refer to instead of what topics one studies under each, demonstrations of encoding, learning, memory, remembering, retrieval and not-forgetting are conceptual variants of each other.

In contrast, consolidation and inhibition are specific claims about processes that differ from and contribute to our understanding of forgetting. Once a memory becomes consolidated, forgetting slows and is less likely to involve individual aspects of the memory which are more strongly bound into a single unit. Questions about the extent to which forgetting is due to active inhibition of material that would otherwise be known are of great theoretical and practical importance.

I now turn to what is usually considered under the concept of forgetting, i.e. the issues that make up the core of what researchers studying forgetting actually study. One key issue is the time course of forgetting, a topic often referred to as a retention function (Rubin and Wenzel 1996) because the quantity measured is the amount retained, not the amount forgotten. A second issue is what, if anything, is ever completely forgotten or how much can be shown to remain under the right circumstances and test measures (Chapter 54, this volume). A subissue is whether information is overwritten by new information or remains to be later revealed (Chapter 55, this volume). A third issue is how best to account theoretically for the nature of forgetting, a question which led to (1) the development of one of the most detailed and quickly forgotten bodies of literature on human memory—interference theory, though the issues it dealt with remain in the literature on false memories; (2) theories based on the nature of errors that occur when what is forgotten is replaced by more schematic material (Bartlett 1932); and (3) theories of what motivates forgetting and if motivated forgetting can be viewed as a form of active inhibition (Freud 1901/1960). For all these issues, forgetting tends to be most appropriately set in a trace theory context in which known accurate information is either remembered or forgotten, as opposed to a more constructive theory in which the process of remembering produces a memory that is often good enough, even if not accurate.

The general view that I find from the study of forgetting is that forgetting occurs to the extent that what is to be recalled cannot be uniquely determined by the effects of current cuing (Watkins 1990; Rubin 1995); disambiguating items is a key aid to lessen forgetting. One can never tell if anything is ever completely forgotten, only that it is forgotten with the effectiveness of the cues at hand, and this effectiveness can change with time and the state of the individual.

Trying to understand forgetting has led to valuable insights, but is the concept of forgetting needed as a key concept in the science of memory? Studying forgetting is one approach to studying memory. At the behavioral level, it highlights the processes of retrieval, consolidation and inhibition, and the interaction of the organism with the environment. At a neural level, it is a means of examining changes in the organism that result in cues to no longer reactivating what were once the neural traces of a memory. Given that, perhaps forgetting deserves a role in the science of memory. However, we do not need all the concepts of forgetting, remembering and retrieval as well as learning and memory. Others may choose to keep forgetting, but I will continue to emphasize remembering. Remembering emphasizes process versus structure, what is, not what is lacking, and the role of the environment as well as the organism. Moreover, it allows memory to be distributed among many systems of the mind and brain in a highly constructive, but often very faithful, fashion (Rubin 1995, 2005).

Acknowledgments

I wish to thank Dorthe Berntsen, Jennifer LeBreque, Heather Rice, Jennifer Talarico and the group at the Science of Memory meeting for their comments, and NIA grant AG023123 for the time to think.

57

Integrative comments
Forgetting: It's not just the opposite of remembering

John T. Wixted

'Philosophy', wrote Wittgenstein (1953), 'is a battle against the bewitchment of our intelligence by means of language' (p. 109). Psychology is involved in that battle as well, and most would probably agree that the language of *forgetting* would have outlived its usefulness if it tended to bewitch the intelligence more than it helped us to think about and understand how our memories change over time. One obvious problem with the word *forgetting* is that is has more than one meaning (as noted by Davis in Chapter 54). To some, it simply means being unable to retrieve sought-after information from memory (e.g. 'I forgot your name'), regardless of why that might be. According to this way of thinking, the word *forgetting* applies if I was once in a position to have encoded the information (e.g. if I was introduced to you at a party) but I am now unable to retrieve it. The information might have been momentarily held in working memory, but it may never have been stored in long-term memory. Alternatively, the trace might have been encoded into long-term memory, but it may now have weakened to the point where it is no longer accessible. Still another possibility is that the available retrieval cues are deficient in some way (e.g. an acquaintance was wearing casual clothes when the introduction took place but is now wearing a uniform). In all of these cases, the word *forgetting* is commonly used, especially by laymen. To the layman, none of these distinctions matter because, in common parlance, forgetting is tantamount to retrieval failure (as noted by Rubin in Chapter 56).

To the psychologists who have long studied the issue of forgetting, however, these distinctions are (or should be) critical. A patient who suffers from bilateral damage of the medial temporal lobes, for example, is unlikely to remember your name a day after meeting you. While that might seem to indicate rapid forgetting (and would be described as such by many), we now know that it probably reflects the failure to lay down a long-term memory trace in the first place (Squire 1992). As the term has long been used in experimental psychology, the failure to encode does not count as an instance of forgetting. Similarly, it is now well known that memory is cue dependent, with the most effective retrieval cue being that which was encoded along with the to-be-remembered information (Tulving and Thomson 1973). Other cues will be less effective, but the mere fact that a less effective cue fails to elicit retrieval does not imply that forgetting has taken place, at least not as many psychologists have used that term for more than a century. The phrase 'cue-dependent forgetting' (Tulving 1974), which could be applied whenever a cue fails to access an available trace, is probably better termed 'cue-dependent retrieval failure' to distinguish it from what I would regard as a more appropriate definition of forgetting. Although Davis (Chapter 54, this volume) seems comfortable subsuming these disparate cases under the concept of forgetting, my own preference would be to establish a more exact definition.

A more rigorous definition of forgetting

When considering the concept of forgetting, an important distinction to keep in mind is whether the memory trace in question is thought to reside in working memory or in long-term memory. The term *forgetting* can be properly applied to each, but it seems important to be clear about which store one is referring to (and to avoid unintentionally intermingling the two). For the most part, I will concern myself here with forgetting from long-term, declarative memory, which refers to encoded traces that are outside the focus of attention (i.e. outside of the window of working memory) and that are reanimated by retrieval cues (as opposed to being refreshed by rehearsal). Note that neuroscientists often partition what I call long-term memory into short-term and long-term components, depending on whether or not the consolidation process has triggered the protein synthesis needed to establish an especially durable trace. However, that distinction is not critical here. For my purposes, long-term memory refers to memories that are not in the focus of attention but that can be revived into conscious awareness by retrieval cues.

As psychologists have generally used the term, *forgetting* from long-term memory refers to the inability to retrieve information that was once consciously accessible under the cuing conditions that are again in effect now. More formally, a particular item i might have been learned in association with a particular retrieval cue, q_i. At time $t1$, we find that the probability of retrieving item i from long-term memory given q_i—denoted $p(R_{i,t1}|q_i)$—is high. Sometime later, at $t2$, we find that the probability of retrieving item i given q_i—$p(R_{i,t2}|q_i)$—is low, i.e. forgetting from long-term, declarative memory is said to occur when $p(R_{i,t1}|q_i) > p(R_{i,t2}|q_i)$. Usually, these probabilities are estimated by testing memory over a set of items, though I will illustrate the point with reference to the forgetting of a particular item. As a concrete example, imagine having dinner at a restaurant called *Maria's Cocina* on Sunday. On Monday, the word *Maria* might occasion the successful retrieval of *Cocina*, but that same cue might fail to do so a month later. That would qualify as an instance of forgetting because it satisfies the criteria set forth above, i.e. we know that the to-be-remembered item (*Cocina*) was encoded into long-term memory because the retrieval cue (*Maria*) effectively retrieved that information 24 h after encoding (well beyond the window of working memory). Later, that same retrieval cue failed to retrieve the sought-after information. Under conditions like that, one would say that forgetting has occurred, at least according to the definition being proposed here.

Note that this definition of forgetting was implicit from the earliest investigations of memory. The famous savings function reported by Ebbinghaus (1885/1913), for example, illustrates the loss of memory that occurs over time even though the cuing conditions in effect during testing were held constant and even though the to-be-remembered information was undoubtedly encoded into long-term memory. Tulving (1974) appears to have had the same definition in mind when he said "Forgetting, as defined here, is the inability to recall something now that could be recalled on an earlier occasion" (p. 74). I am defining forgetting in the same way, except that I would add two caveats: (1) that the instance of recall that occurred on an earlier occasion involved retrieval from a long-term memory store (not working memory); and (2) that the retrieval cue is the same on both occasions.

A key point is that the study of forgetting should be specific to one memory system. The definition that I have proposed here is the one that applies to forgetting from long-term, declarative memory. As an example, Wixted and Ebbesen (1991) studied the forgetting of words over a relatively short period of time (40 s), but they construed their experiment as a study of forgetting from long-term memory because an extremely demanding distractor task was in effect throughout in order to prevent any involvement of working memory. Unless rehearsed, a trace in working memory is usually thought to survive no more than about 2 s (Baddeley 1997).

One could, of course, study the rapid forgetting that is observed for traces held in working memory, in which case one would be studying forgetting from that memory system (not from declarative memory). Similarly, one could study the loss of a learned skill over time, in which case one would be studying forgetting from procedural memory. The essential point is that regardless of which memory system is involved, the word "forgetting" applies if performance at *t1* and *t2* involved retrieval from the same system and under the same conditions. In most studies of forgetting, the system in question is long-term, declarative memory, and for that system forgetting is said to exist when $p(R_{i,t1}|q_i) > p(R_{i,t2}|q_i)$.

Philosophical conundrums to avoid

The concept of forgetting is neutral about *why* $p(R_{i,t1}|q_i) > p(R_{i,t2}|q_i)$. Answering the question of why forgetting occurs once fascinated experimental psychologists, but interest in the question has greatly subsided in recent years. However, the loss of interest seems to be more a function of the field's disillusionment with a particular theory of forgetting (namely, interference theory) than with any inherent problem with the way in which forgetting is conceptualized. The concept of forgetting did not bewitch the intelligence, but an increasingly baroque interference theory of forgetting may have (Tulving and Madigan 1970).

In searching for the answer to the question of why forgetting occurs, it seems best to avoid spending too much time on issues that are inherently untestable and which quickly devolve into the realm of philosophy. For example, the definition of forgetting presented above includes the assumption that the retrieval cue is held constant over time (but information becomes less accessible anyway). One could worry that the retrieval cue used at *t1* is not *exactly* the same as the retrieval cue used at *t2* despite a conscientious effort to keep them the same. As the Greek philosopher Heraclitus once said, you cannot step into the same river twice. Indeed, whenever $p(R_{i,t1}|q_i) > p(R_{i,t2}|q_i)$, one can appeal to this idea to explain forgetting. However, doing so resurrects a long abandoned notion, namely that the mere passage of time causes forgetting. In its new incarnation, the theory would be that no two retrieval cues can ever be the same if they are separated in time because the passage of time itself somehow changes them. This account is not unlike the decay theory of forgetting that McGeoch (1932) once famously argued against. According to the theory he challenged, forgetting was explained by the idea that the memory trace decays with the mere passage of time. However, McGeoch (1932) argued that time itself does not cause the trace to decay any more than it causes metal to rust. Specific intervening activities and events, he argued, must instead be responsible. The same argument could be applied to the idea that retrieval cues change with the passage of time. The mere assertion that retrieval cues are changed with time does not explain forgetting. One would need to show exactly how they are changed as time passes and how that affects retrieval.

Another philosophical issue that may be best avoided by experimental psychology concerns the final status of the memory trace, a point that Michael Davis also addresses in some detail. As he points out, an extreme view of forgetting would hold that true forgetting involves the complete eradication of the memory trace, either because it faded away altogether or because it was entirely overwritten by a new memory trace. However, it would be difficult to establish the complete absence of a trace because it is always possible that an as yet untried retrieval cue would show that some remnant of the trace is still available. Thus, focusing too much time on this definition of forgetting does not seem to be a fruitful course of action (on that, Michael Davis and I agree).

The difference between remembering and forgetting

Remembering, as that word is commonly used, is said to occur when a cue occasions the retrieval of a prior experience that was encoded into long-term memory, i.e. remembering refers to retrieval success. In everyday language, forgetting is the opposite of remembering because, as indicated above, the term *forgetting* is used synonymously with retrieval failure. However, the more technical definition of forgetting that has been in effect since Ebbinghaus first set out to study forgetting refers not to retrieval failure *per se* but to retrieval failure that occurs despite the fact that the retrieval cue being used now once effectively retrieved the information from long-term memory. Thus, as typically used in psychology, forgetting is *not* the opposite of remembering. On this point, I part company with Michael Davis and David Rubin, both of whom see forgetting as equivalent to retrieval failure (in which case forgetting and remembering are tightly connected, reciprocal concepts, as is true in everyday language). Imagine, for example, an experiment in which one group studies a list of 20 words presented at a rate of one word per second. A second group studies a similar list presented at the same rate while also being required to complete a concurrent task. The next day, we might find that the first group recalls more words than the second, i.e. we might find that the second group experienced more retrieval failure than the first. Did that group therefore exhibit more forgetting? Not necessarily, because it is likely that they failed to encode many of the words in the first place due to the concurrent task at encoding. An earlier test of memory (e.g. 10 min after learning) might have shown that to be true and might have shown that the rate of forgetting in the two groups was the same despite a considerable difference in the amount of retrieval failure.

These considerations call to mind a common referential practice in the neuroimaging literature that strikes me as being too casual and imprecise. Often, neural activity is measured by functional magnetic resonance imaging (fMRI) during a recognition task. Typically, neural activity associated with hits (target items that are correctly identified as having appeared on the list) is compared with neural activity associated with misses (target items that are incorrectly identified as being new). The hits are regarded as the remembered items, whereas items that are missed are often referred to as 'forgotten' items (e.g. Davachi *et al.* 2003). What is unclear, though, is whether these items were ever encoded in the first place. Moreover, on a recognition test, whether an item is a hit or a miss depends in large part on where the subject opted to place his or her decision criterion. Had the subject decided to respond in a somewhat more liberal fashion, the hit rate would have been higher (which means that the miss rate would have been lower), and what was labeled as a forgotten item would have instead been labeled as a remembered item. However, this transformation would have taken place despite the fact that the status of the memory trace and the status of the retrieval cue remained unchanged. All that happened was that the subject decided to respond in a more liberal fashion. The subject's d' score (the measure of memory strength) would remain unchanged, and it seems odd to refer to changes in remembering and forgetting taking place despite a constant memory strength. In fact, the terms should not be used in this way. Instead, the field seems best served by reserving the term *forgetting* for items that were once retrievable from long-term memory but no longer are despite using the same retrieval cue in both cases. Applying the term forgetting to misses does not pass this test. Of course, contrasting neural activity for hits versus misses seems appropriate enough, but it is probably better thought of as a comparison between strong and weak memories (not between remembered and forgotten items).

Why do we forget?

With the definition of forgetting from long-term memory suitably framed as $p(R_{i,t1}|q_i) > p(R_{i,t2}|q_i)$, the question then centers on why forgetting happens. Traditionally, the explanations have been that something happens to the retrieval cue (something other than the mere passage of time, that is) or something happens to the memory trace. Interference theory, which has dominated thinking in experimental psychology for decades, essentially holds that forgetting occurs because, during the time between *t1* and *t2*, the retrieval cue becomes associated with additional items, and the more encoded items a retrieval cue subsumes, the less effective it is at retrieving any one of them. This is the 'cue overload' theory of forgetting (Watkins and Watkins 1975). A great deal of convincing experimental evidence demonstrates that overloading a retrieval cue between *t1* and *t2* will, indeed, cause forgetting to happen. However, as noted by Wixted (2004*a,b*, 2005), the evidence that this mechanism accounts for everyday forgetting (i.e. that retrieval cues typically become overloaded with the passage of time) is quite limited.

The other idea, that forgetting occurs because the memory trace becomes degraded in some way between *t1* and *t2*, is standard thinking in the field of neuroscience. As argued by Wixted (2004*a*,*b*), the evidence that the formation of new memories serves to degrade recently formed memories that have yet to consolidate is strong. Still, this is an open question that warrants the attention of the field (though, at present, the field's attention mostly lies elsewhere).

As Loftus points out in Chapter 55, both of these accounts remain viable contenders to explain why the introduction of misinformation between *t1* and *t2* makes the originally encoded information less accessible than it otherwise would have been. Loftus notes that the field has moved away from exploring these fascinating theoretical issues in the area of misinformation, and Wixted (2004*b*) noted that the same is true of the entire area of forgetting. It is unfortunate that, with a few notable exceptions (e.g. Pavlik and Anderson 2005), the field of psychology is feebly ceding the territory of forgetting to the field of neuroscience, where investigations into the issue continue apace. In thinking about the concept of forgetting, the field should also consider whether it has anything interesting to say about why it occurs.

15

Memory systems

That there are functionally and biologically dissociable memory systems is today widely accepted by memory researchers and this concept deeply influences psychological, cognitive, and biological studies of memory. Advancing the study of memory systems requires the integration of behavioral observations with studies delineating cognitive and neural structures and as a result memory systems is a concept rooted by interlevel analysis. Those new to memory research might find it surprising that despite a rich historical record of philosophical musings, clinical observations, and experimental laboratory findings indicating that there were different "kinds" of memory, a clearly articulated description for many of the dissociable systems familiar today dates only from the mid-20th century. While the exact number of different memory systems remains contentious, one posssibility is that memory will follow the "rule of hand" proposed for the number of critical change variables observed in complex adaptive systems. If so, then there is likely to be a small set of memory systems, more than two but less than ten. Of course, the number of dissociable memory systems depends on how one defines "system." Reaching agreement on a final number is not what is conceptually important. Rather, the concept of memory systems is essential for building an organizational structure for interpreting the data converging across multiple levels of analysis. The search for dissociable memory systems generates experimentally answerable questions. Pursuit of such answers could reveal the nature of the cognitive operations and neural systems supporting behavior.

S.M.F.

58

Memory systems: A biological concept

Larry R. Squire

The idea that memory is composed of distinct systems has a long and interesting history. Beginning more than a century ago, one finds expressions of the idea that there is more than one kind of learning, and that there are various types or forms of memory and various memory processes. These early writings were based largely on philosophical considerations and psychological intuition, and did not lead to a single view. What eventually moved the discussion forward was the era of experimental inquiry that began in the middle of the twentieth century. This period began with the demonstration that the severely amnesic patient H.M. could learn a hand–eye coordination skill (tracing the outline of a star in a mirror) over a period of days but did not remember that he had practiced the task before (Milner 1962). This finding showed that memory was not unitary and set the stage for asking biological questions about how the brain accomplishes learning and memory. What are the brain structures damaged in H.M., and what memory capacities are impaired or spared as a result of this damage?

Initially, the prevailing view was that, while motor skills such as mirror drawing may lie outside the province of the medial temporal lobe structures damaged in H.M., H.M.'s impairment extends broadly across the rest of memory, and the rest of memory is therefore of one piece. Subsequently, however, it was discovered that motor skills are but a subset of a large domain of skill-like abilities, all of which are preserved in H.M. and other memory-impaired patients. The first example was the demonstration that amnesic patients could learn to read mirror-reversed print. They learned this perceptual skill at a normal rate despite not remembering the words they had read (Cohen and Squire 1980). This finding broadened the scope of what amnesic patients could do and suggested a distinction between declarative and procedural knowledge systems. This distinction had been proposed earlier to describe two possible ways that information might be represented in artificial systems. The new experimental work suggested that this kind of distinction is honored by the nervous system.

Declarative memory is representational, and what is learned is expressed through recollection. Declarative memory provides a way to model the external world, and in this sense is either true or false. It is the kind of memory that is referred to when the term 'memory' is used in everyday language. Procedural memory is expressed through performance rather than recollection, and it is neither true nor false. Procedural memory reflects the various ways that we have learned to interact with the world. Performance changes as the result of experience, and in this sense deserves the term memory, but performance changes without requiring any conscious memory content or in many cases even awareness that memory is being used.

Soon after this distinction was proposed, new interest was directed towards a different task that amnesic patients could sometimes perform well. In the 1970s, it had been reported that, when word stems were given as cues for previously presented words, patients often produced as many previously presented words as their controls. This was a demonstration of what would later be called priming. However, it took some time to appreciate the crucial role of task instructions, and the significance of these findings was initially overlooked. It turned out that amnesic patients perform well only with nonmemory instructions (use this word stem to form the first word that comes to mind). With conventional memory instructions (use this word stem as a cue to help you remember a study word), amnesic patients do more poorly than controls (Graf *et al.* 1984).

Evidence for the special status of priming also came from studies of normal subjects (Tulving *et al.* 1982). These authors wrote '... we are tempted to think that [these priming effects] reflect the operation of some other, as yet little understood, memory system' (p. 341). Thus, priming came to be viewed as a distinct form of memory, separate from what is impaired in amnesia (Tulving and Schacter 1990; Schacter and Buckner 1998). Perhaps the strongest evidence that priming is independent of declarative memory came with the later demonstration that both perceptual and conceptual priming can be fully intact in severely amnesic patients, even though the patients perform at chance on conventional tests of recognition memory constructed from the same test items (Hamann and Squire 1997; Levy *et al.* 2004).

Due to these and other discoveries, it became unwieldy after the mid-1980s to fit the accumulating facts into a two-part dichotomy, such as one based on declarative and procedural knowledge. In addition to skill learning and priming, other kinds of memory abilities were identified and linked to particular brain systems. The cerebellum was discovered to be essential for simple eye-blink classical conditioning. The neostriatum was identified as important for the gradual, feedback-guided learning that results in habit memory.

Other kinds of learning that involve the attachment of positive or negative valence to a stimulus, as in fear conditioning, were found to depend on the amygdala. Given this variety of memory tasks and brain structures, the mid-1980s saw a shift in perspective towards a framework that accommodated multiple (i.e. more than two) memory systems (Tulving 1985; Squire 1987). The term 'nondeclarative' was introduced with the idea that declarative memory refers to one memory system and that 'nondeclarative memory' is an umbrella term referring to additional memory systems (Squire and Zola-Morgan 1988). Figure 58.1 illustrates a taxonomy that incorporates these ideas (for the earliest version of this diagram, see Squire 1987). Note that one can subdivide declarative memory into two separate types (Tulving 1983), one involved with factual knowledge (semantic memory) and one involved with knowledge about specific events (episodic memory).

The notion of multiple memory systems is now widely accepted (Schacter *et al.* 2000; Eichenbaum and Cohen 2001; Squire *et al.* 2004), even if uncertainty remains about exactly how many memory systems there are. One is struck by the fact that the term 'memory system' did not come into comfortable use until it was possible to place the concept, and related experimental work,

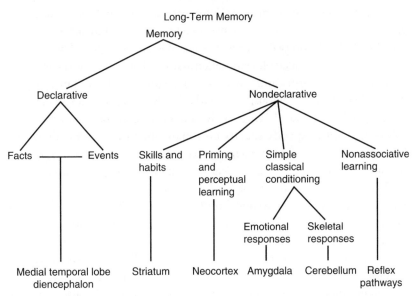

Fig. 58.1 A taxonomy of mammalian long-term memory systems. The taxonomy lists the brain structures thought to be especially important for each form of declarative and nondeclarative memory. In addition to its central role in emotional learning, the amygdala is able to modulate the strength of both declarative and nondeclarative memory.

within a biological framework. The term 'system' has its own tradition within biology (the digestive system, the respiratory system, the nervous system). Even within the nervous system itself, it has been possible for many decades to speak of brain systems as groupings of related structures with defined inputs and outputs, sometimes with identified functional significance (e.g. the cholinergic system, the visual system). The usefulness of the term 'memory system' appears to depend considerably on the extent to which a particular kind of memory can be related to a specific brain system. A memory system is best viewed as a brain system with a significant, though not necessarily exclusive, role in memory function. Emerging biological information has made discussions of memory systems more specific and has helped to define their properties.

History shows that as biological information becomes available about structure and mechanism, explanation becomes more concrete and less dependent on terminology. Terminology is important in psychological science because the concepts tend to be abstract and difficult to pin down. However, terminology is less important when a concept or a function has been related to mechanism. The term 'heredity' may be a little fuzzy, but DNA is not. Whereas one might debate exactly what heredity means, there is no similar argument about DNA. In the case of DNA, one could call it something else. Similarly, in the context of memory systems, 'habit memory' is not easy to define, but there is less difficulty with the 'neostriatum', which has been linked to habit memory (Mishkin *et al.* 1984). The discovery that there are kinds of learning supported by the neostriatum provides considerable clarification and simplification. One can expect to move towards a sharper and more accurate definition of 'habit memory' by considering what kinds of learning, and what kinds of tasks, depend on the neostriatum. Biology provides leverage on the issue of classification and definition.

It is difficult to specify exactly how many memory systems there are. Figure 58.1 lists seven kinds of memory: fact memory, event memory, procedural memory, priming and perceptual learning, emotional learning, conditioning of skeletal responses and nonassociative learning. One can add working memory. That would make eight, but there are a number of uncertain cases. For example, various kinds of nonassociative learning have been demonstrated, even in invertebrates (i.e. habituation and sensitization). These do not constitute memory systems as much as different reflex pathways by which a multiplicity of different stimuli can lead to either diminished or augmented responding. In addition, one could separate priming and perceptual learning, but the difference between priming and perceptual learning seems no more fundamental than the difference, for example, between perceptual and conceptual priming. The point is that there are many kinds of priming and perceptual learning. Fact memory and event memory might merit classification as distinct memory systems, though one could instead take the perspective that these two forms of declarative memory are both products of the medial temporal lobe's interaction with neocortex, and that event memory is different only because it depends on the resources of the frontal lobe to a greater extent than fact memory (Squire 1987). From the perspective of biology, one can identify five basic brain systems that support long-term memory: the medial temporal lobe system, which supports declarative memory; the neostriatum, which supports procedural learning; regions and networks within neocortex, which support varieties of priming and perceptual learning; the amygdala, which supports emotional learning; and the cerebellum, which supports the conditioning of skeletal responses. All these systems can be distinguished in terms of the kinds of information they process, the principles by which they operate, and the brain structures and connections that support them.

At this stage, it is more important and useful to work away at the biology of the various kinds of memory than to debate how many kinds there are. Consider that one does not debate much about how many systems are found in a working automobile. We already know all the parts and how they work. As more is learned about how the brain works, one can expect epistemological questions about what a memory system is and how many there are to become less interesting. In the meantime, it seems reasonable to look for broad principles that can be used to construct a few large categories. Accordingly, one should have in mind on the order of 5–10 memory systems but not, for example, 100. The central idea is that there exist a few major categories, and a few major brain systems, which support the various capacities for experience-dependent behavioral plasticity.

Acknowledgments

This work was supported by the Medical Research Service of the Department of Veterans Affairs, an NIMH grant, and the Metropolitan Life Foundation.

59

Memory systems: Multiple systems in the brain and their interactions

Edmund T. Rolls

Introduction

The aims of this chapter are to show that there are multiple memory systems in the brain; to give an outline of what some of these different memory systems are; to show that the computational principles of the different systems are usually distinct; to consider interactions between different memory systems; to show that some aspects of cognitive functions such as attention arise because of interactions between memory systems; to show how some neurological and neuropsychiatric disorders may be related to impairments in the functions of these memory systems; and to argue that much of brain computation is in a sense related to different types of memory in that what is computed in most brain systems is related to synaptic changes that are induced by learning.

We may define memory systems as 'dissociable brain systems involved in different types of learning and memory'. This definition acknowledges that our concept of what the different memory systems are at a cognitive or behavioral level can be guided by an exact knowledge of what is computed in each neurally defined memory system in the brain, and how it is computed. I note that some memory systems are involved only or primarily in memory, and that others may implement some types of memory, but may have other functions too (e.g. the basal ganglia, implicated in stimulus–response habit memory, but also more generally in motor and other functions). Each memory system may be characterized by its set of input connections, the type of computation it performs on those inputs, and its output connections; which together define the memory function it performs.

Multiple memory systems: some examples, and their computational principles of operation (see Fig. 59.1)

The hippocampus and connected parts of the medial temporal lobe are involved in episodic memory, the memory for a particular event or for

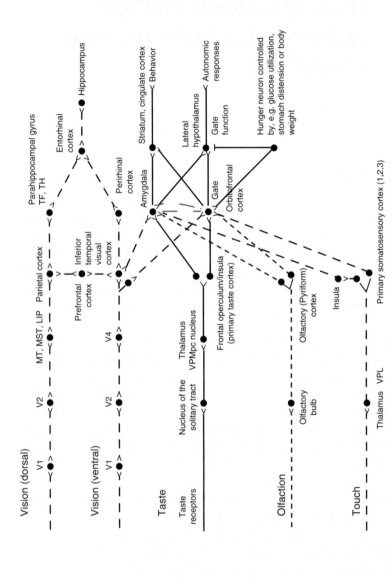

Fig. 59.1 The pathways involved in some different memory systems described in the text. Forward connections start from early cortical areas on the left. To emphasize that backprojections are important in many memory systems, they are made explicit in the synaptic terminals drawn in the upper part of the diagram, but are a property of most of the connections shown.

a sequence of events. This can be tested by, for example, reward–place association learning in primates (remembering the place of a reward in a scene), which is reflected in the activity of hippocampal neurons (Rolls and Treves 1998; Rolls and Kesner 2006). The computational principle may be autoassociation implemented in the CA3 recurrent collateral network, which anatomically could allow inputs derived from the ends of many cortical processing streams that are co-active to be associated together. Retrieval of the memory of the whole episode could be implemented from any part of it within the CA3 network. Backprojections to the neocortex (via CA1 and entorhinal cortex) could allow each part of the memory (e.g. visual object or reward, and place) to be recalled in the appropriate cortical area that originally provided the object or place input to the hippocampus.

The perirhinal cortex is involved in recognition memory (delayed match to sample over long delays, and with intervening stimuli) (Baxter and Murray 2001), and this may be implemented by neurons with larger responses to the sample than to the match stimulus due to a habituation process, with active resetting between trials. The perirhinal cortex is also involved in long-term familiarity memory in that perirhinal neurons' responses increase gradually over 400 presentations of stimuli, and this may be implemented by incremental synaptic enhancement each time the stimulus is seen (Rolls *et al.* 2005).

Semantic memory implemented in the neocortex requires slow learning in order to build in all the constraints that define the semantic representation (McClelland *et al.* 1995). The building of semantic representations may benefit from the recall of episodic memories from the hippocampus to the neocortex, as exemplified by recalling particular (episodic) journeys to build a (semantic) geographical map (Rolls and Kesner 2006). This is an example of an interaction between memory systems.

The prefrontal cortex is involved in short-term/working memory when there are intervening stimuli so that an off-line buffer store is needed. In this situation, the memory cannot be implemented by posterior areas such as the inferior temporal visual cortex and parietal cortex which are committed to ongoing perception (Rolls and Deco 2002). The principle of operation is that attractor networks in the prefrontal cortex can maintain the firing that represents a single item in the memory independently, while posterior perceptual networks continue with ongoing processing of perceptual inputs (Rolls and Deco 2002).

The amygdala is involved in stimulus–reinforcer association learning and therefore in emotion (Rolls 2005). Different amygdala output subsystems are involved in autonomic responses, in effects of conditioned incentives on instrumental behavior, and in freezing. The computational principle may be pattern association learning between the (conditioned) stimulus and the (primary) reinforcer (Rolls 2000, 2005).

The orbitofrontal cortex also implements stimulus–reinforcer (stimulus–stimulus) association learning and is therefore involved in emotion, but it can reverse these associations very rapidly. It is thus more important than the amygdala in implementing changes in emotional and emotional behavior to reflect the changing reinforcers being received (Rolls 2005). The computational principle may be a reversal of an attractor network which holds the current rule active (e.g. the circle is associated with reward), which biases the mapping through sensory to stimulus–reward combination neurons to reward neurons (Deco and Rolls 2005).

The basal ganglia are implicated in stimulus–response habit learning (Rolls 2005), and this may be acquired by reinforcement learning (Doya 1999).

Action–outcome (or response reinforcer) association learning (which is sensitive to devaluation) may involve the cingulate cortex and related areas (Rolls 2005).

The inferior temporal visual cortex is involved in learning view invariant representations of objects, and the learning principle may include associative learning with a short-term memory trace. This learning rule helps each stage of the hierarchy to learn the invariant properties of the stimulus input, which tends to be about the same object on the short time scale due to the temporospatial statistics of viewing objects in the world (Rolls and Deco 2002). A short-term memory trace implemented at each stage of perceptual processing by local cortical recurrent connections may thus be very important in how invariant perceptual representations are built in perceptual systems (Rolls and Deco 2002).

Because there are dissociable systems, there is no single concept of memory. The processes (see below) that implement the memory functions performed by these different systems may be partly similar, but also partly different, so it is important to understand the exact computational and functional properties of each memory system.

Interactions between memory systems are important for understanding many aspects of cognition

Top-down attention can be understood in terms of a top-down bias provided by a short-term memory network which holds the subject of attention active. This top-down bias then acts in a biased competition model on the bottom-up inputs to influence where or to what object attention is paid (Rolls and Deco 2002; Deco and Rolls 2005); or to influence how sensory inputs are gated through prefrontal networks to implement switching of executive function (Deco and Rolls 2003); or to perform stimulus–reinforcer association reversal and thus influence the emotional interpretation of stimuli (Deco and Rolls 2005).

These interactions may be nonlinear and therefore computationally and cognitively interesting, and can be explored formally by integrate-and-fire network models which are consistent with the underlying neuronal firing (Deco and Rolls 2005).

Cognition can influence perceptual processing. An example is that word labels can influence the activations produced by olfactory stimuli in the secondary olfactory cortex in the orbitofrontal cortex (de Araujo *et al.* 2005). These effects are likely to be implemented by top-down signals from the cognitive state held in short-term memory producing biased competition to influence olfactory processing in the orbitofrontal cortex.

Mood states can influence memories, and vice versa. This may be implemented by interactions between attractor networks in brain regions such as the orbitofrontal cortex which represent mood states and attractor networks in memory systems that influence recall (Rolls 2005).

An implication of these points is that the concept of memory systems should be made broad to include many different systems, for it is in fact the case that many aspects of cognitive function can be formally understood computationally as memory systems interacting with each other or with other brain systems (Rolls 2005).

Understanding the interactions between memory systems may be important for understanding some disorders of cognitive function

Depression may be influenced by the interaction between mood states and memories (Rolls 2005). Remembering sad memories is more likely during sadness, and the sad memories may exacerbate the depression. Breaking this positive feedback memory system may be beneficial in depression.

Some of the symptoms of schizophrenia may be understandable in terms of effects of agents (such as pharmacological agents) that influence N-methyl-D-aspartate (NMDA) receptors either directly or via an influence on dopamine receptors, and may thus influence the depth of the basins of attraction of integrate-and-fire attractor neuronal networks (Deco and Rolls 2003; Rolls 2005). These attractor networks appear to be common in the neocortex by virtue of the recurrent collateral connections within a cortical area, and the feedback and feedforward connections between adjacent cortical areas in the hierarchy (Rolls and Deco 2002).

The modification by learning of synaptic connection strengths between neurons is very important for understanding most brain functions

Brain functions are involved in perception, cognition and motor function, and many of these synaptic connections are modifiable as a result of experience. In this sense, a key concept is that the understanding of memory-related synaptic changes in different systems in the brain is fundamental for understanding much of brain function (Rolls and Treves 1998; Rolls and Deco 2002; Rolls 2005). Thus a clear understanding of how memories are left at synapses reflecting previous activity of the coupled neurons may in fact be essential for understanding exactly how different brain systems operate.

Within any memory system there will inevitably be *processes* that take place, such as:

- increasing synaptic strengths (implementing processes such as learning and consolidation);
- overwriting previously modified synapses (contributing to forgetting);
- decay of synaptic strengths (contributing to forgetting);
- alteration of representations as a result of changed synaptic strengths (influencing coding and representation);
- reactivating memory systems which may have emergent properties such as completion of an incomplete memory (implementing processes such as retrieval, recall and remembering); and
- short-term attractor states of the system due to the synaptic modification in recurrently connected circuits that implement processes such as short-term memory and attention.

It appears that some of what have been thought of as core concepts in memory are the *processes* that take place in a memory system and lead to changes in behavior. Part of the science of memory should be to understand these processes by understanding how the synaptic changes underlying memory contribute to the behavior of large populations of neurons, and thus lead to the processes that are observed in the behavior of the organism. These processes will operate differently in different memory systems, due to their different architectures (e.g. pattern associators, autoassociators implementing attractor networks, competitive networks), and to the detailed dynamics of each system which influence how long memories last in each system, how likely it is that previous memories will be overwritten, etc.

Some implications for future research on memory systems

It will be necessary to understand the processes within each memory system in the brain separately in order to capture the real wealth of understanding now possible about our different memory systems (Rolls and Treves 1998; Rolls and Deco 2002; Rolls 2005). Moreover, understanding how different parts of the brain operate as separable systems helps us to define at the behavioral level the large number of dissociable memory systems. To understand how memory and related processes such as attention and decision making actually operate in the brain, it will be necessary to build computational neuroscience models of each memory system based on neuronal activity in each memory system, the details of its internal and external connections, and the effects of selective damage to each system (Rolls and Treves 1998; Rolls and Deco 2002; Deco and Rolls 2005; Rolls 2005).

60

Memory systems: A cognitive construct for analysis and synthesis

Marcia K. Johnson

Memory system is a construct used to refer to the capacity for behavior, thought and emotion to change as a function of experience. It is assumed to be instantiated in biological mechanisms. Because the human memory system is complex, it is useful to think of it as consisting of parts that subserve classes of functions. Depending on an investigator's emphasis, hypothesized parts are defined in terms of conceptual structures (e.g. sensory registers, short-term memory, long-term memory), types of content (e.g. episodic versus semantic memory, habit versus memory, procedural versus declarative memory), types of processes (e.g. shallow versus deep, automatic versus effortful, familiarity versus recollection, perceptual versus reflective), and/or in terms of brain structures (e.g. hippocampus versus striatum). Like the blind men and the elephant, all of these approaches capture some of the truth, and the challenge is to construct the memory system elephant from the ideas and findings yielded by these different perspectives.

One effort—a *multiple-entry, modular memory system (MEM)*—is shown in Fig. 60.1. MEM is a *process*-oriented system that specifies the types of component processes needed for the wide range of memory phenomena demonstrated in human thought and behavior. The MEM architecture organizes these component processes into four functional subsystems. Proposed subsystems P-1 and P-2 consist of perceptual component processes and they record the consequences of these processes. The reflective subsystems R-1 and R-2 consist of component processes of what we generally call 'thought' and 'imagination', allowing us to act mentally on the products of prior perception or reflection and record the consequences. The subsystems are proposed to be modular in the sense that they can engage in some functions without reference to other subsystems, but multiple subsystems are normally operating and interacting in any complex task or situation.

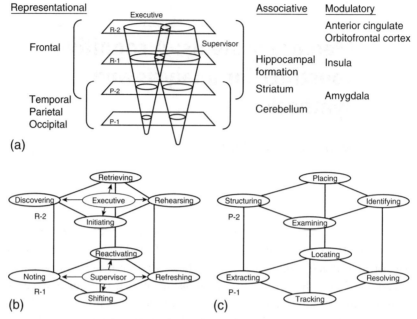

Fig. 60.1 Memory system as a cognitive construct for analysis and synthesis. (a) A multiple-entry, modular memory system composed of two reflective subsystems (R-1 and R-2) and two perceptual subsystems (P-1 and P-2). (b) Component processes of R-1 and R-2. (c) Component processes of P-1 and P-2. Component processes are realized by networks of brain regions: Various cortical regions (frontal, occipital, parietal, temporal) in interaction with each other and with regions in the hippocampal formation, cerebellum, and striatum, and modulated by anterior cingulate cortex, orbitofrontal cortex, insula and amygdala, account for variations in the types of memory that humans display. (From Johnson, M.K. (1991). Reflection, reality-monitoring, and the self. In R. Kunzendorf (Ed.), *Mental imagery* (pp. 3–16). NY: Plenum. Reprinted with permission from Springer Science and Business media.)

We are typically unaware of the perceptual information involved in P-1 processes, for instance the cues in a speech signal that specify a particular vowel or the aspects of a moving stimulus that specify when it is likely to reach a given point in space. Yet, learning via P-1 processes allows us to adjust to a person's accent or to anticipate the trajectory of a baseball. In contrast, we use P-2 processes in learning about the conscious, phenomenal perceptual world of objects such as people, chairs and balls, events such as seeing a person sit down in a chair or catch a ball, and the relations among objects (e.g. a couch is to the left of a chair in the living room).

Reflection allows us to go beyond the immediate consequences of perception, allowing us to sustain, organize, manipulate and revive information. Similar to P-1 compared with P-2 processes, R-1 processes are more automatic than R-2 processes. R-1 processes allow us to refresh (foreground), shift to, note or reactivate relevant information. R-2 processes allow us to rehearse and initiate new strategies (e.g. generate cues) that help us discover relations or retrieve information. Reflective component processes are the mental activities that not only contribute to a sense of remembering but also allow us to anticipate future events, imagine possible alternative pasts and futures, and have the sense that we are taking an active role in our thought and behavior.

The idea of active control of the flow of cognition is often assigned to a central executive in cognitive theories. In MEM, there is no central executive. Rather, perceptual and reflective cognition is guided by agendas, which serve as virtual executives (or supervisors) when active. For example, with an R-1 agenda to listen attentively to a story, you might generate tacit implications of sentences, note relations between one part of the story and an earlier part of which you are reminded, and so forth. With an R-2 agenda to evaluate the story critically, you might generate objections to the logic of events, actively retrieve other stories for comparison, and so forth. That is, agendas (both well-learned and *ad hoc*) activate combinations of reflective and perceptual processes in the service of specific goals and motives, and monitor or evaluate outcomes with respect to these agendas. Agendas can coordinate activity across subsystems (reflected in the cones in Fig. 60.1), as when a goal activates retrieval of information along with related perceptual schemas (e.g. in driving to a party, trying to remember an address while looking for a specific style of house). In MEM, representing agendas separately in each of the two reflective subsystems provides a mechanism for (1) control and monitoring of complex thought and action; (2) self-observation and self-control; and (3) certain forms of consciousness.

The activity of any of these component processes generates changes in memory. Changes in memory can be expressed in behavior (e.g. seeing something that was seen before more easily under degraded conditions) or expressed as phenomenal experiences, such as experiencing a feeling of familiarity, remembering an autobiographical event or knowing a fact.

The component processes of MEM (see Fig. 60.1B and C) are described in terms of mid-level concepts. A component process represents a class of similar operations performed on different data types, for example similar operations occurring in different sensory modalities. Also, because component processes are transactions among brain regions or circuits of activity, they can be disrupted in multiple ways. Because different circuits likely instantiate different versions of a process (e.g. *refreshing* auditory/verbal information may involve a circuit different from *refreshing* visual/pictorial information), considerable specificity of disruption from highly localized brain lesions could occur, depending on where the lesion is located.

Cognitive neuroscience is providing evidence about the relation between proposed cognitive processes and neural mechanisms. For example, for visual information, findings are rapidly accumulating from many laboratories about the roles of different areas of occipital, temporal and parietal cortex in perceptual processing, and about the roles of different areas of frontal cortex in reflective processing (e.g. dorsolateral and ventrolateral prefrontal cortex in *refreshing* and *rehearsing*, respectively). Likewise, we are seeing progress in characterizing how cortical regions, interacting with hippocampal, cerebellar and striatal structures, contribute to memory, and how these circuits are modulated by activity in regions that are sensitive to conflict and emotional and motivational factors (anterior cingulate cortex, orbitofrontal cortex, insula, amygdala). In turn, activity in brain regions associated with motivation and emotion is modulated by past experience and current goals and cognitive contexts. Thus, even at a quite general level of description, the memory system is complex and highly interactive among brain regions and across putative subsystems. Specifying the relations among regions engaged in representing information (e.g. goals, criteria, relations, objects, features) and associative and modulatory regions is a major challenge for cognitive and affective neuroscience.

Science is an effort to understand by analysis and synthesis. MEM subsystems (like concepts such as implicit learning, episodic memory or reflection) are too complex to be the basic units of analysis. For analysis, component processes are a more tractable approach. Hypothesized component processes can be investigated experimentally, both behaviorally and with the tools of cognitive neuroscience that are currently available [e.g. functional magnetic resonance imaging (fMRI), event-related potentoal (ERP), transcranial magnetic stimulation (TMS)]. A cognitive neuroscience of *component processes* aims to: (1) provide operational definitions of processes; (2) identify brain regions subserving a process; (3) distinguish these regions or patterns of activation from regions or patterns of activation subserving other component processes; (4) identify functional correlates of component processes (e.g. impact on long-term memory); (5) demonstrate that disruption of putative function is associated with damage or dysfunction in the presumed brain regions subserving the process; and (6) specify how the process and its neural correlates vary with context (e.g. changes in the types of representations on which the process acts, or changes in the amount of potential interference). In short, understanding a complex psychological phenomenon such as memory involves a graceful alignment between biological perspectives (emphasizing, for example, brain structures) and cognitive perspectives (emphasizing, for example, processes).

As investigators identify more specific neural circuits associated with more specific component processes, and further explicate their interactions, some mid-level conceptual framework that proposes an architecture for component processes should be useful for synthesis. That is, subsystems such as those proposed in MEM help identify and organize relations among the many findings, such as the relation between working memory and long-term memory or why different kinds of brain damage selectively disrupt memory.

Such a general, synthetic framework for characterizing memory subsystems should try to address a number of key issues: (1) the wide range of functions that memory serves (e.g. perceptual learning, recognition, voluntary recall, autobiographical memory, knowledge, prediction); (2) the relation between memory and reality, i.e. the mechanisms that account for both accurate and distorted memory; (3) dissociations among memory measures and variation in phenomenal experience of memory; (4) selective effects of brain damage, aging, fatigue and stress; (5) how subsystems of memory interact; (6) the relation of memory to other cognitive concepts such as attention, perception and consciousness; (7) the relations among cognition, emotion and memory; (8) changes in memory with development; (9) the concept of 'self;' (10) the evolution of memory subsystems; and (11) brain structures and networks subserving memory processes. For further discussion of issues relating to the goals of analysis and synthesis from the MEM perspective, see Johnson (1983, 1990, 1991, 1992, 1997), Johnson *et al.* (1993, 2005), Johnson and Hirst (1991, 1993), Johnson and Chalfonte (1994), Johnson and Multhaup (1992) and Johnson and Reeder (1997).

Acknowledgments

This work has been supported by NIA grants AG09253 and AG15793, and NIH grant MH62196.

61

Integrative comments
Memory systems: An incentive, not an endpoint

Randy L. Buckner

Memory system as a concept is widely accepted and guides much research on memory (e.g. Mishkin 1982; McNaughton and Morris 1987; Squire and Zola-Morgan 1991; LeDoux 1993; Eichenbaum *et al*. 1994). Debate and discovery most often surround identifying new properties of memory systems, their neural bases and dissociations between systems. In the essays prepared for this volume, we focused on how the concept of 'memory system' is used in studies of memory.

An early appearance of the concept and term *memory system* is found in the writings of the noted zoologist John Young (e.g. Boycott and Young 1955; Young 1965). His work is particularly informative for understanding some of the reasons to evoke the concept of a memory system, so I briefly review it here. A broader historical context is provided in Squire's contribution to this volume (Chapter 58; see also Schacter and Tulving 1994).

John Young was a zoologist whose work spanned half a century. His most important contribution was the description of the giant squid fiber system just prior to the Great Depression. This description served as the basis for the preparation later used to unravel the ionic mechanisms of the action potential (Altman 1997). In a second phase of his academic career, Young became immersed in a research program that targeted for understanding how simple learned behaviors in the octopus were instantiated in the anatomy and properties of the nervous system. In his pursuits, Young developed the concept of a memory system.

Influenced by the failed attempts of Karl Lashley to identify the repository of memory and Richard Semon's ideas that a memory repository, or engram (see Chapter 3, this volume), would exist, Young conducted explorations of the memory system of the octopus by making varied lesions and determining their effects on learned attack behaviors (Young 1965). An octopus will instinctively attack a crab. Young taught his subjects that attacks would result in electrical shocks when specific visible cues were present but not in their absence. His motivation was the belief that, much as specialized neurons

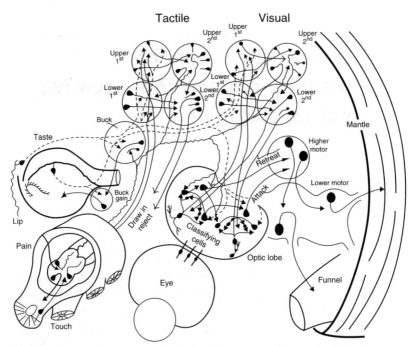

Fig. 61.1 Young's 1965 'visual and tactile memory systems of the octopus'. Young developed the concept of a memory system as a parallel to the idea that the brain contains systems for processing different forms of information. He proposed that, as neural specializations exist to support functions associated with perception and action, similar networks of neural nodes exist to support the persistence of memories. From Young, J.Z. (1965). *The Croonian Lecture, 1965: The organization of a memory system*. Proceedings of the Royal Society of London, Series B, Biological Sciences, **163**, 285–320. Reprinted with permisssion from the Royal Society of London.

existed for processing tactile and visual information, specialized neurons he labeled 'memory cells' would exist to aid the persistence of an experience. Young termed the system containing these specialized mnemonic facilitators a 'memory system' as a natural parallel to the idea that the nervous system contained specialized networks of nodes preferential to visual and tactile processing functions, contained within the visual and tactile systems (Fig. 61.1).

Memory system was used as a concept to describe the network of connections whose function was primarily to facilitate long-lasting persistence of learned environmental cues. The concept was intuitive and drew from common knowledge that systems in machines, and presumably systems in the brain, contained interacting physical structures that did things—memory was such a thing. The concept was probably appealing because other fields, including the fledgling area of computer science, were speaking of systems, even specifically 'memory systems'.

Young's early ideas about the properties of memory system echo many aspects of contemporary usage. Based on retained learning following specific lesions to the octopus, he argued that the octopus memory system was involved in certain long-term forms of retention but not short-term persistence (Boycott and Young 1955). He also postulated the existence of multiple memory systems based on dissociated effects of lesions and distinct anatomical connections (Young 1965). Perhaps most relevant to the present chapter, he argued that the concept was productive because it encouraged further exploration of the nature of memory systems and the memory processes that they subserve. His inquiry began with a behavioral question and turned to biology for clarification:

> ... the study of the connexion pattern of the nervous system of the octopus has given me a feeling of beginning to understand a little about the subject of memory. To study the material organization behind any subject or problem is surely the basis of scientific approach. I shall go so far as to suggest evidence for the existence of a unit of memory or mnemon. The suggestion is made with great hesitation and in full awareness of its dangers. The technique of pushing the analysis of the system as far as possible on the basis of the connexion pattern seems to have brought increasing clarification (p. 285).

Memory system as a concept

In contemporary usage, the concept memory system can be understood heuristically as a collection of interacting brain areas that participate in memory function and dissociate from other systems that participate in distinct forms of memory. As is evident from this definition, the emphasis is on *both* neural and behavioral levels of analysis. Schacter and Tulving's 1994 instructive criteria for defining a memory system include a property list that notes features of the memory system that make it different from other systems. These features will include its neural bases, rules of operation and the kinds of information operated upon.

One question that emerges is the relationship between the concept memory system and the concept of brain system, since all memory systems are, by definition, brain systems. The concept memory system is used when emphasis is placed on the mnemonic properties of the brain system as opposed to information processing that does not emphasize plasticity and experience-dependent change. This is an important distinction to make in that many brain systems contain within them mechanisms for plasticity but are also used for current processing function (e.g. the basal ganglia and the cerebellum). As Nadel (1994) notes in relation to the propensity to propose new, distinct forms of memory: 'One might argue that we have gone too far in this regard: everything the nervous system does could be construed as "memorylike" in some sense, since just about every form of activity in the nervous system leaves some relatively non-transient trace behind' (pp. 40–41). The concept memory system is thus a concept of convenience to highlight the mnemomic properties of brain systems when those properties are the focus of investigation. The concept persists because it is useful for the same reason originally proposed by Young half a century ago: it forces us to push analysis of the memory system as far as possible, and this pursuit has brought clarification.

A number of further aspects of the concept emerged across the views of our authors in this volume. First, there was consensus that there are multiple memory systems as opposed to a unitary memory system. This point is well articulated in the individual essays, so it will not be discussed further here. The only point to be made here is that the concept memory system, while perhaps gaining its recent popularity within the unitary versus multiple memory system debate, is not inherently about whether there is one, two or a dozen memory systems. The concept would apply to an animal that, as far as could be discerned, had only a single memory system.

Secondly, convergent empirical dissociation was agreed upon as a key tool in putting substance to the concept. In fact, while one might seek to idealize a concept in a form that is abstracted from its empirical support, the concept of memory system does not appear to have such a perfect form. Its utility derives, in large part, from the concept's ability to make sense of empirical dissociations. For example, separate memory systems are expected to dissociate based on brain lesions, be sensitive to varied aspects of learning paradigms and test procedures, and contribute in distinct ways to memory performance. Finally, there was broad agreement that we are just beginning to understand the properties of identified memory systems. Thus, the concept is still driving new discovery and debate. It is a tool.

Biological versus cognitive anchoring

A point of divergence among the various essays is the degree to which behavioral versus biological dissociation is the anchoring point. In the end, if a final understanding of all memory systems were accomplished, this would seem an unnecessary point to discuss since there is agreement that memory systems are based on distinct neural structures that express themselves in multiple forms of memory and process. However, knowledge is incomplete, and the practice of using the concept differed among the authors. Marcia Johnson (Chapter 60) described her influential process-oriented memory system that first postulates specific component processes and then seeks understanding of the underlying neural bases (Johnson 1983). In contrast, Larry Squire and Edmund Rolls (Chapters 58 and 59) began with biological dissociations, in particular from lesion–behavior analysis, and constructed descriptions of the memory systems to account for these biological dissociations.

In a previous essay, Sherry and Schacter (1987) took the middle road in their definition using terms that are appropriate to both neural and cognitive mechanisms: 'memory system refers to an interaction among acquisition, retention, and retrieval mechanisms that is characterized by certain rules of operation' (p. 440). I tend toward a biologically anchored version of the concept for the reasons articulated by Rolls, Squire, and Young half a century ago—the biology of the system clarifies and refines description of the memory system. However, in principle, because the defining properties of a memory system contain both its dissociated neural implementation *and* supported memory forms, these two approaches are valid and their utility should be measured by the insights they provide.

Relationship to other concepts

The concept memory system can also be defined based on its relationships to other concepts and by what it is not. As already noted, the concept is intimately tied to the broader concept of a brain system (Chapter 58, this volume). A memory system is a descriptor for a brain system when its mnemonic properties are emphasized. This particular relationship suggests two reasons why the concept will almost certainly persist in having fuzzy boundaries. One obstacle for hard drawn boundaries is that the same brain system will be discussed as a 'memory' or 'brain' system dependent on context and the degree to which the user seeks to emphasize memory as opposed to other processing functions. A second obstacle is that brain systems are themselves inherently fuzzy concepts. The brain contains a complex network of interconnected, specialized processing units organized as pathways that evolved their specializations to be adaptive (Mishkin *et al.* 1983; Van Essen *et al.* 1992). As Sherry and Schacter (1987) note in the context of memory systems 'the evolution of multiple memory systems requires memory systems to be specialized to such a degree that the functional problems each system handles cannot be handled by another system' (p. 439). Some specializations across brain systems provide clear dividing lines between networks of areas based on anatomy, connections, topography and function. Others are blurry. For these reasons, the concept of memory system will remain blurry.

Several things are not memory systems. Behavioral tasks are not memory systems nor are tasks expected to have one-to-one relationships with memory systems (Schacter and Tulving 1994). Most tasks will undoubtedly rely on multiple memory systems much in the same manner that a complex task may draw upon contributions from visual, motor and other brain systems. Use of memory in everyday life certainly does not respect boundaries between memory systems but rather flexibly draws upon multiple available systems to attain goals. Experimental expectations and understanding of disease influences on brain systems should consider this complex relationship. Spikes in a single-unit recording train and activation regions in functional imaging studies are not memory systems. Such observations may reflect the expressions of memory systems in the context of a task, but themselves do not define memory systems. Experimental preparations that reveal molecular mechanisms associated with plasticity are not memory systems, although they may be revealing underlying mechanisms that exist within memory systems to support their mnemonic function. The concept memory system is broader than individual empirical observations. The concept is most useful when employed as a construct to integrate multiple levels of observation, both behavioral and neural, to identify and understand evolved networks of brain structures that support learning and remembering.

Prospective use

The concept memory system has motivated extensive exploration of the structures that support memory function and description of the memory forms that are supported. This use will certainly continue. The concept has encouraged exploration of dissociations among putative memory systems—a powerful experimental approach. However, classification of distinct memory systems should not be the end-point for research. It will be disappointing if the next era of memory research ends with only a clearer taxonomy of the multiple memory systems. Central questions of how processes are performed within memory systems should take center stage. For example, evidence that structures within the medial temporal lobe are part of a memory system that is necessary for remembering is a foundational discovery. Understanding how those structures contribute to the processes involved in remembering and how they interact with brain systems that are part of the larger architecture of cognition is the natural next question. Similarly, future research will undoubtedly see connections with molecular approaches that unravel mechanisms of plasticity and the memory systems that rely upon them. As we succeed in identifying individual memory systems that are agreed upon, the concept will probably be less central in our explorations as the workings of these systems become the focus of investigation rather than dissociations among them.

16

Phylogeny and evolution

Despite their central importance to biological theory, evolutionary concepts tend to be somewhat peripheral to the experimental conduct of the science of memory as it has been traditionally pursued by a majority of psychologists and neuroscientists. Evolutionary concepts, when invoked, have been used principally for phylogenetic hierarchies and ontological development (e.g. procedural memory appears early in evolution and is present in young infants; episodic memory appears later in evolution and emerges with maturity). Memory research could benefit by incorporating a comparative approach carefully considering the cognitive adaptations unique to each species. We can learn much from comparative studies using a broader diversity of species than is experimentally typical in most studies of memory (e.g. rodents, non-human primates, and humans). Looking across a multiplicity of species will help delineate how different brain systems evolve to solve the differing array of computational problems encountered by individual species through the course of evolutionary history. Most importantly, taking the concepts of evolution seriously will lead us to delineate in what ways human memory is unique, what selective pressures might have influenced the emergence of the novel neural architectures required, and what adaptive advantages emerged. Additionally, a broad comparative approach might even reveal unique types of memory that humans lack. We won't know unless we look.

S.M.F.

62

Phylogeny and evolution:
It takes two to tango

Nicola S. Clayton

Darwin (1872) suggested that mental characteristics, including memory, are subject to natural selection in much the same way as morphological traits. Comparative psychologists and neurobiologists have paid considerable attention to Darwin's argument that human memory and other mental traits share many features in common with those of other animals. Indeed, most forms of memory do appear to be common to humans and nonhuman animals, and this has allowed for the development of animal models for the treatment of various memory disorders such as those that arise in Alzheimer's disease. However, in his seminal book '*Elements of Epsiodic Memory*', Tulving (1983) argued that there is one particular type of memory, namely episodic memory, that is unique to humans. Yet when it comes to memory research, considerably less attention has been paid to the metaconcept '*Evolution*'. How does an understanding of evolution, as opposed to simply an acknowledgement of its existence, contribute to the 'science of memory'?

I shall address this question by focusing on three key evolutionary concepts, which have important implications for memory research, particularly within the realm of declarative memory and the question of whether or not episodic memory is a uniquely human trait.

Homology and convergence

The first concept concerns the evolutionary mechanisms by which similarities between animals can arise. Homology refers to similarities between groups of animals that arise because they share a common ancestor who also possessed the same trait(s). In contrast, convergence refers to those similarities that arise as a result of adaptation to similar selection pressures, and the more distantly related the two groups then the stronger the case for convergence.

How does an understanding of whether similarities in a trait arise because of homology or convergence inform the science of memory? Consider the evolution of episodic memory. A number of psychologists have argued that episodic memory is unique to humans, yet there is evidence that one species of bird, the western scrub-jay, can remember the what, where and when of specific past events, which are behavioral markers of episodic memory (Clayton and Dickinson 1998). The term 'episodic-like' is used to describe the scrub-jay's memory because it is unclear as to whether or not animals have the conscious experiences that accompany episodic recollection in humans, namely autonoesis and chronesthesia (Tulving 2005).

So far the most detailed studies of 'episodic-like' memory in animals have been conducted on one member of the corvid (crow) family, the western scrub-jay (for a recent review, see de Kort et al. 2005). Now if episodic-like memory is present in at least one species of corvids and at least one species of ape (i.e. humans), then has this ability arisen through convergence, or do all birds and mammals possess this ability, in which case the parsimonious explanation is evolution by homology? The answer to this question will only be known when studies have been conducted on a wider sample of species. So far there is some evidence to suggest that rhesus monkeys are unable to remember the when of particular past events (Hampton et al. 2005), suggesting that not even all primates possess this ability. In rats, however, the evidence is mixed: some experiments suggest that rats can remember 'what, where and when' (Babb and Crystal 2006), whereas other experiments using rather similar paradigms report their failure to do so (Bird et al. 2003). A key question for future research will be to make sense of these apparently conflicting results using such similar paradigms on the same species. However, this pattern of mixed results also serves as a caution that even species that can remember the what, where and when of a specific past experience may not necessarily express this ability under all conditions.

If convergent evolution is the most likely scenario, then what are the common selective pressures shared between the ape and corvid species? One direction for future research will be to characterize what advantages the possession of episodic memory might have over nonepisodic-like (semantic) declarative memory. This point is taken up by Klein (Chapter 64, this volume), where he discusses the potential importance of integrated episodic memories in humans for coping with the trials and tribulations of social life (see also Chapter 65). It is important to note at this point that similarity arising as a result of convergence need not lead to identical solutions, and therefore episodic-like memory in different groups may have similar functional properties, but not necessarily similar underlying neurobiological structures (de Kort and Clayton 2006). So another important direction for future research will be to ask questions about the brain systems necessary to support the various kinds of memory and the extent to which convergently evolved brain systems are similar in their details. For example, although there is good evidence that the hippocampus plays an important role in spatial memory processing in both birds and mammals, the two types of hippocampi differ in structure, the avian one being nuclear and the mammalian one being laminar (see also Chapter 63 for a comparison between invertebrate and vertebrate brain systems).

Ontogeny recapitulates phylogeny

The second concept concerns the interplay between current developmental patterns and those that occurred during the evolutionary history of our ancestors. Based on patterns of embryonic development, Haeckel (1866) argued that ontogeny recapitulates phylogeny, and therefore that evolutionarily older traits should emerge earlier in development than more recently evolved traits. For example, with regard to embryonic limb development, the fact that cetaceans first develop arms with fingers, which later develop into flippers, suggests that the flippers are a secondarily derived state in these animals.

Haeckel's theory can also be applied to memory systems, particularly the development and evolution of episodic and semantic memory. In humans, semantic memory emerges earlier in cognitive development than episodic memory, so it might be argued that semantic memory is an evolutionarily older trait, one which humans share with many other animals, whereas episodic memory is a trait that evolved later in evolution. Indeed Tulving (2005, p. 20) argues 'it is a fact that humans somehow acquired the ability to remember their experienced past, in addition to their earlier acquired skill of knowing of things in the presence'.

Adaptive specializations

The third concept is that of adaptive specializations (see Chapter 65 for further discussion on this topic). Many have argued that there is good evidence that food-caching birds have an adaptive specialization in brain and behavior in the form of an enlarged hippocampus and a particularly long-lasting and highly accurate spatial memory for retrieving their caches (but see Bolhuis 2005 for an alternative view). One of the most convincing cases comes from studying black-capped chickadees in Alaska and Colorado (Pravosudov and Clayton 2002). In the winter, chickadees living in Alaska have to endure considerably shorter days, much colder temperatures and significantly more snow than in Colorado. Pravosudov and I argued that there would be a greater selection pressure for the Alaskan birds to remember their caches because the harsher the environment, the more dependent the birds will be on efficient cache retrieval in order to avoid death by starvation. We therefore predicted that if enhanced spatial memory and hippocampal enlargement are adaptive specializations for cache retrieval, then the Alaskan population should have larger hippocampi and perform better on spatial memory tasks than the birds from Colorado, even when the birds were housed under identical conditions in the laboratory. We found support for both of these predictions, the Alaskan birds having larger hippocampi, containing more neurons than the Colorado birds, and they also performed more accurately on a series of spatial but not nonspatial memory tasks.

Is it useful to think of different forms of memory as adaptive specializations, and if so might it be helpful to make a distinction between quantitative adaptations, for example enhanced accuracy and/or increased duration of spatial memory, as opposed to qualitative adaptations, such as the possession of an additional kind of memory, such as episodic memory? In the case of quantitative specializations then, the adaptations may lie not so much in the possession of differences in memory mechanisms but in species differences in attention to particular kinds of cues. In the case of episodic memory, one approach would be to compare those species that live in climates where foods perish and cache perishable foods with those that live in colder climates where perishable food is unlikely to perish, or with those species that only cache nonperishable foods, on tasks that require them to remember the what, where and when of specific past events. Additional questions might focus on other kinds of selection pressure that might have been important for the development of episodic memory.

We must be careful in what we assume about the possession of an adaptive specialization, however. Consider the example of adaptive specializations of food-caching birds. The assumption is that the food-caching species possess the adaptive specialization. However, a phylogenetic reconstruction of the ancestral state for caching behavior in corvids shows that the common ancestor was a moderate cacher, and that although caching was secondarily lost twice within the corvids, there were at least two independent transitions from moderate to specialized caching as well (de Kort and Clayton 2006). Thus it is loss of caching and the transition from moderate to specialized cacher that represent the adaptive traits, as opposed to the existence of caching *per se*. This example also serves to highlight the importance of thinking about phylogeny, and the question of convergence versus homology.

Acknowledgments

I thank Selvino de Kort and Sara Shettleworth for comments, and Sara Shettleworth, Randolf Menzel and Stanley Klein for discussion.

63

Phylogeny and evolution: On comparing species at multiple levels

Randolf Menzel

Comparison is the magic tool of evolutionary biology. Darwin applied it to behavioral traits by comparing facial expressions in mammals (Darwin 1872), but how should differences and similarities be interpreted, as evolutionary conserved traits (homologies) or as independent developments under similar ecological pressure (analogies)? Since Thorndike's (1898) comparative analysis of learning in mammals, experimental psychology emphasized the 'general rule' concept, positing that learning processes are basically the same in all animals and apply to all conditions. The underlying assumption was that such universality stems from common evolutionary history, indicating that ancestral species shared the properties of the nervous system's units and, therefore, the basic mechanisms of learning and memory. However, different animal species do not learn the same way (Domjan 1998), and principles of temporal and spatial causation that depend upon species-specific environmental features appear to be incorporated into learning and memory processes. Thus it is quite obvious that some properties of learning may indeed reflect a long-lasting evolutionary history, while others may be novel properties only common to a subgroup of related species. Moreover, behavioral traits may also disappear in the course of evolution, or even serve a different function. Furthermore, arguments in favor of homologies or analogies may apply specifically and differently to various mechanisms underlying a particular form of learning or memory. The key question is how criteria can be developed for distinguishing between homologies and analogies, and how they can be applied to the respective mechanistic levels.

By comparing stereotyped behaviors in closely related species, ethologists reconstructed sequences of transitions between innate behaviors serving basic needs of the animal to ritualized forms of communication (Tinbergen 1963). When such a comparison strategy is applied to learning, however, differences are more obvious than similarities (Shettleworth 1998). The study of learning thus requires experiments with a strict control of the test situation, because behavioral changes need to be attributed in a quantitative way to the contingencies of stimuli and responses. Under this condition, it is the experimenter, and not the animal, who chooses the environment (which may also impose species-specific constraints). The problem of experimental design becomes more relevant when comparing distantly related species, and a strategy called 'systematic variation' (Bitterman 1988) has not helped to tease apart the contribution of learning and nonlearning factors, or the role of different forms of learning, or even the exchangeability of learned and innately programmed behavior, mainly because of the limited information we have about the sensory, motor and motivational capacities of the animal, the value (or salience) of the stimuli applied in the laboratory test and the internal status of the animal. In addition, one often overlooks what the animal can do without learning, and whether learning indeed leads to a more efficient behavioral strategy. Two examples from comparative studies in insects may illustrate how experience-dependent responses and adaptive specializations are tightly interlinked.

(1) *Cotesia glomerata* and *Cotesia flavipes* are two closely related species of parasitic wasps (Geervliet *et al.* 1998) that share a common host, the larvae of *Pieris brassica*. Whereas *C. flavipes* exhibits stereotypic innate preference for the odor of *Pieris* larvae, *C. glomerata* learn the larvae's varying odor profiles that depend on which plants it feeds on. Interestingly, no other behavioral differences were found between these two species of wasps, indicating that innate and experience-dependent responses are two close behavioral strategies unrelated to any major difference between the neural systems involved.

(2) When honeybees (*Apis mellifera*) and bumble bees (*Bombus terrestris*) learn odors, honeybees perform better than bumble bees. Their acquisition is faster and shows a higher asymptote, and their retention is better (Menzel 1990, and unpublished observations). However, when these two species are trained to learn colors signaling the entrance of their colonies, bumble bees are better performers. Odor perception and color vision is rather similar in both species; however, these two species differ in their foraging behavior (i.e., bumble bees simultaneously forage on different flower species while honeybees tend to forage on single flower species) and social organization (i.e., honeybees communicate about foraging opportunities while bumble bees do not). Thus it appears that bumble bees have to probe for changes in the distribution of reward on a regular basis, giving the impression that they are inferior in reward learning.

The lesson from these examples is that the functionality of experience-dependent responses depends upon specific ecological conditions, and that comparative studies usually provide no information about the evolutionary process that led to the gain or loss of specific behavioral traits.

The cellular underpinnings of learning and memory

Since associative learning is found in all animals with a nervous system, it is suggestive to conclude that its evolutionary roots must be at least 1.5 billion years old and reflect a common optimization strategy. However, it needs to be demonstrated that the molecular and cellular bases of associative plasticity, as well as some network properties at least, are indeed conserved across phyla. Support comes from the discovery that several molecules (e.g. cAMP and NMDA receptors) are essential components in associative plasticity. An intriguing issue in evolutionarily guided studies is the relationship between the complexity of learning and memory phenomena, and that of the molecular, cellular and network properties involved (including brain size). For a large battery of associative paradigms, no differences have yet been found between even such varied groups of animals as insects and mammals. Moreover, advanced forms of learning, for example generalization, navigation and rule-based learning, also exist in insects. Bees, for instance, perform such forms of learning that appear as analogs to those of mammals (Menzel and Giurfa 2001) Darwin (1877, p. 89) attributed these achievements to sophisticated instincts, but now we know that learning and memory processing are essential components across Phyla.

However, if small and big brains do not differ so much with respect to the role of learning versus innate behaviors, at which level of neural processing do they differ when predicting the future from previous experience? Since molecular pathways seem to be surprisingly similar, neural wiring and processing may provide a clue. Unfortunately, we do not yet understand the basic requirements for memory storage at the network level. Long-term potentiation (LTP) may constitute an essential component of these requirements, and it has been found in mollusk and insect neurons. However, although such cellular mechanisms may serve the same purposes in small and big brains, their integration into network processing may lead to different properties.

These considerations tell us that arguments in favor of homology cannot be posed by simply adding up similarities across different levels of complexity. Similar molecular building blocks may be implemented in the neural net to produce totally novel forms of neural plasticity. In such a situation, some molecular and cellular components would indicate homologies, while network properties indicate analogies. As noted by Papini (2002), traits can be decoupled in the course of evolution and 'co-opted' through their implementation in a novel environment, imposing novel rules of composition.

A particular helpful tool in evolutionary studies is the comparison between ontogeny and phylogeny. In the marine mollusk *Aplysia*, nonassociative forms of plasticity appear sequentially during the early development of the sensory–motor connection underlying the siphon withdrawal response (Carew 2002), and a comparison between mollusk species of known phylogenetic relationship indicates successive evolution of these phenomena of cellular plasticity (Wright 1998). Such studies need to be extended to network-based forms of learning. It will then be possible to differentiate between homologies at more basic levels of neural function and analogies at the network level.

Memories exist in multiple forms and functions, and are basically referred to as short-term, mid-term and long-term memory, according to their physiological substrates along a temporal scale. The transitions between these memory phases can be sequential or parallel, and these processes are usually referred to as the physiological correlates of consolidation. The widespread occurrence of memory phases in animals ranging from mollusks and insects to humans has been interpreted as reflecting basic properties of the underlying cellular machinery. Although this may be true to some extent, it does not imply that both the structure and dynamics of different memory systems are equally adapted to process any kind of information in all environments. On the contrary, since learning depends upon competing phenotypic sets of traits, it also reflects species-specific adaptations to the requirements posed by the environment. This is well illustrated by the study of appetitive learning in honeybees, where the time courses of successive foraging behaviors match the temporal dynamics of different memory stages (Menzel 1999). Hence, the physiological bases of learning phenomena and the way in which experience-dependent responses are adapted to a given environment are so tightly interconnected that, ideally, one may need to study both aspects simultaneously.

Comparative studies of learning and memory have been dominated so far by two apparently contradictory approaches, the 'general process' and the 'adaptationist view' (Domjan 1998; Papini 2002). Both approaches were of limited success in explaining the evolution of learning and memory phenomena. In this context, the distinction between homologies and analogies analyzed at different levels of neural integration has received little attention. Indeed, the analysis of behavioral phenomena cannot provide the necessary material for distinguishing between homologous and analogous properties. Additional material is required, and this comes from molecular biology, genetics, developmental biology, neurophysiology, ecology, and theoretical behavioral and neuroscience. Based on such material, close species comparison appears to be much more fruitful than comparison between distantly related species, because such studies are less prone to be trapped by intuition about comparable sensory and motor processes, attention and motivational factors. Comparison between distantly related species (e.g. between insects and mammals) can only be made on the basis of a better understanding of the network properties underlying learning and memory.

64

Phylogeny and evolution: Implications for understanding the nature of a memory system

Stanley B. Klein

Evolutionary biology provides theories of the various adaptive problems memory systems evolved to solve, thereby guiding research on their design.

Anatomists dissect organs of the body. Dissection does not imply random cutting; it is a theoretically driven attempt to divide the body's parts into functional units. Psychologists, in contrast, seldom dissect the brain physically; rather, we dissect it conceptually. The goal of our research is to characterize the information-processing architecture of the brain—to dissect the mind into *functional units*. This requires theories of function, yet most psychologists have an impoverished definition of the function and scope of memory: memory as designed to enable the encoding, storage and retrieval of information. While this conceptualization undoubtedly is true, it is too general to be a good guide to research. As a result, psychologists have spent many years studying the processes that encode, store and retrieve information as if they were the same across all domains—as if it makes no difference whether the words you are hearing are unrelated items on a list or your spouse explaining that she/he's fallen in love with someone else. If all memory processes are the same, regardless of content, then it does not matter what content a subject is remembering: word lists are as good as anything else, and afford more experimental control. This assumption has led to an exploration of what memory is *capable* of doing, without allowing any further dissection of memory into *functional* units.

Starting with evolutionary theories of adaptive function results in a very different research program. Consider, for example, the way a behavioral ecologist approaches the study of memory of nonhuman animals. Such research always starts with the adaptive problems facing the organism: a bird may need to learn its species' song and also remember the random locations of hundreds of food items it cached for another season. By starting with a crisp definition of each adaptive problem the animal needs to solve, these researchers quickly became aware that different adaptive problems have different computational requirements when it comes to memory (Sherry and Shacter 1987; Gallistel 1990).

Different memory systems have evolved to solve different problems. On this view, memory processes are not just in the animal's head: memory systems have procedures that are *designed* to use specific cues that are reliably present in the animal's environment (certain songs and not others, seasonal cues to breeding season, presence of mates, etc.). The design of memory can only be understood in the context of the animal's ecology, because natural selection shaped its procedures to exploit some features of that ecology and not others. Just as crucially, each encoding, storage and retrieval feature has co-evolved not just with the environment, but with attention and learning mechanisms that are just as problem-specialized as the more traditional 'memory' features (i.e. encoding, storage and retrieval) and without which these features would be inert.

In what follows, I draw out some implications of this approach with respect to (1) systems, broadly construed, as the conjoining of neurological, biological and ecological components in the service of functional adaptations for survival and reproduction; and (2) a well-studied type of long-term memory—the episodic memory system.

Adaptive functions define what counts as a 'system'

What counts as a 'system'? How are its boundaries drawn? A biological system, defined with respect to functionality, consists of those component processes individually necessary and jointly sufficient to accomplish a specific adaptive task. As an example, the circulatory system consists of parts, for example a heart, a vascular network and the lungs, whose coordinated efforts are required for the transport of biologically important material to and from the host in which the system resides. The functional identity of each part is defined with respect to the job it performs within the system that evolved to perform this adaptive function. Thus, despite the ability to contract rhythmically, the heart is not a pump unless there is fluid to transport and a mechanism for its delivery: it becomes a pump in the context of a system whose function is to ensure the movement of blood through the body.

From this perspective, memory can be viewed as a co-adapted relationship between component processes whose joint efforts are required to perform certain adaptive functions. These processes include the usual suspects— encoding, storage and retrieval—but the way in which they are accomplished may differ for different adaptive problems. Moreover, 'memory' is not limited to those three capabilities. For an organism to behave 'more appropriately' (i.e. more adaptively) at a later time because of experiences at an earlier time, it must be equipped not only with mechanisms that retrieve ontogenetically acquired information but also with mechanisms that use this information to make decisions and drive behavior. Moreover, because decision mechanisms (termed 'decision rules' by Klein *et al.* 2002) often differ in what information they require, different sets of decision rules will activate different search engines (retrieval processes) and may access different data systems (storage systems). Without engines that can search for and retrieve the right information, supplying it to the right decision rule at the right time, an organ designed to store ontogenetically acquired information would be a pointless appendage (for discussion, see Klein *et al.* 2002, 2004).

A system of memory, on this view, can be conceptualized as the *interplay* of a set of computational processes, only some of which involve encoding, storage and retrieval. Many psychological processes will interact, and, through their interaction, will transform stored information into the subjective experience of remembering and the objective behaviors we produce.

An example—the episodic memory system

Episodic memory is held to consist of knowledge of a previously experienced event along with an awareness that the event occurred in one's past (e.g. Tulving 1985; Wheeler *et al.* 1997). However, the fact that scientists have an abstract category, *episodic memory*, which encompasses this type of information, does not guarantee that an ontological correlate can be found in the brain. If episodic memory is a genuine aspect of biological reality, then it exists in its present form because that arrangement solved certain recurrent problems faced by the organism in its evolutionary past. Evolution does not produce new phenotypic systems that are complex and functionally organized by chance; rather, systems acquire their functional organization because they contributed to the organism's ability to survive and reproduce.

My colleagues and I have argued that episodic memory handles functional problems that cannot be handled by other systems of memory. These include, but are not limited to: (1) keeping track of coalitional structure (e.g. social exchange, cheater detection); (2) the creedal value of a person's statements; (3) re-evaluating social knowledge in light of new evidence; and (4) bounding the scope of generalizations about others (for a fuller discussion, see Klein *et al.* 2002). In short, episodic memory enables its owner to navigate more successfully in the complex world of human social interaction (e.g. Klein *et al.* 2002; see also Suddendorf and Corballis 1997). This is not to say that episodic memory is capable of performing only socially relevant tasks. Every system, by virtue of having a particular causal structure, is capable of doing an endless series of things that it was not designed to do. What we argue is that the ability to relive past experiences by mentally traveling back in time is the functional product of an evolved adaptation designed to facilitate interaction in the social world.

Ancestrally, humans lived in small bands and interacted repeatedly with the same set of individuals. To negotiate social interactions with the same set of individuals successfully, a person must be able to represent him or herself as a psychologically coherent entity persisting through time, whose past experiences are remembered as belonging to its present self. Without this ability, a person would be unable to represent past and present states as aspects of the same personal identity, and thus be unable to know that a current mental state refers to an episode or state previously experienced—by the self or others. To experience memory in this manner requires, at a minimum, three capabilities in addition to the traditional triumvirate of encoding/storage/retrieval: (1) a capacity for self-reflection, i.e. the ability to reflect on my own mental states— to know about my own knowing; (2) a sense of personal agency and ownership, i.e. the belief that I am the cause of my thoughts and actions and the feeling that my thoughts and acts *belong to me*; and (3) the ability to think about time as an unfolding of personal happenings centered about the self.

Adopting a functional, systems view, episodic memory can be conceptualized as a conscious state emerging from the finely tuned *interplay* of a set of psychological capacities that transform declarative knowledge into an autobiographical personal experience. It follows that breakdowns in any of these components (i.e. self-reflection, self-agency, self-ownership, personal temporality) should produce, in varying degrees, impairments in episodic recollection. Even if the database of events is intact, amnesia could result from damage to the ability to self-reflect, damage to the machinery that creates a sense of personal agency/ownership or damage to the sense of temporality. Brain trauma, disease or developmental disorders could, in principle, damage one of these components while leaving the others intact. Different amnesic syndromes should result, each characterized by a different pattern of episodic memory impairment, depending on which component (or set of components) is damaged (for reviews, see Klein 2001; Klein *et al.* 2004).

Neuropsychological findings support the conclusion that a number of computational processes—the ability to self-reflect, a sense of personal agency/ ownership and an awareness of the self as being situated within a temporal framework—are involved in the transformation of declarative knowledge into an autobiographical memorial experience. On this view, episodic retrieval— the generation of autobiographical memorial experiences—cannot occur unless *all* of these capacities are intact. By adopting a functional systems approach to memory, phenomena not easily explained within the context of a traditional view of memory as merely the 'encoding, storage and retrieval of information' can be understood in the broader context of a system designed to enable its owner to travel back in time to relive previously experienced personal events, in the service of current decisions about how to interact with others.

65

Integrative comments
Phylogeny and evolution:
Ecology, evolutionary biology,
and the science of memory

Sara J. Shettleworth

What concepts from evolutionary biology might be relevant to a science of memory? In addressing this question, we emphasized two general points. (1) *Ecology* should be part of our topic title, and of our science. Discussions of *adaptation* (a central idea in evolutionary theory), whether of eyes or of memory systems, imply consideration of how a character functions in an environment, i.e. the species' ecology. As Klein (Chapter 64, this volume) emphasizes, psychologists have historically tended to pursue understanding of mechanisms without much thought for what function those mechanisms might be serving in the world outside the laboratory. The proper relationship of functional, or 'what for', considerations to studies of cognitive and brain mechanisms can indeed be debated (see Sherry 2005, for a recent critical summary). However, we all agreed that thinking about how memory functions in a species' ecological niche can be a useful guide to questions about how memory works. The three contributions to this section (Chapters 62–64) provide a rich variety of examples. (2) Our second general point is that the essential tool of evolutionary biologists, and therefore for evolutionarily guided memory research, is *comparison*. This includes both comparisons of closely related species, as in the studies of memory and hippocampus in food-storing birds (Chapter 62) or foraging in honeybees and bumblebees (Chapter 63), and comparisons of very distant relatives, as in analyses of 'episodic-like' memory in birds as compared with humans (Chapters 62 and 64) or studies of associative learning in honeybees and mammals (Chapter 63). Both kinds of comparison can illuminate the evolution and function of memory.

As integrator, I discuss some general issues having to do with the contributions that evolutionary and ecological considerations can make to a science of memory, beginning with a sketch of two approaches to studying evolution

(Shettleworth 1998, Chapter 1; Papini 2002, provide expanded discussions of points in this section). I then consider which approaches or methods are applicable to studying the evolution of memory and/or of the subprocesses identified by the other concepts in this volume. Are there any obstacles to adopting these approaches in the science of memory? What might thinking in terms of evolution, phylogeny and/or ecology contribute to the science of memory?

Ways to study evolution

Evidence about evolution is not obtained only from fossils. Information about how a character is distributed among present-day species along with molecular and other information about phylogeny (i.e. the structure of the evolutionary tree for the group in question) is commonly used to make inferences about evolution. Patterns of distribution in a known phylogeny indicate how far back in the lineage some character appeared and whether present-day species that possess it all inherited it from a common ancestor, i.e. whether it is homologous or evolved convergently due to common selection pressures (analogous). For example, the fact that food storing occurs in three families of birds that are not closely related indicates that food storing evolved independently more than once. This same approach may also reveal the order in which characters appeared in evolution. Papini (2002) discusses an example related to the neurobiology of memory.

Understanding the reasons for observed patterns of evolution can be much more challenging than working out the patterns in the first place. If a character appears in one lineage or disappears in another, presumably that reflects patterns of selection due to changes in the environment. We can rarely be sure what selection pressures operated in the past, and thus there is generally some uncertainty about why evolution took the course it did, but hypotheses about adaptive value can still be tested using modern-day species. One kind of test involves looking at the distribution of the character in question across many species and relating it to their ecology. This approach has been widely used with relative sizes of different brain areas, as in tests of the hypothesis that an enlarged hippocampus is an adaptation to the increased demands on spatial memory experienced by food-storing birds (Chapter 62) and tests of the relationship of relative forebrain size to frequency of innovative behaviors in birds and primates (Reader and Laland 2003). An obstacle to applying this method to specific aspects of memory that must be analyzed in the laboratory is paucity of relevant data. Because memory or learning is inferred from performance and because many motivational, perceptual, and other factors in addition to memory can influence performance, cross-species comparisons of memory in standardized tasks seldom provide entirely clear answers (see Shettleworth 1998). Rigorous comparisons require controlling for or somehow partialling out all the possible nonmemorial factors that can influence performance. This is one reason why the relationship between food storing, memory and the hippocampus in birds is still being debated.

Research on memory and food storing in birds has involved comparing close relatives or even members of the same species living in different habitats (Chapter 62). When available, such within-species comparisons can be valuable for testing ideas about how divergent ecologies may be reflected in divergences of brain and memory because they minimize irrelevant differences between the groups being compared. In contrast, the traditional comparative psychology of learning was primarily concerned with patterns of similarity and difference across widely disparate species. As mentioned by Menzel, the resulting broad survey of the animal kingdom reveals similarities in basic processes of associative learning across virtually all animals, vertebrate and invertebrate. These can be seen as reflecting a fundamental adaptation to basic causal regularities in the world. They also take on new mechanistic significance in the light of discoveries of unexpected commonalities of genetic and developmental mechanisms across species from fruitflies to humans (see Papini 2002; Chapter 63, this volume).

Although modern comparative approaches can tell us something about the evolution, phylogeny and ecology of memory, they have limited value when it comes to the evolution and adaptive value of specific aspects of human memory. The necessary comparative data from our close relatives, i.e. great apes, not to mention early hominids, are generally scanty, as is information about physical and social ecology during human evolution. This is where evolutionary biologists' second, complementary, approach to testing hypotheses about adaptation comes in handy, i.e. by experiment. Tinbergen's classic study of eggshell removal by black-headed gulls is an example of how experiments can be used to test whether a character does serve the function hypothesized for it, i.e. that it could in fact be an adaptation to an hypothesized selection pressure (note, however, that this does not mean it *is* such an adaptation, only that it serves a particular function in the present). Tinbergen and colleagues (1963) tested the hypothesis that removing empty egg shells functions to reduce predation on the nest by comparing predation on two kinds artificial nests set out near a gull colony. Nests with conspicuous white broken shells beside them did in fact suffer more predation than nests without empty eggshells. This finding increased confidence in the hypothesis about the evolution of eggshell removal that had complementary support from comparative studies of species breeding in predator-free environments.

The experimental approach can be applied to test hypotheses about functions of memory. For example, Hollis and her colleagues studied the impact of learning on fitness (number of offspring produced) in blue gourami fish. They compared males exposed to Pavlovian conditioning in which a light signaled presentation of a potential mate behind a barrier to control males for which the light and stimulus female were unpaired. Animals for which learning was possible and presumably functioned to allow them to predict and prepare for mating opportunities, did in fact produce more offspring when the signal was followed by actual contact with a female (Hollis *et al.* 1997). Notice the logic of this experiment. The control fish were deprived of their ability to learn, not by manipulating their genes or their nervous systems but by putting them into an environment in which a particular kind of learning was not possible.

Given the lack of much relevant data for inferring adaptation in human memory from the distribution of memory processes in other species, the experimental approach is particularly useful. For example, if, as hypothesized by Klein *et al.* (2002), priming of memory or of perception is an adaptation to the temporal distribution of information in the environment, one can test whether people (and other species) do worse in some way in experimental environments that lack the hypothesized temporal regularities. One landmark study in evolutionary cognitive psychology took exactly this approach: Cosmides's (1989) test of the hypothesis that the kind of reasoning tested in the Wason selection task was selected for during evolution because it was useful for detecting cheaters on social contracts consists of comparing how people perform on Wason tasks that do versus do not involve cheater detection. The abstract or nonsocial Wason tasks, which people more commonly fail, are claimed, in effect, to be putting the system into an environment to which it is not adapted.

Evolution, phylogeny and ecology in the science of memory

Both commonality and diversity among species define ways in which the science of memory can be enriched by considerations of evolution, phylogeny and ecology. Commonality underlies 'animal models' of memory processes. Fear conditioning in the rat or object recognition in the monkey are useful 'animal models' precisely because rats and monkeys share simple fundamental biological processes with humans. Interestingly, processes are often identified as the same across species in the first place because they function in the same way, i.e. responding adaptively to signals of danger, to objects seen before, and so on. Memory is inferred from specific behaviors, but a rather abstract functional equivalence defines whether the behavioral phenomena in different species are the same in terms of memory. For example, concluding that associative learning is widely shared across species entails accepting that a bee extending its proboscis to an odor paired with sugar water is in some meaningful sense doing the same thing as a rabbit blinking its eye to a tone that signals shock. In the study of associative learning, this approach based on abstract equivalences seems to work very well, but in other cases it is more controversial.

One such case is the research on whether any nonhuman animals have episodic memory (Chapter 62, this volume). This example raises several important points surrounding the study of any aspect of memory from an evolutionary point of view. Among other things, it suggests that for a science of memory truly to integrate an evolutionary approach, core concepts should be defined in a way that permits comparative investigations. For instance, if episodic memory in humans is defined in part by a unique kind of awareness which is assessed by verbal report, then it is *a priori* impossible to study it in a nonverbal animal (or in a human baby). Clayton and colleagues (see de Kort *et al.* 2005) have circumvented this dilemma by calling what they observe in the scrub-jays *episodic-like* memory, meaning that it possesses the behavioral features normally taken as evidence for episodic memory in people, such as evidence of integrated memory for what occurred, where and when. Problems arise because not only is evidence of an integrated what–where–when memory admittedly not sufficient for inferring episodic memory, some researchers (e.g. Eichenbaum *et al.* 2005; Zentall 2005) dispute whether it is even necessary and suggest that other kinds of nonverbal memories qualify equally well as equivalent to human episodic memory. Of course this is not to say that all psychologically interesting aspects of memory should be boiled down to simple behavioral criteria, but it is worth noting that research on the closely related topic of metacognition, or memory awareness, has progressed without such controversies (see Hampton and Schwartz 2004). This may reflect better agreement among researchers on the concept of metacognition than on the concept of episodic memory. As a consequence, it is comparatively easy to agree on what being aware of memory strength means for nonverbal behavior, i.e. what behavior is *functionally similar* to verbal reports of memory awareness.

A second important general issue raised by research on episodic-like memory is the significance of finding the same phenomenon in very distantly related species, particularly if it seems to appear in isolated branches of the evolutionary tree. Clayton (Chapter 62, this volume) argues that episodic-like memory may have a specific function for scrub-jays because they cache a variety of different foods that decay at different rates, that is to say it evolved independently from human episodic memory. Klein (Chapter 64, this volume), however, suggests that episodic memory in humans was selected primarily because it afforded an advantage for survival in solving complex social problems that arose during evolution. Both of these hypotheses can be tested, for example by studying a judicious selection of species that do and do not encounter social and/or nonsocial situations requiring episodic-like memory.

Research on episodic-like memory also illustrates the implications of a comparative approach for studies of memory at the neurobiological level. If birds possess a capacity shared with humans, it must be supported by different brain architectures. At the same time, the fact that a similar capacity has yet to be demonstrated conclusively in a nonhuman primate (see Hampton and Schwartz 2004) suggests that it requires some particular specialization of the primate brain, perhaps accompanying specialized social or foraging behavior. More generally, a broad comparative approach, whether or not it is directed specifically at understanding evolution as such, can provide important challenges to theories about neurobiological mechanisms by providing examples of how similar functions may (or may not) be served by different structures. On the scale of vertebrate–invertebrate differences, Menzel (Chapter 63, this volume) mentions the impressive commonalities between what honey-bees and mammals achieve in terms of learning and memory in spite of very different brains. However, as he points out, even the presence of the same cellular mechanisms in very different species still leaves open the question of similarities at the network level. Thus one needs to look carefully at how deeply similarities extend.

Concluding remarks

A science of memory that truly integrates consideration of evolution, phylogeny and ecology seems a long way off. The required masses of data and specialized knowledge about the behavior of even a reasonable sample of the world's species are just too great. In any case, most memory scientists have their work cut out for them with just one or two species and aspects of memory. However, it seems true to say that information about memory and other aspects of cognition in animals other than rats, mice and monkeys has grown tremendously in recent years and with it awareness of the potential contributions of a comparative perspective. These contributions are still most apparent in relatively few areas of research. However, it is tempting to speculate on what general evolutionary questions a science of memory might eventually address. Do we want to know which processes are shared across species and which are not? Which selection pressures shaped them? Whether shared processes vary across species and in what ways? At what levels, for example genetic, neurobiological, behavioral manifestation, do they vary? What are the implications of the answers to such questions for understanding specific aspects of memory?

66

Remember the future

Susan M. Fitzpatrick

If the *conceptual* focus of this book is not reason enough for readers to treat it as a rarity among collected writings on memory, the inclusion of this chapter might offer another. I doubt that many collections of scientific papers focusing on memory and the products of memory research include a contribution from someone who has never engaged in the study of memory. What can a foundation officer and biochemist, whose research interests (when she was actively engaged in laboratory research) were studies of metabolism in the cerebral cortex add to this collection of essays?

The reasons I initially chose to study metabolic pathways, my later career switch to philanthropy, and my involvement in the *Science of Memory: Concepts* are related, even if not immediately obvious. From my very first introduction to scientific research, I was drawn to the study of metabolism—the interaction of enzymes, substrates and effectors most nonbiochemists only see depicted as the complicated 'roadmap' diagrams hanging on the walls of biology classrooms. I found metabolic pathways, particularly those associated with the production of cellular energy, beautiful. I also had this feeling that it was the right place to be if you wanted to understand how the brain works.

What do I mean, '. . . it felt like the right place to be?' Today, I would mean that the level of analysis occupied by intermediary energy metabolism, the processes that provide the energy needed to fuel the work of the brain, is a necessary span to have in place if we hope to bridge from genes to molecules, to systems, to behavior. Although I did not know it 20 years ago, seeking 'the right place to be' when trying to answer a question would come to define the nature of the work that I do as a foundation officer and the way I think about science.

Thinking about 'the right place to be' is also responsible for initially sparking the conversations that ultimately resulted in the McDonnell Foundation's involvement in the Science of Memory project. I was responsible for developing and teaching a general neuroscience course for students pursuing graduate degrees in the Washington University's School of Occupational Therapy. Designing this course raised several questions for me: What do Occupational Therapists need to know about how the nervous system supports behavior?

What is the right level of detail? How do I connect what is presented in the standard neuroscience texts with their concerns about people living real lives in the real world? How do I cover the required information, at the right depth, in 28 class-days? For some topics, there seemed to be an easily identified 'right place to be'. However, when it came to outlining the two class days devoted to 'memory', I was truly befuddled. Considering the enormous role memory plays in everyday life and the number of ways memory function can be altered by environmental factors, including disease, injury and aging, I agonized over how I was to get it right. The neuroscience text we were using, along with the classic text of neuroscience this course used as a reference, presented a somewhat odd subset (at least to my way of thinking) of what we know about memory—what I have come to call the '*Aplysia*/monkey delayed nonmatch to sample/H.M.' science of memory. Understandably, in two lectures, one can only cover so much, and this selection might not, in some ways, represent a bad choice. What bothered me, however, was that the texts gave the impression that what we knew about habituation in the *Aplysia* flowed seamlessly up to (and offered an explanation for) what we knew about the abilities and disabilities of the famous H.M. The texts, from my reading, suggested that all the richness of the human experience we ascribe to 'memory' could be explained by events occurring at and identified by the molecular level. Of course one can find a richer story in psychology texts, but this was a neuroscience class with the goal of understanding the neurological underpinnings of behavior. Pondering whether my discomfort was primarily due to my naiveté with the full scope of memory research, I did what I usually do when I am not quite certain that my take on a topic is sure-footed. I checked with the experts. Luckily for me, one of the experts willing to listen to my concerns was Endel Tulving. Endel took the nub of what was certainly a naïve discomfort and helped guide it in a direction more interesting and profound. What followed then was a series of conversations beginning with philosopher of science Carl Craver and gradually involving a widening circle of very serious memory scholars willing carefully to consider the question Carl and I posed as a deceptively simple one: Do we have an integrated science of memory? More importantly, the early discussions, culminated in Endel Tulving, Yadin Dudai and Roddy Roediger agreeing to work with the McDonnell Foundation on developing an approach for answering the posed question. A plan emerged to bring together a working group to discuss how concepts of fundamental importance to memory are employed (or not) across various memory research traditions, from the cellular to systems to behavior. (For a discussion on the process for selecting the 16 concepts presented in this volume see Chapter 1.) Our hope was that such an evaluation would identify those places where there are meaningful gaps in our knowledge and would generate interesting new research questions. Such was the rationale behind this volume. From my perspective, some degree of success on both outcomes has been achieved in the essays collected here.

By engaging in the conversations that took place during the project and reading the resulting essays collected in this volume, I see several interesting 'gaps' that could generate new memory research questions. One challenge will be deciding at what levels meaningful biological explanations for the psychology of behavior are likely to be found. (For other discussions along this line, see Chapters 16 and 17).

From my own research perspective, it is worth considering how we can use studies of energy metabolism to further the science of memory. Metabolism occupies a level somewhere in the middle ground between the molecular and the functional. Damage to oxidative metabolic pathways or to the mitochondria (the 'powerhouses of the cell') keeps cropping up as targets in neurological studies of conditions characterized by declining cognitive function. (Mattson and Magnus 2006) However, in my experience, psychological studies of memory rarely consider the constraints of energy demands. Even cognitive neuroscientists employing functional imaging tools that rely on biomarkers such as blood flow changes or rates of oxidative metabolism to study neural correlates of mental function are rarely interested in how the actual energetic demands enhance or constrain the performance of such tasks. In the essays in this volume specifically dealing with evolution, there is little discussion of the metabolic costs that might be associated with the different kinds of memories and/or how energetic considerations may constrain the selection processes by which memory systems evolved. Energy, as we know from our visits to gasoline stations, is expensive. Successful organisms do not waste it.

The science of memory, as represented in this volume, is also missing, along what might be considered a 'biochemical line', a serious discussion of the role of the various neurotransmitter systems. Except for some discussion of inhibitory neural transmission (see Chapter 49), the roles of neurotransmitters is usually mentioned in passing. (There is some mention of neurotransmitters in the essays in Chapters 7, 8, 10 and 36.) From the perspective of a biochemist, items on any future agenda for the science of memory should include integrating energetic demands and limitations and the role of neurotransmitter systems into what we know about the processes and systems that support memory behavior and their evolution. One question could be: have energetic considerations and neurotransmitter functions contributed to the strengths and fallibilities of memory, particularly human memory? Another is: how do we best study such questions?

When I peer out from under the brim of my foundation hat, I see that the science of memory could be enhanced by reaching out to ideas from the science of complex systems. A complex systems approach would mean explicitly studying how different levels of organization within neural, cognitive, and behavioral systems interact (Simon 1974; see also Gunderson and Holling 2001). Too often, the difficulties of interlevel analysis are brushed off with rhetorical handwaving.

While I offer energetic and pharmacological considerations as needed additions to a science of memory—and while my own bias leads me to believe such efforts could enrich the science of memory—I am not suggesting that they are necessarily 'the right place to be'. Since the business of individual neurons is to alter their characteristics in response to experience, it is likely that at lower levels of analysis what we think of as distinct aspects of memory (implicit, explicit, semantic, procedural, and so on) will look fairly similar. (For an alternative view, see Chapters 9 and 58.) This does not mean memory research at molecular levels is unnecessary. However, it does mean that if we want to link cellular and molecular events to behavior, we can only do so by careful study at the intervening levels of analysis, including the neural networks and brain systems at which memory representation is most likely to be coded (see Chapter 11).

A second challenge will be linking the findings from experimental psychology's studies of memory to memory in everyday life—or what might be best described as the 'ordinary bloke's science of memory'. The task for researchers is to decipher how experimental results obtained from laboratory experiments map onto everyday memory (or more broadly, the behaviors supported by memory working in concert with other experimentally isolatable cognitive systems) and what are by-products of the artificial conditions of experimental design (see Chapter 46).

A third area where an investment in effort will yield a wealth of returns is a better understanding and characterization of the uniqueness of human memory (see Chapters 43, 64 and 65). 'Gaps' such as these can only be filled via a broad comparative examination of memory processes in a variety of species and careful evaluation of the similarities and differences. This observation brings me back to energy metabolism. Because the energetic demands of running the human brain are very expensive, there must be a good reason why natural selection settled on costly solutions. Otherwise we could all make do with a tiny, energetically cheap brain and be happy. How does human memory serve uniquely human behaviors?

I have no doubt that those interested in memory will uncover a treasure trove of possible research questions by carefully reading the essays in this volume. Additional questions will surely be revealed by an effort to read between the lines. Even more emerge from what is not covered in the volume at all. Much of what is discussed between the covers of this book focuses almost exclusively on memory research using individual subjects (except perhaps in the essay including bee behavior, Chapter 63). How do we bridge from what is revealed about individual memory to rich traditions of scholarship studying why we create books, visual images, monuments and museums? In what ways do these external repositories of memory mirror the fragilities and/or the robustness of our individual memory systems? How might they make recompense for the sometimes ephemeral nature of our remembrances? A whole field of the humanities (especially in English and history) is concerned with 'memory studies' in which scholars ask questions about memory in very different traditions. In many parts of the world (the Middle East, the Balkans, India and Pakistan), ethnic groups are fighting today because of collective memories of events that happened hundreds or even thousands of years ago. A form of memory spurs these conflicts, even though no one alive today experienced the events that cause such anger and grief in today's world (Wertsch 2002). Will these uses of collective memory ever be linked to and understood through analyses of very different researchers as represented in this volume?

I hope that in 25 years someone initiates a new dialogue on where we are in building an integrated science of memory. I hope those conversations lead to a new Science of Memory project and result in an entirely new and different volume of essays. I hope I am still around. I would very much like to read that book.

References

Aggleton, J.P. and Brown, M.W. (1999) Episodic memory, amnesia, and the hippocampal–anterior thalamic axis. *Behavioral and Brain Sciences*, **22**, 425–489.

Alberini, C.M. (2005) Mechanisms of memory stabilization: are consolidation and reconsolidation similar or distinct processes? *Trends in Neuroscience*, **28**, 51–56.

Allen, N.J. and Barres, B.A. (2005) Signaling between glia and neurons: focus on synaptic plasticity. *Current Opinion in Neurobiology*, **15**, 542–548.

Altman, J. (1997) JZ Young 1907–1997. *Current Biology*, **7**, 456–457.

Amsel, A. (1992) *Frustration Theory: An Analysis of Dispositional Learning and Memory.* Cambridge: Cambridge University Press.

Anderson, M.C. (2003) Rethinking interference theory: executive control and the mechanisms of forgetting. *Journal of Memory and Language*, **49**, 415–445.

Anderson, M.C. and Bjork, R.A. (1994) Mechanisms of inhibition in long-term memory: a new taxonomy. In: Dagenbach, D. and Carr, T.H., eds. *Inhibitory Mechanisms in Attention, Memory and Language.* New York: Academic Press, pp. 265–325.

Anderson, M.C. and Green, C. (2001) Suppressing unwanted memories by executive control. *Nature*, **410**, 366–369.

Anderson, M.C. and Neely, J. (1996) Interference and inhibition in memory retrieval. In: Bjork, E.L. and Bjork, R.A., eds. *Memory. A Volume in the Handbook of Perception and Cognition.* New York: Academic Press, pp. 237–313.

Anderson, M.C. and Spellman, B.A. (1995) On the status of inhibitory mechanisms in cognition: memory retrieval as a model case. *Psychological Review*, **102**, 68–100.

Anderson, M.C., Bjork, R.A. and Bjork, E.L. (1994) Remembering can cause forgetting: retrieval dynamics in long-term memory. *Journal of Experimental Psychology: Learning, Memory, and Cognition*, **20**, 1063–1087.

Anderson, M.C., Bjork, E.L. and Bjork, R.A. (2000) Retrieval-induced forgetting: evidence for a recall-specific mechanism. *Psychonomic Bulletin and Review*, **7**, 522–530.

Anderson, M.C., Ochsner, K., Kuhl, B., Cooper, J., Robertson, E., Gabrieli, S.W., *et al.* (2004) Neural systems underlying the suppression of unwanted memories. *Science*, **303**, 232–235.

Arcediano, F., Escobar, M. and Miller, R.R. (2005) Bidirectional associations in humans and rats. *Journal of Experimental Psychology: Animal Behavior Processes*, **31**, 301–318.

Aristotle (350 BC) *On Memory and Reminiscence.* (Beare, J.I., trans.)

Atick, J.J. (1992) Could information theory provide an ecological theory of sensory processing? *Network* **3**, 213–251.

Atkinson, R. and Shiffrin, R. (1968) Human memory: a proposed system and its control processes. In: Spence, K. and Spence, J., eds. *The Psychology of Learning and Motivation.* New York: Academic Press. pp 89–105.

Ayres, M.S. and Reder, L.M. (1998) A theoretical review of the misinformation effect. *Psychonomic Bulletin and Review*, **5**, 1–21.

Babb, S.J. and Crystal, J.D. (2006) Discrimination of what, when, and where is not based on time of day. *Learning and Motivation*, in press.

Baddeley, A. (1990) *Human Memory: Theory and Practice*. Hove and London: Lawrence Erlbaum Associates.

Baddeley, A. (1992) Working memory: the interface between memory and cognition. *Journal of Cognitive Neuroscience*, 4, 281–288.

Baddeley, A.D. (1997) *Human Memory: Theory and Practice*, revised edn. Hove: Psychology Press.

Baddeley, A.D. (2000) The episodic buffer: a new component of working memory? *Trends in Cognitive Sciences*, 4, 417–423.

Baddeley, A.D. (2007) *Working Memory, Thought and Action*. Oxford: Oxford University Press.

Baddeley A.D. and Hitch, G. (1974) Working memory. In: Bower, G., ed. *The Psychology of Learning and Motivation*, Vol. 8. New York: Academic Press, pp. 47–90.

Baddeley, A.D. and Warrington, E.K. (1970) Amnesia and the distinction between long-and short-term memory. *Journal of Verbal Learning and Behavior*, 9, 176–189.

Baddeley, A.D., Gathercole, S.E. and Papagno, C. (1998) The phonological loop as a language learning device. *Psychological Review*, 105, 158–173.

Baddeley A., Vargha-Khadem, F. and Mishkin, M. (2001*a*) Preserved recognition in a case of developmental amnesia: implications for the acquisition of semantic memory? *Journal of Cognitive Neuroscience*, 13, 357–369.

Baddeley, A.D., Chincotta, D.M. and Adlam, A. (2001*b*) Working memory and the control of action: evidence from task switching. *Journal of Experimental Psychology: General*, 130, 641–657.

Bailey, C.H. and Chen, M. (1983) Morphological basis of long-term habituation and sensitization in Aplysia. *Science*, 220, 91–93.

Bailey, C.H., Bartsch, D. and Kandel, E.R. (1996) Toward a molecular definition of long-term memory storage. *Proceedings of the National Academy of Sciences of the USA*, 93, 13445–13452.

Bailey, C.H., Giustetto, M., Huang, Y.Y., Hawkins, R.D. and Kandel, E.R. (2000) Is heterosynaptic modulation essential for stabilizing Hebbian plasticity and memory? *Nature Reviews Neuroscience* 1, 11–20.

Baker, A.G., Murphy, R., Mehta, R. and Baetu, I. (2005) Mental models of causation: a comparative view. In: Wills, A.J., ed. *New Directions in Human Associative Learning*. Mahwah, NJ: Lawrence Erlbaum, pp. 11–40.

Banghart, M., Borges, K., Isacoff, E., Trauner, D. and Kramer, R.H. (2004) Light-activated ion channels for remote control of neuronal firing. *Nature Neuroscience*, 7, 1381–1386.

Bargh, J.A. and Chartrand, T.L. (1999) The unbearable automaticity of being. *American Psychologist*, 54, 462–479.

Bartlett, F.C. (1932) *Remembering: A Study in Experimental and Social Psychology*. New York: Macmillan.

Barzilai, A., Kennedy, T.E., Sweatt, J.D. and Kandel, E.R. (1989) 5-HT modulates protein synthesis and the expression of specific proteins during long-term facilitation in Aplysia sensory neurons. *Neuron*, 2, 1577–1586.

Bäuml, K. (1996) Revisiting an old issue: retroactive interference as a function of the degree of original and interpolated learning. *Psychonomic Bulletin and Review*, 3, 380–384.

Bäuml, K. (1998) Strong items get suppressed, weak items do not: the role of item strength in output interference. *Psychonomic Bulletin and Review*, **5**, 459–463.

Bauml, K. and Aslan, A. (2004) Part-list cuing as instructed retrieval inhibition. *Memory and Cognition*, **23**, 610–617.

Baxter, M.G. and Murray, E.A. (2001) Opposite relationship of hippocampal and rhinal cortex damage to delayed nonmatching-to-sample deficits in monkeys. *Hippocampus*, **11**, 61–71.

Bechara, A., Tranel, D., Damasio, H., Adolphs, R., Rockland, C. and Damasio, A.R. (1995) Double dissociation of conditioning and declarative knowledge relative to the amygdala and hippocampus in humans. *Science*, **269**, 1115–1118.

Belli, R.F. (1989) Influences of misleading postevent information: misinformation interference and acceptance. *Journal of Experimental Psychology: General*, **118**, 72–85.

Bilodeau, I.M. and Schlosberg, H. (1951) Similarity in stimulating conditions as a variable in retroactive inhibition. *Journal of Experimental Psychology*, **41**, 199–204.

Bird, L.R., Roberts, W.A., Abroms, B., Kit, K.S. and Crupi, C. (2003) Spatial memory for food hidden by rats (*Rattus norvegicus*) on the radial maze: studies of memory for where, what and when. *Journal of Comparative Psychology*, **117**, 1–12.

Bitterman, M.E. (1988) Vertebrate–invertebrate comparisons. *NATO ASI Series—Intelligence and Evolutionary Biology*, **17**, 251–275.

Bjork, E.L. and Bjork, R.A. (2003) Intentional forgetting can increase, not decrease, the residual influences of to-be-forgotten information. *Journal of Experimental Psychology: Learning, Memory and Cognition*, **29**, 524–531.

Bjork, E.L., Bjork, R.A. and Anderson, M.C. (1998) Varieties of goal-directed forgetting. In: Golding, J.M. and MacLeod, C., eds. *Intentional Forgetting: Interdisciplinary Approaches*. Hillsdale, NJ: Lawrence Erlbaum, pp. 103–137.

Bjork, R.A. (1978) The updating of human memory. In: Bower, G.H., ed. *The Psychology of Learning and Motivation*, Vol. 12. New York: Academic Press, pp. 235–259.

Bjork, R.A. (1989) Retrieval inhibition as an adaptive mechanism in human memory. In: Roediger, H.L. and Craik, F.I.M., eds. *Varieties of Memory and Consciousness: Essays in Honour of Endel Tulving*. Hillsdale, NJ: Lawrence Erlbaum, pp. 309–330.

Bjork, R.A. (2001) Recency and recovery in human memory. In: Roediger, H.L., Nairne, J.S., Neath, I. and Surprenant, A.M., eds. *The Nature of Remembering: Essays in Honor of Robert G. Crowder*. Washington, DC: American Psychological Association Press, pp. 211–232.

Bjork, R.A., LaBerge, D. and LeGrande, R. (1968) The modification of short-term memory through instructions to forget. *Psychonomic Science*, **10**, 55–56.

Blanchard, R.J., Fukunaga, F.F. and Blanchard, D.C. (1976) Environmental control of defensive reactions to footshock. *Bulletin of the Psychonomic Society*, **8**, 129–130.

Bliss, T.V.P. and Collingridge, G.L. (1993) A synaptic model of memory: long-term potentiation in the hippocampus. *Nature*, **361**, 31–39.

Bliss, T.V. and Lømo, T. (1973) Long-lasting potentiation of synaptic transmission in the dentate area of the anaesthetized rabbit following stimulation of the performant path. *Journal of Physiology*, **232**, 331–356.

Blumenfeld, R.S. and Ranganath, C. (2006) Dorsolateral prefrontal cortex promotes long-term memory formation through its role in working memory organization. *Journal of Neuroscience*, **26**, 916–925.

Bodner, G.E. and Lindsay, D.S. (2003) Remembering and knowing in context. *Journal of Memory and Language*, **48**, 563–580.

Bolhuis, J.J. (2005) Function and mechanism in neuroecology: looking for clues. *Animal Behaviour*, **55**, 457–490.

Bontempi, B., Jaffard, R. and Destrade, C. (1996) Differential temporal evolution of post-training changes in regional brain glucose metabolism induced by repeated spatial discrimination training in mice: visualization of the memory consolidation process. *European Journal of Neuroscience*, **8**, 2348–2360.

Bourtchuladze, R., Frenguelli, B., Blendy, J., Cioffi, D., Schutz, G. and Silva, A.J. (1994) Deficient long-term memory in mice with a targeted mutation of the cAMP-responsive element-binding protein. *Cell*, **79**, 59–68.

Bouton, M.E. (1993) Context, time, and memory retrieval in the interference paradigms of Pavlovian learning. *Psychological Bulletin*, **114**, 80–99.

Bouton, M.E. (1994*a*) Context, ambiguity, and classical conditioning. *Current Directions in Psychological Science*, **3**, 49–53.

Bouton, M.E. (1994*b*) Conditioning, remembering, and forgetting. *Journal of Experimental Psychology: Animal Behavior Processes*, **20**, 219–231.

Bouton, M.E. (2002) Context, ambiguity, and unlearning: sources of relapse after behavioral extinction. *Biological Psychiatry*, **52**, 976–986.

Bouton, M.E. (2004) Context and behavioral processes in extinction. *Learning and Memory*, **11**, 485–494.

Bouton, M.E. and Bolles, R.C. (1979) Contextual control of the extinction of conditioned fear. *Learn Motiv* **10**, 445–466[ISI].

Bower, G.H. (1981) Mood and memory. *American Psychologist*, **36**, 129–148.

Bower, G.H. and Forgas, J.P. (2000) Affect, memory, and social cognition. In: Eich, E., Kihlstrom, J.F., Bower, G.H., Forgas, J.P. and Niedenthal, P.M., eds. *Cognition and Emotion*. New York: Oxford University Press, pp. 87–168.

Boycott, B.B. and Young, J.Z. (1955) A memory system in *Octopus vulgaris* Lamarck. *Philosophical Transactions of the Royal Society B: Biological Sciences*, **143**, 449–480.

Brainerd, C.J., Reyna, V.F., Wright, R. and Mojardin, A.H. (2003) Recollection rejection: false-memory editing in children and adults. *Psychological Review*, **110**, 762–784.

Breese, B.B. (1899) On inhibition. *Psychological Monographs*, **3**, 1–65.

Brown, J. (1968) Reciprocal facilitation and impairment of free recall. *Psychonomic Science*, **10**, 41–42.

Brown, S.C. and Craik, F.I.M. (2000) Encoding and retrieval of information. In: Tulving, E. and Craik, F.I.M., eds. *The Oxford Handbook of Memory*. New York: Oxford University Press, pp. 93–107.

Brown, T.H., Byrne, J.H., Labar, K.S., LeDoux, J.E., Lindquist, D.H., Thompson, R.F., *et al.* (2004) Learning and memory: Basic Mechanisms. In: Byrne, J.H. and Roberts, J.L., eds. *From Molecules to Networks*. Elsevier Press, USA.

Brunton, T.L. (1883) On the nature of inhibition, and the action of drugs upon it. *Nature*, **27**, 419–422, 436–439, 467–468, 485–487.

Buchsbaum, B.R., Olsen, R.K., Koch, P. and Berman, K.F. (2005) Human dorsal and ventral auditory streams subserve rehearsal-based and echoic processes during verbal working memory. *Neuron*, **48**, 687–697.

Bulevich, J.B., Roediger, H.L., III, Balota, D.A. and Butler, A.C. (2006) Failures to find suppression of episodic memories in the think/mo-think paradigm. *Memory and Cognition*, in press.

Bullock, T.H., Bennett, M.V., Johnston, D., Josephson, R., Marder, E. and Fields, R.D. (2005) The neuron doctrine, redux. *Science*, **310**, 791–793.

Bunge, M. (1967/1998) *Philosophy of Science*, Vol. 1. New Bruswick, NJ: Transaction Publishers.

Buonomano, D.V. and Merzenich, M.M. (1998) Cortical plasticity: from synapses to maps. *Annual Review of Neuroscience*, **21**, 149–186.

Burgess, N. and Hitch, G.J. (1999) Memory for serial order: a network model of the phonological loop and its timing. *Psychological Review*, **106**, 551–581.

Burke, E. (1757/1990) Introduction on taste. In: *A Philosophical Enquiry into the Origin of Our Idea of the Sublime and the Beautiful*. Oxford: Oxford University Press.

Buzsaki, G. (1989) Two-stage model of memory trace formation: a role for 'noisy' brain states. *Neuroscience*, **31**, 551–570.

Buzsaki G. (2005) Similar is different in hippocampal networks. *Science*, **309**, 568–569.

Buzsaki, G. and Chrobak, J.J. (1995) Temporal structure in spatially organized neuronal ensembles: a role for interneuronal networks. *Current Opinion in Neurobiology*, **5**, 504–510.

Buzsaki, G. and Draguhn, A. (2004) Neuronal oscillations in cortical networks. *Science*, **304**, 1926–1929.

Byrne, J.H. (2001) How neuroscientists captured the 2000 Nobel Prize. *Cerebrum*, **3**, 66–79.

Capaldi, E.J. (1994*a*) The sequential view: from rapidly fading stimulus traces to the organization of memory and the abstract concept of number. *Psychonomic Bulletin and Review*, **1**, 156–181.

Capaldi, E.J. (1994*b*) The relation between memory and expectancy as revealed by percentage and sequence of reward investigations. *Psychonomic Bulletin and Review*, **1**, 303–310.

Capaldi, E.J. and Stanley, L.R. (1963) Temporal properties of reinforcement aftereffects. *Journal of Experimental Psychology*, **65**, 169–175.

Capaldi, E.J., Haas, A., Miller, R.M. and Martins, A. (2005) How transitions from nonrewarded to rewarded trials regulate responding in Pavlovian and instrumental learning following extensive acquisition training. *Learning and Motivation*, **36**, 279–296.

Carew, T.J. (2002) Aplysia: development of processes underlying learning. In: Byrne, J.H., ed. *Learning and Memory*. New York: MacMillan Reference Books, pp. 37–41.

Carew, T.J., Menzel, R. and Shatz, C.J., eds. (1998) *Mechanistic Relationships Between Development and Learning*. Chichester: John Wiley.

Ceci, S.J., Ross, D.F. and Toglia, M.P. (1987) Suggestibility of children's memory: psycholegal implications. *Journal of Experimental Psychology: General*, **116**, 38–49.

Challis, B.H., Velichovsky, B.M. and Craik, F.I.M. (1996) Levels-of-processing effects on a variety of memory tasks: new findings and theoretical implications. *Consciousness and Cognition: An International Journal*, **5**, 142–164.

Chandler, C.C. (1991) How memory for an event is influenced by related events: interference in modified recognition tests. *Journal of Experimental Psychology: Learning, Memory and Cognition*, **17**, 115–125.

Charniak, E. and McDermott, D. (1985) *Introduction to Artificial Intelligence*. Reading, MA: Addison Wesley.

Christian, K.M. and Thompson, R.F. (2003) Neural substrates of eyeblink conditioning: acquisition and retention. *Learning and Memory*, **10**, 427–455.

Christian, K.M. and Thompson, R.F. (2005) Long-term storage of an associative memory trace in the cerebellum. *Behavioral Neuroscience*, **119**, 526–537.

Clark, R.E. and Squire, L.R. (1998) Classical conditioning and brain systems: the role of awareness. *Science*, **280**, 77–81.

Clayton, N.S. and Dickinson, A. (1998) Episodic-like memory during cache recovery by scrub jays. *Nature*, **395**, 272–274.

Clayton, N.S., Bussey, T.J. and Dickinson, A. (2003) Can animals recall the past and plan for the future? *Nature Reviews Neuroscience*, **4**, 685–691.

Coffin, J.M. and Woodruff-Pak, D.S. (1993) Delay classical conditioning in young and older rabbits: initial acquisition and retention at 12 an 18 months. *Behavioral Neuroscience*, **107**, 63–71.

Cohen, M.R. and Newsome, W.T. (2004) What electrical microstimulation has revealed about the neural basis of cognition. *Current Opinion in Neurobiology*, **14**, 169–177.

Cohen, N.J. and Eichenbaum, H.E. (1993) *Memory, Amnesia, and the Hippocampal System*. Cambridge, MA: MIT Press.

Cohen, N. and Squire, L.R. (1980) Preserved learning and retention of pattern analyzing skill in amnesia: dissociation of knowing how and knowing that. *Science*, **210**, 207–209.

Cohen, N.J., Poldrack R.A. and Eichenbaum H. (1997) Memory for items and memory for relations in the procedural/declarative memory framework. *Memory*, **5**, 131–178.

Cohen, N.J., Ryan, J., Hunt, C., Romine, L., Wszalek, T. and Nash, C. (1999) Hippocampal system and declarative (relational) memory: summarizing the data from functional neuroimaging studies. *Hippocampus*, **9**, 83–98.

Cohen, R.A. (1993) Neural mechanisms of attention. In: Cohen, R.A., ed. *The Neuropsychology of Attention*. New York: Plenum, pp. 145–176.

Conway, A.R.A., Cowan, N., Bunting, M.F., Therriault, D. and Minkoff, S. (2002) A latent variable analysis of working memory capacity, short term memory capacity, processing speed, and general fluid intelligence. *Intelligence*, **30**, 163–183.

Conway, M.A. (2005) Memory and the self. *Journal of Memory and Language*, **53**, 594–628.

Conway, M.A. and Pleydell-Pearce, C.W. (2000) The construction of autobiographical memories in the self memory system. *Psychological Review*, **107**, 261–288.

Conway, M.A., Collins, A.F., Gathercole, S.E. and Anderson, S.J. (1996) Recollections of true and false autobiographical memories. *Journal of Experimental Psychology: General*, **125**, 69–95.

Cooper, L.N. (1973) A possible organization of animal memory and learning. In: Lundquist, B. and Lundquist, S., eds. *Proceedings of the Nobel Symposium on Collective Properties of Physical Systems*. New York: Academic Press, pp. 252–264.

Corlett, P.R., Aitken, M.R.F., Dickinson, A., Shanks, D.R., Honey, G.D., Honey, R.A.E., *et al.* (2004) Prediction error during retrospective revaluation of causal associations in humans: fMRI evidence in favor of an associative model of learning. *Neuron*, **44**, 877–888.

Cosmides, L. (1989) The logic of social exchange: has natural selection shaped how humans reason? *Cognition*, **31**, 187–276.

Cowan, N. (1993) Activation, attention, and short-term memory. *Memory and Cognition*, **21**, 162–167.

Cowan, N. (2001) The magical number 4 in short-term memory: a reconsideration of mental storage capacity. *Behavioral and Brain Sciences*, **24**, 87.

Craik, F.I.M. (1983) On the transfer of information from temporary to permanent memory. *Philosophical Transactions of the Royal Society B: Biological Sciences*, **302**, 341–359.

Craik, F.I.M. (2002*a*) Human memory and aging. In: Bäckman, L. and von Hofsten, C., eds. *Psychology at the Turn of the Millennium*, Vol. 1. Hove, UK: Psychology Press, pp. 261–280.

Craik, F.I.M. (2002*b*) Levels of processing: Past, present … and future? *Memory*, **10**, 305–318.

Craik, F.I.M. and Lockhart, R.S. (1972) Levels of processing: a framework for memory research. *Journal of Verbal Learning and Verbal Behavior*, **11**, 671–684.

Craik, F.I.M. and Tulving, E. (1975) Depth of processing and the retention of words in episodic memory. *Journal of Experimental Psychology: General*, **104**, 268–294.

Craik, F.I.M. and Watkins, M.J. (1973) The role of rehearsal in short-term memory. *Journal of Verbal Learning and Verbal Behavior*, **12**, 599–607.

Crawley, J.N. and Paylor, R. (1997) A proposed test battery and constellations of specific behavioral paradigms to investigate the behavioral phenotypes of transgenic and knockout mice. *Hormones and Behavior*, **31**, 197–211.

Crowder, R.G. (1976) *Principles of Learning and Memory*. Hillsdale, NJ: Lawrence Erlbaum.

Crowder, R.G. (1982) The demise of short-term memory. *Acta Psychologica*, **50**, 291–323.

Dagenbach, D. and Carr, T.H. (1994) *Inhibitory Processes in Attention, Memory, and Language*. Orlando, FL: Academic Press.

Daneman, M. and Carpenter, P.A. (1980) Individual differences in working memory and reading. *Journal of Verbal Learning and Verbal Behaviour*, **19**, 450–466.

Darwin, C. (1872) *The Expression of the Emotions in Man and Animals*. Chicago: University of Chicago Press.

Darwin, C. (1877) *The Effects of Cross and Self Fertilisation in the Vegetable Kingdom*. London: John Murray

Davachi, L. and Wagner, A.D. (2002) Hippocampal contributions to episodic encoding: insights from relational and item-based learning. *Journal of Neurophysiology*, **88**, 982–990.

Davachi, L., Maril, A. and Wagner, A.D. (2001) When keeping in mind supports later bringing to mind: neural markers of phonological rehearsal predict subsequent remembering. *Journal of Cognitive Neuroscience*, **13**, 1059–1070.

Davachi, L., Mitchell, J.P. and Wagner, A. D. (2003) Multiple routes to memory: distinct medial temporal lobe processes build item and source memories. *Proceedings of the National Academy of Sciences of the USA*, **100**, 2157–2162.

Davies, G.M. and Thomson, D.M., eds. (1988) *Memory in Context: Context in Memory*. Chichester: Wiley.

Davis, H.P. and Squire, L.R. (1984) Protein synthesis and memory: a review. *Psychological Bulletin*, **96**, 518–559.

Dayan, P., Hinton, G.E., Neal, R.M. and Zemel, R.S. (1995) The Helmholtz machine. *Neural Computing*, **7**, 889–904.

de Araujo, I.E.T., Rolls, E.T., Velazco, M.I., Margot, C. and Cayeux, I. (2005) Cognitive modulation of olfactory processing. *Neuron*, **46**, 671–679.

de Hoz, L., Martin, S.J. and Morris, R.G.M. (2004) Forgetting, reminding and remembering: the retrieval of lost spatial memory. *Public Library of Science: Biology*, **2**, **8**, 1–19.

de Kort, S.R. and Clayton, N.S. (2006) An evolutionary perspective on caching by corvids. *Proceedings of the Royal Society B: Biological Sciences*, **273**, 417–423.

de Kort, S.R., Dickinson, A. and Clayton, N.S. (2005) Retrospective cognition by food-caching western scrub-jays. *Learning and Motivation*, **36**, 159–176.

De Zeeuw, C.I. and Yeo, C.H. (2005) Time and tide in cerebellar memory formation. *Current Opinion in Neurobiology*, **15**, 667–674.

De Zeeuw, C.I., Hansel, C., Bian, F., Koekkoek, S.K., van Alphen, A.M., Linden, D.J., *et al.* (1998) Expression of a protein kinase C inhibitor in Purkinje cells blocks cerebellar LTD and adaptation of the vestibulo-ocular reflex. *Neuron*, **20**, 495–508.

Debski, E.A. and Cline, H.T. (2002) Activity-dependent mapping in the retinotectal projection. *Current Opinion in Neurobiology*, **12**, 93–99.

Deco, G. and Rolls, E.T. (2003) Attention and working memory: a dynamical model of neuronal activity in the prefrontal cortex. *European Journal of Neuroscience*, **18**, 2374–2390.

Deco, G. and Rolls, E.T. (2005) Attention, short-term memory, and action selection: a unifying theory. *Progress in Neurobiology*, **76**, 236–256.

Dempster, F.N. and Brainerd, C.J. (1995) *Interference and Inhibition in Cognition*. San Diego, CA: Academic Press.

Denniston, J.C., Savastano, H.I. and Miller, R.R. (2001) The extended comparator hypothesis: learning by contiguity, responding by relative strength. In: Mower, R.R. and Klein, S.B., eds. *Handbook of Contemporary Learning Theories*. Mahwah, NJ: Lawrence Erlbaum, pp. 65–118.

Diamond, S., Balvin, R.S. and Diamond, F.R. (1963) *Inhibition and Choice: A Neurobehavioral Approach to the Problems of Plasticity in Behavior*. New York: Harper and Row, Publishers, Inc.

Dickinson, A. (2001) Causal learning: an associative analysis. *Quarterly Journal of Experimental Psychology*, **54B**, 3–25.

Dodge, R. (1926) The problem of inhibition. *The Psychological Review*, **33**, 1–12.

Dodson, C.S. and Schacter, D.L. (2002) When false recognition meets metacognition: the distinctiveness heuristic. *Journal of Memory and Language*, **46**, 782–803.

Domjan, M. (1998) The Principles of Learning and Behavior. New York: Brooks/Cole.

Doya, K. (1999) What are the computations of the cerebellum, the basal ganglia and the cerebral cortex? *Neural Networks*, **12**, 961–974.

Doya, K. (2002) Metalearning and neuromodulation. *Neural Networks*, **15**, 495–506.

Dudai, Y. (1989) *The Neurobiology of Memory. Concepts, Findings, Trends*. Oxford: Oxford University Press.

Dudai, Y. (1992) Why 'learning' and 'memory' should be redefined (or, an agenda for focused reductionism). *Concepts in Neuroscience*, **3**, 99–121.

Dudai, Y. (2002a) *Memory from A to Z. Keywords, Concepts, and Beyond*. Oxford University Press, Oxford.

Dudai, Y. (2002b) Molecular bases of long-term memories: a question of persistence. *Current Opinions in Neurobiology*, **12**, 211–216.

Dudai, Y. (2004) The neurobiology of consolidations, or, how stable is the engram? *Annual Review of Psychology*, **55**, 51–86.

Dudai, Y. (2006) Reconsolidation: the advantage of being refocused. *Current Opinion in Neurobiology*, **16**, 174–178.

Dudai, Y. and Morris, R.G.M. (2000) To consolidate or not to consolidate: what are the questions? In: Bolhuis, J.J., ed. *Brain, Perception, Memory*. Oxford: Oxford University Press, pp. 149–162.

Dumas, T.C. (2005) Developmental regulation of cognitive abilities: modified composition of a molecular switch turns on associative learning. *Progress in Neurobiology*, **76**, 189–211.

Dweck, C.S. and Wagner, A.R. (1970) Situational cues and correlation between CS and US as determinants of the conditioned emotional response *Psychonomic Science*, **18**, 145–147

Ebbinghaus, H. (1885) *Über das Gedchtnis. Untersuchungen zur experimentellen Psychologie*. Leipzig: Duncker and Humblot.

Ebbinghaus, H. (1913) *Memory. A Contribution to Experimental Psychology*, English edn. New York: Teachers College, Columbia University.

Ebbinghaus, H. (1885/1964) *Memory: A Contribution to Experimental Psychology*. (Ruger, H.A. and Bussenius, C.E., trans.) New York: Dover.

Egorov, A.V., Hamam, B.N., Fransen, E., Hasselmo, M.E. and Alonso, A.A. (2002) Graded persistent activity in entorhinal cortex neurons. *Nature*, **420**, 173–178.

Ehlers, A., Hackmann, A. and Michael, T. (2004) Intrusive re-experiencing in posttraumatic stress disorder: phenomenology, theory, and therapy. *Memory*, **12**, 403–415.

Eich, E. (1980) The cue-dependent nature of state-dependent retrieval. *Memory and Cognition*, **8**, 157–173.

Eich, E. (1995a) Searching for mood dependent memory. *Psychological Science*, **6**, 67–75.

Eich, E. (1995b) Mood as a mediator of place dependent memory. *Journal of Experimental Psychology: General*, **124**, 293–308.

Eich, E. and Macaulay, D. (2007) Cognitive and clinical perspectives on mood dependent memory. In: Forgas, J.P., ed. *Hearts and Minds: Affective Influences on Social Cognition and Behavior*. New York: Psychology Press, in press.

Eichenbaum, H. and Cohen, N.J. (2001) *From Conditioning to Conscious Recollection: Memory Systems of the Brain*. New York: Oxford University Press.

Eichenbaum, H., Otto, T. and Cohen, N.J. (1994) Two functional components of the hippocampal memory system. *Behavioral and Brain Science*, **17**, 449–518.

Eichenbaum, H., Fortin, N.J., Ergorul, C., Wright, S.P. and Agster, K.L. (2005) Episodic recollection in animals: 'If it walks like a duck and quacks like a duck . . .'. *Learning and Motivation*, **36**, 190–207.

Einstein, G.O. and Hunt, R.R. (1980) Levels of processing and organization: additive effects of individual-item and relational processing. *Journal of Experimental Psychology: Human Learning and Memory*, **6**, 588–598.

Elgersma, Y., Fedorov, N.B., Ikonen, S., Choi, E.S., Elgersma, M., Carvalho, O.M., *et al.* (2002) Inhibitory autophosphorylation of CaMKII controls PSD association, plasticity, and learning. *Neuron*, **36**, 493–505.

Ellis, H.C. and Moore, B.A. (1999) Mood and memory. In: Dalgleish, T. and Power, M.J., eds. *Handbook of Cognition and Emotion*. Chichester: Wiley, pp. 193–210.

Engle, R.W. and Kane, M.J. (2004) Executive attention, working memory capacity, and a two-factor theory of cognitive control. In: Ross, B., ed. *The Psychology of Learning and Motivation*, Vol. **44**, New York: Elsevier, pp. 145–199.

Fan, J., Wu, Y., Fossella, J. and Posner, M.I. (2001) Assessing the heritability of attentional networks. *BioMed Central Neuroscience* **2**, 14.

Fanselow, M.S. (1980a) Signaled shock-free periods and preference for signaled shock. Journal of Experimental Psychology: Animal Behavior Processes, 6, 65–80.

Fanselow, M.S. (1980b) Conditional and unconditional components of post-shock freezing in rats. Pavlovian Journal of Biological Sciences, 15, 177–182.

Fanselow, M.S. (1986) Associative vs. topographical accounts of the immediate shock freezing deficit in rats: implications for the response selection rules governing species specific defensive reactions. Learning and Motivation, 17, 16–39.

Fanselow, M.S. and Baackes, M.P. (1982) Conditioned fear-induced opiate analgesia on the formalin test: Evidence for two aversive motivational systems. Learning and Motivation, 13, 200–221.

Fanselow, M.S., Landeira-Fernandez, J., DeCola, J.P. and Kim, J.J. (1994) The immediate-shock deficit and postshock analgesia: implications for the relationship between the analgesia CR and UR. Animal Learning and Behavior, 22, 72–76.

Felleman, D.J. and Van Essen, D.C. (1991) Distributed hierarchical processing in the primate cerebral cortex. Cerebral Cortex, 1, 1–47.

Fisher, R.P. (1977) Interaction between encoding and retrieval operations in cued recall. Journal of Experimental Psychology: Human Learning and Memory, 3, 701–711.

Forgas, J.P. (1995) Mood and judgment: the affect infusion model (AIM). Psychological Bulletin, 117, 39–66.

Fortin, N.J., Wright, S.P. and Eichenbaum, H. (2004) Recollection-like memory retrieval in rats is dependent on the hippocampus. Nature, 431, 188–191.

Frankland, P.W. and Bontempi, B. (2005) The organization of recent and remote memories. Nature Reviews Neuroscience, 6, 119–130.

Frankland, P., O'Brien, C., et al. (2001) Alpha-CaMKII-dependent plasticity in the cortex is required for permanent memory. Nature, 411, 309–313.

Frankland, P.W., Bontempi, B., et al. (2004) The involvement of the anterior cingulate cortex in remote contextual fear memory. Science, 304, 881–883.

Fransen, E., Alonso, A.A. and Hasselmo, M.E. (2002) Simulations of the role of the muscarinic-activated calcium-sensitive non-specific cation current I(NCM) in entorhinal neuronal activity during delayed matching tasks. Journal of Neuroscience, 22, 1081–1097.

Freud, S. (1901/1960) The psychopathology of everyday life. In: The Standard Edition of the Complete Psychological Works of Sigmund Freud, Vol. VI. London: The Hogarth Press.

Freund, T.F. and Buzsaki, G. (1996) Interneurons of the hippocampus. Hippocampus, 6, 347–470.

Frey, U. and Morris, R.G.M. (1997) Synaptic tagging and long-term potentiation. Nature, 385, 533–536.

Funahashi, S., Bruce, C.J. and Goldman-Rakic, P.S. (1989) Mnemonic coding of visual space in the monkey's dorsolateral prefrontal cortex. Journal of Neurophysiology, 61, 331–349.

Funayama, E.S., Grillon, C., Davis, M. and Phelps, E.A. (2001) A double dissociation in the affective modulation of startle in humans: effects of unilateral temporal lobectomy. Journal of Cognitive Neuroscience, 13, 721–729.

Fuster, J.M. (1973) Unit activity in prefrontal cortex during delayed-response performance: neuronal correlates of transient memory. Journal of Neurophysiology, 36, 61–78.

Fuster, J.M. (1997) Network memory. *Trends in Neuroscience*, **20**, 451–459.

Gallistel, C.R. (1990) *The Organization of Learning*. Cambridge, MA: MIT Press.

Gallistel, C.R. and Gibbon, J. (2000) Time, rate, and conditioning. *Psychological Review*, **107**, 289–344.

Gardiner, J.M. (1988) Functional aspects of recollective experience. *Memory and Cognition*, **16**, 309–313.

Gardiner, J.M. and Richardson-Klavehn, A. (1999) Remembering and knowing. In: Tulving, E. and Craik, F.I.M., eds. *Handbook of Memory*. Oxford: Oxford University Press, pp. 229–244.

Gardiner, J.M., Craik, F.I.M. and Bleasdale, F.A. (1973) Retrieval difficulty and subsequent recall. *Memory and Cognition*, **1**, 213–216.

Gazzaley, A., Cooney, J.W., Rissman, J. and D'Esposito, M. (2005) Top-down suppression deficit underlies working memory impairment in normal aging. *Nature Neuroscience*, **8**, 1298–1300.

Geervliet, J.B.F., Vreugdenhil, A.I., Dicke, M. and Vet, L.E.M. (1998) Learning to discriminate between infochemicals from different plant–host complexes by the parasitoids *Cotesia glomerata* and *C. rubecula* (Hym: Braconidae). *Entomologia Experimentalis et Applicata*, **86**, 241–252.

Geiselman, R.E., Bjork, R.A. and Fishman, D. (1983) Disrupted retrieval in directed forgetting: a link with posthypnotic amnesia. *Journal of Experimental Psychology: General*, **112**, 58–72.

Georgopoulos, A.P., Schwartz, A.B., Kettner, R.E. (1986) Neuronal population coding of movement direction. *Science*, **233**, 1416–1419.

Ghirardi, M., Montarolo, P.G. and Kandel, E.R. (1995) A novel intermediate stage in the transition between short- and long-term facilitation in the sensory to motor neuron synapse of Aplysia. *Neuron*, **14**, 413–20.

Gibson, J.J. (1966) *The Senses Considered as Perceptual Systems*. Boston: Houghton Mifflin.

Gibson, J.J. (1979) *The Ecological Approach to Visual Perception*. Boston: Houghton Mifflin.

Gick, M.L. and Holyoak, K.J. (1980) Analogical problem solving. *Cognitive Psycholog*, **12**, 306–355.

Gilboa, A. and Moscovitch, M. (2002) The cognitive neuroscience of confabulation: a review and a model. In: Baddeley, A.D., Wilson, B.A. and Kopelman, M., eds. *Handbook of Memory Disorders*, 2nd edn. London: John Wiley and Sons.

Glenberg, A.M. (1997) What memory is for. *Behavioral and Brain Sciences*, **20**, 1–55.

Godden, D. and Baddeley, A.D. (1975) Context-dependent memory in two natural environments: on land and underwater. *British Journal of Psychology*, **66**, 235–331.

Goldman-Rakic, P.S. (1987) Circuitry of primate prefrontal cortex and regulation of behavior by representational memory. In: Plum, F., ed. *Handbook of Physiology— The Nervous System*. Bethesda, MD: American Physiological Society, pp. 373–417.

Goldsmith, M. and Koriat, A. (2003) Dolphins on the witness stand? The comparative psychology of strategic memory monitoring and control. *Behavioral and Brain Sciences*, **26**, 344–345.

Goldsmith, M., Koriat, A. and Weinberg-Eliezer, A. (2002) Strategic regulation of grain size memory reporting. *Journal of Experimental Psychology: General*, **131**, 73–95.

Goldsmith, M., Koriat, A. and Pansky, A. (2005) Strategic regulation of grain size in memory reporting over time. *Journal of Memory and Language*, **52**, 505–525.

Gonzalez, R.C., Ferry, M. and Powers, R.S. (1974) The adjustment of goldfish to reduction in magnitude of reward in massed trials. *Animal Learning and Behavior*, **2**, 23–26.

Goodlett, C.R., Hamre, K.M. and West, J.R. (1992) Dissociation of spatial navigation and visual guidance performance in Purkinje cell degeneration (pcd) mutant mice. *Behavioral Brain Research*, **47**, 129–141.

Gould, S.J. and Lewontin, R.C. (1979) The spandrels of San Marco and the Panglossian paradigm: a critique of the adaptionist programme. *Proceedings of the Royal Society B: Biological Sciences*, **205**, 581–598.

Gould, T.J. and Steinmetz, J.E. (1996) Changes in rabbit cerebellar cortical and interpositus nucleus activity during acquisition, extinction, and backward classical eyelid conditioning. *Neurobiology of Learning and Memory*, **65**, 17–34.

Grady, C.L., McIntosh, A.R., Horwitz, B., Maisog, J.M., Ungerleider, L.G., Mentis, M.J., *et al.* (1995) Age-related reductions in human recognition memory due to impaired encoding. *Science*, **269**, 218–221.

Graf, P., Squire, L.R. and Mandler, G. (1984) The information that amnesic patients do not forget. *Journal of Experimental Psychology: Learning, Memory and Cognition*, **10**, 164–178.

Gunderson, L. and Holling, C.S. (2001). *Panarchy; understanding transformations in systems of humans and nature.* Island Press, Washington, D.C., USA.

Haag, J. and Borst, A. (2002) Dendro-dendritic interactions between motion-sensitive large-field neurons in the fly. *Journal of Neuroscience*, **22**, 3227–3233.

Haeckel, E. (1866) *Generelle Morphologie der Organismen: Allgemeine Grundzüge der organischen Formen-Wissenschaft, mechanisch begründet durch die von Charles Darwin reformirte Descendenz Theorie.* Berlin: Georg Riemer.

Hall, J. F. (1971) *Verbal learning and retention.* Philadelphia: Lippincott.

Hamann, S.B. and Squire, L.R. (1997) Intact perceptual memory in the absence of conscious memory. *Behavioral Neuroscience*, **111**, 850–854.

Hampton, R.R. and Schwartz, B.L. (2004) Episodic memory in nonhumans: what and where, is when? *Current Opinion in Neurobiology*, **14**, 192–197.

Hampton, R.R., Hampstead, B.M. and Murray, E.A. (2005) Rhesus monkeys (*Macaca mulatta*) demonstrate robust memory for what and where, but not when, in an open-field test of memory. *Learning and Motivation*, **36**, 245–259.

Harlow, H.F. (1949) The formation of learning sets. *Psychological Review*, **56**, 51–65.

Hasher, L. and Griffin, M. (1978) Reconstructive and reproductive processes in memory. *Journal of Experimental Psychology: Human Learning and Memory*, **4**, 318–330.

Hasher, L. and Zacks, R.T. (1979) Automatic and effortful processes in memory. *Journal of Experimental Psychology: General*, **108**, 356–388.

Hasher, L. and Zacks, R.T. (1988) Working memory, comprehension, and aging: a review and a new view. In: Bower, G.H., ed. *The Psychology of Learning and Motivation*, Vol. 22. New York: Academic Press, pp. 193–225.

Hasher, L., Zacks, R.T. and May, C.P. (1999) Inhibitory control, circadian arousal, and age. In: Gopher, D. and Koriat, A., eds. *Attention and Peformance, XVII, Cognitive Regulation of Performance: Interaction of Theory and Application.* Cambridge, MA: MIT Press, pp. 653–675.

Hasher, L., Goldstein, D. and May, C. (2005) It's about time: circadian rhythms, memory and aging. In: Izawa, C. and Ohta, N., eds. *Human Learning and Memory: Advances in Theory and Application: The 4th Tsukuba International Conference on Memory*. Mahwah, NJ: Lawrence Erlbaum Associates, pp. 199–217.

Hasher, L., Lustig, C. and Zacks, R.T. (2007) Inhibitory mechanisms and the control of attention. In: Conway, A., Jarrold, C., Kane, M., Miyake, A. and Towse, J., eds. *Variation in Working Memory*. Oxford: Oxford University Press, in press.

Hasselmo, M.E. (1999) Neuromodulation: acetylcholine and memory consolidation. *Trends in Cognitive Sciences*, **3**, 351–359.

Hasselmo, M.E. and Eichenbaum, H.B. (2005) Hippocampal mechanisms for the context-dependent retrieval of episodes. *Neural Networks*, **18**, 1172–1190.

Hasselmo, M.E. and Stern, C.E. (**2006**). Mechanisms underlying working memory for novel information. *Trends in cognitive sciences*, **10**(11), 487–493.

Hasselmo, M.E., Bodelon, C. and Wyble, B.P. (2002) A proposed function for hippocampal theta rhythm: Separate phases of encoding and retrieval enhance reversal of prior learning. *Neural Computation*, **14**, 793–817.

Hayne, H. (2004) Infant memory development: implications for childhood amnesia. *Developmental Review*, **24**, 33–73.

He, Z. and Koprivica, V. (2004) The Nogo signaling pathway for regeneration block. *Annual Review of Neuroscience*, **27**, 341–368.

Healy, A.F., Wohldmann, E.L. and Bourne, L.E., Jr (2005a) The procedural reinstatement principle: studies on training, retention, and transfer. In: Healy, A.F., ed. *Experimental Cognitive Psychology and its Applications*. Washington, DC: American Psychological Association, pp. 59–71.

Healy, A.F., Wohldmann, E.L., Sutton, E.M. and Bourne, L.E., Jr (2006) Specificity effects in training and transfer of speeded responses. *Journal of Experimental Psychology: Learning, Memory, and Cognition*, **32**, 534–546

Healy, A.F., Wohldmann, E.L., Parker, J.T. and Bourne, L.E., Jr (2005b) Skill training, retention, and transfer: the effects of a concurrent secondary task. *Memory and Cognition*, **33**, 1457–1471

Hearst, E. (1988) Fundamentals of learning and conditioning. In: Atkinson, R.C., Herrnstein, R.J., Lindzey, G., and Luce, R.D., eds. *Stevens' Handbook of Experimental Psychology*, Vol 2. New York: Wiley, pp. 9–27.

Hebb, D.O. (1949) *The Organization of Behavior: A Neuropsychological Theory*. New York: Wiley.

Henson, R. (2001) Neural working memory. In: Andrade, J., ed., *Working Memory in Perspective*. Hove: Psychology Press, pp. 151–174.

Hering, E. (1880/1920) Memory as a universal function of organized matter. In: Butler, S., ed. *Unconscious Memory*. London: Jonathan Cope.

Hildreth-Bearce, K. and Rovee-Collier, C. (2006) Repeated reactivation increases memory accessibility in infants. *Journal of Experimental Child Psychology*, in press.

Hinton, G.E. and Dayan, P. (1996) Varieties of Helmholtz machine. *Neural Networks*, **9**, 1385–1403.

Holland, P.C. (1989) Occasion setting with simultaneous compounds in rats. *Journal of Experimental Psychology: Animal Behavior Processes*, **15**, 183–193.

Holland, P.C. (1992) Occasion setting in Pavlovian conditioning. In: Medin, D.L., ed. *The Psychology of Learning and Motivation*, Vol. 28. San Diego, CA: Academic Press, pp. 69–125.

Holland, P.C. (1997) Brain mechanisms for changes in processing of conditioned stimuli in Pavlovian conditioning: implications for behavior theory. *Animal Learning and Behavior*, **25**, 373–399.

Holland, P.C., Han, J.S. and Gallagher, M. (2000) Lesions of the amygdala central nucleus alter performance on a selective attention task. *Journal of Neuroscience*, **20**, 6701–6706.

Hollis, K.L., Pharr, V.L., Dumas, M.J., Britton, G.B. and Field, J. (1997) Classical conditioning provides paternity advantage for territorial male blue gouramis (*Trichogaster trichopterus*). *Journal of Comparative Psychology*, **111**, 219–225.

Holt, G. and Brush, S.G. (1973) *Introduction to the Concepts and Theories in Physical Science*, 2nd edn. Reading, MA: Addison-Wesley.

Holton, B. (1973) *Introduction to concepts and theories in physical science* (2nd ed.). Reading, MA: Addison-Wesley, 1973.

Holton, G.J. (1973) Thematic origins of scientific thought: Kepler to Einstein. Cambridge, MA: Harvard University Press.

Hubel, D.H. and Wiesel, T.N. (1962) Receptive field, binocular interaction and functional architecture in the cat's visual cortex. *Journal of Physiology*, **160**, 106–54.

Hubel, D.H. and Wiesel, T.N. (2005) *Brain and Visual Perception*. Oxford: Oxford University Press.

Hull, C.L. (1951) *Essentials of Behavior*. New Haven: Yale University Press.

Ito, M. (2002) The molecular organization of cerebellar long-term depression. *Nature Reviews Neuroscience*, **3**, 896–902.

Jacoby, L.L. (1991) A process dissociation framework: separating automatic from intentional uses of memory. *Journal of Memory and Language*, **30**, 513–541.

Jacoby, L.L. and Dallas, M. (1981) On the relationship between autobiographical memory and perceptual learning. *Journal of Experimental Psychology: General*, **3**, 306–340.

Jacoby, L.L., Kelley, C.M. and Dywan, J. (1989) Memory attributions. In: Roediger, H.L. and Craik, F.I.M., eds. *Varieties of Memory and Consciousness: Essays in Honour of Endel Tulving*. Hillsdale, NJ: Erlbaum, pp. 391–422.

Jacoby, L.L., Shimizu, Y., Daniels, K.A. and Rhodes, M.G. (2006) Modes of cognitive control in recognition and source memory: depth of retrieval. *Psychonomic Bulletin and Review*, **12**, 852–857.

James, W. (1890) *The Principles of Psychology*, 1918 edn. New York: Holt.

Jensen, O. and Lisman, J.E. (2005) Hippocampal sequence-encoding driven by a cortical multi-item working memory buffer. *Trends in Neuroscience*, **28**, 67–72.

Ji, R.R., Kohno, T., Moore, K.A. and Woolf, C.J. (2003) Central sensitization and LTP: do pain and memory share similar mechanisms? *Trends in Neuroscience*, **26**, 696–705.

Jobe, J.B., Mellgren, R.L., Feinberg, R.A., Littlejohn, R.L. and Rigby, R.L. (1977) Patterning, partial reinforcement, and N-length as a function of reinstatement of retrieval cues. *Learning and Motivation*, **8**, 77–97.

Johnson, M.K. (1983) A multiple-entry, modular memory system. In: Bower, G.H., ed. *The Psychology of Learning and Motivation*, Vol. 17. New York: Academic Press, pp. 81–123.

Johnson, M.K. (1990) Functional forms of human memory. In: McGaugh, J.L. Weinberger, N.M. and Lynch, G., eds. *Brain Organization and Memory: Cells, Systems and Circuits*. New York: Oxford University Press, pp. 106–134.

Johnson, M.K. (1991) Reflection, reality-monitoring, and the self. In: Kunzendorf, R., ed. *Mental Imagery.* New York: Plenum, pp. 3–16.

Johnson, M.K. (1992) MEM: mechanisms of recollection. *Journal of Cognitive Neuroscience,* **4**, 268–280.

Johnson, M.K. (1997) Identifying the origin of mental experience. In: Myslobodsky, M.S., ed. *The Mythomanias: The Nature of Deception and Self Deception.* Mahwah, NJ: Erlbaum, pp. 133–180.

Johnson, M.K. and Chalfonte, B.L. (1994) Binding complex memories: the role of reactivation and the hippocampus. In: Schacter, D.L. and Tulving, E., eds. *Memory Systems 1994.* Cambridge, MA: MIT Press, pp. 311–350.

Johnson, M.K. and Hirst, W. (1991) Processing subsystems of memory. In: Lister, R.G. and Weingartner, H.J., eds. *Perspectives on Cognitive Neuroscience.* New York: Oxford University Press, pp. 197–217.

Johnson, M.K. and Hirst, W. (1993) MEM: memory subsystems as processes. In: Collins, A.F., Gathercole, S.E., Conway, M.A. and Morris, P.E., eds. *Theories of Memory.* East Sussex, England: Erlbaum, pp. 241–286.

Johnson, M.K. and Multhaup, K.S. (1992) Emotion and MEM. In: Christianson S.-A., ed. *The Handbook of Emotion and Memory: Current Research and Theory.* Hillsdale, NJ: Erlbaum, pp. 33–66.

Johnson, M.K. and Reeder, J.A. (1997) Consciousness as meta-processing. In: Cohen, J.D. and Schooler, J.W., eds. *Scientific Approaches to Consciousness.* Mahwah, NJ: Erlbaum. pp. 261–293).

Johnson, M.K., Hashtroudi, S. and Lindsay, D.S. (1993) Source monitoring. *Psychological Bulletin,* **114**, 3–28.

Johnson, M.K., Raye, C.L., Mitchell, K.J., Greene, E.J., Cunningham, W.A. and Sanislow, C.A. (2005) Using fMRI to investigate a component process of reflection: prefrontal correlates of refreshing a just-activated representation. *Cognitive, Affective, and Behavioral Neuroscience,* **5**, 339–361.

Jonides, J. and Mack, R. (1984) On the cost and benefit of cost and benefit. *Psychological Bulletin,* **96**, 29–44.

Kamin, L.J. (1965) Temporal and intensity characteristics of the conditioned stimulus. In: Prokasy, W.F., ed. *Classical Conditioning.* New York: Appleton-Century-Crofts.

Kandel, E.R. (2004) The molecular biology of memory storage: the dialog between genes and synapses. *Bioscience Reports,* **24**, 477–522.

Kapur, S., Craik, F.I.M., Tulving, E., Wilson, A.A., Houle, S. and Brown, G.M. (1994) Neuroanatomical correlates of encoding in episodic memory: levels of processing effect. *Proceedings of the National Academy of Sciences of the USA,* **91**, 2008–2011.

Kassardjian, C.D., Tan, Y.F., Chung, J.Y.J., Heskin, R., Peterson, M.J. and Broussard, D.M. (2005) The site of a motor memory shifts with consolidation. *Journal of Neuroscience,* **25**, 7979–7985.

Katona, G. (1940) Organizing and Memorizing. New York: Columbia University Press.

Kelley, W.M., Macrae, C.N., Wyland, C.L., Caglar, S., Inati, S. and Heatherton, T.F. (2002) Finding the self? An event-related fMRI study. *Journal of Cognitive Neuroscience,* **14**, 785–794.

Kendler, H.H. and Kendler, T.S. (1962) Vertical and horizontal processes in problem solving. *Psychological Review,* **69**, 1–16.

Keppel, G. and Underwood, B.J. (1962) Proactive inhibition in short-term retention of single items. *Journal of Verbal Learning and Verbal Behavior*, **1**, 153–161.

Kida, S., Josselyn, S.A., *et al.* (2002) CREB required for the stability of new and reactivated fear memories. *Nature Neuroscience*, **5**, 348–55.

Kieras, D.E., Meyer, D.E., Mueller, S. and Seymour, T. (1999) Insights into working memory from the perspective of the EPIC architecture for modeling skilled perceptual-motor and cognitive human performance. In: Miyake, A. and Shah, P., eds. *Models of Working Memory: Mechanisms of Active Maintenance and Executive Control*. Cambridge: Cambridge University Press, pp. 183–223.

Kiernan M.J., Westbrook, R.F. and Cranney, J. (1995) Immediate shock, passive avoidance, and potential startle: implications for the unconditional responses to shock. *Animal Learning and Behavior*, **23**, 22–30.

Kihlstrom, J.F. (1989) On what does mood-dependent memory depend? *Journal of Social Behavior and Personality*, **4**, 23–32.

Kim, J. (1998) *Mind in a Physical World: An Essay on the Mind–Body Problem and Mental Causation*. Cambridge, MA: MIT Press.

Kim, J.J. and Fanselow, M.S. (1992) Modality-specific retrograde amnesia of fear following hippocampal lesions. *Science*, **256**, 675–677.

Kim, J.J., DeCola, J.P., Landeira-Fernandez, J. and Fanselow, M.S. (1991) N-Methyl-D-aspartate receptor antagonist APV blocks acquisition but not expression of fear conditioning. Behavioral Neuroscience, **105**, 160–167.

Kim, J.J., Clark, R.E. and Thompson, R.F. (1995) Hippocampectomy impairs the memory of recently, but not remotely, acquired trace eyeblink conditioned responses. *Behavioral Neuroscience*, **109**, 195–203.

Kimble, G.A. (1961) *Hilgard and Marquis' Conditioning and Learning*. New York: Appleton-Century-Crofts.

Kirwan, C.B. and Stark, C.E. (2004) Medial temporal lobe activation during encoding and retrieval of novel face–name pairs. *Hippocampus*, **14**, 919–930.

Klein, K. and Boals, A. (2001) The relationship of life event stress and working memory capacity. *Applied Cognitive Psychology*, **15**, 565–579.

Klein, R.M. and Taylor, T.L. (1994) Categories of cognitive inhibition with reference to attention. In: Dagenbach, D. and Carr, T.H., eds. *Inhibitory Processes in Attention, Memory, and Language*. San Diego, CA: Academic Press, pp. 113–150.

Klein, S.B. (2001) A self to remember: a cognitive neuropsychological perspective on how self creates memory and memory creates self. In: Sedikides, C. and Brewer, M.B., eds. *Individual Self, Relational Self, and Collective Self*. Philadelphia, PA: Psychology Press, pp. 25–46.

Klein, S.B., Cosmides, L., Tooby, J. and Chance, S. (2002) Decisions and the evolution of memory: multiple systems, multiple functions. *Psychological Review*, **109**, 306–329.

Klein, S.B., German, T.P., Cosmides, L. and Gabriel, R. (2004) A theory of autobiographical memory: necessary components and disorders resulting from their loss. *Social Cognition*, **22**, 460–490.

Knowlton, B.J., Squire, L.R. and Gluck, M. (1994) Probabilistic classification learning in amnesia. *Learning and Memory*, **1**, 106–120.

Knowlton, B.J., Mangels, J.A. and Squire, L.R. (1996) A neostriatal habit learning system in humans. *Science*, **256**, 1399–1402.

Knudsen, E.I. and Knudsen, P.F. (1985) Vision guides the adjustment of auditory localization in young barn owls. *Science*, **230**, 545–548.

Kohler, W. (1947) *Gestalt Psychology*. New York: Liveright.

Kole, J.A. and Healy, A.F. (2006) Using prior knowledge to minimize interference when learning large amounts of information. *Memory and Cognition*, in press.

Kolers, P.A. and Perkins, D.N. (1975) Spatial and ordinal components of form perception and literacy. *Cognitive Psychology*, **7**, 228–267.

Kolers, P.A. and Roediger, H.L., III (1984) Procedures of mind. *Journal of Verbal Learning and Verbal Behavior*, **23**, 425–449.

Koriat, A. (2000) Control processes in remembering. In: Tulving, E. and Craik, F.I.M., eds. *The Oxford Handbook of Memory*. New York: Oxford University Press, pp. 333–346.

Koriat, A. (2007) Metacognition and consciousness. In: Zelazo, P.D., Moscovitch, M. and Thompson, E., eds. *Cambridge Handbook of Consciousness*. New York: Cambridge University Press, pp. 289–325, in press.

Koriat, A. and Goldsmith, M. (1996a) Memory metaphors and the real-life/laboratory controversy: correspondence versus storehouse conceptions of memory. *Behavioral and Brain Sciences*, **19**, 167–228.

Koriat, A. and Goldsmith, M. (1996b) Monitoring and control processes in the strategic regulation of memory accuracy. *Psychological Review*, **103**, 490–517.

Koriat, A., Goldsmith, M. and Pansky, A. (2000) Toward a psychology of memory accuracy. *Annual Review of Psychology*, **51**, 481–537.

Kuhn T. (1962) *The Structure of Scientific Revolutions*. Chicago, IL: University of Chicago Press.

Kushner, S.A., Elgersma, Y., Murphy, G.G., Jaarsma, D., van Woerden, G.M., Hojjati, M.R., *et al.* (2005) Modulation of presynaptic plasticity and learning by the H-ras/extracellular signal-regulated kinase/synapsin I signaling pathway. *Journal of Neuroscience*, **25**, 9721–9734.

LaBar, K.S., LeDoux, J.E., Spencer, D.D. and Phelps, E.A. (1995) Impaired fear conditioning following unilateral temporal lobectomy in humans. *Journal of Neuroscience*, **15**, 6846–6855.

Lang, A.J., Craske, M.G. and Bjork, R.A. (1999) Implications of a new theory of disuse for the treatment of emotional disorders. *Clinical Psychology: Science and Practice*, **6**, 80–94.

Lashley, K.S. (1950) In search of the engram. *Symposia of the Society of Experimental Biology*, **4**, 454–482.

Laurence, S. and Margolis, E. (1999) Concepts and cognitive science. In: Margolis, E. and Laurence, S., eds. *Concepts. Core Readings*. Cambridge, MA: MIT Press, pp. 3–81.

Le Pelley, M.E. (2004) The role of associative history in models of associative learning: a selective review and hybrid model. *Quarterly Journal of Experimental Psychology*, **57B**, 193–243.

Lechner, H.A., Baxter, D.A., Clark, J.W. and Byrne, J.H. (1996) Bistability and its regulation by serotonin in the endogenously bursting neuron R15 in Aplysia. *Journal of Neurophysiology*, **75**, 957–956.

LeDoux, J.E. (1993) Emotional memory systems in the brain. *Behavioural Brain Research*, **58**, 69–79.

LeDoux, J.E. (1996) *The Emotional Brain*. New York: Simon and Schuster.

Levenson, J.M. and Sweatt, J.D. (2005) Epigenetic mechanisms in memory formation. *Nature Reviews Neuroscience*, **6**, 108–18.

Levy, B. and Anderson, M.C. (2002) Inhibitory processes and the control of memory retrieval. *Trends in Cognitive Science*, **6**, 299–305.

Levy, D.A., Stark, C.E.L. and Squire, L.R. (2004) Intact conceptual priming in the absence of declarative memory. *Psychological Science*, **15**, 680–685.

Levy, W.B. and Steward, O. (1983) Temporal contiguity requirements for long-term associative potentiation/depression in the hippocampus. *Neuroscience*, **8**, 791–797.

Lewis, D.J. (1979) Psychobiology of active and inactive memory. *Psychological Bulletin*, **86**, 1054–1083.

Lisman, J., Schulman, H. and Cline, H. (2002) The molecular basis of CaMKII function in synaptic and behavioural memory. *Nature Reviews Neuroscience*, **3**, 175–190.

Loftus, E.F. (2005) A 30-year investigation of the malleability of memory. *Learning and Memory*, **12**, 361–366.

Loftus, E.F. and Hoffman, H.G. (1989) Misinformation and memory: the creation of memory. *Journal of Experimental Psychology: General*, **118**, 100–104.

Loftus, E.F. and Loftus, G.R. (1980) On the permanence of stored information in the human brain. *American Psychologist*, **35**, 409–420.

Loftus, E.F. and Palmer, J.C. (1974) Reconstruction of automobile destruction: an example of the interaction between language and memory. *Journal of Verbal Learning and Verbal Behavior*, **13**, 585–589.

Loftus, E.F., Feldman, J. and Dashiell, R. (1995) The reality of illusory memories. In: Schacter, D.L., Coyle, J.T., Fischbach, G.D., Mesulum, M.M. and Sullivan, L.G., eds. *Memory Distortion: How Minds, Brains, and Societies Reconstruct the Past*. Cambridge, MA: Harvard University Press, pp. 47–68.

Logan, G.D. and Cowan, W.B. (1984) On the ability to inhibit thought and action: a theory of an act of control. *Psychological Review*, **91**, 295–327.

Mackintosh, N.J. (1975) A theory of attention: variations in the associability of stimuli with reinforcement. *Psychological Review*, **82**, 276–298.

MacLeod, C.M. (1998) Directed forgetting. In: Golding, J.M. and MacLeod, C., eds. *Intentional Forgetting: Interdisciplinary Approaches*. Hillsdale, NJ: Erlbaum, pp. 1–57.

MacLeod, C.M., Dodd, M.D., Sheard, E.D., Wilson, D.E. and Bibi, U. (2003) In opposition to inhibition. In: Ross, B.H, ed. *The Psychology of Learning and Motivation*, Vol. 43. San Diego, CA: Academic Press, pp. 163–214.

MacLeod, M.D. and Macrae, C.N. (2001) Gone but not forgotten: the transient nature of retrieval-induced forgetting. *Psychological Science*, **12**, 148–152.

Malenka, R.C. and Bear, M.F. (2004) LTP and LTD: an embarrassment of riches. *Neuron*, **44**, 5–21.

Malinow, R. and Malenka, R.C. (2002) AMPA receptor trafficking and synaptic plasticity. *Annual Review of Neuroscience*, **25**, 103–126.

Mandler, G. (1980) Recognizing: the judgment of previous occurrence. *Psychological Review*, **87**, 252–271.

Marr, D. (1971) Simple memory: a theory for archicortex. *Philosophical Transactions of the Royal Society B: Biological Sciences*, **262**, 23–81.

Martin, K.C., Casadio, A., Zhu, H., Yaping, E., Rose, J.C., Chen, M., *et al.* (1997) Synapse-specific, long-term facilitation of Aplysia sensory to motor synapses: a function for local protein synthesis in memory storage. *Cell*, **91**, 927–938.

Martin, S.J., Grimwood, P.D. and Morris, R.G.M. (2000) Synaptic plasticity and memory: an evaluation of the hypothesis. *Annual Review of Neuroscience*, **23**, 649–711.

Martin, T.A., Keating, J.G., Goodkin, H.P., Bastian, A.J. and Thach, W.T. (1996) Throwing while looking through prisms. I. Focal olivocerebellar lesions impair adaptation, *Brain*, **119**, 1183–1198.

Mattson, M.P. and Magnus, T. (2006) Ageing and neuronal vulnerability. *Nature Reviews Neuroscience* **7**, 278–294.

May, C.P. and Hasher, L. (1998) Synchrony effects in inhibitory control over thought and action. *Journal of Experimental Psychology: Human Perception and Performance*, **24**, 363–379.

May, C.P., Rahhal, T.R., Berry, E. and Leighton (2005) Aging, source memory, and emotion. *Psychology and Aging*, **20**, 571–578, in press.

Mayr, E. (1982) *The Growth of Biological Thought*. Cambridge, MA: Harvard University Press.

McClelland, J.L. and Goddard, N.H. (1996) Considerations arising from a complementary learning systems perspectives on hippocampus and neocortex. *Hippocampus*, **6**, 654–665.

McClelland, J.L. and Rumelhart, D.E. (1985) Distributed memory and the representation of general and specific information. *Journal of Expeirmental Psychology: General*, **114**, 159–188.

McClelland, J.L., McNaughton, B.L. and O'Reilly, R.C. (1995) Why there are complementary learning systems in the hippocampus and neocortex: insights from the successes and failures of connectionist models of learning and memory. *Psychological Reveiw*, **102**, 419–457.

McCloskey, M. and Zaragoza, M. (1985) Misleading postevent information and memory for events: arguments and evidence against memory impairment hypotheses. *Journal of Experimental Psychology: General*, **114**, 1–16.

McDaniel, M.A. and Busemeyer, J.R. (2005) The conceptual basis of function learning and extrapolation: comparison of rule and associative based models. *Psychonomic Bulletin and Review*, **12**, 24–42.

McDaniel, M.A. and Schlager, M.S. (1990) Discovery learning and transfer of problem-solving skills. *Cognition and Instruction*, **7**, 129–159.

McDaniel, M.A., Friedman, A. and Bourne, L.E. (1978) Remembering the levels of information in words. *Memory and Cognition*, **6**, 156–164.

McDermott, K.B., Jones, T.C., Petersen, S.E., Lageman, S.K. and Roediger, H.L. (2000) Retrieval success is accompanied by enhanced activation in anterior prefrontal cortex during recognition memory: an event-related fMRI study. *Journal of Cognitive Neuroscience*, **12**, 965–976.

McEwen, B.S. (2001) Plasticity of the hippocampus: adaptation to chronic stress and allostatic load. *Annals of the New York Academy of Sciences*, **933**, 265–277.

McGaugh, J.L. (2000) Memory—a century of consolidation. *Science*, **287**, 248–251.

McGaugh, J.L. (2004) The amygdala modulates the consolidation of memories of emotionally arousing experiences. *Annual Review of Neuroscience*, **27**, 1–28.

McGeoch, J.A. (1932) Forgetting and the law of disuse. *Psychological Review*, **39**, 352–370.

McGuire, W.J. (1961) A multiprocess model for paired-associate learning. *Journal of Experimental Psychology*, **62**, 335–347.

McIntosh, A.R. (2000) From location to integration: How neural interactions form the basis for human cognition. In: Tulving, E., ed. *Memory, Consciousness, and the Brain: The Tallinn Conference*. Philadelphia: Psychology Press.

McIntosh, A.R. (2004) Contexts and catalysts: a resolution of the localization and integration of function in the brain. *Neuroinfo* **2**, 175–182.

McLaren, I.P.L. and Mackintosh, N.J. (2000) An elemental model of associative learning: I. Latent inhibition and perceptual learning. *Animal Learning and Behavior*, **28**, 211–246.

McNaughton, B.L. (1998) The neurophysiology of reminiscence. *Neurobiology of Learning and Memory*, **70**, 252–267.

McNaughton, B.L. and Morris, R.G. (1987) Hippocampal synaptic enhancement and information-storage within a distributed memory system. *Trends in Neurosciences*, **10**, 408–415.

Melton, A.W. (1963) Implications of short term memory for a general theory of memory. *Journal of Verbal Learning and Verbal Behavior*, **2**, 1–21.

Menzel, R. (1990) Learning, memory, and 'cognition' in honey bees. In: Kesner, R.P. and Olton, D.S., eds. *Neurobiology of Comparative Cognition*. Hillsdale, NJ: Erlbaum Inc., pp. 237–292.

Menzel, R. (2001) Searching for the memory trace in a mini-brain, the honeybee. *Learning and Memory*, **8**, 53–62.

Menzel, R. and Giurfa, M. (2001) Cognitive architecture of a mini-brain: the honeybee. *Trends in Cognitive Sciences*, **5**, 62–71.

Miller, E.K., Erickson, C.A. and Desimone, R. (1996) Neural mechanisms of visual working memory in prefrontal cortex of the macaque. *Journal of Neuroscience*, **16**, 5154–5167.

Miller, G.A. (1956) The magical number seven, plus or minus two: some limits on our capacity for information processing. *Psychological Review*, **63**, 81–97.

Miller, J.S., Jagielo, J.A. and Spear, N.E. (1991) Differential effectiveness of various prior cueing treatments on the reactivation and maintenance of memory. *Journal of Experimental Psychology: Animal Behavior Processes*, **17**, 249–258.

Miller, P., Zhabotinsky, A.M., Lisman, J.E. and Wang, X.J. (2005) The stability of a stochastic CaMKII switch: dependence on the number of enzyme molecules and protein turnover. *PLoS Biology*, **3**, e107.

Miller, R.M. (1999) Sequential effects in humans: extinction performance as a function of discrimination leaning. Unpublished master's thesis, Purdue University, West Lafayette, IN.

Miller, R.M. and Capaldi, E.J. (2006) An analysis of sequential variables in Pavlovian conditioning. *Learning and Motivaton*, in press.

Miller, R.R. and Springer, A.D. (1973) Amnesia, consolidation, and retrieval. *Psychological Review*, **80**, 69–79.

Millin, P.M., Moody, E.W. and Riccio, D.C. (2001) Interpretation of retrograde amnesia. Old problems redux. *Nature Reviews Neuroscience*, **2**, 68–70.

Milner, B. (1962) Les troubles de la mémoire accompagnant des lésions hippocampiques bilatérales. In: *Physiologie de l'Hippocampe*. Paris: Centre National de la Recherche Scientifique, pp. 257–272. (Milner, B.M. and Glickman, S., trans.) Princeton: Van Nostrand, **1965**, pp 97–111.

Ming, G.L. and Song, H. (2005) Adult neurogenesis in the mammalian central nervous system. *Annual Review of Neuroscience*, **28**, 223–250.

Mishkin, M. (1982) A memory system in the monkey. *Philosophical Transactions of the Royal Society B: Biological Sciences*, **298**, 83–95.

Mishkin, M., Ungerleider, L.G. and Macko, K.A. (1983) Object vision and spatial vision: two cortical pathways. *Trends in Neurosciences*, **6**, 414–417.

Mishkin, M., Malamut, B. and Bachevalier, J. (1984) Memories and habits: two neural systems. In: Lynch, G., McGaugh, J.L. and Weinberger, N.M., eds. *Neurobiology of Learning and Memory*. New York: Guilford Press, pp. 65–77.

Miyake, A. and Shah, P. (1999) Toward unified theories of working memory: emerging general consensus, unresolved theoretical issues and future directions. In: Miyake, A. and Shah, P., eds. *Models of Working Memory: Mechanisms of Active Maintenance and Executive Control*. Cambridge: Cambridge University Press, pp. 28–61.

Moita, M.A.P., Rosis, S., Zhou, Y., LeDoux, J.E. and Blair, H.T. (2004) Putting fear in its place: remapping of hippocampal place cells during fear conditioning. *Journal of Neuroscience*, **24**, 7015–7023.

Morgan, C.L. (1891) *Animal Life and Intelligence*. 2nd edn. London: Edward Arnold.

Morris, C.D., Bransford, J.D. and Franks, J.J. (1977) Levels of processing versus transfer appropriate processing. *Journal of Verbal Learning and Verbal Behavior*, **16**, 519–533.

Morris, R.G. (2003) Long-term potentiation and memory. *Philosophical Transactions of the Royal Society B: Biological Sciences*, **358**, 643–647.

Morton, J., Hammersley, R.H. and Bekerian, D.A. (1985) Headed records: a model for memory and its failures. *Cognition*, **20**, 1–23.

Moscovitch, M., Rosenbaum, S., Gilboa, A., Addis, D., Westmacott, R., Grady, C., *et al.* (2005) Functional neuroanatomy of remote episodic (autobiographical), semantic and spatial memory in humans as determined by lesion and functional neuroimaging studies: a unified account based on multiple trace theory. *Journal of Anatomy*, **207**, 35–66.

Moser, M.B., Trommald, M. and Andersen, P. (1994) An increase in dendritic spine density on hippocampal CA1 pyramidal cells following spatial learning in adult rats suggests the formation of new synapses. *Proceedings of the National Academy of Sciences of the USA*, **91**, 12673–12675.

Murphy, G.L. (2002) *The Big Book of Concepts*. Cambridge, MA: MIT Press.

Nadel, L. (1994) Multiple memory systems: what and why, an update. In: Schacter, D.L. and Tulving, E., eds. *Memory Systems 1994*. Cambridge, MA: MIT Press, pp. 39–64.

Nadel, L. and Moscovitch, M. (1997) Memory consolidation, retrograde amnesia and the hippocampal complex. *Current Opinion in Neurobiology*, **7**, 217–227.

Nadel, L. and Moscovitch, M. (1998) Hippocampal contribution to cortical plasticity. *Neuropharmacology*, **37**, 431–440.

Nadel, L. and Wexler, K. (1984) Neurobiology, representations and memory. In: Lynch, G., McGaugh, J.L. and Weinberger, N., eds. *The Neurobiology of Learning and Memory*. New York: The Guilford Press.

Nadel, L., Samsonovitch, A., Ryan, L. and Moscovitch, M. (2000) Multiple trace theory of human memory: computational, neuroimaging and neuropsychological results. *Hippocampus*, **10**, 352–368.

Nader, K. (2003) Memory traces unbound. *Trends in Neurosciences*, **26**, 65–72.

Nader, K., Schafe, G. E. and LeDoux, J. E. (2000a) Fear memories require protein synthesis in the amygdala for reconsolidation after retrieval. *Nature*, **406**, 722–726.

Nader, K., Schafe, G.E. and Le Doux, J.E. (2000*b*) The labile nature of consolidation theory. *Nature Reviews Neuroscience*, **1**, 216–219.

Napier, R.M., Macrae, M. and Kehoe, E.J. (1992) Rapid reacquisition in conditioning of the rabbit's nictitating membrane response. *Journal of Experimental Psychology: Animal Behavior Processes*, **18**, 182–192.

Neisser, U. (1962) Cultural and cognitive discontinuity. In: Gladwin, T.E. and Sturtevant, W., eds, *Anthropology and Human Behavior*. Washington, DC: Anthropological Society of Washington.

Neisser, U. (1967) *Cognitive Psychology*. New York: Appleton Century Crofts.

Neisser, U. (1988) Time present and time past. In: Gruneberg, M.M., Morris, P.E. and Sykes, R.N., eds. *Practical Aspects of Memory: Current Research and Issues*, Vol. 2. Chichester: Wiley, pp. 545–560.

Neisser, U. (1996) Remembering as doing. *Behavioral and Brain Sciences*, **19**, 203–204.

Nelson, A.B., Gittis, A.H. and du Lac, S. (2005) Decreases in CaMKII activity trigger persistent potentiation of intrinsic excitability in spontaneously firing vestibular nucleus neurons. *Neuron*, **46**, 623–631.

Noel, F., Nunez-Regueiro, M., Cook, R., Byrne, J.H. and Eskin, A. (1993) Long-term changes in synthesis of intermediate filament protein, actin and other proteins in pleural sensory neurons of Aplysia produced by an *in vitro* analogue of sensitization training. *Brain Research and Molecular Brain Research*, **19**, 203–210.

Nolan, M.F., Malleret, G., Lee, K.H., Gibbs, E., Dudman, J.T., Santoro, B., *et al.* (2003) The hyperpolarization-activated HCN1 channel is important for motor learning and neuronal integration by cerebellar Purkinje cells. *Cell*, **115**, 551–564.

Norman, D.A. and Bobrow, D.G. (1979) Descriptions an intermediate stage in memory retrieval. *Cognitive Psychology*, **11**, 107–123.

Norman, D.A. and Shallice, T. (1986) Attention to action: willed and automatic control of behaviour. In: Davidson, R.J., Schwarts, G.E. and Shapiro, D., eds. *Consciousness and Self-regulation. Advances in Research and Theory*. Vol. 4. New York: Plenum Press, pp. 1–18.

Nottebohm, F. (2004) The road we traveled: discovery, choreography, and significance of brain replaceable neurons. *Annals of the New York Academy of Sciences*, **1016**, 628–658.

Novick, L.R. (1988) Analogical transfer, problem similarity, and expertise. *Journal of Experimental Psychology: Learning, Memory, and Cognition*, **14**, 510–520.

O'Craven, K.M. and Kanwisher, N. (2000) Mental imagery of faces and places activates corresponding stimulus-specific brain regions. *Journal of Cognitive Neuroscience*, **12**, 1013–23.

Ohman, A. and Mineka, S. (2001) Fears, phobias, and preparedness: toward an evolved module of fear and fear learning. Psychological Review, **108**, 483–522.

O'Reilly, R.C. and McClelland, J.L. (1994) Hippocampal conjunctive encoding, storage, and recall: avoiding a trade-off. *Hippocampus*, **4**, 661–682.

O'Reilly, R.C., Braver, T.S. and Cohen, J.D. (1999) A biologically based computational model of working memory. In: Miyake, A. and Shah, P., eds. *Models of Working Memory: Mechanisms of Active Maintenance and Executive Control*. New York: Cambridge University Press, pp. 375–411.

Osgood, C.E. (1953) *Method and Theory in Experimental Psychology*. New York: Oxford University Press.

Osgood, C.E. (1949) The similarity paradox in human learning: a resolution. *Psychological Review*, **56**, 132–143.

Paller, K.A., Kutas, M. and Mayes, A.R. (1987) Neural correlates of encoding in an incidental learning paradigm. *Electroencephalography and Clinical Neurophysiology*, **67**, 360–371.

Papini, M. (2002) Pattern and process in the evolution of learning. *Psychological Review*, **109**, 186–201.

Pavlik, P.I. and Anderson, J.R. (2005) Practice and forgetting effects on vocabulary memory: an activation-based model of the spacing effect. *Cognitive Science*, **29**, 559–586.

Pavlov, I.P. (1927) *Conditioned Reflexes*. London: Routledge and Kegan Paul.

Pearce, J.M. and Hall, G. (1980) A model for Pavlovian learning: variations in the effectiveness of conditioned but not of unconditioned stimuli. *Psychological Review*, **87**, 532–552.

Penfield, W. (1955) The role of the temporal cortex in certain psychical phenomena. *Journal of Mental Science*, **424**, 1955. A review of this article by John A. Speyrer can be found at http://primal-page.com/penfield.htm.

Pham, K., McEwen, B.S., Ledoux, J.E. and Nader, K. (2005) Fear learning transiently impairs hippocampal cell proliferation. *Neuroscience*, **130**, 17–24.

Phelps, E.A., O'Connor, K.J., Gatenby, J.C., Gore, J.C., Grillon, C. and Davis, M. (2001) Activation of the left amygdala to a cognitive representation of fear. *Nature Neuroscience*, **4**, 437–441.

Pinsker, H., Kupfermann, I., Castellucci, V. and Kandel, E. (1970) Habituation and dishabituation of the gill-withdrawal reflex in Aplysia. Science, **167**,1740–1742.

Plato, Meno 79c,d. In: Hamilton, E. and Cairns, H., eds. *The Collected Dialogues*. Princeton, NJ: Princeton University Press (1961).

Plato, Theaethetus 153b. In: Hamilton, E. and Cairns, H., eds. *The Collected Dialogues*. Princeton, NJ: Princeton University Press (1961).

Poldrack, R.A. (2000) Imaging brain plasticity: conceptual and methodological issues— a theoretical review. *NeuroImage*, **12**, 1–13.

Poldrack, R.A. and Packard, M.G. (2003) Competition among multiple memory systems: converging evidence from animal and human brain studies. *Neuropsychologia*, **41**, 245–51.

Poldrack, R.A., Clark, J., Pare-Blagoex, E.J., Shohamy, D., Moyano, J., Myers, C., *et al.* (2001) Interactive memory system in the human brain. *Nature*, **29**, 546–550.

Posner, M.I. and Petersen, S.E. (1990) The attention system of the human brain. *Annu Rev Neurosci* **13**:25–42.

Posner, M.I. and Cohen, Y. (1984) Components of visual orienting. In: Bouma, D. and Bonwhuis, D., eds. *Attention and Performance X*. Hillsdale, NJ: Lawrence Erlbaum Associates, pp. 531–566.

Postle, B.R., Druzgal, T.J. and D'Esposito, M. (2003) Seeking the neural substrates of visual working memory storage. *Cortex*, **39**, 927–946.

Postman, L.U. and Schwartz, M. (1964) Studies of learning to learn: I. Transfer as a function of method of practice and class of verbal materials. *Journal of Verbal learning and Verbal Behavior*, **3**, 37–49.

Postman, L., Stark, K. and Fraser, J. (1968) Temporal changes in interference. *Journal of Verbal Learning and Verbal Behavior*, **7**, 672–694.

Prabhakaran, V., Narayanan, K., Zhao, Z. and Gabrielli, J.D.E. (2000) Integration of diverse information in working memory in the frontal lobe. *Nature Neuroscience*, **3**, 85–90.

Pravosudov, V.V. and Clayton, N.S. (2002) A test of the adaptive specialization hypothesis: population differences in caching, memory and the hippocampus in black-capped chickadees (*Poecile atricapilla*). *Behavioral Neuroscience*, **16**, 515–522.

Pribram, K.H., Mishkin, M., Rosvold, H.E. and Kaplan, S.J. (1952) Effects on delayed-response performance of lesions of dorsolateral and ventromedial frontal cortex of baboons. Journal of Comparative Physiology and Psychology, **45**, 565–575.

Proust, M. (1925/1981) *Remembrance of Things Past: The Fugitive.* (Scott-Moncrieff, C.K., Kilmartin, T. and Mayor, A., trans.) New York: Random House.

Proust, M. (2000) *Swann's Way.* (Moncrieff, C.K.S., trans.) London: Penguin Books. (Original work published 1913.)

Przybyslawski, J. and Sara, S.J. (1997) Reconsolidation of memory after its reactivation. *Behavioral Brain Research*, **84**, 241–246.

Przybyslawski, J., Roullet, P. and Sara, S.J. (1999) Attenuation of emotional and nonemotional memories after their reactivation: role of beta adrenergic receptors. *Journal of Neuroscience*, **19**, 6623–6628.

Radley, J.J. and Morrison, J.H. (2005) Repeated stress and structural plasticity in the brain. *Age Research Reviews*, **4**, 271–287.

Raichle, M.E., Fiez, J.A., Videen, T.O., MacLeod, A.-M.K., Pardo, J.V., Fox, P.T., *et al.* (1994) Practice-related changes in the human brain functional anatomy during nonmotor learning. *Cerebral Cortex*, **4**, 8–26.

Rajaram, S. (1993) Remembering and knowing: two means of access to the personal past. *Memory and Cognition*, **21**, 89–102.

Rajaram, S. and Roediger, H. L. (1997) Remembering and knowing as states of consciousness during recollection. In: Cohen, J.D. and Schooler, J.W., eds. *Scientific Approaches to the Question of Consciousness.* Hillsdale, NJ: Erlbaum, pp. 213–240.

Rajaram, S., Hamilton, M. and Bolton, A. (2002) Distinguishing states of awareness from confidence during retrieval: evidence from amnesia. *Cognitive, Affective and Behavioral Neuroscience*, **2**, 227–235.

Randich, A. (1981) The US preexposure phenomenon in the conditioned suppression paradigm: a role for conditioned situational stimuli. *Learning and Motivation*, **12**, 321–341

Ranganath, C. and Blumenfeld, R.S. (2005) Doubts about double dissociations between short- and long-term memory. *Trends in Cognitive Science*, **9**, 374–380.

Ranganath, C. and D'Esposito, M. (2001) Medial temporal lobe activity associated with active maintenance of novel information. *Neuron*, **31**, 865–873.

Ranganath, C., Cohen, M.X. and Brozinsky, C.J. (2005) Working memory maintenance contributes to long-term memory formation: neural and behavioral evidence. *Journal of Cognitive Neuroscience*, **17**, 994–1010.

Ranganath, C., Yonelinas, A.P., Cohen, M.X., Dy, C.J., Tom, S.M. and D'Esposito, M. (2004) Dissociable correlates of recollection and familiarity within the medial temporal lobes. *Neuropsychologia*, **42**, 2–13.

Reader, S.M. and Laland, K.N., eds (2003) *Animal Innovation.* Oxford: Oxford University Press.

Redish, A.D., Bataglia, F.P., Chawla, M.K., Ekstrom, A.D., Gerrard, J.L., Lipa, P., *et al.* (2001) Independence of firing correlates of anatomically proximate hippocampal pyramidal cells. *Journal of Neuroscience*, **21**, RC134.

Rescorla, R.A. (1968) Probability of shock in the presence and absence of CS in fear conditioning. *Journal of Comparative and Physiological Psychology*, **66**, 1–5.

Rescorla, R.A. (1980) Simultaneous and successive associations in sensory preconditioning. *Journal of Experimental Psychology: Animal Behavior Processes*, **6**, 207–216.

Rescorla, R.A. (1988) Behavioral studies of Pavlovian conditioning. *Annual Review of Neuroscience*, **11**, 329–352.

Rescorla, R.A. (2001) Experimental extinction. In: Mowrer, R.R. and Klein, S., eds. *Handbook of Contemporary Learning Theories*. Hillsdale, NJ: Erlbaum, pp. 119–154.

Rescorla, R.A. and Holland, P.C. (1976) Some behavioral approaches to the study of learning. In: Rosenzweig, M.R. and Bennett, E.L., eds. *Neural Mechanisms of Learning and Memory*. Cambridge, MA: MIT Press, pp. 165–172.

Rescorla, R.A. and Wagner, A.R. (1972) A theory of Pavlovian conditioning: variations in the effectiveness of reinforcement and nonreinforcement. In: Black A.H. and W.F. Prokasy, eds. *Classical Conditioning II: Current Research and Theory*. New York: Appleton-Century-Crofts, pp. 64–99.

Reus, V.I., Weingartner, H. and Post, R.M. (1979) Clinical implications of state-dependent learning. *American Journal of Psychiatry*, **136**, 927–931.

Richardson-Klavehn, A., Gardiner, J.M. and Java, R.I. (1996) Memory: task dissociations, process dissociations and dissociations of consciousness. In: Underwood, G., ed. *Implicit Cognition*. Oxford: Oxford University Press, pp. 85–158.

Roberson, E.D. and Sweatt, J.D. (1999) A biochemical blueprint for long-term memory. *Learning and Memory*, **6**, 381–388.

Rodrigues, S.M., Schafe, G.E. and LeDoux, J.E. (2004) Molecular mechanisms underlying emotional learning and memory in the lateral amygdala. *Neuron*, **44**, 75–91.

Roediger, H.L. (1980) Memory metaphors in cognitive psychology. *Memory and Cognition*, **8**, 231–246.

Roediger, H.L., III (1996) Memory illusions. *Journal of Memory and Language*, **35**, 76–100

Roediger, H.L. (2000) Why retrieval is the key process in understanding human memory. In: Tulving, E., ed. *Memory, Consciousness, and the Brain: The Tallinn Conference*. Philadelphia, PA: Psychology Press, pp. 52–75.

Roediger, H.L. and Guynn, M.J. (1996) Retrieval processes. In: Bjork, E.L. and Bjork, R.A., eds. *Memory. A Volume in the Handbook of Perception and Cognition*. New York: Academic Press, pp. 197–236.

Roediger, H.L., Weldon, M.S. and Challis, B.H. (1989) Explaining dissociations between implicit and explicit measures of retention: a processing account. In: Roediger, H.L. and Craik, F.I.M., eds. *Varieties of Memory and Consciousness: Essays in Honour of Endel Tulving*. Hillsdale, NJ: Erlbaum, pp. 3–39.

Roediger, H.L., Rajaram, S. and Srininvas, K. (1990) Specifying criteria for postulating memory systems. *Annals of the New York Academy of Sciences*, **608**, 572–589.

Roediger, H.L., Weldon, M.S., Stadler, M.L. and Riegler, G.L. (1992) Direct comparison of two implicit memory tests: word fragment and word stem completion. *Journal of Experimental Psychology: Learning, Memory and Cognition*, **18**, 1251–1269.

Roediger, H.L., Gallo, D.A. and Geraci, L. (2002) Processing approaches to cognition: the impetus from the levels of processing framework. *Memory*, **10**, 319–332.

Rogan, M.T., Staubli, U.V. and LeDoux, J.E. (1997) Fear conditioning induces associative long-term potentiation in the amygdala. *Nature*, **390**, 604–607.

Rolls, E.T. (1992) Neurophysiological mechanisms underlying face processing within and beyond the temporal cortical visual areas. *Philosophical Transactions of the Royal Society B: Biological Sciences*, **335**, 11–20.

Rolls, E.T. (2000) Memory systems in the brain. *Annual Review of Psychology*, **51**, 599–630.

Rolls, E.T. (2005) *Emotion Explained*. Oxford University Press: Oxford.

Rolls, E.T. and Deco, G. (2002) *Computational Neuroscience of Vision*. Oxford University Press: Oxford.

Rolls, E.T. and Kesner, R.P. (2006) A computational theory of hippocampal function, and empirical tests of the theory. *Progress in Neurobiology*, **79**:1–48

Rolls, E.T. and Treves, A. (1998) *Neural Networks and Brain Function*. Oxford University Press: Oxford.

Rolls, E.T., Franco, L. and Stringer, S.M. (2005) The perirhinal cortex and long-term familiarity memory. *Quarterly Journal of Experimental Psychology*, **58B**, 234–245

Rosen, J.B., Fanselow, M.S., Young, S.L., Sitcoske, M. and Maren, S. (1998) Immediate-early gene expression in the amygdala following footshock stress and contextual fear conditioning. *Brain Research*, **796**, 132–142.

Roullet, P. and Sara, S. (1998) Consolidation of memory after its reactivation: involvement of beta noradrenergic receptors in the late phase. *Neural Plasticity*, **6**, 63–68.

Rovee-Collier, C., Hayne, H. and Columbo, M. (2001) *The Development of Implicit and Explicit Memory*. Philadelphia: John Benjamins Publishing Co.

Rowe, G., Valderrama, S., Hasher, L. and Lenartowicz, A. Attention disregulation: a benefit for implicit memory. *Psychology and Aging*, **21**, 826–830.

Rubin, D.C. (1988) Go for the skill. In: Neisser, U. and Winograd, E., eds, *Remembering Reconsidered: Ecological and Traditional Approaches to the Study of Memory*. Cambridge: Cambridge University Press, pp. 374–382.

Rubin, D.C. (1995) *Memory in Oral Traditions: The Cognitive Psychology of Epic, Ballads, and Counting-out Rhymes*. New York: Oxford University Press.

Rubin, D.C. (2005) A basic-systems approach to autobiographical memory. *Current Directions in Psychological Science*, **14**, 79–83.

Rubin, D.C. and Wenzel, A.E. (1996) One hundred years of forgetting: a quantitative description of retention. *Psychological Review*, **103**, 734–760.

Ruiz-Canada, C., Ashley, J., Moeckel-Cole, S., Drier, E., Yin, J. and Budnik, V. (2002) New synaptic bouton formation is disrupted by misregulation of microtubule stability in aPKC mutants. *Neuron*, **42**, 567–580.

Ryan, L., Nadel, L., Keil, K., Putnam, K., Schnyer, D., Trouard, T., *et al.* (2001) The hippocampal complex is equally involved in retrieving recent and very remote autobiographical memories: evidence from functional magnetic resonance imaging in neurologically intact people. *Hippocampus*, **11**, 707–714.

Salaman, E. (1970) *A Collection of Moments: A study of Involuntary Memories*. London, Longman.

Sandquist, T.F., Rohrbaugh, J.W., Syndulko, K. and Lindsley, D.B. (1980) Electrophysiological signs of levels of processing: perceptual analysis and recognition memory. *Psychophysiology*, **17**, 568–576.

Sara, S.J., Lelong, J. and Yeshenko, O. (2005) *Late now print signal from the locus ceruleus for memory consolidation during slow-wave sleep.* Program No. 775.10. 2005 Abstract Viewer/Itinerary Planner. Washington, DC: Society for Neuroscience, 2005. Online.

Sara, S.J. (2000) Retrieval and reconsolidation: toward a neurobiology of remembering. *Learning and Memory,* **7,** 73–84.

Sara, S.J. and Remacle, J.F. (1977) Strychnine-induced passive avoidance facilitation after electroconvulsive shock or undertraining: a retrieval effect. *Behavioral Biology,* **19,** 465–475.

Sara, S.J., David-Remacle, M. and Lefevre, D. (1975) Passive avoidance behavior in rats after electroconvulsive shock: facilitative effect of response retardation. *Journal of Comparative Physiology and Psychology,* **89,** 489–497.

Scavio, M.J. and Thompson, R.F. (1979) Extinction and reacquisition performance alternations of the conditioned nictitating membrane response. *Bulletin of the Psychonomic Society,* **13,** 57–60.

Schacter, D.L. (1996) *Searching for Memory: The Brain, the Mind, and the Past.* New York: Basic Books.

Schacter, D.L. (2001*a*) *Forgotten Ideas, Neglected Pioneers: Richard Semon and the Story of Memory.* Philadelphia: Psychology Press.

Schacter, D.L. (2001*b*) *The Seven Sins of Memory.* New York: Houghton Mifflin.

Schacter, D.L. and Buckner, R.L. (1998) Priming and the brain. *Neuron,* **20,** 185–195.

Schacter, D.L. and Tulving, E. (1994) What are the memory systems of 1994? In: Schacter, D.L. and Tulving, E., eds. Memory. *A Volume in the Handbook of Perception and Cognition.* systems 1994. Cambridge: MIT Press, pp. 1–38.

Schacter, D.L., Dobbins, I.G. and Schnyer, D.M. (2004) Specificity of priming: A cognitive neuroscience perspective. *Nature Reviews Neuroscience,* **5,** 853–862.

Schacter, D.L., Norman, K.A. and Koutstaal, W. (1998) The cognitive neuroscience of constructive memory. *Annual Review of Psychology,* **49,** 289–318.

Schacter, D.L., Wagner, A.D. and Buckner, R.L. (2000) Memory systems of 1999. In: Tulving, E. and Craik, F.I.M., eds. *The Oxford Handbook of Memory.* New York: Oxford University Press, pp. 627–643.

Schafe, G.E., Doye're, V. and LeDoux, J.E. (2005) Tracking the fear engram: the lateral amygdala is an essential locus of fear memory storage. *Journal of Neuroscience,* **25,** 10010 –10015.

Schank, R.C. (1982) *Dynamic Memory.* New York, Cambridge University Press.

Schmader, T. and Johns, M. (2003) Converging evidence that stereotype threat reduces working memory capacity. *Journal of Personality and Social Psychology,* **85,** 440–452.

Schon, K., Atri, A., Hasselmo, M.E., Tricarico, M.D., LoPresti, M.L. and Stern, C.E. (2005) Scopolamine reduces persistent activity related to long-term encoding in the parahippocampal gyrus during delayed matching in humans. *Journal of Neuroscience,* **25,** 9112–9123.

Schultz, W. and Dickinson, A. (2000) Neural coding of prediction errors. *Annual Review of Neuroscience,* **23,** 473–500.

Schultz, W., Dayan, P. and Montague, P.R. (1997) A neural substrate of prediction and reward. *Science,* **275,** 1593–1599.

Schweikert, R. (1993) A multinomial processing tree model for degradation and redintegration in immediate recall. *Memory and Cognition,* **21,** 168–175.

Scoville, W.B. and Milner, B. (1957) Loss of recent memory after bilateral hippocampal lesions. *Journal of Neurology, Neurosurgery and Psychiatry*, **20**, 11–21.

Semon, R. (1904) *Die Mneme*. Leipzig: Wilhelm Engelmann.

Shallice, T., Fletcher, P., Frith, C.D., Grasby, P., Frackowiak, R.S.J. and Dolan, R.J. (1994) Brain regions associated with acquisition and retrieval of verbal episodic memory. *Nature*, **368**, 633–635.

Shallice, T. and Warrington, E.K. (1970) Independent functioning of verbal memory stores: A neuropsychological study. *Quarterly Journal of Experimental Psychology*, **22**, 261–273.

Shannon, C.E. (1948) A mathematical theory of communication. *Bell System Technical Journal*, **27**, 379–**423**, 623–656.

Sherrington, C.S. (1906) *The Integrative Action of the Nervous System*. Cambridge: Yale University Press.

Sherry, D.F. (2005) Do ideas about function help in the study of causation? *Animal Biology*, **55**, 441–456.

Sherry, D.F. and Schacter, D.L. (1987) The evolution of multiple memory systems. *Psychological Review*, **94**, 439–454.

Shettleworth, S.J. (1998) *Cognition, Evolution, and Behavior*. New York: Oxford University Press.

Shors, T.J. and Matzel, L.D. (1997) Long-term potentiation: what's learning got to do with it? *Behavioral and Brain Sciences*, **20**, 597–655.

Siegel, S. (1976) Morphine analgesic tolerance: its situation specificity supports a Pavlovian conditioning model. *Science*, **193**, 323–325

Siegel, S. (2005) Drug tolerance, drug addiction, and drug anticipation. *Current Directions in Psychological Science*, **14**, 296–300.

Silva, A.J., Stevens, C.F., Tonegawa, S. and Wang, Y. (1992a) Deficient hippocampal long-term potentiation in alpha-calcium-calmodulin kinase II mutant mice. *Science*, **257**, 201–206.

Silva, A.J., Paylor, R., Whener, J.M. and Tonegawa, S. (1992b) Impaired spatial learning in alpha-calcium-calmodulin kinase II mutant mice. *Science*, **257**, 206–211.

Silva, A.J., Kogan, J.H., Frankland, P.W. and Kida, S. (1998) CREB and memory. *Annual Review of Neuroscience*, **21**, 127–148.

Simon, H.A. (1974) *The organization of complex systems*. In: HH Pattee, ed. *Hierarchy theory: the challenge of complex systems*. New York: Braziller. pp. 3–27.

Singley, M.K. and Anderson, J.R. (1989) *The Transfer of Cognitive Skill*. Cambridge, MA: Harvard University Press.

Skinner, B.F. (1974) *About Behaviorism*. New York: Alfred A. Knopf.

Slamecka, N.J. (1968) An examination of trace storage in free recall. *Journal of Experimental Psychology*, **76**, 504–513.

Smith, E.E. and Jonides, J. (1997) Working memory: a view from neuroimaging. *Cognitive Psychology*, **33**, 5–42.

Smith, J.D., Shields, W.E. and Washburn, D.A. (2003) A comparative approach to metacognition and uncertainty monitoring. *Behavioral and Brain Sciences*, **26**, 317–339.

Smith, R. (1992) *Inhibition: History and Meaning in the Sciences of Mind and Brain*. Berkeley and Los Angeles, CA: University of California Press.

Smith, S.M. (1979) Remembering in and out of context. *Journal of Experimental Psychology: Human Learning and Memory*, **5**, 460–471.

Smith, S.M. (1988) Environmental context-dependent memory. In: Davies, G.M. and Thomnson, D.M., eds. *Memory in Context: Context in Memory*. Chichester: Wiley, pp. 13–34.

Smith, S.M. and Vela, E. (2001) Environmental context-dependent memory: a review. *Psychonomic Bulletin and Review*, **8**, 203–220.

Smith, S.M., Glenberg, A.M. and Bjork, R.A. (1978) Environmental context and human memory. *Memory and Cognition*, **6**, 342–353.

Somogyi, P., Tamas, G., Lujan, R. and Buhl, E.H. (1998) Salient features of synaptic organisation in the cerebral cortex. *Brain Research and Brain Research Reviews*, **26**, 113–135

Spear, N.E. and Mueller, C.W. (1984) Consolidation as a function of retrieval. In: Weingartner, H. and Parker, E.S., eds. *Memory Consolidation: Psychobiology of Cognition*. Hillsdale, NJ: Erlbaum, pp. 111–147.

Spear, N.E. and Riccio, D.C. (1994) *Memory: Phenomena and Principles*. Needham Heights, MA: Allyn and Bacon.

Spear, N.E., McKinzie, D.L. and Arnold, H.M. (1994) Suggestions from the infant rat about brain dysfunction and memory. In: Delacour, J., ed. *The Memory System of the Brain*. Singapore: World Scientific Publishing, pp. 278–315.

Spencer, W.A., Thompson, R.F. and Neilson, D.R., Jr (1966) Decrement of ventral root electronic and intracellularly recorded PSPs produced by iterated cutaneous afferent volleys. *Journal of Neurophysiology*, **29**, 253–274.

Sporns, O. and Kotter, R. (2004) Motifs in brain networks. *PLoS Biology*, **2**, e369.

Sporns, O. and Zwi, J.D. (2004) The small world of the cerebral cortex. *Neuroinfo*, **2**, 145–162.

Squire, L.R. (1987) *Memory and Brain*. New York: Oxford University Press.

Squire, L.R. (1992) Memory and the hippocampus: a synthesis from findings with rats, monkeys, and humans. *Psychological Review*, **99**, 195–231.

Squire, L.R. (2004) Memory systems of the brain: a brief history and current perspective. *Neurobiology of Learning and Memory*, **82**, 171–177.

Squire, L.R. and Alvarez, P. (1995) Retrograde amnesia and memory consolidation: a neurobiological perspective. *Current Opinion in Neurobiology*, **5**, 169–175.

Squire, L.R. and Kandel, E.R. (1999) *Memory: From Mind to Molecules*. New York: Scientific American Library.

Squire, L.R. and Knowlton, B.J. (2000) The medial temporal lobe, the hippocampus and the memory systems of the brain. In: Gazzaniga, M.S., ed. *The New Cognitive Neurosciences*. Cambridge, MA: MIT Press, pp 765–95.

Squire, L.R. and Zola-Morgan, S. (1988) Memory: brain systems and behavior. *Trends in Neuroscience*, 1988, **11**, 170–175.

Squire, L.R. and Zola-Morgan, S. (1991) The medial temporal lobe memory system. *Science*, **253**, 1380–1386.

Squire, L.R., Cohen, N.J. and Nadel, L. (1984) The medial temporal region and memory consolidation: a new hypothesis. In: Weingartner, H. and Parker, E., eds. *Memory Consolidation*. Hillsdale, NJ: Lawrence Erlbaum Associates.

Squire, L.R., Stark, C.E.L. and Clark, R.E. (2004) The medial temporal lobe. *Annual Review of Neuroscience*, **27**, 279–306.

Stent, G. (1973) A physiological mechanism for Hebb's learning postulate. *Proceedings of the National Academy of Sciences of the USA*, **69**, 997–1001.

Stern, C.E., Sherman, S.J., Kirchhoff, B.A. and Hasselmo, M.E. (2001) Medial temporal and prefrontal contributions to working memory tasks with novel and familiar stimuli. *Hippocampus*, **11**, 337–346.

Storm, B.C., Bjork, E.L. and Bjork, R.A. (2005) Social metacognitive judgments: the role of retrieval-induced forgetting in person memory and impressions. *Journal of Memory and Language*, **52**, 535–550.

Storm, B.C., Bjork, E.L., Bjork, R.A. and Nestojko, J. (2006) Is retrieval success a necessary condition for retrieval-induced forgetting? *Psychonomic Bulletin and Review*, in press.

Suddendorf, T. and Corballis, M. (1997) Mental time travel and the evolution of the human mind. *Genetic, Social, and General Psychology Monographs*, **123**, 133–167.

Sutherland, N.S. and Mackintosh, N.J. (1971) *Mechanisms of Animal Discrimination Learning*. New York: Academic Press.

Sutherland, S. (1996) *The International Dictionary of Psychology*, 2nd edn. New York: Crossroad Publishing Company.

Sutton, M.A., Masters, S.E., Bagnall, M.W. and Carew, T.J. (2001) Molecular mechanisms underlying a unique intermediate phase of memory in Aplysia. *Neuron*, **31**, 143–154.

Sutton, M.A., Ide, J., Masters, S.E. and Carew, T.J. (2002) Interaction between amount and pattern of training in the induction of intermediate- and long-term memory for sensitization in Aplysia. *Learning and Memory*, **9**, 29–40.

Suzuki, W.A., Miller, E.K. and Desimone, R. (1997) Object and place memory in the macaque entorhinal cortex. *Journal of Neurophysics*, **78**, 1062–1081.

Sweatt, J.D. (2003) *Mechanisms of Memory*. Elsevier, London.

Takashima, A., Petersson, K.M., Rutters, F., Tendolkar, I., Jensen, O., Zwarts, M.J., McNaughton, B.L. and Fernanndez, G. (2006) Declarative memory consolidation in humans: a prospective functional magnetic resonance imaging study. *Proceedings of the National Academy of Sciences of the USA*, **103**, 756–761.

Thomas, A.K. and McDaniel, M.A. (in press). The negative cascade of incongruent generative study-test processsing in memory and metacomprehension. *Memory and Cognition*.

Thomas, M.J. and Malenka, R.C. (2003) Synaptic plasticity in the mesolimbic dopamine system. *Philosophical Transactions of the Royal Society B: Biological Sciences*, **358**, 815–819.

Thompson, R.F. and Spencer, W.A. (1966) Habituation: a model phenomenon for the study of neuronal substrates of behavior. *Psychological Review*, **73**, 16–43.

Thorndike, E.L. (1898) Animal intelligence: an experimental study of the associative processes in animals. *Psychological Review*, **2**, 1–109.

Thorndike, E.L. (1906) *The Principles of Teaching: Based on Psychology*. New York: A.G. Seiler.

Thorndike, E.L. and Woodworth, R.S. (1901*a*) The influence of improvement in one mental function upon the efficiency of other functions. (I) *Psychological Review*, **8**, 247–261.

Thorndike, E.L. and Woodworth, R.S. (1901*b*) The influence of improvement in one mental function upon the efficiency of other functions. II. The estimation of magnitudes. *Psychological Review*, **8**, 384–395.

Thorndike, E.L. and Woodworth, R.S. (1901*c*) The influence of improvement in one mental function upon the efficiency of other functions: functions involving attention, observation and discrimination. *Psychological Review*, **8**, 553–564.

Tinbergen, N. (1963) On aims and methods of ethology. *Zeitschrift für Tierpsychologie*, **20**, 410–433.

Tinbergen, N., Broekhuysen, G.J., Feekes, F., Houghton, J.C.W., Kruuk, H. and Szule, E. (1963) Egg shell removal by the black-headed gull, *Larus ridibundus* L.; a behaviour component of camouflage. *Behaviour*, **19**, 74–117.

Tononi, G., Sporns, O. and Edelman, G.M. (1992) Reentry and the problem of integrating multiple cortical areas: simulation of dynamic integration in the visual system. *Cerebral Cortex*, **2**, 310–335.

Tulving, E. (1972) Episodic and semantic memory. In: Tulving, E. and Donaldson, W., eds. *Organization of Memory*. New York: Academic Press, pp. 382–403.

Tulving, E. (1974) Cue-dependent forgetting. *American Scientist*, **62**, 74–82.

Tulving, E. (1983) *Elements of Epsidoc Memory*. Clarendon Press: Oxford.

Tulving, E. (1985a) Memory and consciousness. *Canadian Psychologist*, **26**, 1–12.

Tulving, E. (1985b) How many memory systems are there? *American Psychologist*, **40**, 385–398.

Tulving, E. (2000) Concepts of memory. In: Tulving, E. and Craik, F.I.M., eds. *The Oxford Handbook of Memory*. New York: Oxford University Press, pp. 33–44.

Tulving, E. (2001) Does memory encoding exist? In: Naveh-Benjamin, M., Moscovitch, M. and Roediger, H.L., III, eds. *Perspectives on Human Memory and Cognitive Aging: Essays in Honour of Fergus Craik*. Philadelphia: Psychology Press, pp. 67–80.

Tulving, E. (2002a) Chronesthesia: awareness of subjective time. In: Stuss, D.T. and Knight, R.C., eds. *Principles of Frontal Lobe Function*. New York: Oxford University Press, pp. 311–325.

Tulving, E. (2002b) Episodic memory: from mind to brain. *Annual Review of Psychology*, **53**, 1–25.

Tulving, E. (2005) Episodic memory and autonoesis: uniquely human? In: Terrace, H.S. and Metcalfe, J., eds. *The Missing Link in Cognition: Self-knowing Consciousness in Man and Animals*. New York: Oxford University Press, pp. 3–56.

Tulving, E. and Madigan, S.A. (1970) Memory and verbal learning. *Annual Review of Psychology*, **21**, 437–484.

Tulving, E. and Pearlstone, Z. (1966) Availability versus accessibility in memory for words. *Journal of Verbal Learning and Verbal Behavior*, **5**, 381–391.

Tulving, E. and Schacter, D.L. (1990) Priming and human memory systems. *Science*, **247**, 301–306.

Tulving, E. and Thompson, D.M. (1973) Encoding specificity and retrieval processes in episodic memory. *Psychological Review*, **80**, 352–373.

Tulving, E., Schacter, D.L. and Stark, H.A. (1982) Priming effects in word-fragment completion are independent of recognition memory. *Journal of Experimental Psychology: Learning, Memory and Cognition*, **8**, 336–342.

Tulving, E., Kapur, S., Craik, F.I.M., Moscovitch, M. and Houle, S. (1994) Hemispheric encoding/retrieval asymmetry in episodic memory: positron emission tomography findings. *Proceedings of the National Academy of Sciences of the USA* **91**, 2016–2020.

Turley-Ames, K.J. and Whitfield, M.M. (2003) Strategy training and working memory task performance. *Journal of Memory and Language*, **49**, 446–468.

Turrigiano, G.G. and Nelson, S.B. (2000) Hebb and homeostasis in neuronal plasticity. *Current Opinion in Neurobiology*, **10**, 358–364.

Unsworth, N., Schrock, J.C. and Engle, R.W. (2004) Working memory capacity and the antisaccade task: individual differences in voluntary saccade control. *Journal of Experimental Psychology: Learning, Memory and Cognition*, **30**, 1302–1321.

Van Essen, D.C., Anderson, C.H. and Felleman, D.C. (1992) Information-processing in the primate visual-system—an integrated systems perspective. *Science*, **255**, 419–423.

Vargha-Khadem, F., Gadian, D.G., Watkins, K.E., Connelly, A., Van Paesschen, W. and Mishkin, M. (1997) Differential effects of early hippocampal pathology on episodic and semantic memory. *Science*, **277**, 376–380.

Veling, H. and Van Knippenberg, A. (2004) Remembering can cause inhibition. Retrieval-induced inhibition as a cue independent process. *Journal of Experimental Psychology: Learning, Memory and Cognition*, **30**, 315–318.

von Gersdorff, H. and Borst, J.G. (2002) Short-term plasticity at the calyx of held. *Nature Reviews Neuroscience*, **3**, 53–64.

Vriezen, E., Moscovitch, M. and Bellos, S.A. (1995) Priming effects in semantic classification tasks. *Journal of Experimental Psychology: Learning, Memory and Cognition*, **21**, 933–946.

Vyas, A. and Chttarji, S. (2004) Modulation of different states of anxiety-like behavior by chronic stress. *Behavioral Neuroscience*, **118**, 1450–1454.

Waelti, P., Dickinson, A. and Schultz, W. (2001) Dopamine responses comply with basic assumptions of formal learning learning. *Nature*, **412**, 43–48.

Wagner, A.R. (1981) SOP: a model of automatic memory processing in animal behavior. In: Spear, N.E. and Miller, R.R., eds. *Information Processing in Animals: Memory Mechanisms*. Hillsdale, NJ: Lawrence Erlbaum Associates, pp. 5–47.

Wagner, A.R. and Brandon, S.E. (1989) Evolution of a structured connectionist model of Pavlovian conditioning (AESOP). In: Klein, S.B. and Mowrer, R.R., eds. *Contemporary Learning Theories: Pavlovian Conditioning and the Status of Traditional Learning Theory*. Hillsdale, NJ: Lawrence Erlbaum Associates, pp. 149–190.

Wainwright, M.L., Zhang, H., Byrne, J.H. and Cleary, L.J. (2002) Localized neuronal outgrowth induced by long-term sensitization training in Aplysia. *Journal of Neuroscience*, 22: 4132–41.

Wang, X.J. (2001) Synaptic reverberation underlying mnemonic persistent activity. *Trends in Neurosciences* **24**, 455–463.

Warrington, E.K. and Weiskrantz, L. (1968) New method for testing long-term retention with special reference to amnesic patients. *Nature*, **217**, 972–974.

Warrington, E.K. and Weiskrantz, L. (1970) Amnesic syndrome: consolidation of retrieval? *Nature*, **228**, 628–630.

Watkins, C. and Watkins, M.J. (1975) Buildup of proactive inhibition as a cue overload effect. *Journal of Experimental Psychology: Human Learning and Memory*, **1**, 442–452.

Watkins, M.J. (1990) Mediationism and the obfuscation of memory. *American Psychologist*, **45**, 328–335.

Watkins, O.C. and Watkins, M.J. (1974) Buildup of proactive inhibition as a cue-overload effect. *Journal of Experimental Psychology*, **104**, 442–452.

Weaver, I.C.G., Cervoni, N., Champagne, F.A., D'Alessio, A.C., Sharma, S., Seckl, J.R., *et al.* (2004) Epigenetic programming by maternal behavior. *Nature Neuroscience*, **7**, 847–854.

Wegner, D.M., Eich, E. and Bjork, R.A. (1994) Thought suppression. In: Druckman, D. and Bjork, R.A., eds. *Learning, Remembering, Believing: Enhancing Human Performance*. Washington, DC: National Academy Press, pp. 277–293.

Weiskrantz, L. (1966) Experimental studies of amnesia. In: Whitty, C and Zangwill, O., eds. *Amnesia*. London: Butterworths, pp. 1–31.

Weiskrantz, L. (1987) Neuroanatomy of memory and amnesia: a case for multiple memory systems. *Human Neurobiology*, **6**, 93–105.

Werker, J.F. and Tees, R.C. (1999) Influences on infant speech processing: toward a new synthesis. *Annual Review of Psychology*, **50**, 509–535.

Wertsch, J.V. (2002) *Voices of collective remembering*. Cambridge: Cambridge University Press.

Wheeler, M.A., Stuss, D.T. and Tulving, E. (1997) Toward a theory of episodic memory: the frontal lobes and autonoetic consciousness. *Psychological Bulletin*, **121**, 331–354.

Whittlesea, B.W.A. (2002) Two routes to remembering (and another to remembering not). *Journal of Experimental Psychology: General*, **131**, 325–348.

Wig, G.S., Grafton, S.T., Demos, K.E. and Kelley, W.M. (2005) Reductions in neural activity underlie behavioral components of repetition priming. *Nature Neuroscience*, **8**, 1228–1233.

Wilson, M.A. and McNaughton, B.L. (1993) Dynamics of the hippocampal ensemble code for space. *Science*, **261**, 1055–1058.

Wilson, M.A. and McNaughton, B.L. (1994) Reactivation of hippocampal ensemble memories during sleep. *Science*, **265**, 676–679.

Wiltgen, B.J., Brown, R.A., Talton, L.E. and Silva, A.J. (2004) New circuits for old memories: the role of the neocortex in consolidation. *Neuron*, **44**, 101–108.

Winch, W.H. (1908) The transfer of improvement in memory in school-children. *British Journal of Psychology*, **2**, 284–298.

Winocur, G. and Hasher, L. (2002) Circadian rhythms and memory in aged humans and animals. In: Squire, L. and Schacter, D., eds, *Neuropsychology of Memory*, 3rd edn. New York: Guilford Press, pp. 273–285.

Wittenberg, G.M. and Tsien, J.Z. (2002) An emerging molecular and cellular framework for memory processing by the hippocampus. *Trends in Neurosciences*, **25**, 501–505.

Wittgenstein, L. (1953) *Philosophical Investigations*. Oxford: Basil Blackwell.

Wixted, J.T. (2004a) On common ground: Jost's (1897) law of forgetting and Ribot's (1881) law of retrograde amnesia. *Psychological Review*, **111**, 864–879.

Wixted, J.T. (2004b) The psychology and neuroscience of forgetting. *Annual Review of Psychology*, **55**, 235–269.

Wixted, J.T. (2005) A theory about why we forget what we once knew. *Current Directions in Psychological Science*, **14**, 6–9.

Wixted, J.T. and Ebbesen, E. (1991) On the form of forgetting. *Psychological Science*, **2**, 409–415.

Wolpaw, J.R. (1997) The complex structure of a simple memory. *Trends in Neurosciences* **20**, 588–594.

Woods, T.M., Cusick, C.G., Pons, T.P., Taub, E. and Jones, E.G. (2000) Progressive transneuronal changes in the brainstem and thalamus after long-term dorsal rhizotomies in adult macaque monkeys. *Journal of Neuroscience*, **20**, 3884–99.

Woodworth, R.S. (1938) *Experimental Psychology*. New York: Holt.

Woodworth, R.S. and Schlosberg, H. (1954) *Experimental Psychology*. New York: Henry Holt and Company.

Woolley, C.S., Gould, E., Frankfurt, M. and McEwen, B.S. (1990) Naturally occurring fluctuation in dendritic spine density on adult hippocampal pyramidal neurons. *Journal of Neuroscience*, **10**, 4035–4039.

Wright, W.G. (1998) Evolution of nonassociative learning: behavioral analysis of a phylogenetic lesion. *Neurobiology of Learning and Memory*, **69**, 326–337.

Xu, J., Kang, N., Jiang, L., Nedergaard, M. and Kang, J. (2005) Activity-dependent long-term potentiation of intrinsic excitability in hippocampal CA1 pyramidal neurons. *Journal of Neuroscience*, **25**, 1750–1760.

Yonelinas, A.P. (1994) Receiver-operating characteristics in recognition memory: evidence for a dual-process model. *Journal of Experimental Psychology: Learning, Memory, and Cognition*, **20**, 1341–1354.

Yonelinas, A.P. (2001) Components of episodic memory: the contribution of recollection and familiarity. *Philosophical Transactions of the Royal Society B: Biological Sciences*, **356**, 1363–1374.

Yonelinas, A.P. (2002) The nature of recollection and familiarity: a review of 30 years of research. *Journal of Memory and Language*, **46**, 441–517.

Yonelinas, A.P., Kroll, N.E.A., Dobbins, I.G. and Soltani, M. (1999) Recognition memory for faces: when familiarity supports associative recognition. *Psychonomic Bulletin and Review*, **6**, 418–661.

Young, J.Z. (1965) The Croonian Lecture, 1965: the organization of a memory system. *Proceedings of the Royal Society B: Biological Sciences*, **163**, 285–320.

Young, J.Z. and Nguyen, P. (2005) Homosynaptic and heterosynaptic inhibition of synaptic tagging and capture of LTP by previous synaptic activity. *Journal of Neuroscience*, **25**, 7221–7231.

Young, J.Z. and Nguyen, P.V. (2005) Homosynaptic and heterosynaptic inhibition of synaptic tagging and capture of long-term potentiation by previous synaptic activity. *J. Neurosci.* **25**, 7221–7231.

Young, M.P. and Yamane, S. (1992) Sparse population coding of faces in the inferotemporal cortex. *Science*, **256**, 1327–1331.

Young, R.W. and Lewis, R.L. (1999) The soar cognitive architecture and human working memory. In: Miyake, A. and Shah, P., eds. *Models of Working Memory*. Cambridge: Cambridge University Press.

Yu, A.J. and Dayan, P. (2005) Uncertainty, neuromodulation, and attention. *Neuron*, **46**, 681–692.

Zentall, T.R. (2005) Animals may not be stuck in time. *Learning and Motivation*, **36**, 208–225.

Zhang, W. and Linden, D.J. (2003) The other side of the engram: experience-driven changes in neuronal intrinsic excitability. *Nature Reviews Neuroscience*, **4**, 885–900.

Zhang, W.P., Guzowski, J.F. and Thomas, S.A. (2005) Mapping neuronal activation and the influence of adrenergic signaling during contextual memory retrieval. *Learning and Memory* **12**, 239–247.

Zola-Morgan, S. and Squire, L.R. (1985) Medial temporal lesions in monkeys impair memory on a variety of tasks sensitive to human amnesia. *Behavioral Neuroscience*, **99**, 22–34.

Zucker, R.S. and Regehr, W.G. (2002) Short-term synaptic plasticity. *Annual Review of Physiology* **64**, 355–405.

Author Index

Subject Index